Reading · Mastery

CLASSIC EDITION

Presentation Book C

Level I

Siegfried Engelmann
Elaine C. Bruner

A Division of The McGraw·Hill Companies

Columbus, Ohio

www.sra4kids.com

SRA/McGraw-Hill

A Division of The McGraw-Hill Companies

Send all inquiries to:
SRA/McGraw-Hill
8787 Orion Place
Columbus, OH 43240-4027

Printed in the United States of America.

ISBN 0-07-569289-9

2 3 4 5 6 7 8 9 QGK 06 05 04 03

Table of Contents

Lesson 108

p

d

g

t

SOUNDS

TASK 1   Teaching **p** as in **pat**

a. Point to **p.** Here's a new sound. It's a quick sound.
b. My turn. (Pause.) Touch **p** for an instant, saying: p. Do not say **puuh.**
c. Again. Touch **p** and say: p.
d. Point to **p.** Your turn. When I touch it, you say it. (Pause.) Get ready. Touch **p.** p.
e. Again. Touch **p.** p.
f. Repeat e until firm.

TASK 2   Individual test

Call on different children to identify **p.**

TASK 3   Sounds firm-up

a. Get ready to say the sounds when I touch them.
b. Alternate touching **p** and **d.** Point to the sound. (Pause one second.) Say: Get ready. Touch the sound. *The children respond.*
c. When **p** and **d** are firm, alternate touching **p, g, d,** and **t** until all four sounds are firm.

TASK 4   Individual test

Call on different children to identify **p, g, d,** or **t.**

TASK 5   Sounds firm-up

a. Point to **p.** When I touch the sound, you say it.
b. (Pause.) Get ready. Touch **p.** p.
c. Again. Repeat b until firm.
d. Get ready to say all the sounds when I touch them.
e. Alternate touching **k, v, u, ō, p, sh, h,** and **n** three or four times. Point to the sound. (Pause one second.) Say: Get ready. Touch the sound. *The children respond.*

TASK 6   Individual test

Call on different children to identify one or more sounds in task 5.

p

k

v

u

ō

sh

h

n

1

READING VOCABULARY

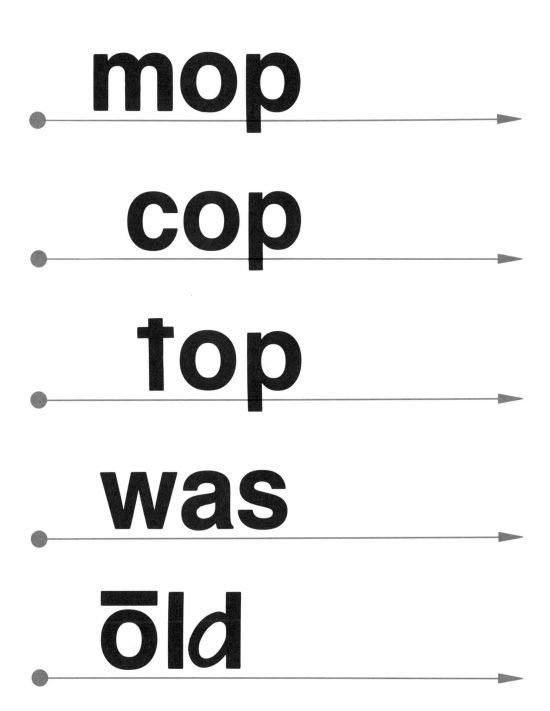

TASK 7   Children rhyme with mop

a. Touch the ball for **mop.** **You're going to read this word the fast way.** (Pause three seconds.) **Get ready.** Move your finger quickly along the arrow. *Mop.*

b. Touch the ball for **cop.** **This word rhymes with** (pause) **mop.** Move to **c,** then quickly along the arrow. *Cop.* **Yes, what word?** (Signal.) *Cop.*

c. Touch the ball for **top.** **This word rhymes with** (pause) **mop.** Move to **t,** then quickly along the arrow. *Top.* **Yes, what word?** (Signal.) *Top.*

TASK 8   Children identify, then sound out an irregular word (was)

a. Touch the ball for **was.** **Everybody, you're going to read this word the fast way.** (Pause three seconds.) **Get ready.** Move your finger quickly along the arrow. *Was.* **Yes, was.**

b. **Now you're going to sound out the word. Get ready.** Quickly touch **w, a, s** as the children say *wwwaaasss.*

c. **Again.** Repeat *b.*

d. **How do we say the word?** (Signal.) *Was.* **Yes, was.**

e. Repeat *b* and *d* until firm.

TASK 9   Individual test

Call on different children to do *b* and *d* in task 8.

TASK 10   Children read the fast way

Touch the ball for **ōld.** **Get ready to read this word the fast way.** (Pause three seconds.) **Get ready.** (Signal.) *Old.*

TASK 11   Children read the words the fast way

Have the children read the words on this page the fast way.

TASK 12   Individual test

Call on different children to read one word the fast way.

108

TASK 13 Children identify, then sound out an irregular word (of)

a. Touch the ball for **of.** Everybody, you're going to read this word the fast way. (Pause three seconds.) Get ready. Move your finger quickly along the arrow. *Of.* Yes, **of**.

b. Now you're going to sound out the word. Get ready. Quickly touch **o, f** as the children say *ooofff.*

c. Again. Repeat *b.*
d. How do we say the word? (Signal.) *Of.* Yes, **of**.
e. Repeat *b* and *d* until firm.
f. Call on different children to do *b* and *d.*

TASK 14 Children identify, then sound out an irregular word (to)

Repeat the procedures in task 13 for **to.**

TASK 15 Children read the fast way

Touch the ball for **that.** Get ready to read this word the fast way. (Pause three seconds.) Get ready. (Signal.) *That.*

TASK 16 Children sound out the word and tell what word

a. Touch the ball for **cōat.** Sound it out.
b. Get ready. Touch **c, ō, t** as the children say *cōōōt.* If sounding out is not firm, repeat *b.*
c. What word? (Signal.) *Coat.* Yes, **coat**.

TASK 17 Children sound out the word and tell what word

a. Touch the ball for **gōat.** Sound it out.
b. Get ready. Touch **g, ō, t** as the children say *gōōōt.* If sounding out is not firm, repeat *b.*
c. What word? (Signal.) *Goat.* Yes, **goat**.

TASK 18 Children read the words the fast way

Have the children read the words on this page the fast way.

TASK 19 Individual test

Call on different children to read one word the fast way.

Do not touch any small letters.

of

to

that

cōₐt

gōₐt

Story 108

TASK 20 First reading—children read the story the fast way

Have the children reread any sentences containing words that give them trouble. Keep a list of these words.

a. Pass out Storybook 1.
b. Open your book to page 37 and get ready to read.
c. We're going to read this story the fast way.
d. Touch the first word. Check children's responses.
e. Reading the fast way. First word. (Pause three seconds.)
Get ready. Clap. *Thē.*
f. Next word. Check children's responses. (Pause three seconds.)
Get ready. Clap. *Old.*
g. Repeat *f* for the remaining words in the first sentence. Pause at least three seconds between claps. The children are to identify each word without sounding it out.
h. Repeat *d* through *g* for the next two sentences. Have the children reread the first three sentences until firm.
i. The children are to read the remainder of the story the fast way, stopping at the end of each sentence.
j. After the first reading of the story, print on the board the words that the children missed more than one time. Have the children sound out each word one time and tell what word.
k. After the group's responses are firm, call on individual children to read the words.

TASK 21 Individual test

a. I'm going to call on different children to read a whole sentence the fast way.
b. Call on different children to read a sentence. Do not clap for each word.

TASK 22 Second reading—children read the story the fast way and answer questions

a. You're going to read the story again the fast way and I'll ask questions.
b. First word. Check children's responses. Get ready. Clap. *Thē.*
c. Clap for each remaining word. Pause at least three seconds between claps. Pause longer before words that gave the children trouble during the first reading.
d. Ask the comprehension questions below as the children read.

After the children read:	You ask:
The old goat had an old coat.	What did she have? (Signal.) *An old coat.*
The old goat said, "I will eat this old coat."	What did she say? (Signal.) *I will eat this old coat.*
So she did.	What did she do? (Signal.) *She ate the old coat.*
"That was fun," she said.	What did she say? (Signal.) *That was fun.*
"I ate the old coat."	What did the goat say? (Signal.) *I ate the old coat.*
"And now I am cold."	What did she say? (Signal.) *And now I am cold.*
Now the old goat is sad.	How does she feel? (Signal.) *Sad.* Why? (Signal.) *The children respond.*

TASK 23 Picture comprehension

a. What do you think you'll see in the picture? *The children respond.*
b. Turn the page and look at the picture.
c. Ask these questions:
1. How does that goat feel? *The children respond.* Cold and sad.
2. Why is she out in the cold without a coat? *The children respond.* Because she ate her coat.
3. Did you ever go outside without a coat when it was cold? *The children respond.*

Take-Home 108

SUMMARY OF INDEPENDENT ACTIVITY

TASK 24 Introduction to independent activity

a. Pass out Take-Home 108 to each child.

b. Everybody, you're going to do this take-home on your own. Tell the children when they will work the items. Let's go over the things you're going to do.

TASK 25 Sentence copying

a. Hold up side 1 of your take-home and point to the first line in the sentence-copying exercise.

b. Everybody, here's the sentence you're going to write on the lines below.

c. Get ready to read the words in this sentence the fast way. First word. Check children's responses. Get ready. Clap. *Thē.*

d. Next word. Check children's responses. Get ready. Clap. *Goat.*

e. Repeat *d* for the remaining words.

f. After you finish your take-home, you get to draw a picture about the sentence, **thē gōat āte thē cōat.**

TASK 26 Sound writing

a. Point to the sound-writing exercise. Here are the sounds you're going to write today. I'll touch the sounds. You say them.

b. Touch each sound. *The children respond.*

c. Repeat the series until firm.

TASK 27 Matching

a. Point to the column of words in the Matching Game.

b. Everybody, you're going to follow the lines and write these words.

c. Reading the fast way.

d. Point to the first word. (Pause.) Get ready. (Signal.) *The children respond.*

e. Repeat *d* for the remaining words.

f. Repeat *d* and *e* until firm.

TASK 28 Cross-out game

Point to the boxed word in the Cross-out Game. Everybody, here's the word you're going to cross out today. What word? (Signal.) *Not.* Yes, **not.**

TASK 29 Pair relations

a. Point to the pair-relations exercise on side 2. You're going to circle the picture in each box that shows what the words say.

b. Point to the space at the top of the page. After you finish, remember to draw a picture that shows **thē gōat āte thē cōat.**

INDIVIDUAL CHECKOUT: STORYBOOK

TASK 30 2½–minute individual checkout — whole story

Make a permanent chart for recording results of individual checkouts. See Teacher's Guide for sample chart.

a. As you are doing your take-home, I'll call on children one at a time to read the **whole story.** If you can read the whole story the fast way in less than two and a half minutes and if you make no more than three errors, I'll put two stars after your name on the chart for lesson 108.

b. If you make too many errors or don't read the story in less than two and a half minutes, you'll have to practice it and do it again. When you do read it in under two and a half minutes with no more than three errors, you'll get one star. Remember, two stars if you can do it the first time, one star if you do it the second or third time you try.

c. Call on a child. Tell the child: Read the whole story very carefully the fast way. Go. Time the child. If the child makes a mistake, quickly tell the child the correct word and permit the child to continue reading. As soon as the child makes more than three errors or exceeds the time limit, tell the child to stop. You'll have to read the story to yourself and try again later. Plan to monitor the child's practice.

d. Record two stars for each child who reads appropriately. Congratulate those children.

e. Give children who do not earn two stars a chance to read the story again before the next lesson is presented. Award one star to each of those children who meet the rate and accuracy criterion.

41 words/2.5 min = 16 wpm [3 errors]

END OF LESSON 108

Lesson 109

SOUNDS

TASK 1 Teaching **p** as in **pat**

a. Point to **p.** My turn. When I touch it, I'll say it. (Pause.)
Touch **p** for an instant, saying: p. Do not say **puuh.**

b. Point to **p.** Your turn. When I touch it, you say it. (Pause.)
Get ready. Touch **p.** *p.*

c. Again. Touch **p.** *p.*
d. Repeat *c* until firm.

p

g

d

k

TASK 2 Sounds firm-up

a. Get ready to say the sounds when I touch them.
b. Alternate touching **g** and **p.** Point to the sound. (Pause one second.)
Say: Get ready. Touch the sound. *The children respond.*
c. When **g** and **p** are firm, alternate touching **d, g, k,** and **p**
until all four sounds are firm.

TASK 3 Individual test

Call on different children to identify **d, g, k,** or **p.**

TASK 4 Teacher introduces cross-out game

a. Use acetate and crayon.
b. I'll cross out the sounds on this part of the page when you can tell me every sound.
c. Remember—when I touch it, you say it.
d. Go over the sounds until the children can identify all the sounds in order.

TASK 5 Individual test

Call on different children to identify two or more sounds in task 4.

TASK 6 Teacher crosses out sounds

a. You told me every sound. Get ready to do it again. This time I'll cross out each sound when you tell me what it is.
b. Point to each sound. (Pause.) Say: Get ready. Touch the sound. *The children respond.* As you cross out the sound, say: Goodbye, ———— .

I

H

p

v

w

a

k

ō

READING VOCABULARY

Do not touch any small letters.

TASK 7 Children read the fast way

a. Get ready to read these words the fast way.
b. Touch the ball for **got.** (Pause three seconds.) Get ready.

(Signal.) *Got.*

c. Repeat *b* for the remaining words on the page.

TASK 8 Children read the fast way again

a. Get ready to do these words again. Watch where I point.
b. Point to a word. (Pause one second.) Say: Get ready. (Signal.)
The children respond. Point to the words in this order:
have, not, got, ship.

c. Repeat *b* until firm.

TASK 9 Individual test

Call on different children to read one word the fast way.

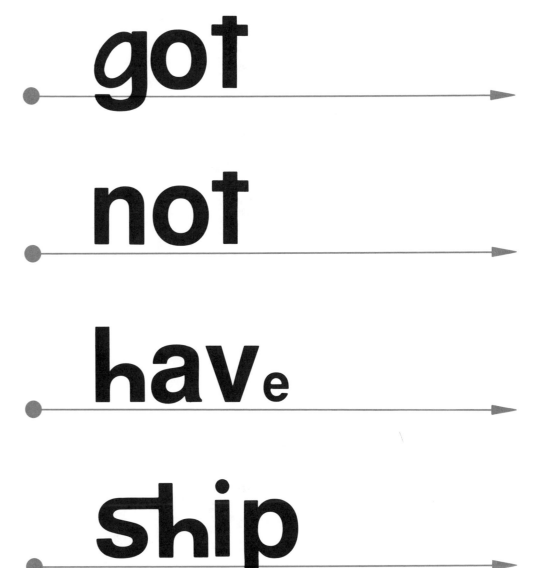

TASK 10 Children identify, then sound out an irregular word (said)

a. Touch the ball for **said.** Everybody, you're going to read this word the fast way. (Pause three seconds.) Get ready. Move your finger quickly along the arrow. *Said.* Yes, **said.**

b. Now you're going to sound out the word. Get ready. Quickly touch **s, a, i, d** as the children say *sssaaaiiid.*

c. Again. Repeat *b.*

d. How do we say the word? (Signal.) *Said.* Yes, **said.**

e. Repeat *b* and *d* until firm.

f. Call on different children to do *b* and *d.*

said

TASK 11 Children sound out the word and tell what word

a. Touch the ball for **cop.** Sound it out.

b. Get ready. Touch **c, o, p** as the children say *cooop.* If sounding out is not firm, repeat *b.*

c. What word? (Signal.) *Cop.* Yes, **cop.**

cop

TASK 12 Children sound out the word and tell what word

Repeat the procedures in task 11 for **dip.**

dip

TASK 13 Children sound out the word and tell what word

Repeat the procedures in task 11 for **down.**

down

TASK 14 Children identify, then sound out an irregular word (of)

a. Touch the ball for **of.** Everybody, you're going to read this word the fast way. (Pause three seconds.) Get ready. Move your finger quickly along the arrow. *Of.* Yes, **of.**

b. Now you're going to sound out the word. Get ready. Quickly touch **o, f** as the children say *ooofff.*

c. Again. Repeat *b.*

d. How do we say the word? (Signal.) *Of.* Yes, **of.**

e. Repeat *b* and *d* until firm.

f. Call on different children to do *b* and *d.*

of

TASK 15 Children read the words the fast way

Have the children read the words on this page the fast way.

Story 109

TASK 16 First reading—children read the story the fast way

Have the children reread any sentences containing words that give them trouble. Keep a list of these words.

a. Pass out Storybook 1.
b. Open your book to page 39 and get ready to read.
c. We're going to read this story the fast way.
d. Touch the first word. Check children's responses.
e. Reading the fast way. First word. (Pause three seconds.)
   Get ready. Clap. Thē.
f. Next word. Check children's responses. (Pause three seconds.)
   Get ready. Clap. Fat.
g. Repeat f for the remaining words in the first sentence. Pause at least three seconds between claps. The children are to identify each word without sounding it out.
h. Repeat d through g for the next two sentences. Have the children reread the first three sentences until firm.
i. The children are to read the remainder of the story the fast way, stopping at the end of each sentence.
j. After the first reading of the story, print on the board the words that the children missed more than one time. Have the children sound out each word one time and tell what word.
k. After the group's responses are firm, call on individual children to read the words.

TASK 17 Individual test

a. Turn back to page 39. I'm going to call on different children to read a whole sentence the fast way.
b. Call on different children to read a sentence. Do not clap for each word.

TASK 18 Second reading—children read the story the fast way and answer questions

a. You're going to read the story again the fast way and I'll ask questions.
b. First word. Check children's responses. Get ready. Clap. Thē.
c. Clap for each remaining word. Pause at least three seconds between claps. Pause longer before words that gave the children trouble during the first reading.
d. Ask the comprehension questions below as the children read.

After the children read:	You say:
The fat man and his fat cow got on a little rock.	Who got on the rock? (Signal.) *The fat man and his fat cow.*
A cat said, "Fat man, that rock will not hold a fat man and his cow."	What did the cat say? (Signal.) *Fat man, that rock will not hold a fat man and his cow.*
"That rock will go down the hill."	What did the cat say? (Signal.) *That rock will go down the hill.*
Did the rock go down the hill with the fat man and his fat cow?	What do you think? *The children respond.*

TASK 19 Picture comprehension

a. Everybody, look at the picture.
b. Ask these questions:
   1. Did the rock go down the hill with the fat man and his fat cow? *Yes.*
   2. How do you think that fat man feels? *The children respond.*
   3. What would you do if you were that fat man? *The children respond.*

Take-Home 160

SUMMARY OF INDEPENDENT ACTIVITY

TASK 19 Introduction to independent activity

a. Pass out sides 1 and 2 of Take-Home 160 to each child.
b. **Everybody, do a good job on your take-home today and I'll give you a bonus take-home.**

c. Hold up side 1 of your take-home. **You're going to do this take-home on your own.** Tell the children when they will work the items. **Let's go over the things you're going to do.**

TASK 20 Story items

a. Point to the story-items exercise.
b. **Everybody, here are items about the story we read today.**
c. **Think about what happened in the story and circle the right answer for each item.**

TASK 21 Picture comprehension

a. Point to the pictures in the picture-comprehension exercise. **Everybody, you're going to look at the picture. Then you're going to read each item and write the missing word.**
b. **Remember—the first sound of each missing word is already written in the blank.**

TASK 22 Reading comprehension

a. Point to the reading-comprehension exercise on side 2.
b. **Everybody, get ready to read the sentences in the box the fast way.**
c. **First word.** Check children's responses. **Get ready.** Clap for each word as the children read the sentences: *He fell in the mud. His nose had mud on it.*
d. Point to items 1 and 2. **These items tell about the story in the box. You're going to read each item and circle the right answer.**

TASK 23 Sound writing

a. Point to the sound-writing exercise. **Here are the sounds you're going to write today. I'll touch the sounds. You say them.**
b. Touch each sound. *The children respond.*
c. Repeat the series until firm.

TASK 24 Sentence copying

a. Point to the dotted sentence in the sentence-copying exercise.
b. **You're going to trace the words in this sentence. Then you're going to write the sentence on the other lines.**
c. **Reading the fast way. First word.** Check children's responses. **Get ready.** Clap for each word.
d. **After you finish your take-home, you get to draw a picture about the sentence, "I ēat fast," hē said. You'll draw your picture on a piece of plain paper.** When the children finish their take-homes, give them sheets of plain paper.

INDIVIDUAL CHECKOUT: STORYBOOK

TASK 25 2½-minute individual checkout

a. **As you are doing your take-home, I'll call on children one at a time to read the whole story. Remember, you get two stars if you read the story in less than two and a half minutes and make no more than three errors.**
b. Call on a child. Tell the child: **Start with the title and read the story carefully the fast way. Go.** Time the child. Tell the child any words the child misses. Stop the child as soon as the child makes the fourth error or exceeds the time limit.
c. If the child meets the rate-accuracy criterion, record two stars on your chart for lesson 160. Congratulate the child. Give children who do not earn two stars a chance to read the story again before the next lesson is presented.

   95 words/2.5 min = 38 wpm [3 errors]

TASK 26 Bonus take-home: sides 3 and 4

After the children have completed their take-home exercises, give them sides 3 and 4 of Take-Home 160. Tell them they may keep the stories and read them.

END OF LESSON 160

END OF PRESENTATION BOOK C

Take-Home 109

SUMMARY OF INDEPENDENT ACTIVITY

TASK 20   Introduction to independent activity

a. Pass out Take-Home 109 to each child.
b. Everybody, you're going to do this take-home on your own.
Tell the children when they will work the items.
Let's go over the things you're going to do.

TASK 21   Sentence copying

a. Hold up side 1 of your take-home and point to the first line in the sentence-copying exercise.
b. Everybody, here's the sentence you're going to write on the lines below.
c. Get ready to read the words in this sentence the fast way.
First word.   Check children's responses. Get ready.   Clap. *A.*
d. Next word.   Check children's responses. Get ready.   Clap. *Cow.*
e. Repeat *d* for the remaining words.
f. After you finish your take-home, you get to draw a picture about the sentence, **a cow got on a rock.**

TASK 22   Sound writing

a. Point to the sound-writing exercise. Here are the sounds you're going to write today. I'll touch the sounds. You say them.
b. Touch each sound. *The children respond.*
c. Repeat the series until firm.

TASK 23   Matching

a. Point to the column of words in the Matching Game.
b. Everybody, you're going to follow the lines and write these words.
c. Reading the fast way.
d. Point to the first word. (Pause.) Get ready.   (Signal.)
The children respond.
e. Repeat *d* for the remaining words.
f. Repeat *d* and *e* until firm.

TASK 24   Cross-out game

Point to the boxed word in the Cross-out Game. Everybody, here's the word you're going to cross out today. What word?   (Signal.)
Man. Yes, **man.**

TASK 25   Pair relations

a. Point to the pair-relations exercise on side 2. You're going to circle the picture in each box that shows what the words say.
b. Point to the space at the top of the page. After you finish, remember to draw a picture that shows **a cow got on a rock.**

INDIVIDUAL CHECKOUT: STORYBOOK

TASK 26   2-minute individual checkout — first page

a. As you are doing your take-home, I'll call on children one at a time to read the **first page** of the story. If you can read the first page of the story the fast way in less than two minutes and if you make no more than three errors, I'll put two stars after your name on the chart for lesson 109.
b. If you make too many errors or don't read the page in less than two minutes, you'll have to practice it and do it again. When you do read it in under two minutes with no more than three errors, you'll get one star. Remember, two stars if you can do it the first time, one star if you do it the second or third time you try.
c. Call on a child. Tell the child: Read the first page of the story very carefully the fast way. Go. Time the child. If the child makes a mistake, quickly tell the child the correct word and permit the child to continue reading. As soon as the child makes more than three errors or exceeds the time limit, tell the child to stop. You'll have to read the page to yourself and try again later. Plan to monitor the child's practice.
d. Record two stars for each child who reads appropriately. Congratulate those children.
e. Give children who do not earn two stars a chance to read the page again before the next lesson is presented. Award one star to each of those children who meet the rate and accuracy criterion.

35 words/2 min = 18 wpm [3 errors]

END OF LESSON 109

Story 160

TASK 15 First reading—children read the title and first three sentences

a. Now you're going to finish the story about the man who went so fast.
b. Everybody, touch the title of the story and get ready to read the words in the title the fast way.
c. First word. Check children's responses. (Pause two seconds.) Get ready. Clap. *A.*
d. Clap for each remaining word in the title.
e. After the children have read the title, ask: What's this story about? (Signal.) *A man liked to go fast.* Yes, **a man liked to go fast.**
f. Everybody, get ready to read this story the fast way.
g. First word. Check children's responses. (Pause two seconds.) Get ready. Clap. *A.*
h. Clap for the remaining words in the first sentence. Pause at least two seconds between claps.
i. Repeat *g* and *h* for the next two sentences. Have the children reread the first three sentences until firm.

TASK 16 Individual children or the group read sentences to complete the first reading

a. I'm going to call on different children to read a sentence. Everybody, follow along and point to the words. If you hear a mistake, raise your hand.
b. Call on a child. Read the next sentence. Do not clap for the words. Let the child read at his own pace, but be sure he reads the sentence correctly.

To correct	Have the child sound out the word. Then return to the beginning of the sentence.

c. Repeat *b* for most of the remaining sentences in the story. Occasionally have the group read a sentence. When the group is to read, say: Everybody, read the next sentence. (Pause two seconds.) Get ready. Clap for each word in the sentence. Pause at least two seconds between claps.

TASK 17 Second reading—individual children or the group read each sentence; the group answer questions

a. You're going to read the story again. This time I'm going to ask questions.
b. Starting with the first word of the title. Check children's responses. Get ready. Clap as the children read the title. Pause at least two seconds between claps.
c. Call on a child. Read the first sentence. *The child responds.*
d. Repeat *b* and *c* in task 16. Present the following comprehension questions to the entire group.

After the children read:	You say:
"I will not do things fast."	What did the man say? *The children respond.* He said, "I will slow down. I will not do things fast."
And he did not eat so fast that he got fish cake on his nose.	Name the things that the man did not do fast any more. *The children respond.* He didn't go fast in his car. He did not walk fast. He did not talk fast. And he did not eat fast.

TASK 18 Picture comprehension

a. What do you think you'll see in the picture? *The children respond.*
b. Turn the page and look at the picture.
c. Ask these questions:
   1. Does the man look like he's going fast in that picture? *No.*
   2. Is his wife happy? *Yes.* Why do you think she doesn't like him to go fast when he eats? *The children respond.*
   3. Did you ever eat so fast that you got food on your nose? *The children respond.*

Lesson 110

SOUNDS

TASK 1   Sounds firm-up

a. Get ready to say the sounds when I touch them.
b. Alternate touching **p** and **t**. Point to the sound. (Pause one second.)
     Say: Get ready. Touch the sound. *The children respond.*
c. When **p** and **t** are firm, alternate touching **g, v, p,** and **t** until all
     four sounds are firm.

p

t

g

v

TASK 2   Individual test

Call on different children to identify **g, v, p,** or **t.**

p

k

n

sh

o

c

ō

u

TASK 3   Sounds firm-up

a. Point to **p.** When I touch the
   sound, you say it.
b. (Pause.) Get ready. Touch **p.** *p.*
c. Again. Repeat *b* until firm.
d. Get ready to say all the sounds
   when I touch them.
e. Alternate touching **k, n, sh, o, c,
   p, ō,** and **u** three or four times.
   Point to the sound.
   (Pause one second.) Say:
   Get ready. Touch the sound.
   The children respond.

TASK 4   Individual test

Call on different children to identify
one or more sounds in task 3.

Read the Items 160

TASK 12 Children read items 1 and 2

a. Pass out Storybook 3.
b. Open your book to page 62.
c. Get ready to read the items and play the game.
d. Finger under the first word of the title. Check children's responses.
e. When I clap, read the title. (Pause.) Get ready. Clap.
                                                      Read the items.
f. Touch item 1 and get ready to read. Check children's responses.
         First word. Clap for each word as the children read: *When the teacher says "Touch your head," hold up your hands.* Repeat until firm.
g. Everybody, get ready to say item 1. (Pause and signal.) *The children say the sentence.* Repeat four times or until firm.
h. Touch item 2 and get ready to read. Check children's responses.
         First word. Clap for each word as the children read: *If the teacher picks up a book, say "Now." Repeat until firm.*
i. Everybody, get ready to say item 2. (Pause and signal.) *The children say the sentence.* Repeat four times or until firm.

TASK 13 Children reread items 1 and 2 and answer questions

a. Everybody, touch item 1. Check children's responses.
b. Read item 1 to yourself. Raise your hand when you know what you're going to do and when you're going to do it.
c. After the children raise their hands, say: Everybody, what are you going to do when I say "**Touch your head**"? (Signal.)
                                                      Hold up my hands.

To correct	1. Everybody, read item 1 out loud. Clap as the children read each word.
	2. What are you going to do when I say "**Touch your head**"? (Signal.) *Hold up my hands.*

d. Everybody, when are you going to **hold up your hands**? (Signal.)
                                  When the teacher says "Touch your head."

To correct	1. Everybody, read item 1 out loud. Clap as the children read each word.
	2. When are you going to **hold up your hands**? (Signal.) *When the teacher says "Touch your head."*

e. Repeat *c* and *d* until firm.

---

f. Everybody, touch item 2. Check children's responses.
g. Read item 2 to yourself. Raise your hand when you know what you're going to do and when you're going to do it.
h. After the children raise their hands, say: Everybody, what are you going to do if I **pick up a book?** (Signal.) *Say "Now."*

To correct	1. Everybody, read item 2 out loud. Clap as the children read each word.
	2. What are you going to do if I **pick up a book?** (Signal.) *Say "Now."*

i. Everybody, when are you going to **say "Now"**? (Signal.)
                                      If the teacher picks up a book.

To correct	1. Everybody, read item 2 out loud. Clap as the children read each word.
	2. When are you going to **say "Now"**? (Signal.) *If the teacher picks up a book.*

j. Repeat *h* and *i* until firm.

TASK 14 Children play the game

a. Everybody, touch item 1. Check children's responses.
b. Read the item to yourself. Raise your hand when you know what you're going to do and when you're going to do it.
c. After the children raise their hands, say: Let's play the game.
         Think about what you're going to do (pause) and when you're going to do it.
d. Hold out your hand. (Pause.) Get ready. **Touch your head.**
         (Pause.) Drop your hand. *(The children hold up their hands immediately.)*

To correct	1. What did I say? (Signal.) *Touch your head.*
	2. What are you supposed to do when I say "**Touch your head**"? (Signal.) *Hold up my hands.*
	3. If the children's responses are not firm, have them read item 1 aloud.
	4. Repeat task 14.

READING VOCABULARY

Do not touch any small letters.

TASK 5   Children read the fast way

a. Get ready to read these words the fast way.
b. Touch the ball for **fog.** (Pause three seconds.) Get ready.

(Signal.) *Fog.*

c. Repeat *b* for the remaining words on the page.

TASK 6   Children read the fast way again

a. Get ready to do these words again. Watch where I point.
b. Point to a word. (Pause one second.) Say: Get ready. (Signal.)
The children respond. Point to the words in this order:

fog, log, lots, sand, ēars.

c. Repeat *b* until firm.

TASK 7   Individual test

Call on different children to read one word the fast way.

fog

sand

ēars

lots

log

TASK 7   Children sound out an irregular word (took)

a. Touch the ball for **took.** Sound it out.
b. Get ready. Quickly touch each sound as the children say *toook.*
c. Again. Repeat *b* until firm.
d. That's how we <u>sound out</u> the word. Here's how we <u>say</u> the word.
                    Took. How do we <u>say</u> the word?   (Signal.) *Took.*
e. Now you're going to <u>sound out</u> the word. Get ready.
                    Touch each sound as the children say *tooook.*
f. Now you're going to say the word. Get ready.   (Signal.) *Took.*
g. Repeat *e* and *f* until firm.
h. Yes, this word is **took.** I **took** your pencil.

TASK 8   Individual test

Call on different children to do *e* and *f* in task 7.

TASK 9   Children sound out the word and tell what word

a. Touch the ball for **moon.** Sound it out.
b. Get ready. Touch **m, oo, n** as the children say *mmmoooonnn.*
                    If sounding out is not firm, repeat *b.*
c. What word?   (Signal.) *Moon.* Yes, **moon.**

TASK 10   Children read the words the fast way

a. Now you get to read the words on this page the fast way.
b. Touch the ball for **moon.** (Pause three seconds.) Get ready.
                    Move your finger quickly along the arrow. *Moon.*
c. Repeat *b* for **took.**

TASK 11   Individual test

Call on different children to read one word the fast way.

TASK 8 Children identify, then sound out an irregular word (to)

a. Touch the ball for **to**. Everybody, you're going to read this word the fast way. (Pause three seconds.) Get ready. Move your finger quickly along the arrow. *To*. Yes, **to**.

b. Now you're going to sound out the word. Get ready. Quickly touch **t, o** as the children say *tooo*.

c. Again. Repeat *b*.

d. How do we say the word? (Signal.) *To*. Yes, **to**.

e. Repeat *b* and *d* until firm.

TASK 9   Individual test

Call on different children to do *b* and *d* in task 8.

TASK 10   Children sound out the word and tell what word

a. Touch the ball for **dog**. Sound it out.

b. Get ready. Touch **d, o, g** as the children say *dooog*.
       If sounding out is not firm, repeat *b*.

c. What word? (Signal.) *Dog*. Yes, **dog**.

TASK 11   Children sound out the word and tell what word

a. Touch the ball for **tāil**. Sound it out.

b. Get ready. Touch **t, ā, l** as the children say *tāāālll*.
       If sounding out is not firm, repeat *b*.

c. What word? (Signal.) *Tail*. Yes, **tail**.

TASK 12   Children read the words the fast way

a. Now you get to read the words on this page the fast way.

b. Touch the ball for **to**. (Pause three seconds.) Get ready. Move your finger quickly along the arrow. *To*.

c. Repeat *b* for each word on the page.

TASK 13   Individual test

Call on different children to read one word the fast way.

Do not touch any small letters.

to

dog

tāil

TASK 4   Children read the fast way

a. Get ready to read these words the fast way.

b. Touch the ball for **bent.** (Pause three seconds.) Get ready.
(Signal.) *Bent.*

c. Repeat *b* for the remaining words on the page.

TASK 5   Children read the fast way again

a. Get ready to do these words again. Watch where I point.

b. Point to a word. (Pause one second.) Say: Get ready. (Signal.)
The children respond. Point to the words in this order:
crȳ, whȳ, room, bent.

c. Repeat *b* until firm.

TASK 6   Individual test

Call on different children to read one word the fast way.

bent

crȳ

room

whȳ

Story 110

TASK 14 First reading—children read the story the fast way

Have the children reread any sentences containing words that give them trouble. Keep a list of these words.

a. Pass out Storybook 1.
b. Open your book to page 42 and get ready to read.
c. We're going to read this story the fast way.
d. Touch the first word. Check children's responses.
e. Reading the fast way. First word. (Pause three seconds.)
Get ready. Clap. Thē.
f. Next word. Check children's responses. (Pause three seconds.)
Get ready. Clap. Rat.
g. Repeat f for the remaining words in the first sentence. Pause at least three seconds between claps. The children are to identify each word without sounding it out.
h. Repeat d through g for the next two sentences. Have the children reread the first three sentences until firm.
i. The children are to read the remainder of the story the fast way, stopping at the end of each sentence.
j. After the first reading of the story, print on the board the words that the children missed more than one time. Have the children sound out each word one time and tell what word.
k. After the group's responses are firm, call on individual children to read the words.

TASK 15 Individual test

a. Look at page 42. I'm going to call on different children to read a whole sentence the fast way.
b. Call on different children to read a sentence. Do not clap for each word.

TASK 16 Second reading—children read the story the fast way and answer questions

a. You're going to read the story again the fast way and I'll ask questions.
b. First word. Check children's responses. Get ready. Clap. Thē.
c. Clap for each remaining word. Pause at least three seconds between claps. Pause longer before words that gave the children trouble during the first reading.
d. Ask the comprehension questions below as the children read.

After the children read:	You say:
The rat had fun.	Who is this story about? (Signal.) *A rat.*
He ran in the sand.	What did he do? (Signal.) *He ran in the sand.*
He had sand on his feet.	Where did he have sand? (Signal.) *On his feet.*
He had sand on his ears.	Tell me all the places he had sand. (Signal.) *On his feet and ears.*
He had sand on his nose.	Tell me all the places he had sand. (Signal.) *On his feet, ears, and nose.*
He had sand on his tail.	Tell me all the places he had sand. (Signal.) *On his feet, ears, nose, and tail.*
He said, "I have a lot of sand on me."	What did he say? (Signal.) *I have a lot of sand on me.*

TASK 17 Picture comprehension

a. What do you think you'll see in the picture? *The children respond.*
b. Turn the page and look at the picture.
c. Show me the little specks of sand.
d. Ask these questions:
   1. What is that rat doing? *The children respond.* Running in the sand.
   2. How do you think it feels to run through the sand?
   The children respond.

Lesson 160

Groups that are firm on Mastery Tests 29 and 30 should skip this lesson.

READING VOCABULARY

TASK 1   Children read the fast way

a. Get ready to read these words the fast way.

b. Touch the ball for **think.** (Pause three seconds.) Get ready. (Signal.) *Think.*

c. Repeat *b* for the remaining words on the page.

TASK 2   Children read the fast way again

a. Get ready to do these words again. Watch where I point.

b. Point to a word. (Pause one second.) Say: Get ready. (Signal.) *The children respond.* Point to the words in this order: **faster, thing, down, slōwer, think.**

c. Repeat *b* until firm.

TASK 3   Individual test

Call on different children to read one word the fast way.

think

thing

faster

slōwer

down

Take-Home 110

SUMMARY OF INDEPENDENT ACTIVITY

TASK 18   Introduction to independent activity

a. Pass out sides 1 and 2 of Take-Home 110 to each child.

b. Everybody, do a good job on your take-home today and I'll give you a bonus take-home.

c. Hold up side 1 of your take-home. You're going to do this take-home on your own. Tell the children when they will work the items. Let's go over the things you're going to do.

TASK 19   Sentence copying

a. Point to the first line in the sentence-copying exercise.

b. Everybody, here's the sentence you're going to write on the lines below.

c. Get ready to read the words in this sentence the fast way. First word. Check children's responses. Get ready. Clap. *He.*

d. Next word. Check children's responses. Get ready. Clap. *Had.*

e. Repeat d for the remaining words.

f. After you finish your take-home, you get to draw a picture about the sentence, **hē had sand on him.**

TASK 20   Sound writing

a. Point to the sound-writing exercise. Here are the sounds you're going to write today. I'll touch the sounds. You say them.

b. Touch each sound. *The children respond.*

c. Repeat the series until firm.

TASK 21   Matching

a. Point to the column of words in the Matching Game.

b. Everybody, you're going to follow the lines and write these words.

c. Reading the fast way.

d. Point to the first word. (Pause.) Get ready. (Signal.)
The children respond.

e. Repeat d for the remaining words.

f. Repeat d and e until firm.

TASK 22   Cross-out game

Point to the boxed word in the Cross-out Game. Everybody, here's the word you're going to cross out today. What word? (Signal.)
Sand. Yes, **sand.**

TASK 23   Pair relations

a. Point to the pair-relations exercise on side 2. You're going to circle the picture in each box that shows what the words say.

b. Point to the space at the top of the page. After you finish, remember to draw a picture that shows **hē had sand on him.**

INDIVIDUAL CHECKOUT: STORYBOOK

TASK 24   2-minute individual checkout — whole story

a. As you are doing your take-home, I'll call on children one at a time to read the **whole story.** Remember, you get two stars if you read the story in less than two minutes and make no more than three errors.

b. Call on a child. Tell the child: Read the whole story very carefully the fast way. Go. Time the child. Tell the child any words the child misses. Stop the child as soon as the child makes the fourth error or exceeds the time limit.

c. If the child meets the rate-accuracy criterion, record two stars on your chart for lesson 110. Congratulate the child. Give children who do not earn two stars a chance to read the story again before the next lesson is presented.

44 words/2 min = 22 wpm **[3 errors]**

TASK 25   Bonus take-home: sides 3 and 4

After the children have completed their take-home exercises, give them sides 3 and 4 of Take-Home 110. Tell them they may keep the stories and read them.

END OF LESSON 110

Before presenting lesson 111, give Mastery Test 21 to each child.
Do not present lesson 111 to any groups that are not firm on this test.

TASK 22   Picture comprehension

a. Everybody, look at the picture.

b. Ask these questions:
1. Does he look like he's going fast? *Yes.* Where's the meat pie? *The children respond.* Yes, it's flying toward his wife.
2. What's that stuff on his feet? *The children respond.* Egg.
3. What's that stuff all over his nose? *The children respond.* Fish cake.

c. I think he'd better slow down. We'll see what happens when we read the rest of the story.

Take-Home 159

SUMMARY OF INDEPENDENT ACTIVITY

TASK 23   Introduction to independent activity

a. Pass out Take-Home 159 to each child.

b. Everybody, you're going to do this take-home on your own. Tell the children when they will work the items. Let's go over the things you're going to do.

TASK 24   Story items

a. Hold up side 1 of your take-home and point to the story-items exercise.

b. Everybody, here are items about the story we read today.

c. Think about what happened in the story and circle the right answer for each item.

TASK 25   Picture comprehension

a. Point to the pictures in the picture-comprehension exercise. Everybody, you're going to look at the picture. Then you're going to read each item and write the missing word.

b. Remember—the first sound of each missing word is already written in the blank.

TASK 26   Reading comprehension

a. Point to the reading-comprehension exercise on side 2.

b. Everybody, get ready to read the sentences in the box the fast way.

c. First word. Check children's responses. Get ready. Clap for each word as the children read the sentences: *A girl walked down the road. She met a big fox.*

d. Point to items 1 and 2. These items tell about the story in the box. You're going to read each item and circle the right answer.

TASK 27   Sound writing

a. Point to the sound-writing exercise. Here are the sounds you're going to write today. I'll touch the sounds. You say them.

b. Touch each sound. *The children respond.*

c. Repeat the series until firm.

TASK 28   Sentence copying

a. Point to the dotted sentence in the sentence-copying exercise.

b. You're going to trace the words in this sentence. Then you're going to write the sentence on the other lines.

c. Reading the fast way. First word. Check children's responses. Get ready. Clap for each word.

d. After you finish your take-home, you get to draw a picture about the sentence, **hē āte a mēat pie.** You'll draw your picture on a piece of plain paper. When the children finish their take-homes, give them sheets of plain paper.

END OF LESSON 159

Mastery Test 21 after lesson 110, before lesson 111

WHAT TO DO

a. Get ready to read these words the fast way.
b. (test item) Touch the ball for **have.** (Pause three seconds.)
Get ready. (Signal.) *Have.*
c. (test item) Touch the ball for **gōats.** (Pause three seconds.)
Get ready. (Signal.) *Goats.*
d. (test item) Touch the ball for **shāve.** (Pause three seconds.)
Get ready. (Signal.) *Shave.*
e. (test item) Touch the ball for **cow.** (Pause three seconds.)
Get ready. (Signal.) *Cow.*
f. (test item) Touch the ball for **was.** (Pause three seconds.)
Get ready. (Signal.) *Was.*

Total number of test items: **5**

A group is weak if more than one-third of the children missed any of the items on the test.

If the group is firm on Mastery Test 21 and was firm on Mastery Test 20:

Skip lesson 111 and present lesson 112 to the group during the next reading period. If more than one child missed any of the items on the test, present the firming procedures specified below to those children.

If the group is firm on Mastery Test 21 but was weak on Mastery Test 20:

Present lesson 111 to the group during the next reading period. If more than one child missed any of the items on the test, present the firming procedures specified below to those children.

If the group is weak on Mastery Test 21:

A. Present these firming procedures to the group during the next reading period.
   1. Lesson 105, Reading Vocabulary, page 312 (Book B), tasks 16, 17.
   2. Lesson 107, Reading Vocabulary, pages 324–325 (Book B), tasks 6 through 16.
   3. Lesson 109, Reading Vocabulary, page 7, tasks 7 through 9.
B. After presenting the above tasks, again give Mastery Test 21 individually to members of the group who failed the test.
C. If the group is firm (less than one-third of the total group missed any items on the retest), present lesson 111 to the group during the next reading period.
D. If the group is still weak (more than one-third of the total group missed any items on the retest), repeat *A* and *B* during the next reading period.

Story 159

TASK 19 First reading—children read the title and first three sentences

a. Look at page 59. You're going to read the first part of this story today.

b. Everybody, touch the title of the story and get ready to read the words in the title the fast way.

c. First word. Check children's responses. (Pause two seconds.) Get ready. Clap. A.

d. Clap for each remaining word in the title.

e. After the children have read the title, ask: What's this story about? (Signal). *A man liked to go fast.* Yes, **a man liked to go fast.**

f. Everybody, get ready to read this story the fast way.

g. First word. Check children's responses. (Pause two seconds.) Get ready. Clap. A.

h. Clap for the remaining words in the first sentence. Pause at least two seconds between claps.

i. Repeat *g* and *h* for the next two sentences. Have the children reread the first three sentences until firm.

TASK 20 Individual children or the group read sentences to complete the first reading

a. I'm going to call on different children to read a sentence. Everybody, follow along and point to the words. If you hear a mistake, raise your hand.

b. Call on a child. Read the next sentence. Do not clap for the words. Let the child read at his own pace, but be sure he reads the sentence correctly.

To correct	Have the child sound out the word. Then return to the beginning of the sentence.

c. Repeat *b* for most of the remaining sentences in the story. Occasionally have the group read a sentence. When the group is to read, say: Everybody, read the next sentence. (Pause two seconds.) Get ready. Clap for each word in the sentence. Pause at least two seconds between claps.

TASK 21 Second reading—individual children or the group read each sentence; the group answer questions

a. You're going to read the story again. This time I'm going to ask questions.

b. Starting with the first word of the title. Check children's responses. Get ready. Clap as the children read the title. Pause at least two seconds between claps.

c. Call on a child. Read the first sentence. *The child responds.*

d. Repeat *b* and *c* in task 20. Present the following comprehension questions to the entire group.

After the children read:	You say:
A man liked to go fast.	What's this story about? (Signal.) *A man liked to go fast.*
He even talked fast.	Name some things that the man did fast. *The children respond.* He went fast in his car. He walked fast and ran fast. He even talked fast.
He sat down to eat an egg and a fish cake and a meat pie.	What did he eat? (Signal.) *An egg, a fish cake, and a meat pie.*
But he ate so fast that the egg slipped and fell on his feet.	What happened? (Signal.) *He ate so fast that the egg slipped and fell on his feet.*
The meat pie hit his wife.	Tell me all the things that happened when he went to eat the fish cake and the meat pie. *The children respond.* His nose went into the fish cake. He hit the meat pie. And the meat pie hit his wife.

Lesson 111

Groups that are firm on Mastery Tests 20 and 21 should skip this lesson and do lesson 112 today.

SOUNDS

TASK 1 Teacher and children play the sounds game

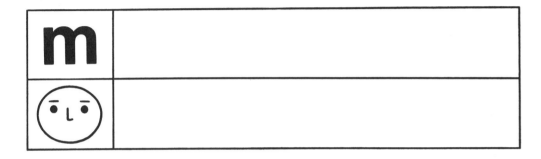

a. Use acetate and crayon. Write the sounds in the symbol box. Keep score in the score box.

b. **I'm smart. I bet I can beat you in a game.**

c. **Here's the rule. When I touch a sound, you say it.**

d. Play the game.
Make one symbol at a time in the symbol box. Use the symbols
l, w, I, and **h.**
Make each symbol quickly.
(Pause.) Touch the symbol.
Play the game for about two minutes.
Then ask: **Who won?** Draw a mouth on the face in the score box.

TASK 2 Teacher introduces cross-out game

a. Use acetate and crayon.

b. **I'll cross out the sounds on this page when you can tell me every sound.**

c. **Remember—when I touch it, you say it.**

d. Go over the sounds until the children can identify all the sounds in order.

TASK 3 Individual test

Call on different children to identify two or more sounds in task 2.

TASK 4 Teacher crosses out sounds

a. **You told me every sound. Get ready to do it again. This time I'll cross out each sound when you tell me what it is.**

b. Point to each sound. (Pause.) Say: **Get ready.** Touch the sound.
The children respond. As you cross out the sound, say:
Goodbye, _____ .

17

Read the Items 159

TASK 16   Children read items 1 and 2

a. Pass out Storybook 3.
b. Open your book to page 58.
c. Get ready to read the items and play the game.
d. Finger under the first word of the title. Check children's responses.
e. When I clap, read the title. (Pause.) Get ready. Clap.
Read the items.
f. Touch item 1 and get ready to read. Check children's responses.
First word. Clap for each word as the children read: *If the teacher says "Touch your nose," touch your feet.* Repeat until firm.
g. Everybody, get ready to say item 1. (Pause and signal.) *The children say the sentence.* Repeat four times or until firm.
h. Touch item 2 and get ready to read. Check children's responses.
First word. Clap for each word as the children read: *When the teacher says, "Give me your book," give the teacher your book.* Repeat until firm.
i. Everybody, get ready to say item 2. (Pause and signal.) *The children say the sentence.* Repeat four times or until firm.

TASK 17   Children reread items 1 and 2 and answer questions

a. Everybody, touch item 1. Check children's responses.
b. Read item 1 to yourself. Raise your hand when you know what you're going to do and when you're going to do it.
c. After the children raise their hands, say: Everybody, what are you going to do if I say "**Touch your nose**"? (Signal.) *Touch my feet.*

To correct	1. Everybody, read item 1 out loud. Clap as the children read each word.
	2. What are you going to do when I say "**Touch your nose**"? (Signal.) *Touch my feet.*

d. Everybody, when are you going to **touch your feet**? (Signal.) *If the teacher says "Touch your nose."*

To correct	1. Everybody, read item 1 out loud. Clap as the children read each word.
	2. When are you going to **touch your feet**? (Signal.) *If the teacher says "Touch your nose."*

e. Repeat *c* and *d* until firm.

f. Everybody, touch item 2. Check children's responses.
g. Read item 2 to yourself. Raise your hand when you know what you're going to do and when you're going to do it.
h. After the children raise their hands, say: Everybody, what are you going to do when I say "**Give me your book**? (Signal.)
Give you my book.

To correct	1. Everybody, read item 2 out loud. Clap as the children read each word.
	2. What are you going to do when I say "**Give me your book**"? (Signal.) *Give you my book.*

i. Everybody, when are you going to **give me your book**? (Signal.) *When the teacher says "Give me your book."*

To correct	1. Everybody, read item 2 out loud. Clap as the children read each word.
	2. When are you going to **give me your book**? (Signal.) *When the teacher says "Give me your book."*

j. Repeat *h* and *i* until firm.

TASK 18   Children play the game

a. Everybody, touch item 1. Check children's responses.
b. Read the item to yourself. Raise your hand when you know what you're going to do and when you're going to do it.
c. After the children raise their hands, say: Let's play the game.
Think about what you're going to do (pause) and when you're going to do it.
d. Hold out your hand. (Pause.) Get ready. **Touch your nose.**
Drop your hand. *(The children touch their feet immediately.)*

To correct	1. What did I say? (Signal.) *Touch your nose.*
	2. What are you supposed to do when I say "**Touch your nose**"? (Signal.) *Touch my feet.*
	3. If the children's responses are not firm, have them read item 1 aloud.
	4. Repeat task 18.

111

READING VOCABULARY

TASK 5   Children read the fast way

a. Get ready to read these words the fast way.
b. Touch the ball for **lots.** (Pause three seconds.) Get ready.
(Signal.) *Lots.*

c. Repeat *b* for the remaining words on the page.

TASK 6   Children read the fast way again

a. Get ready to do these words again. Watch where I point.
b. Point to a word. (Pause one second.) Say: Get ready. (Signal.)
The children respond. Point to the words in this order:
with, us, fog, have, lots.

c. Repeat *b* until firm.

TASK 7   Individual test

Call on different children to read one word the fast way.

Do not touch any small letters.

lots

fog

us

have

with

TASK 12   **Children rhyme with fell and tell**

a. Touch the ball for **fell.** You're going to read this word the fast way.
(Pause three seconds.) Get ready.
Move your finger quickly along the arrow. *Fell.*
b. Touch the ball for **tell.** This word rhymes with (pause) **fell.**
Move to **t,** then quickly along the arrow. *Tell.*
Yes, what word? (Signal.) *Tell.*

TASK 13   **Children sound out the word and tell what word**

a. Touch the ball for **fast.** Sound it out.
b. Get ready. Touch **f, a, s, t** as the children say *fffaaassst.*
If sounding out is not firm, repeat *b.*
c. What word? (Signal.) *Fast.* Yes, **fast.**

TASK 14   **Children read the words the fast way**

a. Now you get to read the words on this page the fast way.
b. Touch the ball for **fell.** (Pause three seconds.) Get ready. Move
your finger quickly along the arrow. *Fell.*
c. Repeat *b* for each word on the page.

TASK 15   **Individual test**

Call on different children to read one word the fast way.

fell

tell

fast

TASK 8 Children rhyme with log

a. Touch the ball for **log**. You're going to read this word the fast way. (Pause three seconds.) Get ready. Move your finger quickly along the arrow. *Log.*

b. Touch the ball for **dog**. This word rhymes with (pause) **log**. Move to **d**, then quickly along the arrow. *Dog.* Yes, what word? (Signal.) *Dog.*

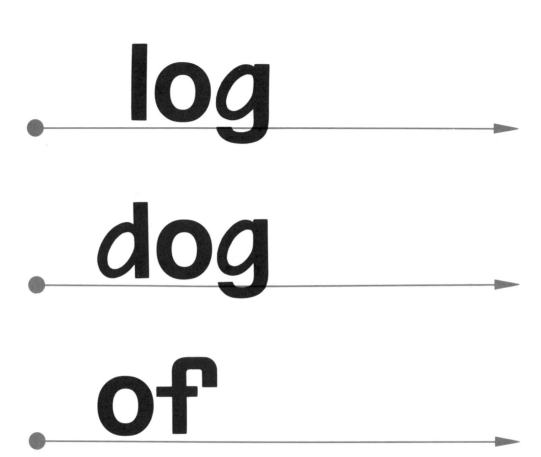

TASK 9 Children identify, then sound out an irregular word (of)

a. Touch the ball for **of**. Everybody, you're going to read this word the fast way. (Pause three seconds.) Get ready. Move your finger quickly along the arrow. *Of.* Yes, **of**.

b. Now you're going to sound out the word. Get ready. Quickly touch **o, f** as the children say *ooofff.*

c. Again. Repeat *b.*

d. How do we say the word? (Signal.) *Of.* Yes, **of**.

e. Repeat *b* and *d* until firm.

TASK 10 Individual test

Call on different children to do *b* and *d* in task 9.

TASK 11 Children read the words the fast way

a. Now you get to read the words on this page the fast way.

b. Touch the ball for **log**. (Pause three seconds.) Get ready. Move your finger quickly along the arrow. *Log.*

c. Repeat *b* for each word on the page.

TASK 12 Individual test

Call on different children to read one word the fast way.

TASK 9   Children read the fast way

a. Get ready to read these words the fast way.
b. Touch the ball for **went.** (Pause three seconds.) Get ready.
(Signal.) *Went.*

c. Repeat *b* for the remaining words on the page.

TASK 10   Children read the fast way again

a. Get ready to do these words again. Watch where I point.
b. Point to a word. (Pause one second.) Say: Get ready. (Signal.)
The children respond. Point to the words in this order:
went, wīpe, slipped, slōw.

c. Repeat *b* until firm.

TASK 11   Individual test

Call on different children to read one word the fast way.

Do not touch any small letters.

went

slōw

slipped

wīpe

Story 111

TASK 13   First reading—children read the story the fast way

Have the children reread any sentences containing words that give them trouble. Keep a list of these words.

a. Pass out Storybook 1.
b. Open your book to page 45 and get ready to read.
c. We're going to read this story the fast way.
d. Touch the first word. Check children's responses.
e. Reading the fast way. First word. (Pause three seconds.)
Get ready. Clap. *She.*
f. Next word. Check children's responses. (Pause three seconds.)
Get ready. Clap. *Said.*
g. Repeat *f* for the remaining words in the first sentence. Pause at least three seconds between claps. The children are to identify each word without sounding it out.
h. Repeat *d* through *g* for the next two sentences. Have the children reread the first three sentences until firm.
i. The children are to read the remainder of the story the fast way, stopping at the end of each sentence.
j. After the first reading of the story, print on the board the words that the children missed more than one time. Have the children sound out each word one time and tell what word.
k. After the group's responses are firm, call on individual children to read the words.

TASK 14   Individual test

a. Turn back to page 45. I'm going to call on different children to read a whole sentence the fast way.
b. Call on different children to read a sentence. Do not clap for each word.

TASK 15   Second reading—children read the story the fast way and answer questions

a. You're going to read the story again the fast way and I'll ask questions.
b. First word. Check children's responses. Get ready. Clap. *She.*
c. Clap for each remaining word. Pause at least three seconds between claps. Pause longer before words that gave the children trouble during the first reading.
d. Ask the comprehension questions below as the children read.

After the children read:	You say:
She said, "I have a fan."	**Who said that?** (Signal.) *She did.*
He said, "I have sand."	**Who had the sand?** (Signal.) *He did.*
She said, "We can run the sand in the fan."	**What did she say?** (Signal.) *We can run the sand in the fan.*
So he ran the fan near the sand.	**What did he do?** (Signal.) *He ran the fan near the sand.*
He had sand in his ears.	**Where did he have sand?** (Signal.) *In his ears.*
He said, "I can not hear."	**What did he say?** (Signal.) *I can not hear.* **Why couldn't he hear?** (Signal.) *He had sand in his ears.*
He had sand on his seat.	**Where did he have sand?** (Signal.) *On his seat.*
She said, "We have sand on us."	**Who said that?** (Signal.) *She did.*

TASK 16   Picture comprehension

a. Everybody, look at the picture.
b. Ask these questions:
   1. Why do they have their hands over their faces? *The children respond.* So they won't get sand in their faces.
   2. Does that look like fun to you? *The children respond.*

READING VOCABULARY

Do not touch any small letters.

TASK 6   Children read the fast way

a. Get ready to read these words the fast way.

b. Touch the ball for **pie.** (Pause three seconds.) Get ready.
(Signal.) *Pie.*

c. Repeat *b* for the remaining words on the page.

TASK 7   Children read the fast way again

a. Get ready to do these words again. Watch where I point.

b. Point to a word. (Pause one second.) Say: Get ready.   (Signal.)
The children respond. Point to the words in this order:
wīfe, pīe, ēven, bent, thing.

c. Repeat *b* until firm.

TASK 8   Individual test

Call on different children to read one word the fast way.

pīe

thing

bent

wīfe

ēven

Take-Home 111

SUMMARY OF INDEPENDENT ACTIVITY

TASK 17   Introduction to independent activity

a. Pass out Take-Home 111 to each child.
b. Everybody, you're going to do this take-home on your own.
Tell the children when they will work the items.
Let's go over the things you're going to do.

TASK 18   Sentence copying

a. Hold up side 1 of your take-home and point to the first line in the sentence-copying exercise.
b. Everybody, here's the sentence you're going to write on the lines below.
c. Reading the fast way. First word.   Check children's responses. **Get ready.**   Clap. *He.*
d. Next word.   Check children's responses. **Get ready.**   Clap. *Ran.*
e. Repeat *d* for the remaining words.
f. After you finish your take-home, you get to draw a picture about the sentence, hē ran thē fan.

TASK 19   Sound writing

a. Point to the sound-writing exercise. **Here are the sounds you're going to write today. I'll touch the sounds. You say them.**
b. Touch each sound. *The children respond.*
c. Repeat the series until firm.

TASK 20   Matching

a. Point to the column of words in the Matching Game.
b. Everybody, you're going to follow the lines and write these words.
c. Reading the fast way.
d. Point to the first word. (Pause.) **Get ready.**   (Signal.)
The children respond.
e. Repeat *d* for the remaining words.
f. Repeat *d* and *e* until firm.

TASK 21   Cross-out game

Point to the boxed word in the Cross-out Game. **Everybody, here's the word you're going to cross out today. What word?**   (Signal.)
Run. Yes, **run.**

TASK 22   Pair relations

a. Point to the pair-relations exercise on side 2. **You're going to circle the picture in each box that shows what the words say.**
b. Point to the space at the top of the page. **After you finish, remember to draw a picture that shows hē ran thē fan.**

END OF LESSON 111

Lesson 159

Groups that are firm on Mastery Tests 29 and 30 should skip this lesson.

SOUNDS

TASK 1 Teaching ū as in ūse

a. Point to **ū**. **My turn.** (Pause.) Touch **ū** and say: ūūū.
b. Point to **ū**. **Your turn. When I touch it, you say it.** (Pause.) **Get ready.** Touch **ū**. ūūū. Lift your finger.
c. **Again.** Touch **ū**. ūūūū. Lift your finger.
d. Repeat *c* until firm.

TASK 2 Sounds firm-up

a. **Get ready to say the sounds when I touch them.**
b. Alternate touching **ū** and **oo**. Point to the sound. (Pause one second.) Say: **Get ready.** Touch the sound. *The children respond.*
c. When **ū** and **oo** are firm, alternate touching **ū, oo, u,** and **z** until all four sounds are firm.

TASK 3 Individual test

Call on different children to identify **ū, oo, u,** or **z.**

TASK 4 Sounds firm-up

a. Point to **ū**. **When I touch the sound, you say it.**
b. (Pause.) **Get ready.** Touch **ū**. *uuu.*
c. **Again.** Repeat *b* until firm.
d. **Get ready to say all the sounds when I touch them.**
e. Alternate touching **ū, qu, ȳ, wh, j, y, er,** and **ī** three or four times. Point to the sound. (Pause one second.) Say: **Get ready.** Touch the sound. *The children respond.*

TASK 5 Individual test

Call on different children to identify one or more sounds in task 4.

Lesson 112

SOUNDS

TASK 1   Teacher and children play the sounds game

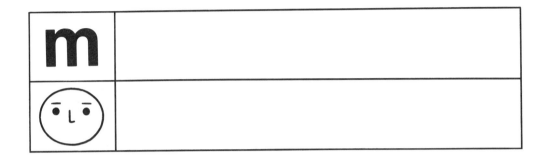

a. Use acetate and crayon. Write the sounds in the symbol box. Keep score in the score box.

b. **I'm smart. I bet I can beat you in a game.**

c. **Here's the rule. When I touch a sound, you say it.**

d. Play the game.
Make one symbol at a time in the symbol box. Use the symbols **ē, i, n, and ā.**
Make each symbol quickly. (Pause.) Touch the symbol.
Play the game for about two minutes.
Then ask: **Who won?** Draw a mouth on the face in the score box.

TASK 2   Child plays teacher

a. Use acetate and crayon.

b. **[Child's name] is going to be the teacher.**

c. **[He or She] is going to touch the sounds. When [he or she] touches a sound, you say it.**

d. The child points to and touches the sounds. You circle any sound that is not firm.

e. After the child has completed the page, present all the circled sounds to the children.

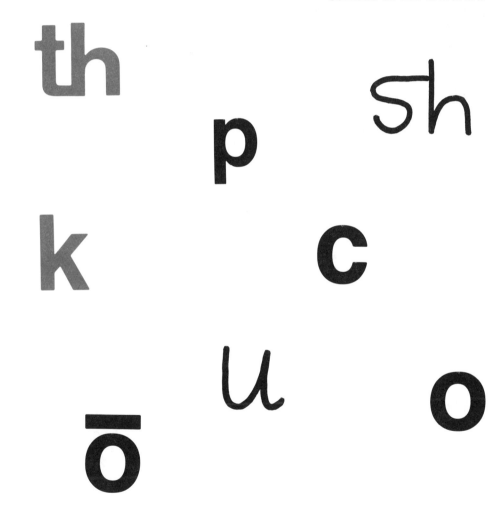

TASK 3   Individual test

Call on different children. **If you can say the sound when I call your name, you may cross it out.**

TASK 30   Picture comprehension

a. Everybody, look at the picture.
b. Ask these questions:
  1. What's the fat eagle doing? *The children respond.*
      He's jumping on top of the tiger. I'll bet that hurts.
  2. What's the tiger going to do? *The children respond.*
      Run far away. Look at how happy the other eagles are.
      I sure am glad the tiger didn't get that little eagle.

Take-Home 158

SUMMARY OF INDEPENDENT ACTIVITY

TASK 31   Introduction to independent activity

a. Pass out Take-Home 158 to each child.
b. Everybody, you're going to do this take-home on your own.
      Tell the children when they will work the items.
      Let's go over the things you're going to do.

TASK 32   Story items

a. Hold up side 1 of your take-home and point to the story-items
                                                    exercise.
b. Everybody, here are items about the story we read today.
c. Think about what happened in the story and circle the right answer
                                                    for each item.

TASK 33   Picture comprehension

a. Point to the pictures in the picture-comprehension exercise.
      Everybody, you're going to look at the picture. Then you're going
                to read each item and write the missing word.
b. Remember—the first sound of each missing word is already written
                                                    in the blank.

TASK 34   Reading comprehension

a. Point to the reading-comprehension exercise on side 2.
b. Everybody, get ready to read the sentences in the box the fast way.
c. First word. Check children's responses. Get ready. Clap for each
      word as the children read the sentences: *A tiger sat under a tree.*
                                      He was looking for rabbits.
d. Point to items 1 and 2. These items tell about the story in the
      box. You're going to read each item and circle the right answer.

TASK 35   Sound writing

a. Point to the sound-writing exercise. Here are the sounds you're
                going to write today. I'll touch the sounds. You say them.
b. Touch each sound. *The children respond.*
c. Repeat the series until firm.

TASK 36   Sentence copying

a. Point to the dotted sentence in the sentence-copying exercise.
b. You're going to trace the words in this sentence. Then you're
                going to write the sentence on the other lines.
c. Reading the fast way. First word. Check children's responses.
                Get ready. Clap for each word.
d. After you finish your take-home, you get to draw a picture about
      the sentence, **they give him cāke.** You'll draw your picture on
      a piece of plain paper. When the children finish their take-homes,
                give them sheets of plain paper.

END OF LESSON 158

READING VOCABULARY

Do not touch any small letters.

TASK 4   Children sound out an irregular word (are)

a. Touch the ball for **are.**   Sound it out.

b. Get ready. Quickly touch each sound as the children say *aaarrr.*

c. Again. Repeat *b* until firm.

d. That's how we <u>sound out</u> the word. Here's how we <u>say</u> the word.

   Are. How do we <u>say</u> the word? (Signal.) *Are.*

e. Now you're going to <u>sound out</u> the word. Get ready.

   Touch each sound as the children say *aaarrr.*

f. Now you're going to <u>say</u> the word. Get ready. (Signal.) *Are.*

g. Repeat *e* and *f* until firm.

are

TASK 5   Children rhyme with an irregular word (are)

a. Touch the ball for **are.**   Everybody, you're going to read this

   word the fast way. Get ready. (Signal.) *Are.*

b. Touch the ball for **car.**   This word rhymes with (pause) **are.**

   Get ready. Move to **c,** then quickly along the arrow. *Car.*

c. Touch the ball for **tar.**   This word rhymes with (pause) **are.**

   Get ready. Move to **t,** then quickly along the arrow. *Tar.*

d. Repeat *a* through *c* until firm.

car

TASK 6   Children sound out car and tar

a. Have the children sound out **car.** *Caaarrr.*   How do we say the word?

   (Signal.) *Car.*   Yes, **car.** Ride in my **car.**

b. Have the children sound out **tar.** *Taaarrr.*   How do we say the word?

   (Signal.) *Tar.*   Yes, **tar. Tar** is black.

tar

Story 158

TASK 27 First reading—children read the title and first three sentences

a. Now you're going to finish the story about the fat eagle.
b. Everybody, touch the title of the story and get ready to read the words in the title the fast way.
c. First word. Check children's responses. (Pause two seconds.) Get ready. Clap. *The.*
d. Clap for each remaining word in the title.
e. After the children have read the title, ask: What's this story about? (Signal.) *The fat eagle.* Yes, **the fat eagle.**
f. Everybody, get ready to read this story the fast way.
g. First word. Check children's responses. (Pause two seconds.) Get ready. Clap. *A.*
h. Clap for the remaining words in the first sentence. Pause at least two seconds between claps.
i. Repeat *g* and *h* for the next two sentences. Have the children reread the first three sentences until firm.

TASK 28 Individual children or the group read sentences to complete the first reading

a. I'm going to call on different children to read a sentence. Everybody, follow along and point to the words. If you hear a mistake, raise your hand.
b. Call on a child. Read the next sentence. Do not clap for the words. Let the child read at his own pace, but be sure he reads the sentence correctly.

To correct	Have the child sound out the word. Then return to the beginning of the sentence.

c. Repeat *b* for most of the remaining sentences in the story. Occasionally have the group read a sentence. When the group is to read, say: Everybody, read the next sentence. (Pause two seconds.) Get ready. Clap for each word in the sentence. Pause at least two seconds between claps.

TASK 29 Second reading—individual children or the group read each sentence; the group answer questions

a. You're going to read the story again. This time I'm going to ask questions.
b. Starting with the first word of the title. Check children's responses. Get ready. Clap as the children read the title. Pause at least two seconds between claps.
c. Call on a child. Read the first sentence. *The child responds.*
d. Repeat *b* and *c* in task 28. Present the following comprehension questions to the entire group.

After the children read:	You say:
"I must save the little eagle."	What did the fat eagle say? (Signal.) *I must save the little eagle.* I wonder what he can do to save the little eagle.
He came down like a fat rock on the tiger.	What did the fat eagle do? (Signal.) *He came down like a fat rock on the tiger.* Do you suppose the tiger liked that? *The children respond.*
And the tiger ran far away.	What did the tiger do? (Signal.) *He ran far away.*
They give him cake and ham and corn.	What do the other eagles do? (Signal.) *They give him cake and ham and corn.* Why don't they make fun of him any more? *The children respond.* Because he saved the little eagle.

TASK 7 Children identify, then sound out an irregular word (of)

a. Touch the ball for **of.** **Everybody, you're going to read this word the fast way.** (Pause three seconds.) **Get ready.** Move your finger quickly along the arrow. *Of.* **Yes, of.**

b. Now you're going to sound out the word. Get ready. Quickly touch **o, f** as the children say *ooofff.*

c. Again. Repeat *b*.

d. How do we say the word? (Signal.) *Of.* **Yes, of.**

e. Repeat *b* and *d* until firm.

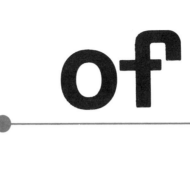

TASK 8 Individual test

Call on different children to do *b* and *d* in task 7.

TASK 9 Children sound out the word and tell what word

a. Touch the ball for **dog.** **Sound it out.**

b. Get ready. Touch **d, o, g** as the children say *dooog.* If sounding out is not firm, repeat *b*.

c. What word? (Signal.) *Dog.* **Yes, dog.**

TASK 10 Children sound out the word and tell what word

a. Touch the ball for **pot.** **Sound it out.**

b. Get ready. Touch **p, o, t** as the children say *pooot.* If sounding out is not firm, repeat *b*.

c. What word? (Signal.) *Pot.* **Yes, pot.**

TASK 11 Children read the words the fast way

a. Now you get to read the words on this page the fast way.

b. Touch the ball for **of.** (Pause three seconds.) **Get ready.** Move your finger quickly along the arrow. *Of.*

c. Repeat *b* for each word on the page.

TASK 12 Individual test

Call on different children to read one word the fast way.

Read the Items 158

TASK 24 Children read items 1 and 2

a. Pass out Storybook 3.

b. Open your book to page 55.

c. Get ready to read the items and play the game.

d. Finger under the first word of the title. Check children's responses.

e. When I clap, read the title. (Pause.) Get ready. Clap.

Read the items.

f. Touch item 1 and get ready to read. Check children's responses.

First word. Clap for each word as the children read:

When the teacher says "Touch your feet," stand up. Repeat until firm.

g. Everybody, get ready to say item 1. (Pause and signal.) *The children say the sentence.* Repeat four times or until firm.

h. Touch item 2 and get ready to read. Check children's responses.

First word. Clap for each word as the children read:

If the teacher says "Go," touch your ears. Repeat until firm.

i. Everybody, get ready to say item 2. (Pause and signal.) *The children say the sentence.* Repeat four times or until firm.

TASK 25 Children reread items 1 and 2 and answer questions

a. Everybody, touch item 1. Check children's responses.

b. Read item 1 to yourself. Raise your hand when you know what you're going to do and when you're going to do it.

c. After the children raise their hands, say: Everybody, what are you going to do when I say "**Touch your feet**"? (Signal.) *Stand up.*

To correct	1. Everybody, read item 1 out loud. Clap as the children read each word. 2. What are you going to do when I say "**Touch your feet**"? (Signal.) *Stand up.*

d. Everybody, when are you going to **stand up**? (Signal.) *When the teacher says "Touch your feet."*

To correct	1. Everybody, read item 1 out loud. Clap as the children read each word. 2. When are you going to **stand up**? (Signal.) *When the teacher says "Touch your feet."*

e. Repeat *c* and *d* until firm.

f. Everybody, touch item 2. Check children's responses.

g. Read item 2 to yourself. Raise your hand when you know what you're going to do and when you're going to do it.

h. After the children raise their hands, say: Everybody, what are you going to do if I say "**Go**"? (Signal.) *Touch my ears.*

To correct	1. Everybody, read item 2 out loud. Clap as the children read each word. 2. What are you going to do when I say "**Go**"? (Signal.) *Touch my ears.*

i. Everybody, when are you going to **touch your ears**? (Signal.) *If the teacher says "Go."*

To correct	1. Everybody, read item 2 out loud. Clap as the children read each word. 2. When are you going to **touch your ears**? (Signal.) *If the teacher says "Go."*

j. Repeat *h* and *i* until firm.

TASK 26 Children play the game

a. Everybody, touch item 1. Check children's responses.

b. Read the item to yourself. Raise your hand when you know what you're going to do and when you're going to do it.

c. After the children raise their hands, say: Let's play the game.

Think about what you're going to do (pause) and when you're going to do it.

d. Hold out your hand. (Pause.) Get ready. **Touch your feet**. (Pause.) Drop your hand. *(The children stand up immediately.)*

To correct	1. What did I say? (Signal.) *Touch your feet.* 2. What are you supposed to do when I say "**Touch your feet**"? (Signal.) *Stand up.* 3. If the children's responses are not firm, have them read item 1 aloud. 4. Repeat task 26.

TASK 13 Children read the fast way

a. Get ready to read these words the fast way.
b. Touch the ball for **us.** (Pause three seconds.) Get ready.
(Signal.) *Us.*
c. Touch the ball for **log.** (Pause three seconds.) Get ready.
(Signal.) *Log.*

us

TASK 14 Children identify, then sound out an irregular word (to)

a. Touch the ball for **to.** Everybody, you're going to read this
word the fast way. (Pause three seconds.) Get ready.
Move your finger quickly along the arrow. *To.* Yes, **to.**
b. Now you're going to sound out the word. Get ready.
Quickly touch **t, o** as the children say *tooo.*
c. Again. Repeat *b.*
d. How do we say the word? (Signal.) *To.* Yes, **to.**
e. Repeat *b* and *d* until firm.

log

TASK 15 Individual test

Call on different children to do *b* and *d* in task 14.

to

TASK 16 Children read the words the fast way

a. Now you get to read the words on this page the fast way.
b. Touch the ball for **us.** (Pause three seconds.) Get ready.
Move your finger quickly along the arrow. *Us.*
c. Repeat *b* for each word on the page.

TASK 17 Individual test

Call on different children to read one word the fast way.

TASK 18   Children sound out an irregular word (took)

a. Touch the ball for **took.** Sound it out.

b. Get ready. Quickly touch each sound as the children say *toook.*

c. Again. Repeat *b* until firm.

d. That's how we <u>sound out</u> the word. Here's how we <u>say</u> the word.
           Took. How do we <u>say</u> the word? (Signal.) *Took.*

e. Now you're going to <u>sound out</u> the word. Get ready.
           Touch each sound as the children say *tooook.*

f. Now you're going to say the word. Get ready. (Signal.) *Took.*

g. Repeat *e* and *f* until firm.

h. Yes, this word is **took**. She **took** my book.

TASK 19   Individual test

Call on different children to do *e* and *f* in task 18.

TASK 20   Children sound out the word and tell what word

a. Touch the ball for **head.** Sound it out.

b. Get ready. Touch **h, e, d** as the children say *heeed.*
           If sounding out is not firm, repeat *b.*

c. What word? (Signal.) *Head.* Yes, **head.**

TASK 21   Children read the fast way

Touch the ball for **thing.** Get ready to read this word the fast way.
           (Pause three seconds.) Get ready. (Signal.) *Thing.*

TASK 22   Children read the words the fast way

Have the children read the words on this page the fast way.

TASK 23   Individual test

Call on different children to read one word the fast way.

Do not touch any small letters.

Story 112

TASK 18   First reading—children read the story the fast way

Have the children reread any sentences containing words that give them trouble. Keep a list of these words.

a. Pass out Storybook 1.
b. Open your book to page 48 and get ready to read.
c. We're going to read this story the fast way.
d. Touch the first word. Check children's responses.
e. Reading the fast way. First word. (Pause three seconds.)
Get ready. Clap. A.

f. Next word. Check children's responses. (Pause three seconds.)
Get ready. Clap. Dog.

g. Repeat <i>f</i> for the remaining words in the first sentence. Pause at least three seconds between claps. The children are to identify each word without sounding it out.
h. Repeat <i>d</i> through <i>g</i> for the next two sentences. Have the children reread the first three sentences until firm.
i. The children are to read the remainder of the story the fast way, stopping at the end of each sentence.
j. After the first reading of the story, print on the board the words that the children missed more than one time. Have the children sound out each word one time and tell what word.
k. After the group's responses are firm, call on individual children to read the words.

TASK 19   Individual test

a. I'm going to call on different children to read a whole sentence the fast way.
b. Call on different children to read a sentence. Do not clap for each word.

TASK 20   Second reading—children read the story the fast way and answer questions

a. You're going to read the story again the fast way and I'll ask questions.
b. First word. Check children's responses. Get ready. Clap. <i>A.</i>
c. Clap for each remaining word. Pause at least three seconds between claps. Pause longer before words that gave the children trouble during the first reading.
d. Ask the comprehension questions below as the children read.

After the children read:	You say:
<i>A dog sat in a little car.</i>	What did the dog do? (Signal.) <i>He sat in a little car.</i>
<i>The dog said, "I need to eat."</i>	What did he say? (Signal.) <i>I need to eat.</i>
<i>Will the dog eat a fish?</i>	What do you think? <i>The children respond.</i> Let's read and find out.
<i>No.</i>	Will he eat a fish? (Signal.) <i>No.</i>
<i>Will the dog eat a log?</i>	What do you think? <i>The children respond.</i> Let's read and find out.
<i>No.</i>	Will he eat a log? (Signal.) <i>No.</i>
<i>Will the dog eat a pot of tar?</i>	What's a pot of tar? <i>The children respond.</i> Let's see if he'll eat that.
<i>No.</i>	Will he eat a pot of tar? (Signal.) <i>No.</i>
<i>The dog will eat the car.</i>	What will he do? (Signal.) <i>He will eat the car.</i> That's silly.

TASK 15   Children read the fast way

a. Get ready to read these words the fast way.
b. Touch the ball for **under.** (Pause three seconds.) Get ready.

(Signal.) *Under.*

c. Repeat *b* for the remaining words on the page.

TASK 16   Children read the fast way again

a. Get ready to do these words again. Watch where I point.
b. Point to a word. (Pause one second.) Say: Get ready.   (Signal.)
The children respond. Point to the words in this order:
shōw, ōver, under, fast, after.

c. Repeat *b* until firm.

TASK 17   Individual test

Call on different children to read one word the fast way.

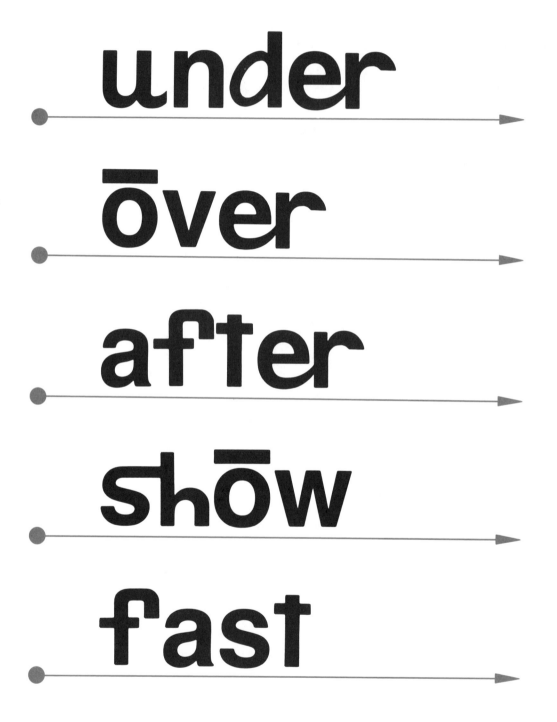

TASK 21 Picture comprehension

a. Everybody, look at the picture.
b. Ask these questions:
   1. Is he eating part of the car? *Yes.* What part?
                 The children respond. The steering wheel.
   2. Do you think that silly dog will eat the whole car?
       The children respond. I don't think a car would taste very good.

Take-Home 112

SUMMARY OF INDEPENDENT ACTIVITY

TASK 22 Introduction to independent activity

a. Pass out Take-Home 112 to each child.
b. Everybody, you're going to do this take-home on your own.
            Tell the children when they will work the items.
            Let's go over the things you're going to do.

TASK 23 Sentence copying

a. Hold up side 1 of your take-home and point to the first line in the
                    sentence-copying exercise.
b. Everybody, here's the sentence you're going to write on the lines
                            below.
c. Reading the fast way. First word. Check children's responses.
                Get ready. Clap. *Thē.*
d. Next word. Check children's responses. Get ready. Clap. *Dog.*
e. Repeat *d* for the remaining words.
f. After you finish your take-home, you get to draw a picture about
                    the sentence, **thē dog āte thē car.**

TASK 24 Sound writing

a. Point to the sound-writing exercise. Here are the sounds you're
               going to write today. I'll touch the sounds. You say them.
b. Touch each sound. *The children respond.*
c. Repeat the series until firm.

TASK 25 Matching

a. Point to the column of words in the Matching Game.
b. Everybody, you're going to follow the lines and write these words.
c. Reading the fast way.
d. Point to the first word. (Pause.) Get ready. (Signal.)
                          The children respond.
e. Repeat *d* for the remaining words.
f. Repeat *d* and *e* until firm.

TASK 26 Cross-out game

Point to the boxed word in the Cross-out Game. Everybody, here's
           the word you're going to cross out today. What word? (Signal.)
                         Hand. Yes, **hand.**

TASK 27 Pair relations

a. Point to the pair-relations exercise on side 2. You're going to
            circle the picture in each box that shows what the words say.
b. Point to the space at the top of the page. After you finish,
           remember to draw a picture that shows **thē dog āte thē car.**

END OF LESSON 112

TASK 9   Children identify, then sound out an irregular word (look)

a. Touch the ball for **look.** **Everybody, you're going to read this word the fast way.** (Pause three seconds.) **Get ready.** Move your finger quickly along the arrow. *Look.* **Yes, look.**

b. Now you're going to sound out the word. Get ready. Quickly touch **l, oo, k** as the children say *lllooook.*

c. Again. Repeat *b*.

d. How do we say the word? (Signal.) *Look.* **Yes, look.**

e. Repeat *b* and *d* until firm.

TASK 10   Individual test

Call on different children to do *b* and *d* in task 9.

TASK 11   Children rhyme with wīfe and līfe

a. Touch the ball for **wīfe.** **You're going to read this word the fast way.** (Pause three seconds.) **Get ready.** Move your finger quickly along the arrow. *Wife.*

b. Touch the ball for **līfe.** **This word rhymes with** (pause) **wife.** Move to **l,** then quickly along the arrow. *Life.* **Yes, what word?** (Signal.) *Life.*

TASK 12   Children sound out the word and tell what word

a. Touch the ball for **picks.** **Sound it out.**

b. Get ready. Touch **p, i, c, s** as the children say *piiicsss.* **If sounding out is not firm, repeat *b.***

c. What word? (Signal.) *Picks.* **Yes, picks.**

TASK 13   Children read the words the fast way

Have the children read the words on this page the fast way.

TASK 14   Individual test

Call on different children to read one word the fast way.

Do not touch any small letters.

Lesson 113

ch

sh

c

th

SOUNDS

TASK 1   Teaching ch as in chat

a. Point to **ch**. Here's a new sound. It's a quick sound.
b. My turn. (Pause.) Touch **ch** for an instant, saying: ch.
Do not say chuh.
c. Again. Touch **ch** and say: ch.
d. Point to **ch**. Your turn. When I touch it, you say it. (Pause.) Get ready. Touch **ch**. *ch.*
e. Again. Touch **ch**. *ch.*
f. Repeat *e* until firm.

TASK 2   Individual test

Call on different children to identify **ch**.

TASK 3   Sounds firm-up

a. Get ready to say the sounds when I touch them.
b. Alternate touching **ch** and **sh**. Point to the sound. (Pause one second.)
Say: Get ready. Touch the sound. *The children respond.*
c. When **ch** and **sh** are firm, alternate touching **ch, c, sh,** and **th** until all four sounds are firm.

TASK 4   Individual test

Call on different children to identify **ch, c, sh,** or **th**.

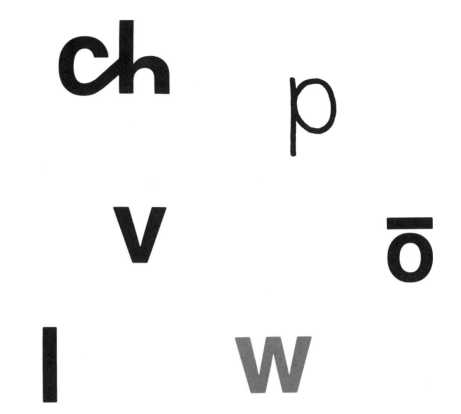

TASK 5   Sounds firm-up

a. Point to **ch**. When I touch the sound, you say it.
b. (Pause.) Get ready. Touch **ch**. *ch.*
c. Again. Repeat *b* until firm.
d. Get ready to say all the sounds when I touch them.
e. Alternate touching **p, v, ō, l, w, k, r,** and **ch** three or four times. Point to the sound.
(Pause one second.) Say:
Get ready. Touch the sound.
The children respond.

TASK 6   Individual test

Call on different children to identify one or more sounds in task 5.

28

READING VOCABULARY

TASK 5   Children read a word beginning with two consonants (slōw)

a. Cover **s.** Point to **lōw.** You're going to read this part of the word the fast way. (Pause three seconds.) Get ready. (Signal.)
Lōw. Yes, **lōw.**

b. Uncover **s.** Point to **s.** You're going to say this first. Move your finger quickly under **lōw.** Then you're going to say (pause) **low.**

c. Point to **s.** What are you going to say first? (Signal.) *sss.* What are you going to say next? (Signal.) *Lōw.*

d. Repeat *c* until firm.

e. Touch the ball for **slōw.** Get ready. Move to **s,** then quickly along the arrow. *Ssslow.*

f. Say it fast. (Signal.) *Slow.* Yes, what word? (Signal.) *Slow.* Yes, **slow.** Good reading.

g. Again. Repeat *e* and *f* until firm.

h. Now you're going to sound out (pause) **slow.** Get ready. Touch **s, l, ō, w** as the children say *sssIllōōōwww.* What word? (Signal.)
Slow. Yes, **slow.**

TASK 6   Children read the fast way

a. Get ready to read these words the fast way.

b. Touch the ball for **when.** (Pause three seconds.) Get ready.
(Signal.) *When.*

c. Repeat *b* for the remaining words on the page.

TASK 7   Children read the fast way again

a. Get ready to do these words again. Watch where I point.

b. Point to a word. (Pause one second.) Say: Get ready. (Signal.)
The children respond. Point to the words in this order:
when, from, then.

c. Repeat *b* until firm.

TASK 8   Individual test

Call on different children to read one word on the page the fast way.

slōw

when

then

from

READING VOCABULARY

Do not touch any small letters.

TASK 7   Children sound out an irregular word (car)

a. Touch the ball for **car.** Sound it out.
b. Get ready.   Quickly touch each sound as the children say *caaarrr.*
c. Again.   Repeat *b* until firm.
d. That's how we <u>sound out</u> the word. Here's how we <u>say</u> the word.
                    Car. How do we <u>say</u> the word?   (Signal.) *Car.*
e. Now you're going to <u>sound out</u> the word. Get ready.
                    Touch each sound as the children say *caaarrr.*
f . Now you're going to say the word. Get ready.   (Signal.) *Car.*
g. Repeat *e* and *f* until firm.
h. Yes, this word is **car.** A dog sat in the **car.**

TASK 8   Individual test

Call on different children to do *e* and *f* in task 7.

TASK 9   Children sound out the word and tell what word

a. Touch the ball for **cāme.** Sound it out.
b. Get ready.   Touch **c, ā, m** as the children say *cāāāmmm.*
                    If sounding out is not firm, repeat *b.*
c. What word?   (Signal.) *Came.* Yes, **came.**

TASK 10   Children sound out the word and tell what word

Repeat the procedures in task 9 for **chops.**

TASK 11   Children read the words the fast way

a. Now you get to read the words on this page the fast way.
b. Touch the ball for **car.** (Pause three seconds.) Get ready.
                    Move your finger quickly along the arrow. *Car.*
c. Repeat *b* for each word on the page.

TASK 12   Individual test

Call on different children to read one word the fast way.

Lesson 158

SOUNDS

TASK 1   Teacher firms up u

a. Point to **u.** Everybody, get ready to tell me this sound. Get ready.

Touch **u.** *uuu.*

b. Point to **ū.** Everybody, look at the line over this sound.

This is not **uuu.** Is it **uuu**? (Signal.) *No.*

c. Point to each sound and ask: Is this **uuu**? *The children respond.*

d. Repeat *c* until firm.

ū

ū

ū

u

ū

u

ō

ȳ

z

TASK 2   Teaching ū as in ūse; children discriminate u—ū

a. Point to the first **ū.** Everybody, this is **ūūū.**

b. When I touch it, you say it. (Pause.) Get ready. Touch **ū.** *ūūū.*

c. Again. Touch **ū.** *ūūū.*

d. Repeat *c* until firm.

e. Get ready to do all these sounds. When I touch the sound, you say it. Alternate touching the sounds. Before touching each **ū,** trace the line and say: Remember—this is not **uuu.**

f. Repeat *e* until all the sounds are firm.

TASK 3   Sounds firm-up

a. Point to **ū.** When I touch the sound, you say it.

b. (Pause.) Get ready. Touch **ū.** *ūūū.*

c. Again. Repeat *b* until firm.

d. Get ready to say all the sounds when I touch them.

e. Alternate touching **ū, ō, ȳ, z, qu,** and **j** three or four times. Point to the sound. (Pause one second.) Say: Get ready. Touch the sound. *The children respond.*

TASK 4   Individual test

Call on different children to identify one or more sounds in task 3.

TASK 13   Children sound out an irregular word (are)

a. Touch the ball for **are.** Sound it out.
b. Get ready. Quickly touch each sound as the children say *aaarrr.*
c. Again. Repeat *b* until firm.
d. That's how we sound out the word. Here's how we say the word.
   Are. How do we <u>say</u> the word? (Signal.) *Are.*
e. Now you're going to <u>sound out</u> the word. Get ready.
   Touch each sound as the children say *aaarrr.*
f. Now you're going to say the word. Get ready. (Signal.) *Are.*
g. Repeat *e* and *f* until firm.
h. Yes, this word is **are. Are** you working hard?

TASK 14   Individual test

Call on different children to do *e* and *f* in task 13.

TASK 15   Children read the fast way

a. Get ready to read these words the fast way.
b. Touch the ball for **shops.** (Pause three seconds.) Get ready.
   (Signal.) *Shops.*

c. Repeat *b* for the remaining words on the page.

TASK 16   Children read the fast way again

a. Get ready to do these words again. Watch where I point.
b. Point to a word. (Pause one second.) Say: Get ready. (Signal.)
   The children respond. Point to the words in this order:
   cops, shops, dog.

c. Repeat *b* until firm.

TASK 17   Individual test

Call on different children to read one word on the page the fast way.

Do not touch any small letters.

are

shops

dog

cops

TASK 28   Picture comprehension

a. What do you think you'll see in the picture? *The children respond.*
b. Turn the page and look at the picture.
c. Ask these questions:
   1. Where's the little eagle? *The children respond.* Under the tree.
   2. Where's the fat eagle? *The children respond.* In the tree.
   3. Where is the tiger? *The children respond.* Behind the tree.
   4. What's he doing? *The children respond.* He's getting ready to grab the little eagle. It looks bad for that little eagle.

Take-Home 157

SUMMARY OF INDEPENDENT ACTIVITY

TASK 29   Introduction to independent activity

a. Pass out Take-Home 157 to each child.
b. Everybody, you're going to do this take-home on your own.
   Tell the children when they will work the items.
   Let's go over the things you're going to do.

TASK 30   Story items

a. Hold up side 1 of your take-home and point to the story-items exercise.
b. Everybody, here are items about the story we read today.
c. Think about what happened in the story and circle the right answer for each item.

TASK 31   Picture comprehension

a. Point to the pictures in the picture-comprehension exercise.
   Everybody, you're going to look at the picture. Then you're going to read each item and write the missing word.
b. Remember—the first sound of each missing word is already written in the blank.

TASK 32   Reading comprehension

a. Point to the reading-comprehension exercise on side 2.
b. Everybody, get reaay to read the sentences in the box the fast way.
c. First word.   Check children's responses. Get ready.   Clap for each word as the children read the sentences: *A girl liked to talk.*
                She talked to the mail man.
d. Point to items 1 and 2. These items tell about the story in the box.
   You're going to read each item and circle the right answer.

TASK 33   Sound writing

a. Point to the sound-writing exercise. Here are the sounds you're going to write today. I'll touch the sounds. You say them.
b. Touch each sound. *The children respond.*
c. Repeat the series until firm.

TASK 34   Sentence copying

a. Point to the dotted sentence in the sentence-copying exercise.
b. You're going to trace the words in this sentence. Then you're going to write the sentence on the other lines.
c. Reading the fast way. First word. Check children's responses.
                Get ready.   Clap for each word.
d. After you finish your take-home, you get to draw a picture about the sentence, **a fat ēagle sat**. You'll draw your picture on a piece of plain paper.   When the children finish their take-homes, give them sheets of plain paper.

END OF LESSON 157

TASK 18   Children sound out an irregular word (art)

a. Touch the ball for **art.**   Sound it out.
b. Get ready. Quickly touch each sound as the children say *aaarrrt.*
c. Again. Repeat *b* until firm.
d. That's how we <u>sound out</u> the word. Here's how we <u>say</u> the word.
     Art. How do we <u>say</u> the word? (Signal.) *Art.*
e. Now you're going to <u>sound out</u> the word. Get ready.
     Touch each sound as the children say *aaarrrt.*
f. Now you're going to <u>say</u> the word. Get ready. (Signal.) *Art.*
g. Repeat *e* and *f* until firm.

art

TASK 19   Children rhyme with an irregular word (art)

a. Touch the ball for **art.**   Everybody, you're going to read this word
     the fast way. Get ready. (Signal.) *Art.*
b. Touch the ball for **part.**   This word rhymes with (pause) **art.**
     Get ready. Move to **p,** then quickly along the arrow. *Part.*
c. Repeat *a* and *b* until firm.

part

TASK 20   Children sound out part

Have the children sound out **part.** *Paaarrrt.* How do we say the word?
     (Signal.) *Part.* Yes, part. This part of the pencil is the point.

Story 157

TASK 25 First reading—children read the title and first three sentences

a. You're going to read the first part of this story today.

b. Everybody, touch the title of the story and get ready to read the words in the title the fast way.

c. First word. Check children's responses. (Pause two seconds.)
Get ready. Clap. *The.*

d. Clap for each remaining word in the title.

e. After the children have read the title, ask: What's this story about? (Signal.) *The fat eagle.* Yes, **the fat eagle**.

f. Everybody, get ready to read this story the fast way.

g. First word. Check children's responses. (Pause two seconds.)
Get ready. Clap. *An.*

h. Clap for the remaining words in the first sentence. Pause at least two seconds between claps.

i. Repeat *g* and *h* for the next two sentences. Have the children reread the first three sentences until firm.

TASK 26 Individual children or the group read sentences to complete the first reading

a. I'm going to call on different children to read a sentence.
Everybody, follow along and point to the words. If you hear a mistake, raise your hand.

b. Call on a child. Read the next sentence. Do not clap for the words. Let the child read at his own pace, but be sure he reads the sentence correctly.

To correct	Have the child sound out the word. Then return to the beginning of the sentence.

c. Repeat *b* for most of the remaining sentences in the story. Occasionally have the group read a sentence. When the group is to read, say: Everybody, read the next sentence. (Pause two seconds.) Get ready. Clap for each word in the sentence. Pause at least two seconds between claps.

TASK 27 Second reading—individual children or the group read each sentence; the group answer questions

a. You're going to read the story again. This time I'm going to ask questions.

b. Starting with the first word of the title. Check children's responses. Get ready. Clap as the children read the title. Pause at least two seconds between claps.

c. Call on a child. Read the first sentence. *The child responds.*

d. Repeat *b* and *c* in task 26. Present the following comprehension questions to the entire group.

After the children read:	You say:
The fat eagle.	What's this story about? (Signal.) *The fat eagle.*
He ate cake and ham and corn.	What did he eat? (Signal.) *Cake and ham and corn.*
He ate and ate, and he got fatter and fatter.	What happened? (Signal.) *He ate and ate, and he got fatter and fatter.* Why did he get fatter? (Signal.) *Because he ate and ate.*
"Ho ho."	What did the other eagles say? *The children respond.*
A little eagle sat under a tree.	Where was the little eagle? (Signal.) *Under a tree.* Where was the fat eagle? (Signal.) *In a tree.* And what was the tiger doing? (Signal.) *Hunting for eagles.* Better watch out, little eagle.
The other eagles yelled and yelled, but the little eagle did not hear them.	Who was yelling? (Signal.) *The other eagles.* Why? *The children respond.* Did the little eagle hear them? (Signal.) *No.* Poor little eagle. We'll see what happens when we finish the story.

Story 113

TASK 21 First reading—children read the story the fast way

Have the children reread any sentences containing words that give them trouble. Keep a list of these words.

a. Pass out Storybook 1.
b. Open your book to page 50 and get ready to read.
c. We're going to read this story the fast way.
d. Touch the first word. Check children's responses.
e. Reading the fast way. First word. (Pause three seconds.)
                                        Get ready. Clap. *A.*
f. Next word. Check children's responses. (Pause three seconds.)
                                        Get ready. Clap. *Dog.*
g. Repeat *f* for the remaining words in the first sentence. Pause at least three seconds between claps. The children are to identify each word without sounding it out.
h. Repeat *d* through *g* for the next two sentences. Have the children reread the first three sentences until firm.
i. The children are to read the remainder of the story the fast way, stopping at the end of each sentence.
j. After the first reading of the story, print on the board the words that the children missed more than one time. Have the children sound out each word one time and tell what word.
k. After the group's responses are firm, call on individual children to read the words.

TASK 22 Individual test

a. Look at page 50. I'm going to call on different children to read a whole sentence the fast way.
b. Call on different children to read a sentence. Do not clap for each word.

TASK 23 Second reading—children read the story the fast way and answer questions

a. You're going to read the story again the fast way and I'll ask questions.
b. First word. Check children's responses. Get ready. Clap. *A.*
c. Clap for each remaining word. Pause at least three seconds between claps. Pause longer before words that gave the children trouble during the first reading.
d. Ask the comprehension questions below as the children read.

After the children read:	You say:
A dog was in the fog.	What's a fog? *The children respond.*
A goat was in the fog.	Name everybody who was in the fog. (Signal.) *A dog, a cat, and a goat.*
The cat and the dog sat on the log.	Who sat on the log? (Signal.) *The cat and the dog.* Who didn't sit on the log? (Signal.) *The goat.*
"Ha-ha."	What did the goat say? *The children respond.* How could he be in the log? *The children respond.*

TASK 24 Picture comprehension

a. What do you think you'll see in the picture? *The children respond.*
b. Turn the page and look at the picture.
c. Ask these questions:
   1. Is the goat in the log? *The children respond.* Yes, that log is hollow.
   2. Did you ever see a hollow log? *The children respond.*
   3. Did you ever see an animal go into a hollow log? *The children respond.*

Read the Items 157

TASK 22   Children read items 1 and 2

a. Pass out Storybook 3.

b. Open your book to page 52.

c. Get ready to read the items and play the game.

d. Finger under the first word of the title. Check children's responses.

e. When I clap, read the title. (Pause.) Get ready. Clap.
Read the items.

f. Touch item 1 and get ready to read. Check children's responses.
First word. Clap for each word as the children read:
If the teacher stands up, touch your hand. Repeat until firm.

g. Everybody, get ready to say item 1. (Pause and signal.) *The children say the sentence.* Repeat four times or until firm.

h. Touch item 2 and get ready to read. Check children's responses.
First word. Clap for each word as the children read:
If the teacher says "Stand up," touch your nose. Repeat until firm.

i. Everybody, get ready to say item 2. (Pause and signal.) *The children say the sentence.* Repeat four times or until firm.

TASK 23   Children reread items 1 and 2 and answer questions

a. Everybody, touch item 1. Check children's responses.

b. Read item 1 to yourself. Raise your hand when you know what you're going to do and when you're going to do it.

c. After the children raise their hands, say: Everybody, what are you going to do if I **stand up**? (Signal.) *Touch my hand.*

To correct	1. Everybody, read item 1 out loud. Clap as the children read each word.
	2. What are you going to do if I **stand up**? (Signal.) *Touch my hand.*

d. Everybody, when are you going to **touch your hand**? (Signal.) *If the teacher stands up.*

To correct	1. Everybody, read item 1 out loud. Clap as the children read each word.
	2. When are you going to **touch your hand**? (Signal.) *If the teacher stands up.*

e. Repeat *c* and *d* until firm.

f. Everybody, touch item 2. Check children's responses.

g. Read item 2 to yourself. Raise your hand when you know what you're going to do and when you're going to do it.

h. After the children raise their hands, say: Everybody, what are you going to do if I say "**Stand up**"? (Signal.) *Touch my nose.*

To correct	1. Everybody, read item 2 out loud. Clap as the children read each word.
	2. What are you going to do if I say "**Stand up**"? (Signal.) *Touch my nose.*

i. Everybody, when are you going to **touch your nose**? (Signal.) *If the teacher says "Stand up."*

To correct	1. Everybody, read item 2 out loud. Clap as the children read each word.
	2. When are you going to **touch your nose**? (Signal.) *If the teacher says "Stand up."*

j. Repeat *h* and *i* until firm.

TASK 24   Children play the game

a. Everybody, touch item 1. Check children's responses.

b. Read the item to yourself. Raise your hand when you know what you're going to do and when you're going to do it.

c. After the children raise their hands, say: Let's play the game.
Think about what you're going to do (pause) and when you're going to do it.

d. Hold out your hand. (Pause.) Get ready. Stand up. (Pause.)
Drop your hand. *(The children touch their hands immediately.)*

To correct	1. What did I do? (Signal.) *Stand up.*
	2. What are you supposed to do if I **stand up**? (Signal.) *Touch my hand.*
	3. If the children's responses are not firm, have them read item 1 aloud.
	4. Repeat task 24.

Take-Home 113

SUMMARY OF INDEPENDENT ACTIVITY

TASK 25   Introduction to independent activity

a. Pass out Take-Home 113 to each child.

b. Everybody, you're going to do this take-home on your own.
Tell the children when they will work the items.
Let's go over the things you're going to do.

TASK 26   Sentence copying

a. Hold up side 1 of your take-home and point to the first line in the
sentence-copying exercise.

b. Everybody, here's the sentence you're going to write on the lines
below.

c. Reading the fast way. First word. Check children's responses.
Get ready. Clap. *Thē.*

d. Next word. Check children's responses. Get ready. Clap. *Goat.*

e. Repeat *d* for the remaining words.

f. After you finish your take-home, you get to draw a picture about
the sentence, **thē goat sat on a log.**

TASK 27   Sound writing

a. Point to the sound-writing exercise. Here are the sounds you're
going to write today. I'll touch the sounds. You say them.

b. Touch each sound. *The children respond.*

c. Repeat the series until firm.

TASK 28   Matching

a. Point to the column of words in the Matching Game.

b. Everybody, you're going to follow the lines and write these words.

c. Reading the fast way.

d. Point to the first word. (Pause.) Get ready. (Signal.)
The children respond.

e. Repeat *d* for the remaining words.

f. Repeat *d* and *e* until firm.

TASK 29   Cross-out game

Point to the boxed word in the Cross-out Game. Everybody, here's
the word you're going to cross out today. What word? (Signal.)
Dog. Yes, **dog.**

TASK 30   Pair relations

a. Point to the pair-relations exercise on side 2. You're going to
circle the picture in each box that shows what the words say.

b. Point to the space at the top of the page. After you finish,
remember to draw a picture that shows **thē gōat sat on a log.**

END OF LESSON 113

TASK 21   Children read a word beginning with two consonants (slōw)

a. Cover **s**. Point to **lōw**. You're going to read this part of the word the fast way. (Pause three seconds.) Get ready. (Signal.) *Lōw*. Yes, **lōw**.

b. Uncover **s**. Point to **s**. You're going to say this first. Move your finger quickly under **lōw**. Then you're going to say (pause) **lōw**.

c. Point to **s**. What are you going to say first? (Signal.) *sss*. What are you going to say next? (Signal.) *Lōw*.

d. Repeat *c* until firm.

e. Touch the ball for **slōw**. Get ready. Move to **s**, then quickly along the arrow. *Ssslow*.

f. Say it fast. (Signal.) *Slow*. Yes, what word? (Signal.) *Slow*. Yes, **slow**. Good reading.

g. Again. Repeat *e* and *f* until firm.

h. Now you're going to sound out (pause) **slow**. Get ready. Touch **s, l, ō, w** as the children say *ssslllōōōwww*. What word? (Signal.) *Slow*. Yes, **slow**.

Lesson 114

SOUNDS

TASK 1 Teaching **ch** as in **chat**

a. Point to **ch.** My turn. When I touch it, I'll say it. (Pause.)
Touch **ch** for an instant, saying: ch.

b. Point to **ch.** Your turn. When I touch it, you say it. (Pause.)
Get ready. Touch **ch.** ch.

c. Again. Touch **ch.** ch.
d. Repeat c until firm.

TASK 2 Sounds firm-up

a. Get ready to say the sounds when I touch them.
b. Alternate touching **g** and **ch.** Point to the sound. (Pause one second.)
Say: Get ready. Touch the sound. *The children respond.*
c. When **g** and **ch** are firm, alternate touching **g, th, ch,** and **sh**
until all four sounds are firm.

TASK 3 Individual test

Call on different children to identify **g, th, ch,** or **sh.**

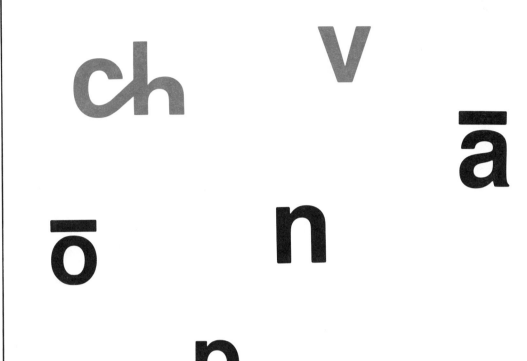

TASK 4 Sounds firm-up

a. Point to **ch.** When I touch the sound, you say it.
b. (Pause.) Get ready. Touch **ch.** ch.
c. Again. Repeat b until firm.
d. Get ready to say all the sounds when I touch them.
e. Alternate touching **v, ā, ō, n, p, d, k,** and **ch** three or four times. Point to the sound. (Pause one second.) Say: Get ready. Touch the sound. *The children respond.*

TASK 5 Individual test

Call on different children to identify one or more sounds in task 4.

TASK 17   Children read a word beginning with two consonants (tr̄e̅e̅)

a. Cover **t.** Run your finger under **r̄e̅e̅.** You're going to sound out this part. Get ready. Touch **r,** between the **e̅**'s as the children say *rrr̄e̅e̅.*

b. Say it fast. (Signal.) *R̄e̅e̅.* Yes, this part is **r̄e̅e̅.**

c. Uncover **t.** Point to **t.** You're going to say this first. Move your finger quickly under **r̄e̅e̅.** Then you're going to say (pause) **r̄e̅e̅.**

d. Point to **t.** What are you going to say first? (Signal.) *t.* What are you going to say next? (Signal.) *R̄e̅e̅.*

e. Repeat *d* until firm.

f. Touch the ball for **tr̄e̅e̅.** Get ready. Move to **t,** then quickly along the arrow. *Tree.*

g. Say it fast. (Signal.) *Tree.* Yes, what word? (Signal.) *Tree.* Yes, **tree.** Good reading.

h. Again. Repeat *f* and *g* until firm.

i. Now you're going to sound out (pause) **tree.** Get ready. Touch **t, r,** between the **e̅**'s as the children say *trrr̄e̅e̅.* What word? (Signal.) *Tree.* Yes, **tree.**

TASK 18   Children sound out the word and tell what word

a. Touch the ball for **things.** Sound it out.

b. Get ready. Touch **th, ing, s** as the children say *thththiiingsss.* If sounding out is not firm, repeat *b.*

c. What word? (Signal.) *Things.* Yes, **things.**

TASK 19   Children sound out the word and tell what word

Repeat the procedures in task 18 for **ēven.**

TASK 20   Children read the words the fast way

a. Now you get to read the words on this page the fast way.

b. Touch the ball for **things.** (Pause three seconds.) Get ready. Move your finger quickly along the arrow. *Things.*

c. Repeat *b* for **tr̄e̅e̅.**

Individual test

Call on different children to read one word the fast way.

READING VOCABULARY

TASK 6   Children sound out an irregular word (car)

a. Touch the ball for **car.** Sound it out.
b. Get ready. Quickly touch each sound as the children say *caaarrr*.
c. Again. Repeat *b* until firm.
d. That's how we <u>sound out</u> the word. Here's how we <u>say</u> the word.
                Car. How do we <u>say</u> the word? (Signal.) *Car.*
e. Now you're going to <u>sound out</u> the word. Get ready.
               Touch each sound as the children say *caaarrr*.
f. Now you're going to say the word. Get ready. (Signal.) *Car.*
g. Repeat *e* and *f* until firm.
h. Yes, this word is **car.** A **car** has wheels.

TASK 7   Individual test—Have children do *e* and *f* in task 6.

TASK 8   Children sound out the word and tell what word

a. Touch the ball for **chips.** Sound it out.
b. Get ready. Touch **ch, i, p, s** as the children say *chiiipsss*.
                 If sounding out is not firm, repeat *b*.
c. What word? (Signal.) *Chips.* Yes, **chips.**

TASK 9   Children sound out an irregular word (far)

a. Touch the ball for **far.** Sound it out.
b. Get ready. Quickly touch each sound as the children say *fffaaarrr*.
c. Again. Repeat *b* until firm.
d. That's how we <u>sound out</u> the word. Here's how we <u>say</u> the word.
              Far. How do we <u>say</u> the word? (Signal.) *Far.*
e. Now you're going to <u>sound out</u> the word. Get ready.
             Touch each sound as the children say *fffaaarrr*.
f. Now you're going to say the word. Get ready. (Signal.) *Far.*
g. Repeat *e* and *f* until firm.
h. Yes, this word is **far.** I live **far** from here.

TASK 10   Individual test—Have children do *e* and *f* in task 9.

TASK 11   Children read the words the fast way

Have the children read the words on this page the fast way.

TASK 12   Individual test—Have children read one word the fast way.

TASK 14   Children read the fast way

a. Get ready to read these words the fast way.

b. Touch the ball for **under.** (Pause three seconds.)   Get ready.

(Signal.) *Under.*

c. Repeat *b* for the remaining words on the page.

TASK 15   Children read the fast way again

a. Get ready to do these words again. Watch where I point.

b. Point to a word. (Pause one second.) Say: Get ready. (Signal.)
The children respond. Point to the words in this order:
fast, tēēth, tīger, whȳ, under.

c. Repeat *b* until firm.

TASK 16   Individual test

Call on different children to read one word the fast way.

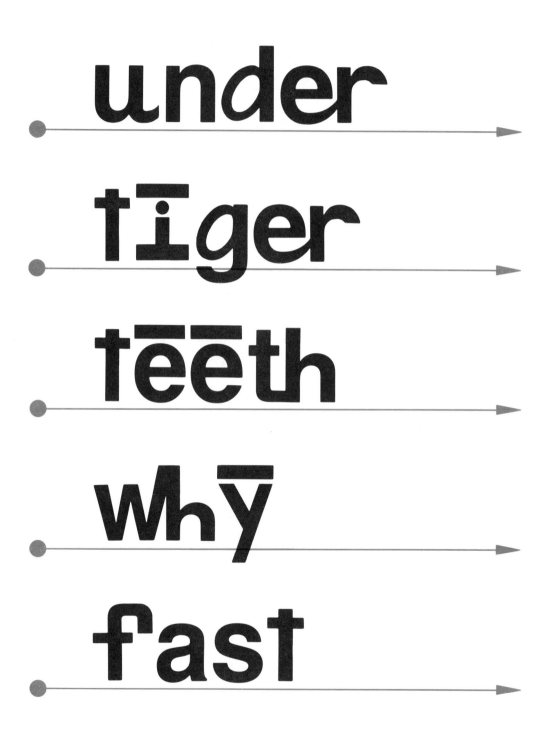

114

TASK 13 Children read the fast way

a. Get ready to read these words the fast way.
b. Touch the ball for **ships.** (Pause three seconds.) Get ready.

(Signal.) *Ships.*

c. Repeat *b* for the remaining words on the page.

TASK 14 Children read the fast way again

a. Get ready to do these words again. Watch where I point.
b. Point to a word. (Pause one second.) Say: Get ready.   (Signal.)
The children respond. Point to the words in this order:
rōad, ships, sō, gō.

c. Repeat *b* until firm.

TASK 15 Individual test

Call on different children to read one word the fast way.

Do not touch any small letters.

ships

gō

rōad

sō

TASK 10   Children read a word beginning with two consonants
(**stands**)

a. Cover **s.** Run your finger under **tands.** You're going to sound
out this part. Get ready. Touch **t, a, n, d, s** as the children
say *taaannndsss.*

b. Say it fast. (Signal.) *Tands.* Yes, this part is **tands.**
c. Uncover **s.** Point to **s.** You're going to say this first.
Move your finger quickly under **tands.** Then you're going to say
(pause) **tands.**

d. Point to **s. What are you going to say first?** (Signal.) *sss.*
What are you going to say next? (Signal.) *Tands.*

e. Repeat *d* until firm.
f. Touch the ball for **stands. Get ready.** Move to **s,** then quickly along
the arrow. *Ssstands.*

g. Say it fast. (Signal.) *Stands.* Yes, what word? (Signal.) *Stands.*
Yes, **stands. Good reading.**

h. Again. Repeat *f* and *g* until firm.
i. Now you're going to sound out (pause) **stands.** Get ready.
Touch **s, t, a, n, d, s** as the children say *ssstaaannndsss.*
What word? (Signal.) *Stands.* Yes, **stands.**

TASK 11   Children read the fast way

a. Get ready to read these words the fast way.
b. Touch the ball for **after.** (Pause three seconds.) **Get ready.**
(Signal.) *After.*

c. Repeat *b* for the remaining words on the page.

TASK 12   Children read the fast way again

a. Get ready to do these words again. Watch where I point.
b. Point to a word. (Pause one second.) Say: **Get ready.** (Signal.)
The children respond. Point to the words in this order:
smile, after, ēagle.

c. Repeat *b* until firm.

TASK 13   Individual test

Call on different children to read one word on the page the fast way.

Do not touch any small letters.

stands

after

smīle

ēagle

TASK 16   Children sound out an irregular word (farm)

a. Touch the ball for **farm.** Sound it out.
b. Get ready.   Quickly touch each sound as the children say
fffaaarrrmmm.

c. Again.   Repeat *b* until firm.
d. That's how we <u>sound out</u> the word. Here's how we <u>say</u> the word.
Farm. How do we <u>say</u> the word?   (Signal.) *Farm.*
e. Now you're going to <u>sound out</u> the word. Get ready.
Touch each sound as the children say *fffaaarrrmmm.*
f. Now you're going to say the word. Get ready.   (Signal.) *Farm.*
g. Repeat *e* and *f* until firm.
h. Yes, this word is **farm.** We see cows on a **farm.**

TASK 17   Individual test

Call on different chiidren to do *e* and *f* in task 16.

TASK 18   Children sound out an irregular word (are)

a. Touch the ball for **are.** Sound it out.
b. Get ready.   Quickly touch each sound as the children say *aaarrr.*
c. Again.   Repeat *b* until firm.
d. That's how we <u>sound out</u> the word. Here's how we <u>say</u> the word.
Are. How do we <u>say</u> the word?   (Signal.) *Are.*
e. Now you're going to <u>sound out</u> the word. Get ready.
Touch each sound as the children say *aaarrr.*
f. Now you're going to say the word. Get ready.   (Signal.) *Are.*
g. Repeat *e* and *f* until firm.
h. Yes, this word is **are.** You **are** in school.

TASK 19   Individual test

Call on different children to do *e* and *f* in task 18.

TASK 20   Children read the words the fast way

a. Now you get to read the words on this page the fast way.
b. Touch the ball for **farm.** (Pause three seconds.)   Get ready.
Move your finger quickly along the arrow. *Farm.*
c. Repeat *b* for **are.**

TASK 21   Individual test

Call on different children to read one word the fast way.

Do not touch any small letters.

READING VOCABULARY

Do not touch any small letters.

TASK 6 **Children read a word beginning with two consonants (steps)**

a. Cover **s.** Run your finger under **teps.** You're going to sound out this part. Get ready. Touch **t, e, p, s** as the children say *teeepsss.*

b. Say it fast. (Signal.) *Teps.* Yes, this part is **teps.**

c. Uncover **s.** Point to **s.** You're going to say this first. Move your finger quickly under **teps.** Then you're going to say (pause) **teps.**

d. Point to **s.** What are you going to say first? (Signal.) *sss.* What are you going to say next? (Signal.) *Teps.*

e. Repeat *d* until firm.

f. Touch the ball for **steps.** Get ready. Move to **s,** then quickly along the arrow. *Sssteps.*

g. Say it fast. (Signal.) *Steps.* Yes, what word? (Signal.) *Steps.* Yes, **steps.** Good reading.

h. Again. Repeat *f* and *g* until firm.

i. Now you're going to sound out (pause) **steps.** Get ready. Touch **s, t, e, p, s** as the children say *sssteeepsss.* What word? (Signal.) *Steps.* Yes, **steps.**

TASK 7 **Children read the fast way**

a. Get ready to read these words the fast way.

b. Touch the ball for **when.** (Pause three seconds.) Get ready. (Signal.) *When.*

c. Repeat *b* for the remaining words on the page.

TASK 8 **Children read the fast way again**

a. Get ready to do these words again. Watch where I point.

b. Point to a word. (Pause one second.) Say: Get ready. (Signal.) *The children respond.* Point to the words in this order: **where, there, when.**

c. Repeat *b* until firm.

TASK 9 **Individual test**

Call on different children to read one word on the page the fast way.

steps

when

where

there

Story 114

TASK 22 First reading—children read the story the fast way

Have the children reread any sentences containing words that give them trouble. Keep a list of these words.

a. Pass out Storybook 1.
b. Open your book to page 53 and get ready to read.
c. We're going to read this story the fast way.
d. Touch the first word. Check children's responses.
e. Reading the fast way. First word. (Pause three seconds.)
Get ready. Clap. *Thē.*
f. Next word. Check children's responses. (Pause three seconds.)
Get ready. Clap. *Fat.*
g. Repeat *f* for the remaining words in the first sentence. Pause at least three seconds between claps. The children are to identify each word without sounding it out.
h. Repeat *d* through *g* for the next two sentences. Have the children reread the first three sentences until firm.
i. The children are to read the remainder of the story the fast way, stopping at the end of each sentence.
j. After the first reading of the story, print on the board the words that the children missed more than one time. Have the children sound out each word one time and tell what word.
k. After the group's responses are firm, call on individual children to read the words.

TASK 23 Individual test

a. Turn back to page 53. I'm going to call on different children to read a whole sentence the fast way.
b. Call on different children to read a sentence. Do not clap for each word.

TASK 24 Second reading—children read the story the fast way and answer questions

a. You're going to read the story again the fast way and I'll ask questions.
b. First word. Check children's responses. Get ready. Clap. *Thē.*
c. Clap for each remaining word. Pause at least three seconds between claps. Pause longer before words that gave the children trouble during the second reading.
d. Ask the comprehension questions below as the children read.

After the children read:	You say:
The fat man and his dog had a car.	What did the fat man and his dog have? (Signal.) *A car.*
The car did not run.	What was wrong with the car? (Signal.) *It didn't run.*
The fat man and his dog sat on the goat.	Who sat on the goat? (Signal.) *The fat man and his dog.*
The fat man said, "The goat will not go."	What did the fat man say? (Signal.) *The goat will not go.*
So the fat man and his dog sat on the road.	What happened? (Signal.) *The fat man and his dog sat on the road.*

TASK 25 Picture comprehension

a. Everybody, look at the picture.
b. Ask these questions:
1. Who's sitting on the road? *The children respond.* *A fat man and his dog.*
2. What's the goat doing? *The children respond.*
3. What would you do if you were that dog? *The children respond.*

Lesson 157

Groups that are firm on Mastery Tests 29 and 30 should skip this lesson and do lesson 158 today.

SOUNDS

TASK 1   Teaching **z** as in **zoo**

a. Point to **z.** My turn. (Pause.) Touch **z** and say: zzz.
b. Point to **z.** Your turn. When I touch it, you say it. (Pause.)
              Get ready. Touch **z.** *zzz.* Lift your finger.
c. Again. Touch **z.** *zzzz.* Lift your finger.
d. Repeat *c* until firm.

TASK 2   Sounds firm-up

a. Get ready to say the sounds when I touch them.
b. Alternate touching **z** and **v.** Point to the sound. (Pause one second.)
       Say: Get ready. Touch the sound. *The children respond.*
c. When **z** and **v** are firm, alternate touching **z, v, s,** and **qu** until
                all four sounds are firm.

z

v

s

qu

TASK 3   Individual test

Call on different children to identify **z, v, s,** or **qu.**

z   ā

u   qu

J   g

 wh

ȳ

TASK 4   Sounds firm-up

a. Point to **z.** When I touch the sound, you say it.
b. (Pause.) Get ready. Touch **z.** zzz.
c. Again. Repeat *b* until firm.
d. Get ready to say all the sounds when I touch them.
e. Alternate touching **z, ā, u, qu, j, g, wh,** and **ȳ** three or four times. Point to the sound. (Pause one second.) Say: Get ready. Touch the sound. *The children respond.*

TASK 5   Individual test

Call on different children to identify one or more sounds in task 4.

Take-Home 114

PAIR RELATIONS
The children will need pencils.

TASK 26 Children draw a line through the incorrect words

a. Pass out Take-Home 114 to each child.

b. Point to the picture of the ear in the pair-relations exercise on side 2. **Everybody, what does this picture show?** (Signal.) *An ear.*

c. Point to the words next to the picture. **Let's find the word that tells about this picture. Reading the fast way.**

d. Point to the word **nōse.** (Pause.) **Everybody, what word?** (Signal.) *Nose.* **Does that word tell about this picture?** (Signal.) *No.* **It's wrong. So I'll draw a line through it.** Do it.

e. Point to the word **tēēth.** (Pause.) **Everybody, what word?** (Signal.) *Teeth.* **Does that word tell about this picture?** (Signal.) *No.* **It's wrong. So I'll draw a line through it.** Do it.

f. Point to the word **ēar.** (Pause.) **Everybody, what word?** (Signal.) *Ear.* **Does that word tell about this picture?** (Signal.) *Yes.* **It's right. So I won't draw a line through it.**

g. Point to the word **car.** (Pause.) **Everybody, what word?** (Signal.) *Car.* **Does that word tell about this picture?** (Signal.) *No.* **So what do I do?** (Signal.) *Draw a line through it.* **Yes, I'll draw a line through it.** Do it.

h. Point to the picture of the ear. **Everybody, draw a line through the words that do not tell about this picture.** Check children's responses.

i. Hold up your take-home. Point to the picture of the cow. **Everybody, what does this picture show?** (Signal.) *A cow.* **Yes, a cow. Draw a line through the words that do not tell about this picture.** Check children's responses.

j. **You'll do the rest of the boxes later.**

SUMMARY OF INDEPENDENT ACTIVITY

TASK 27 Introduction to independent activity

a. Hold up Take-Home 114.

b. **Everybody, you're going to finish this take-home on your own.** Tell the children when they will work the remaining items. **Let's go over the things you're going to do.**

TASK 28 Sentence copying

a. Point to the first line in the sentence-copying exercise on side 1.

b. **Everybody, here's the sentence you're going to write on the lines below.**

c. **Reading the fast way. First word.** Check children's responses. **Get ready.** Clap. *A.*

d. **Next word.** Check children's responses. **Get ready.** Clap. *Man.*

e. Repeat *d* for the remaining words.

f. **After you finish your take-home, you get to draw a picture about the sentence, a man sat on a gōat.**

TASK 29 Sound writing

a. Point to the sound-writing exercise. **Here are the sounds you're going to write today. I'll touch the sounds. You say them.**

b. Touch each sound. *The children respond.*

c. Repeat the series until firm.

TASK 30 Matching

a. Point to the column of words in the Matching Game.

b. **Everybody, you're going to follow the lines and write these words.**

c. **Reading the fast way.**

d. Point to the first word. (Pause.) **Get ready.** (Signal.) *The children respond.*

e. Repeat *d* for the remaining words.

f. Repeat *d* and *e* until firm.

TASK 31 Cross-out game

Point to the boxed word in the Cross-out Game. **Everybody, here's the word you're going to cross out today. What word?** (Signal.) *Pot.* **Yes, pot.**

TASK 32 Pair relations

a. Point to the pair-relations exercise on side 2. **Remember—you're going to draw a line through the words in each box that do not tell about the picture.**

b. Point to the space at the top of the page. **After you finish, remember to draw a picture that shows a man sat on a gōat.**

END OF LESSON 114

Take-Home 156

SUMMARY OF INDEPENDENT ACTIVITY

TASK 30   Introduction to independent activity

a. Pass out Take-Home 156 to each child.

b. Everybody, you're going to do this take-home on your own. Tell the children when they will work the items. Let's go over the things you're going to do.

TASK 31   Story items

a. Hold up side 1 of your take-home and point to the story-items exercise.

b. Everybody, here are items about the story we read today.

c. Think about what happened in the story and circle the right answer for each item.

TASK 32   Picture comprehension

a. Point to the pictures in the picture-comprehension exercise. Everybody, you're going to look at the picture. Then you're going to read each item and write the missing word.

b. Remember—the first sound of each missing word is already written in the blank.

TASK 33   Reading comprehension

a. Point to the reading-comprehension exercise on side 2.

b. Everybody, get ready to read the sentences in the box the fast way.

c. First word. Check children's responses. Get ready. Clap for each word as the children read the sentences: *Bill went to the park. He went in the big pool.*

d. Point to items 1 and 2. These items tell about the story in the box. You're going to read each item and circle the right answer.

TASK 34   Sound writing

a. Point to the sound-writing exercise. Here are the sounds you're going to write today. I'll touch the sounds. You say them.

b. Touch each sound. *The children respond.*

c. Repeat the series until firm.

TASK 35   Sentence copying

a. Point to the dotted sentence in the sentence-copying exercise.

b. You're going to trace the words in this sentence. Then you're going to write the sentence on the other lines.

c. Reading the fast way. First word. Check children's responses. Get ready. Clap for each word.

d. After you finish your take-home, you get to draw a picture about the sentence, **the girl smiled**. You'll draw your picture on a piece of plain paper. When the children finish their take-homes, give them sheets of plain paper.

END OF LESSON 156

Lesson 115

SOUNDS

TASK 1   Sounds firm-up

a. Get ready to say the sounds when I touch them.

b. Alternate touching **ch** and **c.** Point to the sound. (Pause one second.) Say: Get ready. Touch the sound. *The children respond.*

c. When **ch** and **c** are firm, alternate touching **h, c, v,** and **ch** until all four sounds are firm.

ch

c

h

v

TASK 2   Individual test

Call on different children to identify **h, c, v,** or **ch.**

TASK 3   Teacher introduces cross-out game

a. Use acetate and crayon.

b. I'll cross out the sounds on this part of the page when you can tell me every sound.

c. Remember—when I touch it, you say it.

d. Go over the sounds until the children can identify all the sounds in order.

TASK 4   Individual test

Call on different children to identify two or more sounds in task 3.

TASK 5   Teacher crosses out sounds

a. You told me every sound. Get ready to do it again. This time I'll cross out each sound when you tell me what it is.

b. Point to each sound. (Pause.) Say: Get ready. Touch the sound. *The children respond.* As you cross out the sound, say: Goodbye, _____ .

p

w

k

ō

ch

r

i

u

Story 156

TASK 26 First reading—children read the title and first three sentences

a. Now you're going to finish the story about the girl and her red tooth brush.

b. Everybody, touch the title of the story and get ready to read the words in the title the fast way.

c. First word. Check children's responses. (Pause two seconds.) Get ready. Clap. *The.*

d. Clap for each remaining word in the title.

e. After the children have read the title, ask: What's this story about? (Signal.) *The red tooth brush.* Yes, **the red tooth brush.**

f. Everybody, get ready to read this story the fast way.

g. First word. Check children's responses. (Pause two seconds.) Get ready. Clap. *A.*

h. Clap for the remaining words in the first sentence. Pause at least two seconds between claps.

i. Repeat *g* and *h* for the next two sentences. Have the children reread the first three sentences until firm.

TASK 27 Individual children or the group read sentences to complete the first reading

a. I'm going to call on different children to read a sentence. Everybody, follow along and point to the words. If you hear a mistake, raise your hand.

b. Call on a child. Read the next sentence. Do not clap for the words. Let the child read at his own pace, but be sure he reads the sentence correctly.

To correct	Have the child sound out the word. Then return to the beginning of the sentence.

c. Repeat *b* for most of the remaining sentences in the story. Occasionally have the group read a sentence. When the group is to read, say: Everybody, read the next sentence. (Pause two seconds.) Get ready. Clap for each word in the sentence. Pause at least two seconds between claps.

TASK 28 Second reading—individual children or the group read each sentence; the group answer questions

a. You're going to read the story again. This time I'm going to ask questions.

b. Starting with the first word of the title. Check children's responses. Get ready. Clap as the children read the title. Pause at least two seconds between claps.

c. Call on a child. Read the first sentence. *The child responds.*

d. Repeat *b* and *c* in task 27. Present the following comprehension questions to the entire group.

After the children read:	You say:
The girl went back to her room.	What did she do? (Signal.) *She went back to her room.*
She slipped on her dog.	What did she slip on? (Signal.) *Her dog.*
Her dog was brushing his teeth with her red tooth brush.	What was that dog doing? (Signal.) *He was brushing his teeth with her red tooth brush.*
They said, "Now we both have teeth that shine like the moon."	What did they say? (Signal.) *Now we both have teeth that shine like the moon.*

TASK 29 Picture comprehension

a. Everybody, look at the picture.

b. Ask these questions:

1. Look at those teeth. They really shine. What did the girl and the dog say about their teeth? *The children respond.* Yes, **we both have teeth that shine like the moon.**

2. What would you do if you had a dog that used your tooth brush? *The children respond.*

READING VOCABULARY

Do not touch any small letters.

TASK 6   Children identify, then sound out an irregular word (**are**)

a. Touch the ball for **are**. Everybody, you're going to read this word the fast way. (Pause three seconds.) Get ready. Move your finger quickly along the arrow. *Are.* Yes, **are**.

b. Now you're going to sound out the word. Get ready. Quickly touch **a, r** as the children say *aaarrr.*

c. Again. Repeat *b.*

d. How do we say the word? (Signal.) *Are.* Yes, **are**.

e. Repeat *b* and *d* until firm.

TASK 7   Individual test

Call on different children to do *b* and *d* in task 6.

TASK 8   Children read the fast way

a. Get ready to read these words the fast way.

b. Touch the ball for **ēach**. (Pause three seconds.) Get ready. (Signal.) *Each.*

c. Repeat *b* for the remaining words on the page.

TASK 9   Children read the fast way again

a. Get ready to do these words again. Watch where I point.

b. Point to a word. (Pause one second.) Say: Get ready. (Signal.) *The children respond.* Point to the words in this order: **cop, ēach, lots.**

c. Repeat *b* until firm.

TASK 10   Individual test

Call on different children to read one word on the page the fast way.

Read the Items 156

TASK 23   Children read items 1 and 2

a. Pass out Storybook 3.

b. Open your book to page 49.

c. Get ready to read the items and play the game.

d. Finger under the first word of the title.   Check children's responses.

e. When I clap, read the title.   (Pause.) Get ready.   Clap.

Read the items.

f. Touch item 1 and get ready to read.   Check children's responses.

First word.   Clap for each word as the children read:

When the teacher says "Stand up," pick up your book.

Repeat until firm.

g. Everybody, get ready to say item 1.   (Pause and signal.)

The children say the sentence. Repeat four times or until firm.

h. Touch item 2 and get ready to read.   Check children's responses.

First word.   Clap for each word as the children read:

If the teacher says "Now," hold up your hands. Repeat until firm.

i. Everybody, get ready to say item 2.   (Pause and signal.) *The children say the sentence.* Repeat four times or until firm.

TASK 24   Children reread items 1 and 2 and answer questions

a. Everybody, touch item 1.   Check children's responses.

b. Read item 1 to yourself. Raise your hand when you know what you're going to do and when you're going to do it.

c. After the children raise their hands, say: Everybody, what are you going to do when I say "Stand up"?   (Signal.) *Pick up my book.*

| To correct | 1. Everybody, read item 1 out loud.   Clap as the children read each word. |
| | 2. What are you going to do when I say "Stand up"?   (Signal.) *Pick up my book.* |

d. Everybody, when are you going to **pick up your book**?   (Signal.) *When the teacher says "Stand up."*

| To correct | 1. Everybody, read item 1 out loud.   Clap as the children read each word. |
| | 2. When are you going to **pick up your book**?   (Signal.) *When the teacher says "Stand up."* |

e. Repeat *c* and *d* until firm.

---

f. Everybody, touch item 2.   Check children's responses.

g. Read item 2 to yourself. Raise your hand when you know what you're going to do and when you're going to do it.

h. After the children raise their hands, say: Everybody, what are you going to do if I say "**Now**"?   (Signal.) *Hold up my hands.*

| To correct | 1. Everybody, read item 2 out loud.   Clap as the children read each word. |
| | 2. What are you going to do if I say "**Now**"?   (Signal.) *Hold up my hands.* |

i. Everybody, when are you going to **hold up your hands**?   (Signal.) *If the teacher says "Now."*

| To correct | 1. Everybody, read item 2 out loud.   Clap as the children read each word. |
| | 2. When are you going to **hold up your hands**?   (Signal.) *If the teacher says "Now."* |

j. Repeat *h* and *i* until firm.

TASK 25   Children play the game

a. Everybody, touch item 1.   Check children's responses.

b. Read the item to yourself. Raise your hand when you know what you're going to do and when you're going to do it.

c. After the children raise their hands, say: Let's play the game.

Think about what you're going to do   (pause) and when you're going to do it.

d. Hold out your hand. (Pause.) Get ready. Stand up.   (Pause.)

Drop your hand. *(The children pick up their books immediately.)*

To correct	1. What did I say? (Signal.) *Stand up.*
	2. What are you supposed to do when I say "**Stand up**"? (Signal.) *Pick up my book.*
	3. If the children's responses are not firm, have them read item 1 aloud.
	4. Repeat task 25.

TASK 11 Children sound out an irregular word (arm)

a. Touch the ball for **arm. Sound it out.**

b. Get ready. Quickly touch each sound as the children say *aaarrrmmm.*

c. Again. Repeat *b* until firm.

d. That's how we <u>sound out</u> the word. Here's how we <u>say</u> the word. Arm. How do we <u>say</u> the word? (Signal.) *Arm.*

e. Now you're going to <u>sound out</u> the word. Get ready. Touch each sound as the children say *aaarrrmmm.*

f. Now you're going to <u>say</u> the word. Get ready. (Signal.) *Arm.*

g. Repeat *e* and *f* until firm.

TASK 12 Children rhyme with an irregular word (arm)

a. Touch the ball for **arm. Everybody, you're going to read this word the fast way. Get ready.** (Signal.) *Arm.*

b. Touch the ball for **farm. This word rhymes with** (pause) **arm. Get ready.** Move to **f,** then quickly along the arrow. *Farm.*

c. Repeat *a* and *b* until firm.

TASK 13 Children sound out farm

Have the children sound out **farm.** *Fffaaarrrmmm.* **How do we say the word?** (Signal.) *Farm.* **Yes, farm. Do you live on a farm?**

TASK 14 Children sound out the word and tell what word

a. Touch the ball for **tēach. Sound it out.**

b. Get ready. Touch **t, ē, ch** as the children say *tēēēch.* If sounding out is not firm, repeat *b.*

c. What word? (Signal.) *Teach.* **Yes, teach.**

TASK 15 Children read the words the fast way

a. Now you get to read the words on this page the fast way.

b. Touch the ball for **arm.** (Pause three seconds.) **Get ready.** Move your finger quickly along the arrow. *Arm.*

c. Repeat *b* for each word on the page.

TASK 16 Individual test

Call on different children to read one word the fast way.

Do not touch any small letters.

TASK 19   Children sound out an irregular word (looked)

a. Touch the ball for **looked.** Sound it out.
b. Get ready. Quickly touch each sound as the children say *Illooookd.*
c. Again. Repeat *b* until firm.
d. That's how we <u>sound out</u> the word. Here's how we <u>say</u> the word. **Looked.** How do we <u>say</u> the word? (Signal.) *Looked.*
e. Now you're going to <u>sound out</u> the word. Get ready. Touch each sound as the children say *Illooookd.*
f. Now you're going to say the word. Get ready. (Signal.) *Looked.*
g. Repeat *e* and *f* until firm.
h. Yes, this word is **looked.** I **looked** under the chair.
i. Call on different children to do *e* and *f.*

TASK 20   Children read fat and fatter

a. Touch the ball for **fat.** You're going to read this word the fast way. (Pause three seconds.) Get ready. Move your finger quickly along the arrow. *Fat.*
b. Return to the ball for **fat.** Yes, this word is **fat.**
c. Touch the ball for **fatter.** So this must be **fat** . . . . Touch **er.** *Er.* What word? (Signal.) *Fatter.* Yes, **fatter.**
d. Again. Repeat *b* and *c* until firm.
e. Touch the ball for **fat.** This word is **fat.**
f. Touch the ball for **fatter.** So this must be . . . . Quickly run your finger under **fat** and tap **er.** *Fatter.* Yes, **fatter.**
g. Again. Repeat *e* and *f* until firm.
h. Now you're going to sound out (pause) **fatter.** Get ready. Touch **f, a,** between the **t**'s, **er** as the children say *fffaaaterrr.* Yes, what word? (Signal.) *Fatter.* Yes, **fatter.**

TASK 21   Children read the fast way

Touch the ball for **broom.** Get ready to read this word the fast way. (Pause three seconds.) Get ready. (Signal.) *Broom.*

TASK 22   Children read the words the fast way

Have the children read the words on this page the fast way.

Individual test

Call on different children to read one word the fast way.

Do not touch any small letters.

looked

fat

fatter

broom

TASK 17   Children identify, then sound out an irregular word (of)

a. Touch the ball for **of.** Everybody, you're going to read this word the fast way.   (Pause three seconds.) Get ready. Move your finger quickly along the arrow. *Of.* Yes, **of.**

b. Now you're going to sound out the word. Get ready.   Quickly touch **o, f** as the children say *ooofff.*

c. Again.   Repeat *b.*

d. How do we say the word?   (Signal.) *Of.* Yes, **of.**

e. Repeat *b* and *d* until firm.

TASK 18   Individual test

Call on different children to do *b* and *d* in task 17.

TASK 19   Children sound out an irregular word (cars)

a. Touch the ball for **cars.** Sound it out.

b. Get ready.   Quickly touch each sound as the children say *caaarrrsss.*

To correct	If the children do not say the sounds you touch
	1. Say: **You've got to say the sounds I touch.**
	2. Repeat *a* and *b* until firm.

c. Again.   Repeat *b* until firm.

d. That's how we <u>sound out</u> the word. Here's how we <u>say</u> the word. **Cars**. How do we <u>say</u> the word?   (Signal.) *Cars.*

e. Now you're going to <u>sound out</u> the word. Get ready. Touch each sound as the children say *caaarrrsss.*

f. Now you're going to say the word. Get ready.   (Signal.) *Cars.*

g. Repeat *e* and *f* until firm.

h. Yes, this word is **cars. Cars** can go fast.

TASK 20   Individual test

Call on different children to do *e* and *f* in task 19.

TASK 15 Children sound out the word and tell what word

a. Touch the ball for **yelled.** Sound it out.
b. Get ready. Touch **y, e**, between the l's, **d** as the children say
   yyyeeellld. If sounding out is not firm, repeat *b*.
c. What word? (Signal.) *Yelled.* Yes, **yelled.**

TASK 16 Children sound out the word and tell what word

Repeat the procedures in task 15 for **after.**

TASK 17 Children read the fast way

a. Get ready to read these words the fast way.
b. Touch the ball for **slipped.** (Pause three seconds.) Get ready.
   (Signal.) *Slipped.*
c. Repeat *b* for the remaining words on the page.

TASK 18 Children read the words the fast way

a. Now you get to read the words on this page the fast way.
b. Touch the ball for **yelled.** (Pause one second.) Get ready.
   Move your finger quickly along the arrow. *Yelled.*
c. Repeat *b* for each word on the page.

Individual test

Call on different children to read one word the fast way.

Do not touch any small letters.

yelled

after

slipped

under

jumped

Story 115

TASK 21   Teacher introduces the title

a. Pass out Storybook 1.
b. Open your book to page 56.
c. Hold up your reader. Point to the title. **These words are called the title of the story. These words tell what the story is about. I'll read the title the fast way.**
d. Point to the words as you read: **Lots of cars.**
e. **Everybody, what is this story about?** (Signal.) *Lots of cars.* **Yes, lots of cars. This story is going to tell something about lots of cars.**

TASK 22   First reading—children read the story the fast way

Have the children reread any sentences containing words that give them trouble. Keep a list of these words.

a. **Everybody, touch the title of the story and get ready to read the words in the title the fast way.**
b. **First word.** Check children's responses. (Pause three seconds.) **Get ready.** Clap. *Lots.*
c. **Next word.** Check children's responses. (Pause three seconds.) **Get ready.** Clap. *Of.*
d. Repeat c for the word **cars.**
e. After the children have read the title, ask: **What's this story about?** (Signal.) *Lots of cars.* **Yes, lots of cars.**
f. **Everybody, touch the first word of the story.** Check children's responses.
g. **Get ready to read this story the fast way.**
h. **First word.** (Pause three seconds.) **Get ready.** Clap. *A.*
i. **Next word.** Check children's responses. (Pause three seconds.) **Get ready.** Clap. *Man.*
j. Repeat *i* for the remaining words in the first sentence. Pause at least three seconds between claps. The children are to identify each word without sounding it out.
k. Repeat *h* through *j* for the next two sentences. Have the children reread the first three sentences until firm.
l. The children are to read the remainder of the story the fast way, stopping at the end of each sentence.

m. After the first reading of the story, print on the board the words that the children missed more than one time. Have the children sound out each word one time and tell what word.
n. After the group's responses are firm, call on individual children to read the words.

TASK 23   Individual test

a. **Look at page 56. I'm going to call on different children to read a whole sentence the fast way.**
b. Call on different children to read a sentence. Do not clap for each word.

TASK 24   Second reading—children read the story the fast way and answer questions

a. **You're going to read the story again the fast way and I'll ask questions.**
b. **Starting with the first word of the title.** Check children's responses. **Get ready.** Clap. *Lots.*
c. Clap for each remaining word. Pause at least three seconds between claps. Pause longer before words that gave the children trouble during the first reading.
d. Ask the comprehension questions below as the children read.

After the children read:	You say:
Lots of cars.	**What's this story about?** (Signal.) *Lots of cars.*
A man on a farm has lots of cars.	**What does he have?** (Signal.) *Lots of cars.*
He has little cars.	**What kind of cars does he have?** (Signal.) *Old cars and little cars.*
Are his cars for goats?	**What do you think?** *The children respond.* **Let's read and find out.**
No.	**Are they for goats?** (Signal.) *No.*
He has lots of cop cars.	**What kind of cars does he have?** (Signal.) *Cop cars.*

**TASK 10 Children read a word beginning with two consonants
(tree)**

a. Cover **t.** Run your finger under **rēē.** You're going to sound out
this part. Get ready. Touch **r,** between the **ē**'s as the children
say *rrrēēē.*

b. Say it fast. (Signal.) *Rēē.* Yes, this part is **rēē.**

c. Uncover **t.** Point to **t.** You're going to say this first.
Move your finger quickly under **rēē.** Then you're going to say
(pause) **rēē.**

d. Point to **t.** What are you going to say first? (Signal.) *t.*
What are you going to say next? (Signal.) *Rēē.*

e. Repeat *d* until firm.

f. Touch the ball for **trēē.** Get ready. Move to **t,** then quickly along
the arrow. *Tree.*

g. Say it fast. (Signal.) *Tree.* Yes, what word? (Signal.) *Tree.*
Yes, **tree.** Good reading.

h. Again. Repeat *f* and *g* until firm.

i. Now you're going to sound out (pause) **tree.** Get ready.
Touch **t, r,** between the **ē**'s as the children say *trrrēēē.*
What word? (Signal.) *Tree.* Yes, **tree.**

tree

TASK 11 Children sound out the word and tell what word

a. Touch the ball for **from.** Sound it out.

b. Get ready. Touch **f, r, o, m** as the children say *fffrrrooommm.*
If sounding out is not firm, repeat *b.*

c. What word? (Signal.) *From.* Yes, **from.**

from

TASK 12 Children sound out the word and tell what word

Repeat the procedures in task 11 for **tīger.**

tīger

TASK 13 Children read the words the fast way

Have the children read the words on this page the fast way.

TASK 14 Individual test

Call on different children to read one word the fast way.

TASK 25   Picture comprehension

a. What do you think you'll see in the picture? *The children respond.*

b. Turn the page and look at the picture.

c. Ask these questions:
   1. Do you see lots of cop cars? *Yes.*
   2. What would you do if you had all those cop cars?
      The children respond.

Take-Home 115

PAIR RELATIONS

The children will need pencils.

TASK 26   Children draw a line through the incorrect words

a. Pass out sides 1 and 2 of Take-Home 115 to each child.

b. Everybody, do a good job on your take-home today and I'll give
   you a bonus take-home.

c. Hold up side 2 of your take-home. Point to the picture of the car
   in the pair-relations exercise. Everybody, what does this picture
   show? (Signal.) *A car.*

d. Point to the words next to the picture. Let's find the word that
   tells about this picture. Reading the fast way.

e. Point to the word **man.** (Pause.) Everybody, what word? (Signal.)
   Man. Does that word tell about this picture? (Signal.) *No.*
   It's wrong. So I'll draw a line through it. Do it.

f. Point to the word **cat.** (Pause.) Everybody, what word? (Signal.)
   Cat. Does that word tell about this picture? (Signal.) *No.*
   It's wrong. So I'll draw a line through it. Do it.

g. Point to the word **tāil.** (Pause.) Everybody, what word? (Signal.)
   Tail. Does that word tell about this picture? (Signal.) *No.*
   So what do I do? (Signal.) *Draw a line through it.*
   Yes, I'll draw a line through it. Do it.

h. Point to the word **car.** (Pause.) Everybody, what word? (Signal.)
   Car. Does that word tell about this picture? (Signal.) *Yes.*
   It's right. So I won't draw a line through it.

i. Point to the picture of the car. Everybody, draw a line through
   the words that do not tell about this picture.
   Check children's responses.

j. Hold up your take-home. Point to the picture of the rat.
   Everybody, what does this picture show? (Signal.) *A rat.*
   Yes, a rat. Draw a line through the words that do not tell about
   this picture. Check children's responses.

k. You'll do the rest of the boxes later.

READING VOCABULARY

Do not touch any small letters.

TASK 7   Children read the fast way

a. Get ready to read these words the fast way.
b. Touch the ball for **where.** (Pause three seconds.) Get ready.
(Signal.) *Where.*

c. Repeat *b* for the remaining words on the page.

TASK 8   Children read the fast way again

a. Get ready to do these words again. Watch where I point.
b. Point to a word. (Pause one second.) Say: Get ready. (Signal.)
The children respond. Point to the words in this order:
there, when, where, whȳ.

c. Repeat *b* until firm.

TASK 9   Individual test

Call on different children to read one word the fast way.

where

there

when

whȳ

SUMMARY OF INDEPENDENT ACTIVITY

TASK 27 Introduction to independent activity

a. Hold up Take-Home 115.
b. You're going to finish this take-home on your own.
Tell the children when they will work the remaining items.
Let's go over the things you're going to do.

TASK 28 Sentence copying

a. Point to the first line in the sentence-copying exercise.
b. Everybody, here's the sentence you're going to write on the lines below.
c. Reading the fast way. First word. Check children's responses.
Get ready. Clap. *He*.
d. Next word. Check children's responses. Get ready. Clap. *Has*.
e. Repeat *d* for the remaining words.
f. After you finish your take-home, you get to draw a picture about the sentence, **hē has lots of cars**.

TASK 29 Sound writing

a. Point to the sound-writing exercise. Here are the sounds you're going to write today. I'll touch the sounds. You say them.
b. Touch each sound. *The children respond.*
c. Repeat the series until firm.

TASK 30 Matching

a. Point to the column of words in the Matching Game.
b. Everybody, you're going to follow the lines and write these words.
c. Reading the fast way.
d. Point to the first word. (Pause.) Get ready. (Signal.)
The children respond.
e. Repeat *d* for the remaining words.
f. Repeat *d* and *e* until firm.

TASK 31 Cross-out game

Point to the boxed word in the Cross-out Game. Everybody, here's the word you're going to cross out today. What word? (Signal.)
Fish. Yes, **fish**.

TASK 32 Pair relations

a. Point to the pair-relations exercise on side 2. Remember—you're going to draw a line through the words in each box that do not tell about the picture.
b. Point to the space at the top of the page. After you finish, remember to draw a picture that shows **hē has lots of cars**.

INDIVIDUAL CHECKOUT: STORYBOOK

TASK 33 2-minute individual checkout — whole story from title

a. As you are doing your take-home, I'll call on children one at a time to read the **whole story**. Remember, you get two stars if you read the story in less than two minutes and make no more than three errors.
b. Call on a child. Tell the child: Start with the title and read the story carefully the fast way. Go. Time the child. Tell the child any words the child misses. Stop the child as soon as the child makes the fourth error or exceeds the time limit.
c. If the child meets the rate-accuracy criterion, record two stars on your chart for lesson 115. Congratulate the child. Give children who do not earn two stars a chance to read the story again before the next lesson is presented.

49 words/2 min = 25 wpm [3 errors]

TASK 34 Bonus take-home: sides 3 and 4

After the children have completed their take-home exercises, give them sides 3 and 4 of Take-Home 115. Tell them they may keep the stories and read them.

END OF LESSON 115

Before presenting lesson 116, give Mastery Test 22 to each child.
Do not present lesson 116 to any groups that are not firm on this test.

Lesson 156

z

s

SOUNDS

TASK 1   Teaching z as in zoo

a. Point to **z**. Here's a new sound.
b. My turn. (Pause.) Touch **z** and say: **zzz**.
c. Again. Touch **z** for a longer time. **zzzzz**. Lift your finger.
d. Point to **z**. Your turn. When I touch it, you say it. (Pause.) Get ready. Touch **z**. **zzz**. Lift your finger.
e. Again. Touch **z**. **zzzzzz**. Lift your finger.
f. Repeat e until firm.

TASK 2   Individual test

Call on different children to identify **z**.

TASK 3   Sounds firm-up

a. Get ready to say the sounds when I touch them.
b. Alternate touching **z** and **s**. Point to the sound. (Pause one second.) Say: Get ready. Touch the sound. *The children respond.*
c. When **z** and **s** are firm, alternate touching **z, s, x,** and **th** until all four sounds are firm.

TASK 4   Individual test—Have children identify **z, s, x,** or **th.**

TASK 5   Sounds firm-up

a. Point to **z**. When I touch the sound, you say it.
b. (Pause.) Get ready. Touch **z**. *zzz*.
c. Again. Repeat *b* until firm.
d. Get ready to say all the sounds when I touch them.
e. Alternate touching **z, qu, ȳ, wh, j, er, b,** and **y** three or four times.
      Point to the sound. (Pause one second.) Say: Get ready.
      Touch the sound. *The children respond.*

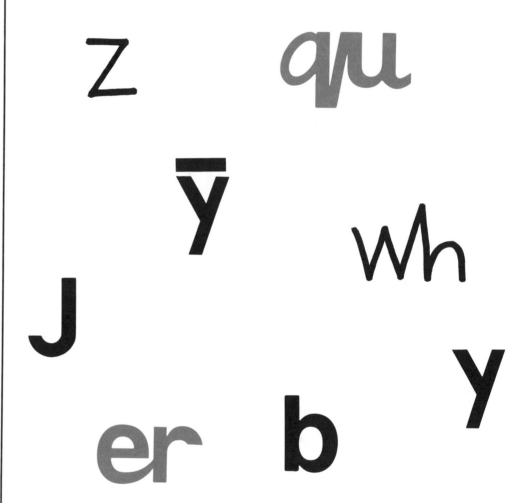

TASK 6   Individual test

Call on different children to identify one or more sounds in task 5.

Mastery Test 22 after lesson 115, before lesson 116

a. You're going to read this story the fast way.
b. Touch the first word. *(The child responds.)*
c. **(test item)** (Pause three seconds.) Get ready. Clap. *A.*
d. **(test item)** Next word. (Pause three seconds.) Get ready. Clap. *Dog.*
e. **(test item)** Next word. (Pause three seconds.) Get ready. Clap. *Sat.*
f. **(11 test items)** Repeat e for the remaining eleven words in the story.

Total number of test items: **14**

A group is weak if more than one-third of the children missed two or more words on the test.

WHAT TO DO

If the group is firm on Mastery Test 22 and was firm on Mastery Test 21:

Skip lesson 116 and present lesson 117 to the group during the next reading period. If more than one child missed two or more words on the test, present the firming procedures specified in the next column to those children.

If the group is firm on Mastery Test 22 but was weak on Mastery Test 21:

Present lesson 116 to the group during the next reading period. If more than one child missed two or more words on the test, present the firming procedures specified below to those children.

If the group is weak on Mastery Test 22:

A. Present these firming procedures to the group during the next reading period. Present each story until the children make no more than three mistakes. Then proceed to the next story.
   1. Lesson 113, Story, page 32, tasks 21, 22.
   2. Lesson 114, Story, page 38, tasks 22, 23.
   3. Lesson 115, Story, page 44, tasks 22, 23.
B. After presenting the above tasks, again give Mastery Test 22 individually to members of the group who failed the test.
C. If the group is firm (less than one-third of the total group missed two or more words in the story on the retest), present lesson 116 to the group during the next reading period.
D. If the group is still weak (more than one-third of the total group missed two or more words in the story on the retest), repeat A and B during the next reading period.

a dog sat in a

littl℮ car. th℮̄ dog

said, "I nē℮̄d to ℮̄at."

Mastery Test 30 after lesson 155, before lesson 156

Read this story the fast way. Do not clap for the words. Let the child read at his own pace.

Total number of test items: **18**

A group is weak if more than one-third of the children missed two or more words on the test.

WHAT TO DO

If the group is firm on Mastery Test 30 and was firm on Mastery Test 29:

Present lesson 156, skip lesson 157, present lesson 158, and skip lessons 159 and 160. If more than one child missed two or more words on the test, present the firming procedures specified in the next column to those children.

If the group is firm on Mastery Test 30 but was weak on Mastery Test 29:

Present lesson 156 to the group during the next reading period. If more than one child missed two or more words on the test, present the firming procedures specified below to those children.

If the group is weak on Mastery Test 30:

A. Present these firming procedures to the group during the next reading period. Present each story until the children make no more than three mistakes. Then proceed to the next story.
   1. Lesson 153, Story, page 288, tasks 26, 27.
   2. Lesson 154, Story, page 296, tasks 24, 25.
   3. Lesson 155, Story, page 304, tasks 27, 28.
B. After presenting the above tasks, again give Mastery Test 30 individually to members of the group who failed the test.
C. If the group is firm (less than one-third of the total group missed two or more words in the story on the retest), present lesson 156 to the group during the next reading period.
D. If the group is still weak (more than one-third of the total group missed two or more words in the story on the retest), repeat A and B during the next reading period.

some girls went to the

moon in a moon ship.

a girl said, "I will

find some fun."

Lesson 116

Groups that are firm on Mastery Tests 21 and 22 should skip this lesson and do lesson 117 today.

SOUNDS

TASK 1   Teacher and children play the sounds game

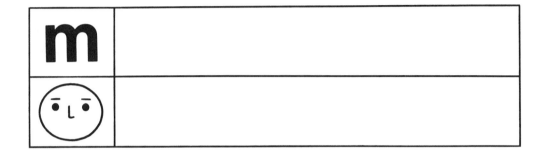

a. Use acetate and crayon. Write the sounds in the symbol box. Keep score in the score box.

b. **I'm smart. I bet I can beat you in a game.**

c. **Here's the rule. When I touch a sound, you say it.**

d. Play the game.
Make one symbol at a time in the symbol box. Use the symbols **p, h, th,** and **d.**
Make each symbol quickly. (Pause.) Touch the symbol.
Play the game for about two minutes.
Then ask: **Who won?** Draw a mouth on the face in the score box.

TASK 2   Sounds firm-up

a. Point to **ch.** **When I touch the sound, you say it.**

b. (Pause.) **Get ready.** Touch **ch.** *ch.*

c. **Again.** Repeat *b* until firm.

d. **Get ready to say all the sounds when I touch them.**

e. Alternate touching **ō, k, o, u, n, ē, ch** and **l** three or four times.
Point to the sound. (Pause one second.) Say: **Get ready.**
Touch the sound. *The children respond.*

TASK 3   Individual test

Call on different children to identify one or more sounds in task 2.

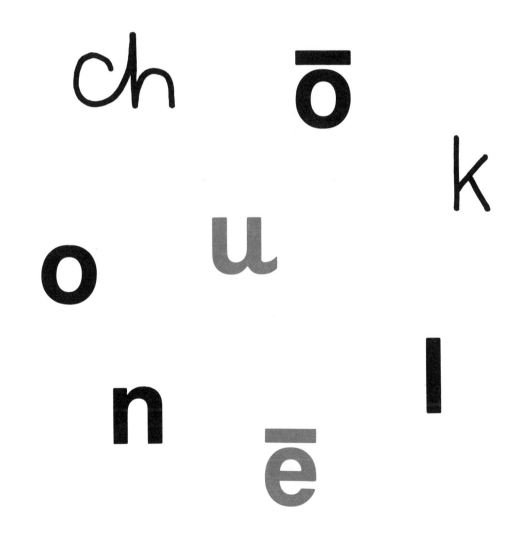

TASK 30   Picture comprehension

a. What do you think you'll see in the picture?   *The children respond.*
b. Turn the page and look at the picture.
c. Ask these questions:
  1. Who's the girl talking to in the picture?   *The children respond.*
                                                                    Her mother.
  2. What's the girl saying?   *The children respond.*
                                            Yes, I need my red tooth brush.
  3. Do you have a tooth brush?   *The children respond.*
                                          What color is it?   *The children respond.*

Take-Home 155

SUMMARY OF INDEPENDENT ACTIVITY

TASK 31   Introduction to independent activity

a. Pass out sides 1 and 2 of Take-Home 155 to each child.
b. Everybody, do a good job on your take-home today and I'll give you a bonus take-home.
c. Hold up side 1 of your take-home. You're going to do this take-home on your own. Tell the children when they will work the items. Let's go over some of the things you're going to do.

TASK 32   Reading comprehension

a. Point to the reading-comprehension exercise on side 2.
b. Everybody, get ready to read the sentences in the box the fast way.
c. First word. Check children's responses. Get ready. Clap for each word as the children read the sentences: *Bill had a brush.*
                                            It was not a tooth brush.
d. Point to items 1 and 2. These items tell about the story in the box. You're going to read each item and circle the right answer.

TASK 33   Sentence copying

a. Point to the dotted sentence in the sentence-copying exercise.
b. You're going to trace the words in this sentence. Then you're going to write the sentence on the other lines.
c. Reading the fast way. First word. Check children's responses. Get ready. Clap for each word.
d. After you finish your take-home, you get to draw a picture about the sentence, **I need a tooth brush**. You'll draw your picture on a piece of plain paper. When the children finish their take-homes, give them sheets of plain paper.

TASK 34   Other independent activity: sides 1, 2, 3, 4

Remember to do all the parts of the take-home and to read all the parts carefully. After you draw your picture, I'll give you a bonus take-home.

INDIVIDUAL CHECKOUT: STORYBOOK

TASK 35   2½-minute individual checkout

a. As you are doing your take-home, I'll call on children one at a time to read the **whole story.** Remember, you get two stars if you read the story in less than two and a half minutes and make no more than three errors.
b. Call on a child. Tell the child: Start with the title and read the story carefully the fast way. Go. Time the child. Tell the child any words the child misses. Stop the child as soon as the child makes the fourth error or exceeds the time limit.
c. If the child meets the rate-accuracy criterion, record two stars on your chart for lesson 155. Congratulate the child. Give children who do not earn two stars a chance to read the story again before the next lesson is presented.

100 words/**2.5 min** = 40 wpm **[3 errors]**

END OF LESSON 155

Before presenting lesson 156, give Mastery Test 30 to each child.
Do not present lesson 156 to any groups that are not firm on this test.

READING VOCABULARY

Do not touch any small letters.

TASK 4   Children identify, then sound out an irregular word (to)

a. Touch the ball for **to.** Everybody, you're going to read this word the fast way. (Pause three seconds.) Get ready. Move your finger quickly along the arrow. *To.* Yes, **to.**

b. Now you're going to sound out the word. Get ready. Quickly touch **t, o** as the children say *tooo.*

c. Again. Repeat *b.*

d. How do we say the word? (Signal.) *To.* Yes, **to.**

e. Repeat *b* and *d* until firm.

TASK 5   Individual test

Call on different children to do *b* and *d* in task 4.

TASK 6   Children sound out the word and tell what word

a. Touch the ball for **cāves.** Sound it out.

b. Get ready. Touch **c, ā, v, s** as the children say *cāāāvvvsss.* If sounding out is not firm, repeat *b.*

c. What word? (Signal.) *Caves.* Yes, **caves.**

TASK 7   Children sound out the word and tell what word

Repeat the procedures in task 6 for **tēach.**

TASK 8   Children read the fast way

Touch the ball for **will.** Get ready to read this word the fast way. (Pause three seconds.) Get ready. (Signal.) *Will.*

TASK 9   Children read the words the fast way

Have the children read the words on this page the fast way.

TASK 10   Individual test

Call on different children to read one word the fast way.

to

cāves

tēach

will

Story 155

TASK 27 First reading—children read the title and first three sentences

a. You're going to read the first part of this story today.

b. Everybody, touch the title of the story and get ready to read the words in the title the fast way.

c. First word. Check children's responses. (Pause two seconds.) Get ready. Clap. *The.*

d. Clap for each remaining word in the title.

e. After the children have read the title, ask: What's this story about? (Signal.) *The red tooth brush.* Yes, **the red tooth brush.**

f. Everybody, get ready to read this story the fast way.

g. First word. Check children's responses. (Pause two seconds.) Get ready. Clap. *A.*

h. Clap for the remaining words in the first sentence. Pause at least two seconds between claps.

i. Repeat *g* and *h* for the next two sentences. Have the children reread the first three sentences until firm.

TASK 28 Individual children or the group read sentences to complete the first reading

a. I'm going to call on different children to read a sentence. Everybody, follow along and point to the words. If you hear a mistake, raise your hand.

b. Call on a child. Read the next sentence. Do not clap for the words. Let the child read at his own pace, but be sure he reads the sentence correctly.

To correct	Have the child sound out the word. Then return to the beginning of the sentence.

c. Repeat *b* for most of the remaining sentences in the story. Occasionally have the group read a sentence. When the group is to read, say: Everybody, read the next sentence. (Pause two seconds.) Get ready. Clap for each word in the sentence. Pause at least two seconds between claps.

TASK 29 Second reading—individual children or the group read each sentence; the group answer questions

a. You're going to read the story again. This time I'm going to ask questions.

b. Starting with the first word of the title. Check children's responses. Get ready. Clap as the children read the title. Pause at least two seconds between claps.

c. Call on a child. Read the first sentence. *The child responds.*

d. Repeat *b* and *c* in task 28. Present the following comprehension questions to the entire group.

After the children read:	You say:
The red tooth brush.	What's this story about? (Signal.) *The red tooth brush.*
She brushed her teeth six times a day.	What did she do? (Signal.) *She brushed her teeth six times a day.* What did she use to brush her teeth? (Signal.) *Her red tooth brush.*
"They are so white they shine like the moon."	What did she say? *The children respond.* She said, "My teeth are white. They are so white they shine like the moon." Why were her teeth so white? (Signal.) *She brushed them six times a day.*
But her mother said, "I do not have your red tooth brush."	What did her mother say? (Signal.) *I do not have your red tooth brush.* I wonder how she'll brush her teeth without her red tooth brush.

TASK 11   Children sound out an irregular word (girl)

a. Touch the ball for **girl. Sound it out.**
b. Get ready. Quickly touch each sound as the children say *giiirrrlll.*

To correct	If the children do not say the sounds you touch
	1. Say: **You've got to say the sounds I touch.**
	2. Repeat *a* and *b* until firm.

c. Again. Repeat *b* until firm.
d. That's how we sound out **the word. Here's how we** say **the word.**
            Girl. **How do we** say **the word?** (Signal.) *Girl.*
e. Now you're going to sound out **the word. Get ready.**
            Touch each sound as the children say *giiirrrlll.*
f. Now you're going to say the word. Get ready. (Signal.) *Girl.*
g. Repeat *e* and *f* until firm.
h. Yes, this word is girl. She is a girl.

TASK 12   Individual test

Call on different children to do *e* and *f* in task 11.

TASK 13   Children identify, then sound out an irregular word (car)

a. Touch the ball for **car. Everybody, you're going to read this**
            word the fast way. (Pause three seconds.) **Get ready.**
            Move your finger quickly along the arrow. *Car.* **Yes, car.**
b. Now you're going to sound out the word. Get ready.
            Quickly touch **c, a, r** as the children say *caaarrr.*
c. Again. Repeat *b.*
d. How do we say the word? (Signal.) *Car.* **Yes, car.**
e. Repeat *b* and *d* until firm.

TASK 14   Individual test

Call on different children to do *b* and *d* in task 13.

Read the Items 155

TASK 24   Children read items 1 and 2

---

a. Pass out Storybook 3.

b. Open your book to page 46.

c. Get ready to read the items and play the game.

d. Finger under the first word of the title. Check children's responses.

e. When I clap, read the title. (Pause.) Get ready. Clap.

Read the items.

f. Touch item 1 and get ready to read. Check children's responses.

First word. Clap for each word as the children read:

When the teacher says "Go," pat your ears. Repeat until firm.

g. Everybody, get ready to say item 1. (Pause and signal.) *The children say the sentence.* Repeat four times or until firm.

h. Touch item 2 and get ready to read. Check children's responses.

First word. Clap for each word as the children read:

When the teacher says "Do it," touch your feet.

Repeat until firm.

i. Everybody, get ready to say item 2. (Pause and signal.) *The children say the sentence.* Repeat four times or until firm.

TASK 25   Children reread items 1 and 2 and answer questions

a. Everybody, touch item 1. Check children's responses.

b. Read item 1 to yourself. Raise your hand when you know what you're going to do and when you're going to do it.

c. After the children raise their hands, say: Everybody, what are you going to do when I say "Go"? (Signal.) *Pat my ears.*

To correct	1. Everybody, read item 1 out loud. Clap as the children read each word.
	2. What are you going to do when I say "Go"? (Signal.) *Pat my ears.*

d. Everybody, when are you going to **pat your ears**? (Signal.) *When the teacher says "Go."*

To correct	1. Everybody, read item 1 out loud. Clap as the children read each word.
	2. When are you going to **pat your ears**? (Signal.) *When the teacher says "Go."*

e. Repeat *c* and *d* until firm.

---

f. Everybody, touch item 2. Check children's responses.

g. Read item 2 to yourself. Raise your hand when you know what you're going to do and when you're going to do it.

h. After the children raise their hands, say: Everybody, what are you going to do when I say "**Do it**"? (Signal.) *Touch my feet.*

To correct	1. Everybody, read item 2 out loud. Clap as the children read each word.
	2. What are you going to do when I say "**Do it**"? (Signal.) *Touch my feet.*

i. Everybody, when are you going to **touch your feet**? (Signal.) *When the teacher says "Do it."*

To correct	1. Everybody, read item 2 out loud. Clap as the children read each word.
	2. When are you going to **touch your feet**? (Signal.) *When the teacher says "Do it."*

j. Repeat *h* and *i* until firm.

TASK 26   Children play the game

a. Everybody, touch item 1. Check children's responses.

b. Read the item to yourself. Raise your hand when you know what you're going to do and when you're going to do it.

c. After the children raise their hands, say: Let's play the game. Think about what you're going to do (pause) and when you're going to do it.

d. Hold out your hand. (Pause.) Get ready. Go. (Pause.) Drop your hand. *(The children pat their ears immediately.)*

To correct	1. What did I say? (Signal.) *Go.*
	2. What are you supposed to do when I say "**Go**"? (Signal.) *Pat my ears.*
	3. If the children's responses are not firm, have them read item 1 aloud.
	4. Repeat task 26.

TASK 15 **Children rhyme with wāves**

a. Touch the ball for **wāves.** You're going to read this word the fast way. (Pause three seconds.) Get ready. Move your finger quickly along the arrow. *Waves.*

b. Touch the ball for **sāves.** This word rhymes with (pause) **waves.** Move to **s,** then quickly along the arrow. *Saves.* Yes, what word? (Signal.) *Saves.*

TASK 16 **Children read the words the fast way**

a. Now you get to read the words on this page the fast way.

b. Touch the ball for **sāves.** (Pause three seconds.) Get ready. Move your finger quickly along the arrow. *Saves.*

c. Repeat *b* for **wāves.**

TASK 17 **Individual test**

Call on different children to read one word the fast way.

Do not touch any small letters.

wāveS

sāveS

TASK 21 Children read sm͞ile and sm͞iled

Do not touch any small letters.

a. Cover **s.** Point to **m͞ile.** You're going to read this part of the word the fast way. (Pause three seconds.) Get ready. (Signal.) *M͞ile.* Yes, **m͞ile.**

b. Uncover **s.** Point to **s.** You're going to say this first. Move your finger quickly under **m͞ile.** Then you're going to say (pause) **m͞ile.**

c. Point to **s.** What are you going to say first? (Signal.) *sss.* What are you going to say next? (Signal.) *M͞ile.*

d. Repeat *c* until firm.

e. Touch the ball for **sm͞ile.** Get ready. Move to **s,** then quickly along the arrow. *Sssmile.*

f. Say it fast. (Signal.) *Smile.* Yes, what word? (Signal.) *Smile.* Yes, **smile.** Good reading.

g. Again. Repeat *e* and *f* until firm.

h. Return to the ball for **sm͞ile.** Yes, this word is **smile.**

i. Touch the ball for **sm͞iled.** So this must be **smile . . . .** Touch **d.** *d.* What word? (Signal.) *Smiled.* Yes, **smiled.**

j. Again. Repeat *h* and *i* until firm.

k. Touch the ball for **sm͞ile.** This word is **smile.** Touch the ball for **sm͞iled.** So this must be . . . . Quickly run your finger under **sm͞ile** and tap **d.** *Smiled.* Yes, **smiled.**

l. Again. Repeat *k* until firm.

m. Now you're going to sound out (pause) **smiled.** Get ready. Touch **s, m, ͞i, l, d** as the children say *sssmmm͞iiillld.* Yes, what word? (Signal.) *Smiled.* Yes, **smiled.**

sm͞ile

sm͞iled

TASK 22 Children read the words the fast way

a. Now you get to read the words on this page the fast way.

b. Touch the ball for **sm͞iled.** (Pause three seconds.) Get ready. Move your finger quickly along the arrow. *Smiled.*

c. Repeat *b* for **sm͞ile.**

TASK 23 Individual test

Call on different children to read one word the fast way.

Story 116

TASK 18   Teacher introduces the title

a. Pass out Storybook 1.

b. Open your book to page 59.

c. Hold up your reader. Point to the title. These words are called the title of the story. These words tell what the story is about. I'll read the title the fast way.

d. Point to the words as you read: Thē girl and thē dog.

e. Everybody, what is this story about? (Signal.) *Thē girl and thē dog.* Yes, thē girl and thē dog. This story is going to tell something about thē girl and thē dog.

TASK 19   First reading—children read the story the fast way

Have the children reread any sentences containing the words that give them trouble. Keep a list of these words.

a. Everybody, touch the title of the story and get ready to read the words in the title the fast way.

b. First word. Check children's responses. (Pause three seconds.) Get ready. Clap. *Thē.*

c. Next word. Check children's responses. (Pause three seconds.) Get ready. Clap. *Girl.*

d. Repeat c for the words and, thē, dog.

e. After the children have read the title, ask: What's this story about? (Signal.) *Thē girl and thē dog.* Yes, thē girl and thē dog.

f. Everybody, touch the first word of the story. Check children's responses.

g. Get ready to read this story the fast way.

h. First word. (Pause three seconds.) Get ready. Clap. *Thē.*

i. Next word. Check children's responses. (Pause three seconds.) Get ready. Clap. *Girl.*

j. Repeat *i* for the remaining words in the first sentence. Pause at least three seconds between claps. The children are to identify each word without sounding it out.

k. Repeat *h* through *j* for the next two sentences. Have the children reread the first three sentences until firm.

l. The children are to read the remainder of the story the fast way, stopping at the end of each sentence.

m. After the first reading of the story, print on the board the words that the children missed more than one time. Have the children sound out each word one time and tell what word.

n. After the group's responses are firm, call on individual children to read the words.

TASK 20   Individual test

a. Turn back to page 59. I'm going to call on different children to read a whole sentence the fast way.

b. Call on different children to read a sentence. Do not clap for each word.

TASK 21   Second reading—children read the story the fast way and answer questions

a. You're going to read the story again the fast way and I'll ask questions.

b. Starting with the first word of the title. Check children's responses. Get ready. Clap. *Thē.*

c. Clap for each remaining word. Pause at least three seconds between claps. Pause longer before words that gave the children trouble during the first reading.

d. Ask the comprehension questions below as the children read.

After the children read:	You say:
The girl and the dog.	What's this story about? (Signal.) *The girl and the dog.*
The girl said, "I can teach the dog to run."	What did she say? (Signal.) *I can teach the dog to run.*
The girl said, "I will teach the dog to run."	What did she say? (Signal.) *I will teach the dog to run.*
"Ha-ha."	What did the dog say? (Signal.) *The children respond.* Why couldn't the girl teach him to run? *The children respond.* Yes, he already knew how to run. Was this story about the girl and the dog? (Signal.) *Yes.*

TASK 16   Children read a word beginning with two consonants (flȳ)

Do not touch any small letters.

a. Cover **f.** Run your finger under **lȳ.** **You're going to sound out this part. Get ready.** Touch **l, ȳ** as the children say *lllȳȳȳ.*

b. **Say it fast.** (Signal.) *Lȳ.* **Yes, this part is lȳ.**

c. Uncover **f.** Point to **f.** **You're going to say this first. Move your finger quickly under lȳ. Then you're going to say** (pause) **lȳ.**

d. Point to **f.** **What are you going to say first?** (Signal.) *fff.* **What are you going to say next?** (Signal.) *Lȳ.*

e. **Repeat** *d* **until firm.**

f. Touch the ball for **flȳ.** **Get ready.** Move to **f,** then quickly along the arrow. *Ffflȳ.*

g. **Say it fast.** (Signal.) *Fly.* **Yes, what word?** (Signal.) *Fly.* **Yes, fly. Good reading.**

h. **Again.** **Repeat** *f* **and** *g* **until firm.**

i. **Now you're going to sound out** (pause) **fly. Get ready.** Touch **f, l, ȳ** as the children say *ffflllȳȳȳ.* **What word?** (Signal.) *Fly.* **Yes, fly.**

TASK 17   Children sound out the word and tell what word

a. Touch the ball for **tooth.** **Sound it out.**

b. **Get ready.** Touch **t, oo, th** as the children say *toooothththth.* If sounding out is not firm, repeat *b.*

c. **What word?** (Signal.) *Tooth.* **Yes, tooth.**

TASK 18   Children sound out the word and tell what word

a. Touch the ball for **where.** **Sound it out.**

b. **Get ready.** Touch **wh, e, r** as the children say *whwhwheeerrr.* If sounding out is not firm, repeat *b.*

c. **What word?** (Signal.) *Where.* **Yes, where. She didn't know where to go.**

TASK 19   Children read the words the fast way

Have the children read the words on this page the fast way.

TASK 20   Individual test

Call on different children to read one word the fast way.

TASK 22   Picture comprehension

a. Everybody, look at the picture.
b. Ask these questions:
   1. Does that girl look happy? *No.* Why not? *The children respond.*
   2. Why does the girl want to teach the dog to run?
                                                   The children respond.
   3. Did you ever teach a dog to do tricks? *The children respond.*

Take-Home 116

SUMMARY OF INDEPENDENT ACTIVITY

TASK 23   Introduction to independent activity

a. Pass out Take-Home 116 to each child.
b. Everybody, you're going to do this take-home on your own.
                  Tell the children when they will work the items.
                  Let's go over the things you're going to do.

TASK 24   Sentence copying

a. Hold up side 1 of your take-home and point to the first line in the
                                                   sentence-copying exercise.
b. Everybody, here's the sentence you're going to write on the lines
                                                   below.
c. Reading the fast way. First word.   Check children's responses.
                                 Get ready.   Clap. *Thē.*
d. Next word.   Check children's responses. Get ready.   Clap. *Dog.*
e. Repeat *d* for the remaining words.
f. After you finish your take-home, you get to draw a picture about
                              the sentence, **thē dog said**, "**nō.**"

TASK 25   Sound writing

a. Point to the sound-writing exercise. Here are the sounds you're
                              going to write today. I'll touch the sounds. You say them.
b. Touch each sound. *The children respond.*
c. Repeat the series until firm.

TASK 26   Matching

a. Point to the column of words in the Matching Game.
b. Everybody, you're going to follow the lines and write these words.
c. Reading the fast way.
d. Point to the first word. (Pause.) Get ready.   (Signal.)
                                                   The children respond.
e. Repeat *d* for the remaining words.
f. Repeat *d* and *e* until firm.

TASK 27   Cross-out game

Point to the boxed word in the Cross-out Game. Everybody, here's
                  the word you're going to cross out today. What word? (Signal.)
                                                   Girl. Yes, **girl**.

TASK 28   Pair relations

a. Point to the pair-relations exercise on side 2. Remember—you're
                  going to draw a line through the words in each box that do not
                                                   tell about the picture.
b. Point to the space at the top of the page. After you finish,
                  remember to draw a picture that shows **thē dog said**, "**nō.**"

END OF LESSON 116

TASK 12 Children read a word beginning with two consonants (stand)

a. Cover **s**. Run your finger under **tand**. You're going to sound out this part. Get ready. Touch **t, a, n, d** as the children say *taaannnd*.

b. Say it fast. (Signal.) *Tand.* Yes, this part is **tand**.

c. Uncover **s**. Point to **s**. You're going to say this first.
Move your finger quickly under **tand**. Then you're going to say (pause) **tand**.

d. Point to **s**. What are you going to say first? (Signal.) *sss.*
What are you going to say next? (Signal.) *Tand.*

e. Repeat *d* until firm.

f. Touch the ball for **stand**. Get ready. Move to **s**, then quickly along the arrow. *Ssstand.*

g. Say it fast. (Signal.) *Stand.* Yes, what word? (Signal.) *Stand.*
Yes, **stand**. Good reading.

h. Again. Repeat *f* and *g* until firm.

i. Now you're going to sound out (pause) **stand**. Get ready.
Touch **s, t, a, n, d** as the children say *ssstaaannnd*.
What word? (Signal.) *Stand.* Yes, **stand**.

TASK 13 Children rhyme with mȳ

a. Touch the ball for **mȳ**. You're going to read this word the fast way.
(Pause three seconds.) Get ready. Move your finger quickly along the arrow. *My.*

b. Touch the ball for **whȳ**. This word rhymes with (pause) **my.**
Move to **wh**, then quickly along the arrow. *Why.*
Yes, what word? (Signal.) *Why.*

TASK 14 Children read the words the fast way

a. Now you get to read the words on this page the fast way.

b. Touch the ball for **stand**. (Pause three seconds.) Get ready.
Move your finger quickly along the arrow. *Stand.*

c. Repeat *b* for each word on the page.

TASK 15 Individual test

Call on different children to read one word the fast way.

Lesson 117

SOUNDS

TASK 1   Teacher and children play the sounds game

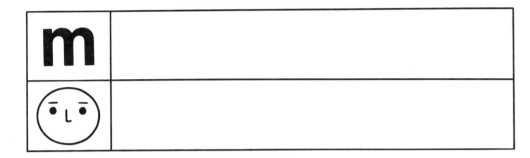

a. Use acetate and crayon. Write the sounds in the symbol box. Keep score in the score box.
b. I'm smart. I bet I can beat you in a game.
c. Here's the rule. When I touch a sound, you say it.
d. Play the game.
   Make one symbol at a time in the symbol box. Use the symbols **ō, o, i,** and **ā.**
   Make each symbol quickly. (Pause.) Touch the symbol.
   Play the game for about two minutes.
   Then ask: Who won? Draw a mouth on the face in the score box.

TASK 2   Child plays teacher

a. Use acetate and crayon.
b. [Child's name] is going to be the teacher.
c. [He or She] is going to touch the sounds. When [he or she] touches a sound, you say it.
d. The child points to and touches the sounds. You circle any sound that is not firm.
e. After the child has completed the page, present all the circled sounds to the children.

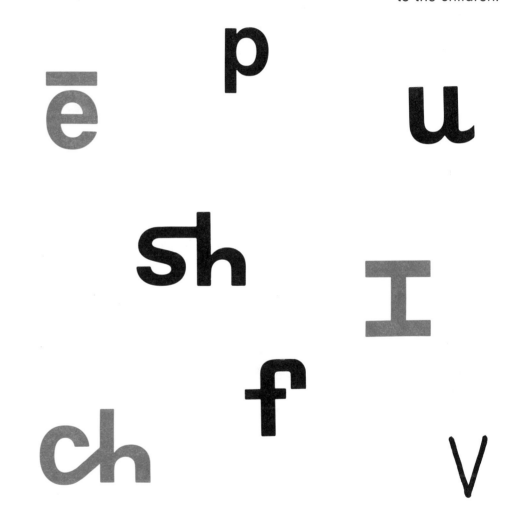

TASK 3   Individual test

Call on different children. If you can say the sound when I call your name, you may cross it out.

READING VOCABULARY

Do not touch any small letters.

TASK 7   Children sound out an irregular word (touch)

a. Touch the ball for **touch.** Sound it out.
b. Get ready. Quickly touch each sound as the children say *tooouuuch.*
c. Again. Repeat *b* until firm.
d. That's how we <u>sound out</u> the word. Here's how we <u>say</u> the word.
           Touch. How do we <u>say</u> the word? (Signal.) *Touch.*
e. Now you're going to <u>sound out</u> the word. Get ready.
           Touch each sound as the children say *tooouuuch.*
f. Now you're going to say the word. Get ready. (Signal.) *Touch.*
g. Repeat *e* and *f* until firm.
h. Yes, this word is **touch.** I can **touch** my nose.

TASK 8   Individual test

Call on different children to do *e* and *f* in task 7.

TASK 9   Children read the fast way

a. Get ready to read these words the fast way.
b. Touch the ball for **six.** (Pause three seconds.) Get ready.
                                                         (Signal.) *Six.*

c. Repeat *b* for the remaining words on the page.

TASK 10   Children read the fast way again

a. Get ready to do these words again. Watch where I point.
b. Point to a word. (Pause one second.) Say: Get ready. (Signal.)
           The children respond. Point to the words in this order:
                white, six, shīne, brushed.

c. Repeat *b* until firm.

TASK 11   Individual test

Call on different children to read one word on the page the fast way.

touch

six

shīne

whīte

brushed

READING VOCABULARY

Do not touch any small letters.

TASK 4   Children read the fast way

a. Get ready to read these words the fast way.
b. Touch the ball for **cows.** (Pause three seconds.) Get ready.
(Signal.) *Cows.*
c. Repeat *b* for the remaining words on the page.

TASK 5   Children read the fast way again

a. Get ready to do these words again. Watch where I point.
b. Point to a word. (Pause one second.) Say: Get ready. (Signal.)
The children respond. Point to the words in this order:
with, cāves, cows, will, cats.
c. Repeat *b* until firm.

TASK 6   Individual test

Call on different children to read one word the fast way.

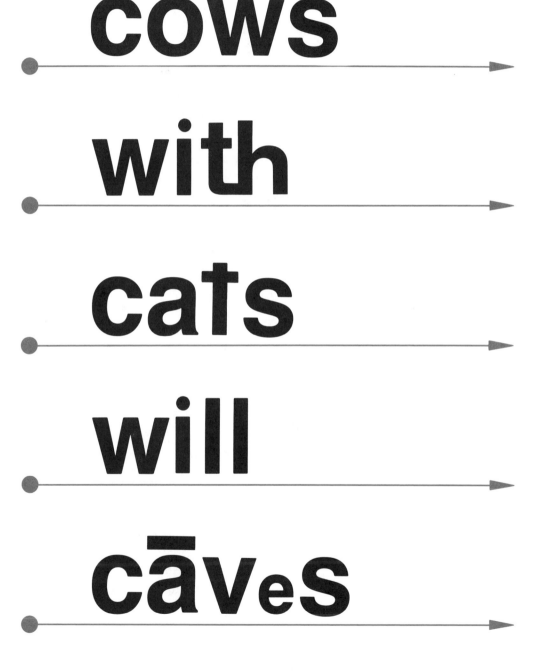

Lesson 155

SOUNDS

TASK 1   Teaching **qu** as in **quick**

a. Point to **qu.** My turn. When I touch it, I'll say it. (Pause.)
Touch **qu** for an instant, saying: *qu.*

b. Point to **qu.** Your turn. When I touch it, you say it. (Pause.)
Get ready. Touch **qu.** *qu.*

c. Again. Touch **qu.** *qu.*
d. Repeat *c* until firm.

TASK 2   Sounds firm-up

a. Get ready to say the sounds when I touch them.
b. Alternate touching **qu** and **wh.** Point to the sound. (Pause one second.) Say: Get ready. Touch the sound. *The children respond.*
c. When **qu** and **wh** are firm, alternate touching **qu, wh, p,** and **k** until all four sounds are firm.

TASK 3   Individual test

Call on different children to identify **qu, wh, p,** or **k.**

TASK 4   Teacher introduces cross-out game

a. Use acetate and crayon.
b. I'll cross out the sounds on this part of the page when you can tell me every sound.
c. Remember—when I touch it, you say it.
d. Go over the sounds until the children can identify all the sounds in order.

TASK 5   Individual test

Call on different children to identify two or more sounds in task 4.

TASK 6   Teacher crosses out sounds

a. You told me every sound. Get ready to do it again. This time I'll cross out each sound when you tell me what it is.
b. Point to each sound. (Pause.) Say: Get ready. Touch the sound. *The children respond.* As you cross out the sound, say: Goodbye, _____.

TASK 7   Children sound out an irregular word (do)

a. Touch the ball for **do.** Sound it out.
b. Get ready. Quickly touch each sound as the children say *dooo.*

To correct	If the children do not say the sounds you touch
	1. Say: You've got to say the sounds I touch.
	2. Repeat *a* and *b* until firm.

c. Again. Repeat *b* until firm.
d. That's how we <u>sound out</u> the word. Here's how we <u>say</u> the word.
    Do. How do we <u>say</u> the word? (Signal.) *Do.*
e. Now you're going to <u>sound out</u> the word. Get ready.
    Touch each sound as the children say *dooo.*
f. Now you're going to say the word. Get ready. (Signal.) *Do.*
g. Repeat *e* and *f* until firm.
h. Yes, this word is **do. Do** you have a penny?

TASK 8   Individual test

Call on different children to do *e* and *f* in task 7.

TASK 9   Children sound out an irregular word (girl)

a. Touch the ball for **girl.** Sound it out.
b. Get ready. Quickly touch each sound as the children say *giiirrrlll.*
c. Again. Repeat *b* until firm.
d. That's how we <u>sound out</u> the word. Here's how we <u>say</u> the word.
    Girl. How do we <u>say</u> the word? (Signal.) *Girl.*
e. Now you're going to <u>sound out</u> the word. Get ready.
    Touch each sound as the children say *giiirrrlll.*
f. Now you're going to say the word. Get ready. (Signal.) *Girl.*
g. Repeat *e* and *f* until firm.
h. Yes, this word is **girl.** Raise your hand if you're a **girl.**

TASK 10   Individual test

Call on different children to do *e* and *f* in task 9.

TASK 27 Picture comprehension

a. Everybody, look at the picture.
b. Ask these questions:
  1. What's happening in the picture? *The children respond.*
                    The eagle is riding on the old horse.
  2. Does the eagle look like he's having fun? *The children respond.*
    Yes, he does. What about the horse? *The children respond.*
                                He looks happy too.
  3. Which would you rather do, fly like an eagle or ride a horse?
                                The children respond.

Take-Home 154

SUMMARY OF INDEPENDENT ACTIVITY

TASK 28 Introduction to independent activity

a. Pass out Take-Home 154 to each child.
b. Everybody, you're going to do this take-home on your own.
          Tell the children when they will work the items.
            Let's go over the things you're going to do.

TASK 29 Story items

a. Hold up side 1 of your take-home and point to the story-items
                                exercise.
b. Everybody, here are items about the story we read today.
c. Think about what happened in the story and circle the right answer
                            for each item.

TASK 30 Picture comprehension

a. Point to the pictures in the picture-comprehension exercise.
      Everybody, you're going to look at the picture. Then you're going
                  to read each item and write the missing word.
b. Remember—the first sound of each missing word is already written
                            in the blank.

TASK 31 Reading comprehension

a. Point to the reading-comprehension exercise on side 2.
b. Everybody, get ready to read the sentences in the box the fast way.
c. First word. Check children's responses. Get ready. Clap for each
          word as the children read the sentences: *An old car did not run.*
                                The girl got mad at the car.
d. Point to items 1 and 2. These items tell about the story in the box.
            You're going to read each item and circle the right answer.

TASK 32 Sound writing

a. Point to the sound-writing exercise. Here are the sounds you're
                going to write today. I'll touch the sounds. You say them.
b. Touch each sound. *The children respond.*
c. Repeat the series until firm.

TASK 33 Sentence copying

a. Point to the dotted sentence in the sentence-copying exercise.
b. You're going to trace the words in this sentence. Then you're
                going to write the sentence on the other lines.
c. Reading the fast way. First word. Check children's responses.
                        Get ready. Clap for each word.
d. After you finish your take-home, you get to draw a picture about
              the sentence, **the hōrse ran**. You'll draw your picture
          on a piece of plain paper. When the children finish their
                take-homes, give them sheets of plain paper.

END OF LESSON 154

TASK 11 **Children identify, then sound out an irregular word (farm)**

a. Touch the ball for **farm.** Everybody, you're going to read this word the fast way. (Pause three seconds.) Get ready. Move your finger quickly along the arrow. *Farm.* Yes, **farm.**

b. Now you're going to sound out the word. Get ready. Quickly touch **f, a, r, m** as the children say *fffaaarrrmmm.*

c. Again. Repeat *b.*

d. How do we say the word? (Signal.) *Farm.* Yes, **farm.**

e. Repeat *b* and *d* until firm.

TASK 12 **Individual test**

Call on different children to do *b* and *d* in task 11.

TASK 13 **Children sound out the word and tell what word**

a. Touch the ball for **pots.** Sound it out.

b. Get ready. Touch **p, o, t, s** as the children say *poootsss.* If sounding out is not firm, repeat *b.*

c. What word? (Signal.) *Pots.* Yes, **pots.**

TASK 14 **Children sound out the word and tell what word**

a. Touch the ball for **gāme.** Sound it out.

b. Get ready. Touch **g, ā, m** as the children say *gāāāmmm.* If sounding out is not firm, repeat *b.*

c. What word? (Signal.) *Game.* Yes, **game.**

TASK 15 **Children read the words the fast way**

a. Now you get to read the words on this page the fast way.

b. Touch the ball for **farm.** (Pause three seconds.) Get ready. Move your finger quickly along the arrow. *Farm.*

c. Repeat *b* for **pots** and **gāme.**

TASK 16 **Individual test**

Call on different children to read one word the fast way.

Story 154

TASK 24 First reading—children read the title and first three sentences

a. Now you're going to finish the story about the old horse and the eagle.

b. Everybody, touch the title of the story and get ready to read the words in the title the fast way.

c. First word. Check children's responses. (Pause two seconds.)
Get ready. Clap. *An.*

d. Clap for each remaining word in the title.

e. After the children have read the title, ask: What's this story about?
(Signal.) *An old horse and an eagle.*
Yes, **an old horse and an eagle.**

f. Everybody, get ready to read this story the fast way.

g. First word. Check children's responses. (Pause two seconds.)
Get ready. Clap. *An.*

h. Clap for the remaining words in the first sentence. Pause at least two seconds between claps.

i. Repeat *g* and *h* for the next two sentences. Have the children reread the first three sentences until firm.

TASK 25 Individual children or the group read sentences to complete the first reading

a. I'm going to call on different children to read a sentence.
Everybody, follow along and point to the words. If you hear a mistake, raise your hand.

b. Call on a child. Read the next sentence. Do not clap for the words.
Let the child read at his own pace, but be sure he reads the sentence correctly.

To correct	Have the child sound out the word. Then return to the beginning of the sentence.

c. Repeat *b* for most of the remaining sentences in the story.
Occasionally have the group read a sentence. When the group is to read, say: Everybody, read the next sentence. (Pause two seconds.) Get ready. Clap for each word in the sentence. Pause at least two seconds between claps.

TASK 26 Second reading—individual children or the group read each sentence; the group answer questions

a. You're going to read the story again. This time I'm going to ask questions.

b. Starting with the first word of the title. Check children's responses.
Get ready. Clap as the children read the title. Pause at least two seconds between claps.

c. Call on a child. Read the first sentence. *The child responds.*

d. Repeat *b* and *c* in task 25. Present the following comprehension questions to the entire group.

After the children read:	You say:
And he did.	Do you think the horse will fly to the top of the car? *The children respond.* Let's read and find out.
He ran into the side of the car.	Did the horse fly to the top of the car? (Signal.) *No.* What did he do? (Signal.) *He ran into the side of the car.*
"I can not fly."	What did the horse say? *The children respond.*
The horse said, "I can run with an eagle on my back, and that is fun."	What did the horse say? (Signal.) *I can run with an eagle on my back, and that is fun.* Does that sound like fun? *The children respond.*
"Yes, this is fun," they said.	What did they say? (Signal.) *Yes, this is fun.* Who said that? (Signal.) *The old horse and the eagle.*

Story 117

TASK 17 Teacher introduces the title

a. Pass out Storybook 1.
b. Open your book to page 62.
c. Hold up your reader. Point to the title. These words are called the title of the story. These words tell what the story is about. I'll read the title the fast way.
d. Point to the words as you read: A girl in a cave.
e. Everybody, what is this story about? (Signal.) A girl in a cave. Yes, **a girl in a cave.** This story is going to tell something about **a girl in a cave.**

TASK 18 First reading—children read the story the fast way

Have the children reread any sentences containing words that give them trouble. Keep a list of these words.

a. Everybody, touch the title of the story and get ready to read the words in the title the fast way.
b. First word. Check children's responses. (Pause three seconds.) Get ready. Clap. A.
c. Next word. Check children's responses. (Pause three seconds.) Get ready. Clap. Girl.
d. Repeat c for the words **in, a, cāve.**
e. After the children have read the title, ask: What's this story about? (Signal.) A girl in a cave. Yes, **a girl in a cave.**
f. Everybody, touch the first word of the story. Check children's responses.
g. Get ready to read this story the fast way.
h. First word. (Pause three seconds.) Get ready. Clap. A.
i. Next word. Check children's responses. (Pause three seconds.) Get ready. Clap. Girl.
j. Repeat i for the remaining words in the first sentence. Pause at least three seconds between claps. The children are to identify each word without sounding it out.
k. Repeat h through j for the next two sentences. Have the children reread the first three sentences until firm.
l. The children are to read the remainder of the story the fast way, stopping at the end of each sentence.

m. After the first reading of the story, print on the board the words that the children missed more than one time. Have the children sound out each word one time and tell what word.
n. After the group's responses are firm, call on individual children to read the words.

TASK 19 Individual test

a. Look at page 62. I'm going to call on different children to read a whole sentence the fast way.
b. Call on different children to read a sentence. Do not clap for each word.

TASK 20 Second reading—children read the story the fast way and answer questions

a. You're going to read the story again the fast way and I'll ask questions.
b. Starting with the first word of the title. Check children's responses. Get ready. Clap. A.
c. Clap for each remaining word. Pause at least three seconds between claps. Pause longer before words that gave the children trouble during the first reading.
d. Ask the comprehension questions below as the children read.

After the children read:	You say:
A girl in a cave.	What's this story about? (Signal.) A girl in a cave.
A girl was in a cave.	What's a cave? The children respond.
A wave came in the cave.	What's a wave? The children respond.
The girl said, "Save me, save me."	What did she say? (Signal.) Save me, save me.
She said, "I will save that girl."	What did the fish say? (Signal). I will save that girl. Do you think the fish will save her? The children respond. Let's read and find out.
And she did.	Did the fish save the girl? (Signal.) Yes.
So she gave the girl a seed and a ham.	What did the fish give her? (Signal.) A seed and a ham.

58

Read the Item 154

TASK 21 Children read item 1

a. Pass out Storybook 3.

b. Open your book to page 43.

c. Point to the title **rēad the ītem**. **Everybody, touch this title.**
Check children's responses.

d. I'll read the title. You point to the words I read. (Pause.)
Get ready. **Read** (pause) **the** (pause) **item**.

e. Your turn to read the title. First word. Check children's responses.
Get ready. Clap for each word as the children read *read the item*.

f. Everybody, say the title. (Pause and signal.) Without looking at the
words, the children say *read the item*. Repeat until firm.

g. You're going to read the item. Touch item 1 and get ready to read.
Check children's responses.

h. First word. Clap for each word as the children read:
When the teacher says "Do it," pick up your book.
Repeat three times or until firm.

i. Everybody, get ready to say item 1 with me. (Pause and signal.)
Without looking at the words, you and the children say, When the
teacher says "Do it," (pause one second) pick up your book.
Repeat four times or until firm.

j. All by yourselves. Say item 1. (Signal.)
When the teacher says "Do it," pick up your book.
Repeat four times or until firm.

TASK 22 Children reread item 1 and answer questions

a. Everybody, touch item 1 again. Check children's responses.

b. Read item 1 to yourself. Raise your hand when you know what
you're going to do and when you're going to do it.

c. After the children raise their hands, say: Everybody, what are you
going to do when I say "**Do it**"? (Signal.) *Pick up my book.*

| To correct | 1. Everybody, read item 1 out loud. Clap as the children read each word. |
| | 2. What are you going to do when I say "**Do it**"? (Signal.) *Pick up my book.* |

d. Everybody, when are you going to **pick up your book**? (Signal.)
When the teacher says "Do it."

| To correct | 1. Everybody, read item 1 out loud. Clap as the children read each word. |
| | 2. When are you going to **pick up your book**? (Signal.) *When the teacher says "Do it."* |

e. Repeat *c* and *d* until firm.

TASK 23 Children play the game

a. Everybody, touch item 1. Check children's responses.

b. Read the item to yourself. Raise your hand when you know what
you're going to do and when you're going to do it.

c. After the children raise their hands, say: Let's play the game.
Think about what you're going to do (pause) and when you're
going to do it.

d. Hold out your hand. (Pause.) Get ready. **Do it.** (Pause.)
Drop your hand. *(The children pick up their books immediately.)*

To correct	1. What did I say? (Signal.) *Do it.*
	2. What are you supposed to do when I say "**Do it**"? (Signal.) *Pick up my book.*
	3. If the children's responses are not firm, have them read item 1 aloud.
	4. Repeat task 23.

TASK 21   Picture comprehension

a. What do you think you'll see in the picture? *The children respond.*
b. Turn the page and look at the picture.
c. Ask these questions:
  1. Who is in the cave? *The children respond.* The fish and the girl.
  2. What is the girl eating? *The children respond.*
                                        Yes, a piece of ham.
  3. Have you ever been in a cave? *The children respond.*

Take-Home 117

SUMMARY OF INDEPENDENT ACTIVITY

TASK 22   Introduction to independent activity

a. Pass out Take-Home 117 to each child.
b. Everybody, you're going to do this take-home on your own.
                    Tell the children when they will work the items.
                    Let's go over the things you're going to do.

TASK 23   Sentence copying

a. Hold up side 1 of your take-home and point to the first line in the
                                        sentence-copying exercise.
b. Everybody, here's the sentence you're going to write on the lines
                                        below.
c. Reading the fast way. First word. Check children's responses.
                                        Get ready. Clap. *A.*
d. Next word. Check children's responses. Get ready. Clap. *Girl.*
e. Repeat *d* for the remaining words.
f. After you finish your take-home, you get to draw a picture about
                    the sentence, **a girl was in a cave**.

TASK 24   Sound writing

a. Point to the sound-writing exercise. Here are the sounds you're
                    going to write today. I'll touch the sounds. You say them.
b. Touch each sound. *The children respond.*
c. Repeat the series until firm.

TASK 25   Matching

a. Point to the column of words in the Matching Game.
b. Everybody, you're going to follow the lines and write these words.
c. Reading the fast way.
d. Point to the first word. (Pause.) Get ready. (Signal.)
                                        The children respond.
e. Repeat *d* for the remaining words.
f. Repeat *d* and *e* until firm.

TASK 26   Cross-out game

Point to the boxed word in the Cross-out Game. Everybody, here's
    the word you're going to cross out today. What word? (Signal.)
                                        Farm. Yes, **farm**.

TASK 27   Pair relations

a. Point to the pair-relations exercise on side 2. Remember—you're
                    going to draw a line through the words in each box that do not
                                        tell about the picture.
b. Point to the space at the top of the page. After you finish,
                    remember to draw a picture that shows **a girl was in a cāve**.

END OF LESSON 117

TASK 16   Children sound out an irregular word (**took**)

a. Touch the ball for **took.** Sound it out.
b. Get ready. Quickly touch each sound as the children say *tooook.*
c. Again. Repeat *b* until firm.
d. That's how we <u>sound out</u> the word. Here's how we <u>say</u> the word.
    Took. How do we <u>say</u> the word? (Signal.) *Took.*
e. Now you're going to <u>sound out</u> the word. Get ready.
    Touch each sound as the children say *tooook.*
f. Now you're going to say the word. Get ready. (Signal.) *Took.*
g. Repeat *e* and *f* until firm.

took

TASK 17   Children rhyme with an irregular word (**took**)

a. Touch the ball for **took.** Everybody, you're going to read this word
    the fast way. Get ready. (Signal.) *Took.*
b. Touch the ball for **look.** This word rhymes with (pause) **took.**
    Get ready. Move to **l**, then quickly along the arrow. *Look.*
c. Touch the ball for **book.** This word rhymes with (pause) **took.**
    Get ready. Move to **b**, then quickly along the arrow. *Book.*
d. Repeat *a* through *c* until firm.

look

TASK 18   Children sound out **look** and **book**

a. Have the children sound out **look.** *Lllooook.* How do we say
    the word? (Signal.) *Look.* Yes, **look.**
b. Have the children sound out **book.** *Booook.* How do we say
    the word? (Signal.) *Book.* Yes, **book.**

book

TASK 19   Children read the words the fast way

a. Now you get to read the words on this page the fast way.
b. Touch the ball for **took.** (Pause three seconds.) Get ready.
    Move your finger quickly along the arrow. *Took.*
c. Repeat *b* for each word on the page.

TASK 20   Individual test

Call on different children to read one word the fast way.

Lesson 118

ē

e

ē

ē

e

e

i

ch

ō

SOUNDS

TASK 1 Teacher firms up ē

a. Point to ē. Everybody get ready to tell me this sound. Get ready. Touch ē. *ēēē.*

b. Point to the space over **e.** Everybody, there's no line over this sound. This is not ēēē. Is it ēēē? (Signal.) *No.*

c. Point to each sound and ask: Is this ēēē? *The children respond.*

d. Repeat c until firm.

TASK 2 Teaching e as in end; children discriminate ē—e

a. Point to the first **e.** Everybody, this is **eee.**

b. When I touch it, you say it. (Pause.) Get ready. Touch **e.** *eee.*

c. Again. Touch **e.** *eee.*

d. Repeat c until firm.

e. Get ready to say these sounds. When I touch the sound, you say it.

Alternate touching the sounds. Before touching each **e,** point to the space over **e** and say: Remember—this is not ēēē.

f. Repeat e until all the sounds are firm.

TASK 3 Sounds firm-up

a. Point to **e.** When I touch the sound, you say it.

b. (Pause.) Get ready. Touch **e.** *eee.*

c. Again. Repeat b until firm.

d. Get ready to say all the sounds when I touch them.

e. Alternate touching **ch, e, i** and ō three or four times.
Point to the sound.
(Pause one second.) Say:
Get ready. Touch the sound.
The children respond.

TASK 4 Individual test

Call on different children to identify one or more sounds in task 3.

TASK 13 Children read the fast way

a. Get ready to read these words the fast way.
b. Touch the ball for **when.** (Pause three seconds.) Get ready.

(Signal.) *When.*

c. Repeat *b* for the remaining words on the page.

TASK 14 Children read the fast way again

a. Get ready to do these words again. Watch where I point.
b. Point to a word. (Pause one second.) Say: Get ready. (Signal.)
The children respond. Point to the words in this order:
when, brush, tooth, brushing, tēēth.
c. Repeat *b* until firm.

TASK 15 Individual test

Call on different children to read one word the fast way.

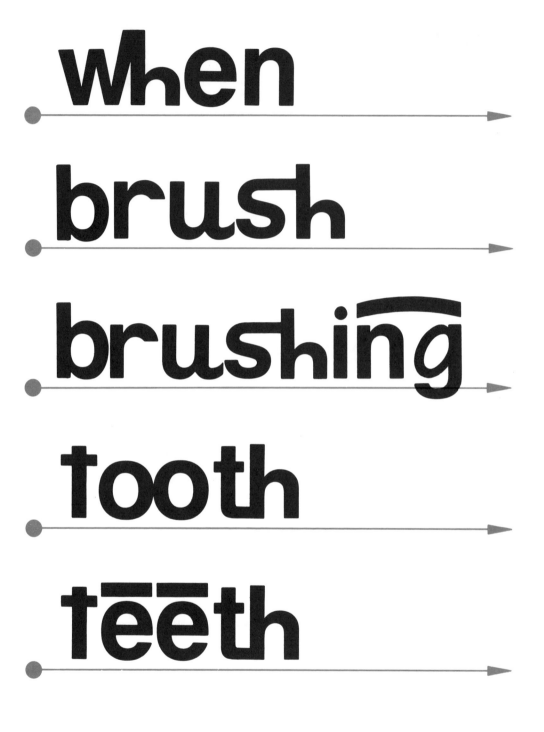

TASK 5   Children read the fast way

a. Get ready to read these words the fast way.
b. Touch the ball for **fish.** (Pause three seconds.) Get ready.
(Signal.) *Fish.*
c. Repeat *b* for the remaining words on the page.

TASK 6   Children read the fast way again

a. Get ready to do these words again. Watch where I point.
b. Point to a word. (Pause one second.) Say: Get ready. (Signal.)
The children respond. Point to the words in this order:
top, pots, with, tops, fish.
c. Repeat *b* until firm.

TASK 7   Individual test

Call on different children to read one word the fast way.

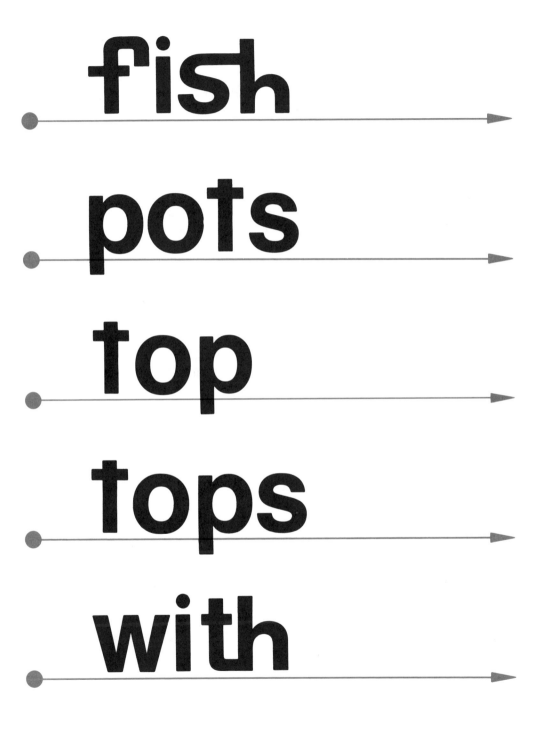

TASK 12   Children read slip and slipped

Do not touch any small letters.

a. Cover **s.** Point to **lip.**   You're going to read this part of the word the fast way. (Pause three seconds.)   **Get ready.** (Signal.) *Lip.*
Yes, lip.

b. Uncover **s.** Point to **s.**   You're going to say this first.
Move your finger quickly under **lip.**   Then you're going to say (pause) **lip.**

c. Point to **s.**   What are you going to say first? (Signal.) *sss.*
What are you going to say next? (Signal.) *Lip.*

d. Repeat *c* until firm.

e. Touch the ball for **slip.**   **Get ready.** Move to **s,** then quickly along the arrow. *Ssslip.*

f. **Say it fast.** (Signal.) *Slip.*   Yes, what word? (Signal.) *Slip.*
Yes, **slip. Good reading.**

g. **Again.** Repeat *e* and *f* until firm.

h. Return to the ball for **slip.**   Yes, this word is **slip.**

i. Touch the ball for **slipped.**   So this must be **slip** . . . .
Touch **d.** *d.*   What word? (Signal.) *Slipped.*   Yes, **slipped.**

j. **Again.** Repeat *h* and *i* until firm.

k. Touch the ball for **slip.**   This word is **slip.**
Touch the ball for **slipped.**   So this must be . . . .
Quickly run your finger under **slip** and tap **d.** *Slipped.*
Yes, **slipped.**

l. **Again.** Repeat *k* until firm.

m. **Now you're going to sound out** (pause) **slipped.** Get ready.
Touch **s, l, i,** between the **p**'s, **d** as the children say *sssllliiipd.*
Yes, what word? (Signal.) *Slipped.*   Yes, **slipped.**

slip

slipped

118

TASK 8 Children identify, then sound out an irregular word (of)

a. Touch the ball for **of.** Everybody, you're going to read this word the fast way. (Pause three seconds.) Get ready. Move your finger quickly along the arrow. *Of.* Yes, **of.**

b. Now you're going to sound out the word. Get ready. Quickly touch **o, f** as the children say *ooofff.*

c. Again. Repeat *b.*
d. How do we say the word? (Signal.) *Of.* Yes, **of.**
e. Repeat *b* and *d* until firm.
f. Call on different children to do *b* and *d.*

TASK 9 Children sound out the word and tell what word

a. Touch the ball for **hōme.** Sound it out.
b. Get ready. Touch **h, ō, m** as the children say *hōōōmmm.* If sounding out is not firm, repeat *b.*
c. What word? (Signal.) *Home.* Yes, **home.**

TASK 10 Children sound out an irregular (do)

a. Touch the ball for **do.** Sound it out.
b. Get ready. Quickly touch each sound as the children say *dooo.*
c. Again. Repeat *b* until firm.
d. That's how we <u>sound out</u> the word. Here's how we <u>say</u> the word. **Do.** How do we <u>say</u> the word? (Signal.) *Do.*
e. Now you're going to <u>sound out</u> the word. Get ready. Touch each sound as the children say *dooo.*
f. Now you're going to say the word. Get ready. (Signal.) *Do.*
g. Repeat *e* and *f* until firm.
h. Yes, this word is **do.** I **do** not run fast.
i. Call on different children to do *e* and *f.*

TASK 11 Children read the fast way

Touch the ball for **fōr.** Get ready to read this word the fast way. (Pause three seconds.) Get ready. (Signal.) *For.*

TASK 12 Children read the words the fast way

Have the children read the words on this page the fast way.

READING VOCABULARY

Do not touch any small letters.

TASK 7 Children read t̄ime and t̄imes

a. Touch the ball for t̄ime. You're going to read this word the fast way. (Pause three seconds.) Get ready. Move your finger quickly along the arrow. *Time.*

b. Return to the ball for t̄ime. Yes, this word is **time**.

c. Touch the ball for t̄imes. So this must be **time** . . . . Touch **s.** *s.* What word? (Signal.) *Times.* Yes, **times**.

d. Again. Repeat *b* and *c* until firm.

e. Touch the ball for t̄ime. This word is **time**.

f. Touch the ball for t̄imes. So this must be . . . . Quickly run your finger under t̄ime and tap **s.** *Times.* Yes, **times**.

g. Again. Repeat *e* and *f* until firm.

h. Now you're going to sound out (pause) **times**. Get ready. Touch **t, ī, m, s** as the children say *tiiimmmsss.* Yes, what word? (Signal.) *Times.* Yes, **times**.

TASK 8 Children sound out the word and tell what word

a. Touch the ball for **where**. Sound it out.

b. Get ready. Touch **wh, e, r** as the children say *whwhwheeerrr.* If sounding out is not firm, repeat *b*.

c. What word? (Signal.) *Where.* Yes, **where**. **Where** is my pencil?

TASK 9 Children sound out the word and tell what word

Repeat the procedures in task 8 for **wh̄ite**.

TASK 10 Children read the words the fast way

Have the children read the words on this page the fast way.

TASK 11 Individual test

Call on different children to read one word the fast way.

Story 118

TASK 13 Teacher introduces the title

a. Pass out Storybook 2.
b. Open your book to page 1.
c. Hold up your reader. Point to the title. These words are called the title of the story. These words tell what the story is about. I'll read the title the fast way.
d. Point to the words as you read: Lots of pots.
e. Everybody, what is this story about? (Signal.) Lots of pots. Yes, lots of pots. This story is going to tell something about lots of pots.

TASK 14 First reading—children read the story the fast way

Have the children reread any sentences containing words that give them trouble. Keep a list of these words.

a. Everybody, touch the title of the story and get ready to read the words in the title the fast way.
b. First word. Check children's responses. (Pause three seconds.) Get ready. Clap. Lots.
c. Next word. Check children's responses. (Pause three seconds.) Get ready. Clap. Of.
d. Repeat c for the word pots.
e. After the children have read the title, ask: What's this story about? (Signal.) Lots of pots. Yes, lots of pots.
f. Everybody, touch the first word of the story. Check children's responses.
g. Get ready to read this story the fast way.
h. First word. (Pause three seconds.) Get ready. Clap. A.
i. Next word. Check children's responses. (Pause three seconds.) Get ready. Clap. Girl.
j. Repeat i for the remaining words in the first sentence. Pause at least three seconds between claps. The children are to identify each word without sounding it out.
k. Repeat h through j for the next two sentences. Have the children reread the first three sentences until firm.
l. The children are to read the remainder of the story the fast way, stopping at the end of each sentence.

m. After the first reading of the story, print on the board the words that the children missed more than one time. Have the children sound out each word one time and tell what word.
n. After the group's responses are firm, call on individual children to read the words.

TASK 15 Individual test

a. Turn back to page 1. I'm going to call on different children to read a whole sentence the fast way.
b. Call on different children to read a sentence. Do not clap for each word.

TASK 16 Second reading—children read the story the fast way and answer questions

a. You're going to read the story again the fast way and I'll ask questions.
b. Starting with the first word of the title. Check children's responses. Get ready. Clap. Lots.
c. Clap for each remaining word. Pause at least three seconds between claps. Pause longer before words that gave the children trouble during the first reading.
d. Ask the comprehension questions below as the children read.

After the children read:	You say:
Lots of pots.	What's this story about? (Signal.) Lots of pots.
He has pots with no tops.	What kind of pots did the man have? (Signal.) Pots with tops and pots with no tops.
"I have fish in pots."	What did the man say? (Signal.) I have fish in pots.
The girl said, "Can I have a pot for a little fish?"	What did the girl want? (Signal.) A pot for a little fish.
The man said, "This is a pot for a little fish."	Did the man have a pot for a little fish? (Signal.) Yes.
And she did.	Did the girl take the pot home with her? (Signal.) Yes.

Lesson 154

SOUNDS

TASK 1 Teaching **qu** as in **quick**

a. Point to **qu.** Here's a new sound. It's a quick sound.

b. My turn. (Pause.) Touch **qu** for an instant, saying: **qu (koo).**

c. Again. Touch **qu** and say: qu.

d. Point to **qu.** Your turn. When I touch it, you say it. (Pause.) Get ready. Touch **qu.** *qu.*

e. Again. Touch **qu.** *qu.*

f. Repeat *e* until firm.

TASK 2 Individual test

Call on different children to identify **qu.**

TASK 3 Sounds firm-up

a. Get ready to say the sounds when I touch them.

b. Alternate touching **qu** and **k.** Point to the sound. (Pause one second.) Say: Get ready. Touch the sound. *The children respond.*

c. When **qu** and **k** are firm, alternate touching **qu, k, wh,** and **ch** until all four sounds are firm.

TASK 4 Individual test

Call on different children to identify **qu, k, wh,** or **ch.**

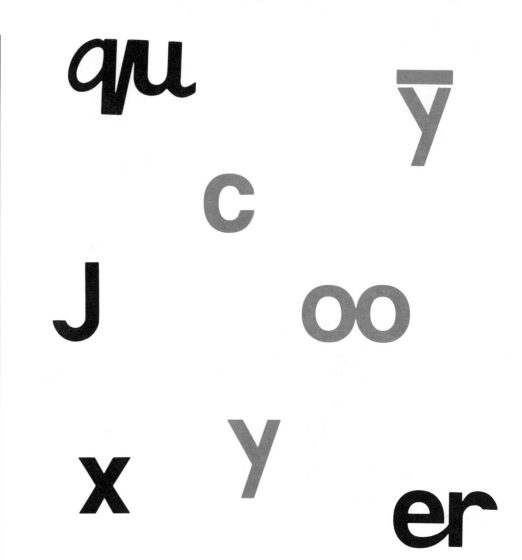

TASK 5 Sounds firm-up

a. Point to **qu.** When I touch the sound, you say it.

b. (Pause.) Get ready. Touch **qu.** *qu.*

c. Again. Repeat *b* until firm.

d. Get ready to say all the sounds when I touch them.

e. Alternate touching **qu, c, ȳ, j, oo, x, y,** and **er** three or four times. Point to the sound. (Pause one second.) Say: Get ready. Touch the sound. *The children respond.*

TASK 6 Individual test

Call on different children to identify one or more sounds in task 5.

TASK 17   Picture comprehension

a. Everybody, look at the picture.
b. Ask these questions:
 1. Look at all those pots. Which pot do you think is for a little fish?
 The children respond.

 2. Have you ever had a pet fish?   *The children respond.*

Take-Home 118

SUMMARY OF INDEPENDENT ACTIVITY

TASK 18   Introduction to independent activity

a. Pass out Take-Home 118 to each child.
b. Everybody, you're going to do this take-home on your own.
 Tell the children when they will work the items.
 Let's go over the things you're going to do.

TASK 19   Sentence copying

a. Hold up side 1 of your take-home and point to the first line in the
 sentence-copying exercise.
b. Everybody, here's the sentence you're going to write on the lines
 below.
c. Reading the fast way. First word.   Check children's responses.
 Get ready.   Clap. *He.*
d. Next word.   Check children's responses. Get ready.   Clap. *Has.*
e. Repeat *d* for the remaining words.
f. After you finish your take-home, you get to draw a picture about
 the sentence, **hē has lots of pots.**

TASK 20   Sound writing

a. Point to the sound-writing exercise. Here are the sounds you're
 going to write today. I'll touch the sounds. You say them.
b. Touch each sound. *The children respond.*
c. Repeat the series until firm.

TASK 21   Matching

a. Point to the column of words in the Matching Game.
b. Everybody, you're going to follow the lines and write these words.
c. Reading the fast way.
d. Point to the first word. (Pause.) Get ready. (Signal.)
 The children respond.
e. Repeat *d* for the remaining words.
f. Repeat *d* and *e* until firm.

TASK 22   Cross-out game

Point to the boxed word in the Cross-out Game. Everybody, here's
 the word you're going to cross out today. What word? (Signal.)
 Cars. Yes, **cars.**

TASK 23   Pair relations

a. Point to the pair-relations exercise on side 2. Remember—you're
 going to draw a line through the words in each box that do not
 tell about the picture.
b. Point to the space at the top of the page. After you finish,
 remember to draw a picture that shows **hē has lots of pots.**

END OF LESSON 118

TASK 29   Picture comprehension

a. What do you think you'll see in the picture?*The children respond.*
b. Turn the page and look at the picture.
c. Ask these questions:
 1. What's the horse doing in that picture?
  The children respond.   Running into the side of the barn.
 2. Where is the eagle?*The children respond.*
  Yes, on top of the barn.

Take-Home 153

SUMMARY OF INDEPENDENT ACTIVITY

TASK 30   Introduction to independent activity

a. Pass out Take-Home 153 to each child.
b. Everybody, you're going to do this take-home on your own.
  Tell the children when they will work the items.
  Let's go over the things you're going to do.

TASK 31   Story items

a. Hold up side 1 of your take-home and point to the story-items
  exercise.
b. Everybody, here are items about the story we read today.
c. Think about what happened in the story and circle the right answer
  for each item.

TASK 32   Picture comprehension

a. Point to the pictures in the picture-comprehension exercise.
  Everybody, you're going to look at the picture. Then you're going
  to read each item and write the missing word.
b. Remember—the first sound of each missing word is already
  written in the blank.

TASK 33   Reading comprehension

a. Point to the reading-comprehension exercise on side 2.
b. Everybody, get ready to read the sentences in the box the fast way.
c. First word.Check children's responses.   Get ready.Clap for each
  word as the children read the sentences: *An eagle liked to fly.*
  He did not sit in a tree.
d. Point to items 1 and 2.   These items tell about the story in the box.
  You're going to read each item and circle the right answer.

TASK 34   Sound writing

a. Point to the sound-writing exercise.   Here are the sounds you're
  going to write today. I'll touch the sounds. You say them.
b. Touch each sound. *The children respond.*
c. Repeat the series until firm.

TASK 35   Sentence copying

a. Point to the dotted sentence in the sentence-copying exercise.
b. You're going to trace the words in this sentence. Then you're
  going to write the sentence on the other lines.
c. Reading the fast way. First word.Check children's responses.
  Get ready.Clap for each word.
d. After you finish your take-home, you get to draw a picture about
  the sentence, **an ēagle līkes to flȳ**. You'll draw your picture on
  a piece of plain paper.When the children finish their take-homes,
  give them sheets of plain paper.

END OF LESSON 153

Lesson 119

SOUNDS

TASK 1   Teaching e as in **end**

a. Point to **e.** My turn. (Pause.) Touch **e** and say: *eee.*
b. Point to **e.** Your turn. When I touch it, you say it. (Pause.)
Get ready. Touch **e.** *eee.* Lift your finger.
c. Again. Touch **e.** *eeee.* Lift your finger.
d. Repeat *c* until firm.

TASK 2   Sounds firm-up

a. Get ready to say the sounds when I touch them.
b. Alternate touching **e** and **u.** Point to the sound. (Pause one second.)
Say: Get ready. Touch the sound. *The children respond.*
c. When **e** and **u** are firm, alternate touching **ē, o, e,** and **u** until all
four sounds are firm.

TASK 3   Individual test

Call on different children to identify **ē, o, e,** or **u.**

TASK 4   Sounds firm-up

a. Point to **e.** When I touch the
sound, you say it.
b. (Pause.) Get ready. Touch **e.**
eee.
c. Again. Repeat *b* until firm.
d. Get ready to say all the sounds
when I touch them.
e. Alternate touching **i, p, v, ō, w,
e, k,** and **ch** three or four times.
Point to the sound.
(Pause one second.) Say:
Get ready. Touch the sound.
The children respond.

TASK 5   Individual test

Call on different children to identify
one or more sounds in task 4.

Story 153

TASK 26   First reading—children read the title and first three sentences

a. You're going to read the first part of this story today.

b. Everybody, touch the title of the story and get ready to read the words in the title the fast way.

c. First word. Check children's responses. (Pause two seconds.) Get ready. Clap. *An.*

d. Clap for each remaining word in the title.

e. After the children have read the title, ask: What's this story about? (Signal.) *An old horse and an eagle.* Yes, **an old horse and an eagle.**

f. Everybody, get ready to read this story the fast way.

g. First word. Check children's responses. (Pause two seconds.) Get ready. Clap. *An.*

h. Clap for the remaining words in the first sentence. Pause at least two seconds between claps.

i. Repeat *g* and *h* for the next two sentences. Have the children reread the first three sentences until firm.

TASK 27   Individual children or the group read sentences to complete the first reading

a. I'm going to call on different children to read a sentence. Everybody, follow along and point to the words. If you hear a mistake, raise your hand.

b. Call on a child. Read the next sentence. Do not clap for the words. Let the child read at his own pace, but be sure he reads the sentence correctly.

To correct	Have the child sound out the word. Then return to the beginning of the sentence.

c. Repeat *b* for most of the remaining sentences in the story. Occasionally have the group read a sentence. When the group is to read, say: Everybody, read the next sentence. (Pause two seconds.) Get ready. Clap for each word in the sentence. Pause at least two seconds between claps.

TASK 28   Second reading—individual children or the group read each sentence; the group answer questions

a. You're going to read the story again. This time I'm going to ask questions.

b. Starting with the first word of the title. Check children's responses. Get ready. Clap as the children read the title. Pause at least two seconds between claps.

c. Call on a child. Read the first sentence. *The child responds.*

d. Repeat *b* and *c* in task 27. Present the following comprehension questions to the entire group.

After the children read:	You say:
An old horse and an eagle.	What's this story about? (Signal.) *An old horse and an eagle.*
"And I like to fly."	Who did the eagle say likes to fly? *The children respond.*
The old horse said, "Can you teach me how to fly?"	What did the old horse say? (Signal.) *Can you teach me how to fly?* That's silly. Can horses fly? *The children respond.*
The old horse said, "I will fly to the top of the barn."	What did the old horse say? (Signal.) *I will fly to the top of the barn.* Do you think he'll do that? *The children respond.* Let's read and find out.
And he ran into the side of the barn.	Did he fly to the top of the barn? (Signal.) *No.* What did he do? (Signal.) *He ran into the side of the barn.*
He said, "You did not teach me how to fly."	What did the horse say? (Signal.) *You did not teach me how to fly.* This is a silly story. I don't think that eagle can ever teach the horse how to fly.

119

READING VOCABULARY

Do not touch any small letters.

TASK 6 Children sound out the word and tell what word

a. Touch the ball for **cōrn.** Sound it out.
b. Get ready. Touch **c, ō, r, n** as the children say *cōōōrrrnnn.*
If sounding out is not firm, repeat *b.*
c. What word? (Signal.) *Corn.* Yes, **corn.**

TASK 7 Children sound out the word and tell what word

Repeat the procedures in task 6 for **tāke.**

TASK 8 Children sound out the word and tell what word

Repeat the procedures in task 6 for **pigs.**

TASK 9 Children sound out the word and tell what word

Repeat the procedures in task 6 for **hēre.**

TASK 10 Children identify, then sound out an irregular word (do)

a. Touch the ball for **do.** Everybody, you're going to read this
word the fast way. (Pause three seconds.) Get ready.
Move your finger quickly along the arrow. *Do.* Yes, **do.**
b. Now you're going to sound out the word. Get ready.
Quickly touch **d, o** as the children say *dooo.*
c. Again. Repeat *b.*
d. How do we say the word? (Signal.) *Do.* Yes, **do.**
e. Repeat *b* and *d* until firm.

TASK 11 Individual test

Call on different children to do *b* and *d* in task 10.

TASK 12 Children read the words the fast way

Have the children read the words on this page the fast way.

TASK 13 Individual test

Call on different children to read one word the fast way.

cōrn

tāke

pigs

hēre

do

66

Read the Item 153

TASK 23   Children read item 1

a. Pass out Storybook 3.

b. Open your book to page 40.

c. Point to the title **rēad the ītem.** Everybody, touch this title.
Check children's responses.

d. I'll read the title. You point to the words I read. (Pause.)
Get ready. **Read** (pause) **the** (pause) **item.**

e. Your turn to read the title. First word.
Check children's responses. Get ready.
Clap for each word as the children read *read the item.*

f. Everybody, say the title. (Pause and signal.)
Without looking at the words, the children say *read the item.*
Repeat until firm.

g. You're going to read the item. Touch item 1 and get ready to read.
Check children's responses.

h. First word. Clap for each word as the children read:
If the teacher says "Now," hold up your hands.
Repeat three times or until firm.

i. Everybody, get ready to say item 1 with me. (Pause and signal.)
Without looking at the words, you and the children say: If the
teacher says "Now," (pause one second) hold up your hands.
Repeat four times or until firm.

j. All by yourselves. Say item 1. (Signal.)
If the teacher says "Now," hold up your hands.
Repeat four times or until firm.

TASK 24   Children reread item 1 and answer questions

a. Everybody, touch item 1 again. Check children's responses.

b. Read item 1 to yourself. Raise your hand when you know what
you're going to do and when you're going to do it.

c. After the children raise their hands, say: Everybody, what are you
going to do if I say "**Now**"? (Signal.) *Hold up my hands.*

To correct	1. Everybody, read item 1 out loud. Clap as the children read each word.
	2. What are you going to do if I say "**Now**"? (Signal.) *Hold up my hands.*

d. Everybody, when are you going to **hold up your hands**? (Signal.)
If the teacher says "Now."

To correct	1. Everybody, read item 1 out loud. Clap as the children read each word.
	2. When are you going to **hold up your hands**? (Signal.) *If the teacher says "Now."*

e. Repeat *c* and *d* until firm.

TASK 25   Children play the game

a. Everybody, touch item 1. Check children's responses.

b. Read the item to yourself. Raise your hand when you know what
you're going to do and when you're going to do it.

c. After the children raise their hands, say: Let's play the game.
Think about what you're going to do (pause) and when you're
going to do it.

d. Hold out your hand. (Pause.) Get ready. **Now.** (Pause.)
Drop your hand. *(The children hold up their hands immediately.)*

To correct	1. What did I say? (Signal.) *Now.*
	2. What are you supposed to do if I say "**Now**"? (Signal.) *Hold up my hands.*
	3. If the children's responses are not firm, have them read item 1 aloud.
	4. Repeat task 25.

TASK 14   Children identify, then sound out an irregular word (car)

a. Touch the ball for **car.** Everybody, you're going to read this word the fast way. (Pause three seconds.) Get ready. Move your finger quickly along the arrow. *Car.* Yes, **car.**

b. Now you're going to sound out the word. Get ready. Quickly touch **c, a, r** as the children say *caaarrr.*

c. Again. Repeat *b*.

d. How do we say the word? (Signal.) *Car.* Yes, **car.**

e. Repeat *b* and *d* until firm.

TASK 15   Individual test

Call on different children to do *b* and *d* in task 14.

TASK 16   Children read the fast way

a. Get ready to read these words the fast way.

b. Touch the ball for **fōr.** (Pause three seconds.) Get ready. (Signal.) *For.*

c. Repeat *b* for the remaining words on the page.

TASK 17   Children read the fast way again

a. Get ready to do these words again. Watch where I point.

b. Point to a word. (Pause one second.) Say: Get ready. (Signal.) *The children respond.* Point to the words in this order: **fōr, lāke, car, ōld, mōre.**

c. Repeat *b* until firm.

TASK 18   Individual test

Call on different children to read one word the fast way.

Do not touch any small letters.

car

fōr

mōre

lāke

ōld

TASK 18   Children sound out an irregular word (look)

a. Touch the ball for **look.** Sound it out.
b. Get ready. Quickly touch each sound as the children say *llllooook.*
c. Again. Repeat *b* until firm.
d. That's how we <u>sound out</u> the word. Here's how we <u>say</u> the word.
              Look. How do we <u>say</u> the word? (Signal.) *Look.*
e. Now you're going to <u>sound out</u> the word. Get ready.
              Touch each sound as the children say *llllooook.*
f. Now you're going to say the word. Get ready. (Signal.) *Look.*
g. Repeat *e* and *f* until firm.

look

TASK 19   Children rhyme with an irregular word (look)

a. Touch the ball for **look.** Everybody, you're going to read
              this word the fast way. Get ready. (Signal.) *Look.*
b. Touch the ball for **book.** This word rhymes with (pause) **look.**
        Get ready. Move to **b,** then quickly along the arrow. *Book.*
c. Repeat *a* and *b* until firm.

book

TASK 20   Children sound out book

Have the children sound out **book.** *Booook.* How do we say the word?
              (Signal.) *Book.* Yes, **book.**

TASK 21   Children read the words the fast way

a. Now you get to read the words on this page the fast way.
b. Touch the ball for **book.** (Pause three seconds.) Get ready.
              Move your finger quickly along the arrow. *Book.*
c. Repeat *b* for **look.**

TASK 22   Individual test

Call on different children to read one word the fast way.

Story 119

TASK 19   First reading—children read the story the fast way

Have the children reread any sentences containing words that give them trouble. Keep a list of these words.

a. Pass out Storybook 2.
b. Open your book to page 4.
c. Everybody, touch the title of the story and get ready to read the words in the title the fast way.
d. First word. Check children's responses. (Pause two seconds.) Get ready. Clap. *Al.*
e. Clap for each remaining word in the title.
f. After the children have read the title, ask: What's this story about? (Signal.) *Al and Sal.* Yes, Al and Sal.
g. Everybody, get ready to read this story the fast way.
h. First word. Check children's responses. (Pause two seconds.) Get ready. Clap. *Al.*
i. Clap for the remaining words in the first sentence. Pause at least two seconds between claps.
j. Repeat *h* and *i* for the next two sentences. Have the children reread the first three sentences until firm.
k. The children are to read the remainder of the story the fast way, stopping at the end of each sentence.
l. After the first reading of the story, print on the board the words that the children missed more than one time. Have the children sound out each word one time and tell what word.
m. After the group's responses are firm, call on individual children to read the words.

TASK 20   Individual test

a. Look at page 4. I'm going to call on different children to read a whole sentence.
b. Call on different children to read a sentence. Do not clap for each word.

TASK 21   Second reading—children read the story the fast way and answer questions

a. You're going to read the story again the fast way and I'll ask questions.
b. Starting with the first word of the title. Check children's responses. Get ready. Clap. *Al.*
c. Clap for each remaining word. Pause at least two seconds between claps. Pause longer before words that gave the children trouble during the first reading.
d. Ask the comprehension questions below as the children read.

After the children read:	You say:
Al and Sal.	What's this story about? (Signal.) *Al and Sal.*
Al said, "Will we go home?"	What did Al say? (Signal.) *Will we go home?*
Sal said, "No. We will go to that farm."	What did Sal say? (Signal.) *We will go to that farm.*
"We can sit in the lake."	Name the things Sal said they could do on the farm. (Signal.) *Run with a cow, eat corn, feed pigs, and sit in the lake.*
Al said, "I hate to sit in lakes."	What did Al say? (Signal.) *I hate to sit in lakes.*
Sal and Al had fun with the pigs.	Did Sal and Al sit in the lake? (Signal.) *No.* What did they do? (Signal.) *Had fun with the pigs.*

TASK 22   Picture comprehension

a. What do you think you'll see in the picture? *The children respond.* Let's see.
b. Turn the page and look at the picture.
c. Ask these questions:
   1. What are that boy and girl doing? *The children respond.* Yes, they're feeding the pigs.
   2. Will they get dirty feeding the pigs? *The children respond.*
   3. What will their daddy say if they get dirty? *The children respond.*
   4. Did you ever get dirty? *The children respond.*

TASK 12 Children identify, then sound out an irregular word (barn)

a. Touch the ball for **barn.** Everybody, you're going to read this
word the fast way. (Pause three seconds.) Get ready.
Move your finger quickly along the arrow. *Barn.* Yes, **barn.**

b. Now you're going to sound out the word. Get ready.
Quickly touch **b, a, r, n** as the children say *baaarrrnnn.*

c. Again. Repeat *b.*

d. How do we say the word? (Signal.) *Barn.* Yes, **barn.**

e. Repeat *b* and *d* until firm.

TASK 13 Individual test

Call on different children to do *b* and *d* in task 12.

TASK 14 Children identify, then sound out an irregular word (into)

a. Touch the ball for **into.** Everybody, you're going to read this
word the fast way. (Pause three seconds.) Get ready.
Move your finger quickly along the arrow. *Into.* Yes, **into.**

b. Now you're going to sound out the word. Get ready.
Quickly touch **i, n, t, o** as the children say *iiinnntooo.*

c. Again. Repeat *b.*

d. How do we say the word? (Signal.) *Into.* Yes, **into.**

e. Repeat *b* and *d* until firm.

TASK 15 Individual test

Call on different children to do *b* and *d* in task 14.

TASK 16 Children read the words the fast way

Have the children read the words on this page the fast way.

TASK 17 Individual test

Call on different children to read one word the fast way.

Take-Home 119

SUMMARY OF INDEPENDENT ACTIVITY

TASK 23   Introduction to independent activity

a. Pass out Take-Home 119 to each child.
b. Everybody, you're going to do this take-home on your own.
> Tell the children when they will work the items.
> Let's go over the things you're going to do.

TASK 24   Sentence copying

a. Hold up side 1 of your take-home and point to the first line in the
> sentence-copying exercise.
b. Everybody, here's the sentence you're going to write on the lines
> below.
c. Reading the fast way. First word. Check children's responses.
> Get ready. Clap. *She.*
d. Next word. Check children's responses. Get ready. Clap. *Sat.*
e. Repeat *d* for the remaining words.
f. After you finish your take-home, you get to draw a picture about
> the sentence, **shē sat in the lāke.**

TASK 25   Sound writing

a. Point to the sound-writing exercise. Here are the sounds you're
> going to write today. I'll touch the sounds. You say them.
b. Touch each sound. *The children respond.*
c. Repeat the series until firm.

TASK 26   Matching

a. Point to the column of words in the Matching Game.
b. Everybody, you're going to follow the lines and write these words.
c. Reading the fast way.
d. Point to the first word. (Pause.) Get ready. (Signal.)
> *The children respond.*

e. Repeat *d* for the remaining words.
f. Repeat *d* and *e* until firm.

TASK 27   Cross-out game

Point to the boxed word in the Cross-out Game. Everybody, here's
> the word you're going to cross out today. What word? (Signal.)
> *Will.* Yes, **will.**

TASK 28   Pair relations

a. Point to the pair-relations exercise on side 2. Remember—you're
> going to draw a line through the words in each box that do not tell
> about the picture.
b. Point to the space at the top of the page. After you finish,
> remember to draw a picture that shows **shē sat in the lāke.**

END OF LESSON 119

TASK 11   Children read brush and brushed

Do not touch any small letters.

a. Cover **b.** Point to **rush.** You're going to read this part of the word the fast way. (Pause three seconds.) Get ready. (Signal.) *Rush.* Yes, **rush.**

b. Uncover **b.** Point to **b.** You're going to say this first. Move your finger quickly under **rush.** Then you're going to say (pause) **rush.**

c. Point to **b.** What are you going to say first? (Signal.) *b.* What are you going to say next? (Signal.) *Rush.*

d. Repeat *c* until firm.

e. Touch the ball for **brush.** Get ready. Move to **b,** then quickly along the arrow. *Brush.*

f. Say it fast. (Signal.) *Brush.* Yes, what word? (Signal.) *Brush.* Yes, **brush.** Good reading.

g. Again. Repeat *e* and *f* until firm.

h. Now you're going to sound out (pause) **brush.** Get ready. Touch **b, r, u, sh** as the children say *brrruuushshsh.* What word? (Signal.) *Brush.* Yes, **brush.**

i. Point to **brush.** This word is **brush.**

j. Tap under **d** in **brushed.** So this must be . . . . Touch the ball for **brushed** and move your finger quickly along the arrow. *Brushed.* Yes, **brushed.**

k. Repeat *i* and *j* until firm.

l. Now you're going to sound out (pause) **brushed.** Get ready. Touch **b, r, u, sh, d** as the children say *brrruuushshshd.* What word? (Signal.) *Brushed.* Yes, **brushed.**

brush

brushed

Lesson 120

SOUNDS

TASK 1 Teaching e as in **end**

a. Point to **e**. My turn. (Pause.) Touch **e** and say: eee.
b. Point to **e**. Your turn. When I touch it, you say it. (Pause.)
Get ready. Touch **e**. *eee.* Lift your finger.
c. Again. Touch **e**. *eee.* Lift your finger.
d. Repeat *c* until firm.

TASK 2 Sounds firm-up

a. Get ready to say the sounds when I touch them.
b. Alternate touching **i** and **e**. Point to the sound. (Pause one second.)
Say: Get ready. Touch the sound. *The children respond.*
c. When **i** and **e** are firm, alternate touching **i**, **ē**, **o**, and **e**
until all four sounds are firm.

TASK 3 Individual test

Call on different children to identify **i**, **ē**, **o**, or **e**.

TASK 4 Teacher introduces cross-out game

a. Use acetate and crayon.
b. I'll cross out the sounds on this part of the page when you can tell me every sound.
c. Remember—when I touch it, you say it.
d. Go over the sounds until the children can identify all the sounds in order.

TASK 5 Individual test

Call on different children to identify two or more sounds in task 4.

TASK 6 Teacher crosses out sounds

a. You told me every sound. Get ready to do it again. This time I'll cross out each sound when you tell me what it is.
b. Point to each sound. (Pause.) Say: Get ready. Touch the sound. *The children respond.* As you cross out the sound, say: Goodbye, _____ .

READING VOCABULARY

Do not touch any small letters.

TASK 6   Children sound out an irregular word (touch)

a. Touch the ball for **touch.**   Sound it out.

b. Get ready. Quickly touch each sound as the children say *tooouuuch.*

To correct	If the children do not say the sounds you touch **1.** Say: **You've got to say the sounds I touch.** **2.** Repeat *a* and *b* until firm.

c. Again. Repeat *b* until firm.

d. That's how we <u>sound out</u> the word. Here's how we <u>say</u> the word.
         Touch. How do we <u>say</u> the word? (Signal.) *Touch.*

e. Now you're going to <u>sound out</u> the word. Get ready.
         Touch each sound as the children say *tooouuuch.*

f. Now you're going to say the word. Get ready. (Signal.) *Touch.*

g. Repeat *e* and *f* until firm.

h. Yes, this word is **touch. Touch** your ears.

TASK 7   Individual test

Call on different children to do *e* and *f* in task 6.

TASK 8   Children read the fast way

a. Get ready to read these words the fast way.

b. Touch the ball for **ēagle.** (Pause three seconds.)   Get ready.
                                          (Signal.) *Eagle.*

c. Repeat *b* for the remaining words on the page.

TASK 9   Children read the fast way again

a. Get ready to do these words again. Watch where I point.

b. Point to a word. (Pause one second.) Say: Get ready.   (Signal.)
         The children respond. Point to the words in this order:
                                          ēagle, six, tēach.

c. Repeat *b* until firm.

TASK 10   Individual test

Call on different children to read one word on the page the fast way.

touch

ēagle

tēach

six

READING VOCABULARY

Do not touch any small letters.

TASK 7 Children identify, then sound out an irregular word (do)

a. Touch the ball for **do**. Everybody, you're going to read this word the fast way. (Pause three seconds.) Get ready. Move your finger quickly along the arrow. *Do*. Yes, **do**.

b. Now you're going to sound out the word. Get ready. Quickly touch **d, o** as the children say *dooo*.

c. Again. Repeat *b*.

d. How do we say the word? (Signal.) *Do*. Yes, **do**.

e. Repeat *b* and *d* until firm.

f. Call on different children to do *b* and *d*.

TASK 8 Children read the fast way

a. Get ready to read these words the fast way.

b. Touch the ball for **cōat**. (Pause three seconds.) Get ready.

(Signal.) *Coat.*

c. Repeat *b* for the remaining words on the page.

TASK 9 Children read the fast way again

a. Get ready to do these words again. Watch where I point.

b. Point to a word. (Pause one second.) Say: Get ready. (Signal.) *The children respond.* Point to the words in this order: **fōr, rāin, met, cōat.**

c. Repeat *b* until firm.

TASK 10 Individual test

Call on different children to read one word the fast way.

do

cōat

rāin

met

fōr

Lesson 153

Groups that are firm on Mastery Tests 28 and 29 should skip this lesson and do lesson 154 today.

SOUNDS

Task 1   Teaching wh as in why

a. Point to **wh**. My turn. (Pause.) Touch **wh** and say: whwhwh.

b. Point to **wh**. Your turn. When I touch it, you say it. (Pause.) Get ready. Touch **wh**. whwhwh. Lift your finger.

c. Again. Touch **wh**. whwhwhwh. Lift your finger.

d. Repeat c until firm.

TASK 2   Sounds firm-up

a. Get ready to say the sounds when I touch them.

b. Alternate touching **wh** and **ȳ**. Point to the sound. (Pause one second.) Say: Get ready. Touch the sound. *The children respond.*

c. When **wh** and **ȳ** are firm, alternate touching **wh, ȳ, w,** and **r** until all four sounds are firm.

TASK 3   Individual test

Call on different children to identify **wh, ȳ, w,** or **r.**

TASK 4   Sounds firm-up

a. Point to **wh**. When I touch the sound, you say it.

b. (Pause.) Get ready. Touch **wh**. whwhwh.

c. Again. Repeat b until firm.

d. Get ready to say all the sounds when I touch them.

e. Alternate touching **wh, h, j, oo, x, ī, e,** and **ing** three or four times. Point to the sound. (Pause one second.) Say: Get ready. Touch the sound. *The children respond.*

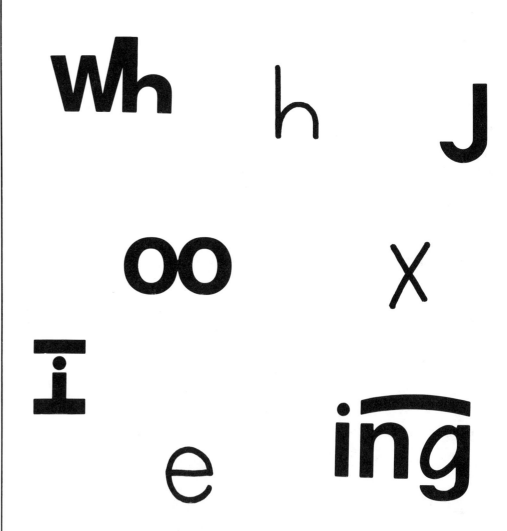

TASK 5   Individual test

Call on different children to identify one or more sounds in task 4.

120

TASK 11   Children sound out the word and tell what word

a. Touch the ball for **there.**   Sound it out.

b. Get ready. Touch **th, e, r** as the children say *thththeeerrr.*
                          If sounding out is not firm, repeat *b.*

c. What word? (Signal.) *There.*   Yes, **there. There** are swings in
                                                          the yard.

TASK 12   Children sound out the word and tell what word

Repeat the procedures in task 11 for **wet.**

TASK 13   Children sound out the word and tell what word

Repeat the procedures in task 11 for **went.**

TASK 14   Children rhyme with let

a. Touch the ball for **let.**   You're going to read this word the fast way.
                          (Pause three seconds.)   Get ready.
                  Move your finger quickly along the arrow. *Let.*

b. Touch the ball for **get.**   This word rhymes with (pause) **let.**
                  Move to **g,** then quickly along the arrow. *Get.*
                          Yes, what word? (Signal.) *Get.*

TASK 15   Children read the words the fast way

Have the children read the words on this page the fast way.

TASK 16   Individual test

Call on different children to read one word the fast way.

Do not touch any small letters.

ther_e

wet

went

let

get

Take-Home 152

SUMMARY OF INDEPENDENT ACTIVITY

TASK 30 Introduction to independent activity

a. Pass out Take-Home 152 to each child.

b. Everybody, you're going to do this take-home on your own.
Tell the children when they will work the items.
Let's go over the things you're going to do.

Task 31 Story items

a. Hold up side 1 of your take-home and point to the story-items
exercise.

b. Everybody, here are items about the story we read today.

c. Think about what happened in the story and circle the right answer
for each item.

TASK 32 Picture comprehension

a. Point to the pictures in the picture-comprehension exercise.
Everybody, you're going to look at the picture. Then you're going
to read each item and write the missing word.

b. Remember—the first sound of each missing word is already written
in the blank.

TASK 33 Reading comprehension

a. Point to the reading-comprehension exercise on side 2.

b. Everybody, get ready to read the sentences in the box the fast way.

c. First word. Check children's responses. Get ready. Clap for each
word as the children read the sentences: *A man went in a sail boat.*
He had a lot of fun.

d. Point to items 1 and 2. These items tell about the story in the box.
You're going to read each item and circle the right answer.

TASK 34 Sound writing

a. Point to the sound-writing exercise. Here are the sounds you're
going to write today. I'll touch the sounds. You say them.

b. Touch each sound. *The children respond.*

c. Repeat the series until firm.

TASK 35 Sentence copying

a. Point to the dotted sentence in the sentence-copying exercise.

b. You're going to trace the words in this sentence. Then you're
going to write the sentence on the other lines.

c. Reading the fast way. First word. Check children's responses.
Get ready. Clap for each word.

d. After you finish your take-home, you get to draw a picture about
the sentence, "**it is gōld**," **hē said.** You'll draw your picture on
a piece of plain paper. When the children finish their take-homes,
give them sheets of plain paper.

END OF LESSON 152

TASK 17 Children read the fast way

a. Get ready to read these words the fast way.
b. Touch the ball for **the.** (Pause three seconds.) **Get ready.**

(Signal.) *The.*

c. Repeat *b* for the remaining words on the page.

TASK 18 Children read the fast way again

a. Get ready to do these words again. Watch where I point.
b. Point to a word. (Pause one second.) Say: **Get ready.** (Signal.)
The children respond. Point to the words in this order:
that, the, shē, thōse.

c. Repeat *b* until firm.

TASK 19 Individual test

Call on different children to read one word the fast way.

Do not touch any small letters.

the

shē

thōse

that

Story 152

TASK 26 First reading—children read the title and first three sentences

a. Now you're going to finish the story about Bill and the old box.

b. Everybody, touch the title of the story and get ready to read the words in the title the fast way.

c. First word. Check children's responses. (Pause two seconds.)
Get ready. Clap. *Bill.*

d. Clap for each remaining word in the title.

e. After the children have read the title, ask: What's this story about? (Signal.) *Bill went fishing.* Yes, **Bill went fishing**.

f. Everybody, get ready to read this story the fast way.

g. First word. Check children's responses. (Pause two seconds.)
Get ready. Clap. *Bill.*

h. Clap for the remaining words in the first sentence. Pause at least two seconds between claps.

i. Repeat *g* and *h* for the next two sentences. Have the children reread the first three sentences until firm.

TASK 27 Individual children or the group read sentences to complete the first reading

a. I'm going to call on different children to read a sentence. Everybody, follow along and point to the words. If you hear a mistake, raise your hand.

b. Call on a child. Read the next sentence. Do not clap for the words. Let the child read at his own pace, but be sure he reads the sentence correctly.

To correct	Have the child sound out the word. Then return to the beginning of the sentence.

c. Repeat *b* for most of the remaining sentences in the story. Occasionally have the group read a sentence. When the group is to read, say: Everybody, read the next sentence. (Pause two seconds.) Get ready. Clap for each word in the sentence. Pause at least two seconds between claps.

TASK 28 Second reading—individual children or the group read each sentence; the group answer questions

a. You're going to read the story again. This time I'm going to ask questions.

b. Starting with the first word of the title. Check children's responses. Get ready. Clap as the children read the title. Pause at least two seconds between claps.

c. Call on a child. Read the first sentence. *The child responds.*

d. Repeat *b* and *c* in task 27. Present the following comprehension questions to the entire group.

After the children read:	You say:
"You have an old box."	What did the other boys say? (Signal.) *You have an old box.*
And Bill said, "That box is filled with gold."	What did Bill say? (Signal.) *That box is filled with gold.*
	I wonder if Bill will still be sad. *The children respond.*
	What's the title of this story? (Signal.) *Bill went fishing.*
	And what happened in the story? (Signal.) *Bill went fishing.*
	Did Bill catch fish? (Signal.) *No.*
	What did he catch when he went fishing? (Signal.) *An old box filled with gold.*

TASK 29 Picture comprehension

a. Everybody, look at the picture.

b. Ask these questions:

1. What's in that box? *Gold.*
2. Are the other boys making fun of Bill now? *No.*
3. Which would you rather have, nine fish or a great big box filled with gold? *The children respond.*
4. What would you do with all that gold? *The children respond.*

Story 120

TASK 20 First reading—children read the story the fast way

Have the children reread any sentences containing words that give them trouble. Keep a list of these words.

a. Pass out Storybook 2.
b. Open your book to page 7.
c. Everybody, touch the title of the story and get ready to read the words in the title the fast way.
d. First word. Check children's responses. (Pause two seconds.) Get ready. Clap. *A*.
e. Clap for each remaining word in the title.
f. After the children have read the title ask: What's this story about? (Signal.) *A fish in the rain.* Yes, **a fish in the rain.**
g. Everybody, get ready to read this story the fast way.
h. First word. Check children's responses. (Pause two seconds.) Get ready. Clap. *A*.
i. Clap for the remaining words in the first sentence. Pause at least two seconds between claps.
j. Repeat *h* and *i* for the next two sentences. Have the children reread the first three sentences until firm.
k. The children are to read the remainder of the story the fast way, stopping at the end of each sentence.
l. After the first reading of the story, print on the board the words that the children missed more than one time. Have the children sound out each word one time and tell what word.
m. After the group's responses are firm, call on individual children to read the words.

TASK 21 Individual test

a. Turn back to page 7. I'm going to call on different children to read a whole sentence.
b. Call on different children to read a sentence. Do not clap for each word.

TASK 22 Second reading—children read the story the fast way and answer questions

a. You're going to read the story again the fast way and I'll ask questions.
b. Starting with the first word of the title. Check children's responses. Get ready. Clap. *A*.
c. Clap for each remaining word. Pause at least two seconds between claps. Pause longer before words that gave the children trouble during the first reading.
d. Ask the comprehension questions below as the children read.

After the children read:	You say:
A fish in the rain.	What's this story about? (Signal.) *A fish in the rain.*
Ron said, "This is not fun."	What did Ron say? (Signal.) *This is not fun.*
Pat said, "This is fun."	Did Pat like getting wet? (Signal.) *Yes.*
So she got a fish and gave it to him.	What did she do? (Signal). *She got a fish and gave it to him.*
Ron said, "It is fun to get wet if we get fish."	What did Ron say? (Signal.) *It is fun to get wet if we get fish.*

TASK 23 Picture comprehension

a. Everybody, look at the picture.
b. Ask these questions:
   1. How do you know they are in the rain? *The children respond.*
   2. What is Pat giving to Ron? *A fish.*
   3. Do you like to have wet feet and walk through puddles when it's raining? *The children respond.*

Read the Item 152

TASK 23   Children read item 1

a. Pass out Storybook 3.
b. Open your book to page 37.
c. Point to the title **rēad the ītem.** Everybody, touch this title.
Check children's responses.

d. I'll read the title. You point to the words I read. (Pause.)
Get ready. **Read** (pause) **the** (pause) **item.**

e. Your turn to read the title. First word. Check children's responses.
Get ready. Clap for each word as the children read *read the item.*

f. Everybody, say the title. (Pause and signal.)
Without looking at the words, the children say *read the item.*
Repeat until firm.

g. You're going to read the item. Touch item 1 and get ready to read.
Check children's responses.

h. First word. Clap for each word as the children read:
If the teacher says "Now," hold up your hand.
Repeat three times or until firm.

i. Everybody, get ready to say item 1 with me. (Pause and signal.)
Without looking at the words, you and the children say: If the teacher says "Now," (pause one second) hold up your hand.
Repeat four times or until firm.

j. All by yourselves. Say item 1. (Signal.) *If the teacher says "Now," hold up your hand.* Repeat four times or until firm.

TASK 24   Children reread item 1 and answer questions

a. Everybody, touch item 1 again. Check children's responses.
b. Read item 1 to yourself. Raise your hand when you know what
you're going to do and when you're going to do it.
c. After the children raise their hands, say: Everybody, what are you
going to do if I say "**Now**"? (Signal.) *Hold up my hand.*

To correct	1. Everybody, read item 1 out loud. Clap as the children read each word.
	2. What are you going to do if I say "**Now**"? (Signal.) *Hold up my hand.*

d. Everybody, when are you going to **hold up your hand**? (Signal.)
If the teacher says "Now."

To correct	1. Everybody, read item 1 out loud. Clap as the children read each word.
	2. When are you going to **hold up your hand**? (Signal.) *If the teacher says "Now."*

e. Repeat *c* and *d* until firm.

TASK 25   Children play the game

a. Everybody, touch item 1. Check children's responses.
b. Read the item to yourself. Raise your hand when you know what
you're going to do and when you're going to do it.
c. After the children raise their hands, say: Let's play the game.
Think about what you're going to do (pause) and when you're going to do it.
d. Hold out your hand. (Pause.) Get ready. **Now**. (Pause.)
Drop your hand. *(The children hold up their hands immediately.)*

To correct	1. What did I say? (Signal.) *Now.*
	2. What are you supposed to do if I say "**Now**"? (Signal.) *Hold up my hand.*
	3. If the children's responses are not firm, have them read item 1 aloud.
	4. Repeat task 25.

Take-Home 120

READING COMPREHENSION
The children will need pencils.

TASK 24   Children choose the correct words to complete the sentences

---

a. Pass out sides 1 and 2 of Take-Home 120 to each child.

b. Everybody do a good job on your take-home today and I'll give you a bonus take-home.

c. Hold up side 1 of your take-home. Point to the sentences in the box in the reading-comprehension exercise.

d. Everybody, touch this box on your take-home. Check children's responses.

e. Get ready to read the words in the box the fast way. First word. Check children's responses. Get ready. Clap for each word in the first sentence as the children read *ron was in the rain.* Pause at least two seconds between claps.

f. Have the children reread the sentence until firm.

g. Get ready to read the next sentence. First word. Check children's responses. Get ready. Clap for each word as the children read *he got wet.*

h. Have the children reread the sentence until firm.

i. Listen. **Ron was in the rain.** (Pause.) **He got wet.** Everybody, get ready to tell me the answers. **Ron was in the** . . . . (Signal.) *Rain.* Yes, **rain.** **He got** . . . . (Signal.) *Wet.* Yes, **wet.**

j. Repeat *i* until firm.

k. Everybody, touch item 1 below the box. Check children's responses. This item tells about the story in the box. Everybody, get ready to read item 1 the fast way. First word. Check children's responses. Get ready. Clap as the children read *ron was in the* . . . .

l. Touch the word **rat** on the next line. Check children's responses. Did the story say Ron was in the rat? (Signal.) *No.*

To correct	Have the children reread the first sentence in the box. Then repeat the question.

Touch the word **rain.** Check children's responses. Did the story say Ron was in the rain? (Signal.) *Yes.*

Touch the word **sand.** Check children's responses. Did the story say Ron was in the sand? (Signal.) *No.*

m. Which word is right? (Signal.) *Rain.* Yes, **rain.** Draw a circle around it. Check children's responses.

n. I'll read the sentences in the box. **Ron was in the rain. He got wet.**

o. Everybody, get ready to read item 2. First word. Check children's responses. Clap as the children read *he got* . . . .

p. Touch the word **fat** on the next line. Check children's responses. Did the story say he got fat? (Signal.) *No.*

Touch the word **sick.** Check children's responses. Did the story say he got sick? (Signal.) *No.*

Touch the word **wet.** Check children's responses. Did the story say he got wet? (Signal.) *Yes.*

q. Which word is right? (Signal.) *Wet.* Yes, **wet.** So what do you do with **wet**? (Signal.) *Draw a circle around it.* Yes, draw a circle around it. Do it. Check children's responses.

PAIR RELATIONS

TASK 25   Children draw a line through the incorrect sentences

---

a. Point to the sentences below the first picture in the pair-relations exercise on side 2.

b. One of these sentences tells about the picture. Everybody, touch the first sentence. Check children's responses.

c. Reading the fast way.

d. First word. Check children's responses. Get ready. Clap for each word as the children read *the man has a sack.*

e. Does that sentence tell about the picture? (Signal.) *No.* So do you draw a line through it? (Signal.) *Yes.* Do it. Check children's responses.

f. Next sentence. First word. Check children's responses. Get ready. Clap for each word as the children read *he has a mitt.*

g. Does that sentence tell about the picture? (Signal.) *Yes.* So do you draw a line through it? (Signal.) *No.*

h. Next sentence. Repeat *d* and *e* for the remaining sentences.

i. Everybody, you'll do the rest of the boxes later. Remember—draw a line through the sentences that do not tell about the picture.

75

TASK 18 **Children sound out the word and tell what word**

a. Touch the ball for **filled.** Sound it out.
b. Get ready.   Touch **f, i,** between the l's, **d,** as the children say *fffiiillld.*
                              If sounding out is not firm, repeat b.
c. What word?   (Signal.) *Filled.* Yes, **filled.**

Do not touch any small letters.

TASK 19 **Children read the fast way**

Touch the ball for **mȳ.** Get ready to read this word the fast way.
                  (Pause three seconds.) Get ready.   (Signal.) *My.*

TASK 20 **Children read a word beginning with two consonants (flȳ)**

a. Cover **f.** Run your finger under **lȳ.** You're going to sound out
              this part. Get ready.   Touch **l, ȳ** as the children say *lllȳȳȳ.*
b. Say it fast.   (Signal.) *Lȳ.* Yes, this part is **lȳ.**
c. Uncover **f.** Point to **f.** You're going to say this first.
              Move your finger quickly under **lȳ.** Then you're going to say
                                          (pause) **lȳ.**
d. Point to **f.** What are you going to say first?   (Signal.) *fff.*
                  What are you going to say next?   (Signal.) *Lȳ.*
e. Repeat *d* until firm.
f. Touch the ball for **fly.** Get ready.   Move to **f,** then quickly along the
                                          arrow. *Ffflȳ.*
g. Say it fast.   (Signal.) *Fly.* Yes, what word?   (Signal.) *Fly.*
                              Yes, **fly.** Good reading.
h. Again.   Repeat *f* and *g* until firm.
i. Now you're going to sound out   (pause) **fly.** Get ready.
                      Touch **f, l, ȳ** as the children say *ffflllȳȳȳ.*
                      What word?   (Signal.) *Fly.* Yes, **fly.**

TASK 21 **Children read the words the fast way**

a. Now you get to read the words on this page the fast way.
b. Touch the ball for **filled.** (Pause three seconds.) Get ready.
                      Move your finger quickly along the arrow. *Filled.*
c. Repeat *b* for each word on the page.

TASK 22 **Individual test**—Have children read one word the fast way.

SUMMARY OF INDEPENDENT ACTIVITY

The children will need plain paper.

TASK 26   Introduction to independent activity

a. Hold up side 1 of Take-Home 120.
b. Everybody, you're going to finish this take-home on your own.
Tell the children when they will work the remaining items.
Let's go over the things you're going to do.

TASK 27   Sentence copying

a. Point to the dotted sentence in the sentence-copying exercise.
b. You're going to trace the words in this sentence.
Then you're going to write the sentence on the other lines.
c. Reading the fast way. First word.   Check children's responses.
Get ready.   Clap. *The.*
d. Next word.   Check children's responses. Get ready.   Clap. *Girl.*
e. Repeat *d* for the remaining words.
f. After you finish your take-home, you get to draw a picture about
the sentence, **the girl got wet.** You'll draw your picture on a
piece of plain paper.

TASK 28   Cross-out game

Point to the boxed word in the Cross-out Game. Everybody, here's
the word you're going to cross out today. What word?   (Signal.)
Girl. Yes, **girl.**

TASK 29   Sound writing

a. Point to the sound-writing exercise on side 2. Here are the
sounds you're going to write today. I'll touch the sounds.
You say them.
b. Touch each sound. *The children respond.*
c. Repeat the series until firm.

TASK 30   Pair relations

a. Point to the pair-relations exercise. Remember—you're going to
draw a line through the sentences in each box that do not tell
about the picture.
b. When the children finish their take-homes, give them sheets of
plain paper. Remind them to draw a picture that shows **the girl
got wet.**

INDIVIDUAL CHECKOUT: STORYBOOK

TASK 31   2-minute individual checkout — first page

a. As you are doing your take-home, I'll call on children one at a time
to read the **first page** of the story. Remember, you get two stars if
you read the first page of the story in less than two minutes and
make no more than three errors.
b. Call on a child. Tell the child: Start with the title and read the first
page of the story carefully the fast way. Go.   Time the child. Tell
the child any words the child misses. Stop the child as soon as the
child makes the fourth error or exceeds the time limit.
c. If the child meets the rate-accuracy criterion, record two stars on
your chart for lesson 120. Congratulate the child. Give children who
do not earn two stars a chance to read the page again before the
next lesson is presented.

44 words/2 min = 22 wpm [3 errors]

TASK 32   Bonus take-home: sides 3 and 4

After the children have drawn their pictures, give them sides 3 and 4
of Take-Home 120. Tell them they may keep the stories and read them.

END OF LESSON 120

Before presenting lesson 121, give Mastery Test 23 to each child.
Do not present lesson 121 to any groups that are not firm on this test.

TASK 10   Children sound out an irregular word (your)

a. Touch the ball for **your.** Sound it out.

b. Get ready. Quickly touch each sound as the children say

yyyooouuurrr.

c. Again. Repeat *b* until firm.

d. That's how we <u>sound out</u> the word. Here's how we <u>say</u> the word.
Your. How do we <u>say</u> the word? (Signal.) *Your.*

e. Now you're going to <u>sound out</u> the word. Get ready.
Touch each sound as the children say *yyyooouuurrr.*

f. Now you're going to say the word. Get ready. (Signal.) *Your.*

g. Repeat *e* and *f* until firm.

h. Yes, this word is **your.** I like **your** new dress.

TASK 11   Individual test—Have children do *e* and *f* in task 10.

TASK 12   Children sound out an irregular word (book)

Repeat the procedures in task 10 for **book.**

TASK 13   Individual test—Have children sound out and say **book.**

TASK 14   Children identify, then sound out an irregular word (says)

a. Touch the ball for **says.** Everybody, you're going to read this
word the fast way. (Pause three seconds.) Get ready.
Move your finger quickly along the arrow. *Says.* Yes, **says.**

b. Now you're going to sound out the word. Get ready.
Quickly touch **s, a, y, s** as the children say *sssaaayyysss.*

c. Again. Repeat *b.*

d. How do we say the word? (Signal.) *Says.* Yes, **says.**

e. Repeat *b* and *d* until firm.

TASK 15   Individual test—Have children do *b* and *d* in task 14.

TASK 16   Children read the words the fast way

Have the children read the words on this page the fast way.

TASK 17   Individual test—Have children read one word the fast way.

your

book

says

Mastery Test 23 after lesson 120, before lesson 121

a. When I touch the sound, you say it.
b. (test item) Point to **ō.** Get ready. Touch **ō.** *ōōō.*
c. (test item) Point to **v.** Get ready. Touch **v.** *vvv.*
d. (test item) Point to **p.** Get ready. Touch **p.** *p.*
e. (test item) Point to **ch.** Get ready. Touch **ch.** *ch.*
f. (test item) Point to **e.** Get ready. Touch **e.** *eee.*

Total number of test items: **5**

A group is weak if more than one-third of the children missed any of the items on the test.

v

ō

p

ch

e

WHAT TO DO

If the group is firm on Mastery Test 23:

Present lesson 121 to the group during the next reading period. If more than one child missed any of the items on the test, present the firming procedures specified below to those children.

If the group is weak on Mastery Test 23:

A. Present these firming procedures to the group during the next reading period.
   1. Lesson 118, Sounds, page 60, tasks 1 through 4.
   2. Lesson 118, Reading Vocabulary, page 61, tasks 5, 6, 7.
   3. Lesson 119, Sounds, page 65, tasks 4, 5.
   4. Lesson 119, Reading Vocabulary, page 67, tasks 14 through 18.
   5. Lesson 120, Sounds, page 70, tasks 4, 5.
B. After presenting the above tasks, again give Mastery Test 23 individually to members of the group who failed the test.
C. If the group is firm (less than one-third of the total group missed any items on the retest), present lesson 121 to the group during the next reading period.
D. If the group is still weak (more than one-third of the total group missed any items on the retest), repeat *A* and *B* during the next reading period.

READING VOCABULARY

Do not touch any small letters.

TASK 7 **Children read the fast way**

a. Get ready to read these words the fast way.
b. Touch the ball for **brush.** (Pause three seconds.) Get ready.
(Signal.) *Brush.*

c. Repeat *b* for the remaining words on the page.

TASK 8 **Children read the fast way again**

a. Get ready to do these words again. Watch where I point.
b. Point to a word. (Pause one second.) Say: Get ready. (Signal.)
The children respond. Point to the words in this order:
brush, tēach, ēagle, tug, gōld.

c. Repeat *b* until firm.

TASK 9 **Individual test**

Call on different children to read one word the fast way.

brush

tug

tēach

ēagle

gōld

Planning Pages: For Lessons 121–140

Making Progress

	Since Lesson 1	Since Lesson 101
Word Reading	27 sounds 210 regular words 19 irregular words Reading words the fast way Reading stories the fast way	4 sounds 49 regular words 17 irregular words Reading stories the fast way
Comprehension	**Picture Comprehension** Predicting what the picture will show Answering questions about the picture **Story Comprehension** Answering *who, what, when, where* and *why* questions orally Making predictions about the story Finding periods, question marks, and quotation marks	

What to Use

Teacher	Students

Presentation Book C (pages 78–203)
Teacher's Guide (pages 52)
Teacher's Take-Home Book and Answer Key
Spelling Book
	Storybook 2 (pages 10–64)
	  Lessons 121–138
	Storybook 2 (pages 1–6)
	  Lessons 139–140
	Take-Home Book C
	plain paper (Sentence picture)
	lined paper (Spelling)

What's Ahead in Lessons 121–140

New Skills
- Story length will increase from 82 to 106 words.
- Children begin to sound out words beginning with blends.
- Beginning at Lesson 140, individuals take turns on the first reading.
- Children begin answering written comprehension questions.
- Children write a sentence from dictation during spelling lesson.

New Sounds
- Lesson 121 – **b** as in *bag* (quick sound)
- Lesson 124 – **ing** as in *sing*
- Lesson 127 – **ī** as in *ice*
- Lesson 131 – **y** as in *yes*
- Lesson 135 – **er** as in *her*
- Lesson 139 – **x** as in *ox*

New Vocabulary
- *Regular words:*

(121) them, red, sent	(132) having, slide, slid, time, tell
(122) paint, men, shots, up, lift	(133) stops, rich, stopping, digging, led, boy
(123) chicks, pig, bug, duck, ducks	(134) told, hole, yes, line, live, dig
(124) going, kissed	(135) dad, they, find
(125) eating	(136) hunt, hunting, ride, gun
(126) be, big, bed, bit, getting, bugs	(137) deer
(127) sleeping, fishing, leaf, slam, let's, but, slip	(138) her
(128) pond, back, bus	(139) beans, ever, shopping, never, toys
(129) bite, tub, stop	(140) hop, shop
(130) dive, like, sliding	
(131) rabbit, sitting	

- *Irregular words:*

(128) walk, talk	(137) other, mother, brother, love
(130) talking	(138) card
(132) doing	(140) come, some
(133) into, you, dark	
(134) yard	

Lesson 152

SOUNDS

TASK 1 Teaching **wh** as in **why**

a. Point to **wh.** Here's a new sound.

b. My turn. (Pause.) Touch **wh** and say: whwhwh.

c. Again. Touch **wh** for a longer time. whwhwhwhwh. Lift your finger.

d. Point to **wh.** Your turn. When I touch it, you say it. (Pause.) Get ready. Touch **wh.** *whwhwh.* Lift your finger.

e. Again. Touch **wh.** *whwhwhwhwh.* Lift your finger.

f. Repeat *e* until firm.

TASK 2 Individual test

Call on different children to identify **wh.**

TASK 3 Sounds firm-up

a. Get ready to say the sounds when I touch them.

b. Alternate touching **wh** and **w.** Point to the sound. (Pause one second.) Say: Get ready. Touch the sound. *The children respond.*

c. When **wh** and **w** are firm, alternate touching **wh, w, oo,** and **r** until all four sounds are firm.

TASK 4 Individual test

Call on different children to identify **wh, w, oo,** or **r.**

TASK 5 Sounds firm-up

a. Point to **wh.** When I touch the sound, you say it.

b. (Pause.) Get ready. Touch **wh.** *whwhwh.*

c. Again. Repeat *b* until firm.

d. Get ready to say all the sounds when I touch them.

e. Alternate touching **wh, ch, ȳ, j, er, x, y,** and **h** three or four times. Point to the sound. (Pause one second.) Say: Get ready. Touch the sound. *The children respond.*

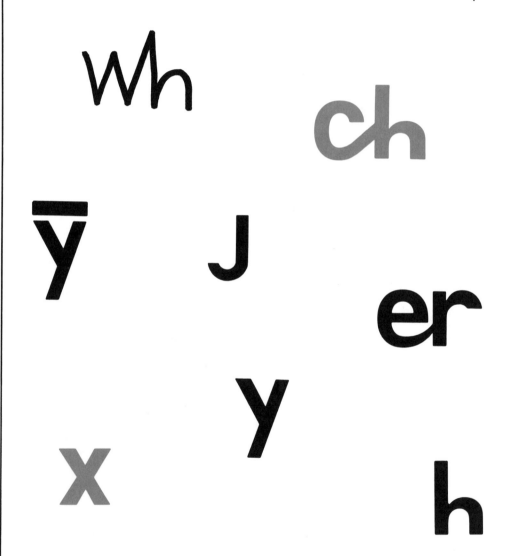

TASK 6 Individual test

Call on different children to identify one or more sounds in task 5.

Look Ahead

Mastery Tests

Skill Tested	Implications
Test 24 (Lesson 125) Reading a story the fast way	Use these tests along with Checkouts to determine if any reading vocabulary or stories should be repeated.
Test 25 (Lesson 130) Reading words the fast way	
Test 26 (Lesson 135) Reading the story the fast way	
Test 27 (Lesson 140) Reading words the fast way	
At Lesson 140	Beginning at Lesson 140, children begin taking turns on the first reading. Having the group read is an option; you may want to mix group and individual turns to help maintain the children's attention.

Reading Checkouts
(Lessons 125, 130, 135, 140)

Skills

Lessons 121-140	
Word Reading	6 sounds
	73 regular words
	15 irregular words
	Individuals take turns reading
Comprehension	**Story Comprehension** Answering written comprehension questions about the day's story and short passages

Reading Activities

Help children develop decoding and comprehension skills by using the following activities.

Beginning-Middle-End
(Lessons 121–140)

After completing stories 121–140, have the children fold a piece of drawing paper lengthwise into thirds. Have children choose a story and write the title of the story across the top of the page and then draw and/or write in each section of the paper what happened in the beginning, the middle, and the end of the story. As an additional activity, have children make up a new ending for the story.

Same or Different
(Lessons 124, 126, 128)

After completing a lesson, have children make a book of opposites using descriptions from a story. Children fold a piece of white drawing paper into four parts and cut on the folds. Then children draw and write a description on one side and its opposite on the other side. Direct children to make a decorated cover and title it. The contents of this activity for Lesson 124 with a title and opposite pairs is shown below. The same activity can be done with similarities for some other stories.

Paint That Nose

fat dog - little dog

red nose - black nose

clean ear - dirty ear

happy dog - sad dog

TASK 26 Picture comprehension

a. What do you think you'll see in the picture? *The children respond.*
b. Turn the page and look at the picture.
c. Show me the boy who has five fish. *(The children respond.)*
d. Show me the boy who has nine fish. *(The children respond.)*
e. Ask these questions:
   1. What's Bill pulling out of the water? *The children respond.*

An old box.

   2. How many fish does Bill have? *None.*

Take-Home 151

SUMMARY OF INDEPENDENT ACTIVITY

TASK 27 Introduction to independent activity

a. Pass out Take-Home 151 to each child.
b. Everybody, you're going to do this take-home on your own.

Tell the children when they will work the items.

Let's go over the things you're going to do.

TASK 28 Story items

a. Hold up side 1 of your take-home and point to the story-items

exercise.

b. Everybody, here are items about the story we read today.
c. Think about what happened in the story and circle the right answer

for each item.

TASK 29 Picture comprehension

a. Point to the pictures in the picture-comprehension exercise.

Everybody, you're going to look at the picture. Then you're going
to read each item and write the missing word.

b. Remember—the first sound of each missing word is already written

in the blank.

TASK 30 Reading comprehension

a. Point to the reading-comprehension exercise on side 2.
b. Everybody, get ready to read the sentences in the box the fast way.
c. First word. Check children's responses. Get ready. Clap for each

word as the children read the sentences: *A girl went fishing.*

She got five fish.

d. Point to items 1 and 2. These items tell about the story in the box.

You're going to read each item and circle the right answer.

TASK 31 Sound writing

a. Point to the sound-writing exercise. Here are the sounds you're

going to write today. I'll touch the sounds. You say them.

b. Touch each sound. *The children respond.*
c. Repeat the series until firm.

TASK 32 Sentence copying

a. Point to the dotted sentence in the sentence-copying exercise.
b. You're going to trace the words in this sentence. Then you're

going to write the sentence on the other lines.

c. Reading the fast way. First word. Check children's responses.

Get ready. Clap for each word.

d. After you finish your take-home, you get to draw a picture about

the sentence, **Bill did not get fish.** You'll draw your picture on
a piece of plain paper. When the children finish their take-homes,

give them sheets of plain paper.

END OF LESSON 151

Lesson 121

SOUNDS

TASK 1 Teaching b as in bag

a. Point to **b.** Here's a new sound. It's a quick sound.
b. My turn. (Pause.) Touch **b** for an instant, saying: b.

Do not say **buuh.**

c. Again. Touch **b** and say: b.
d. Point to **b.** Your turn. When I touch it, you say it. (Pause.)

Get ready. Touch **b.** *b.*

e. Again. Touch **b.** *b.*
f. Repeat *e* until firm.

TASK 2 Individual test

Call on different children to identify **b.**

TASK 3 Sounds firm-up

a. Get ready to say the sounds when I touch them.
b. Alternate touching **b** and **d.** Point to the sound. (Pause one second.)

Say: Get ready. Touch the sound. *The children respond.*

c. When **b** and **d** are firm, alternate touching **b, d, p,** and **t**

until all four sounds are firm.

TASK 4 Individual test

Call on different children to identify **b, d, p,** or **t.**

TASK 5 Sounds firm-up

a. Point to **b.** When I touch the sound, you say it.
b. (Pause.) Get ready. Touch **b.** *b.*
c. Again. Repeat *b* until firm.
d. Get ready to say all the sounds when I touch them.
e. Alternate touching **v, e, ch, ē, ō, r, ā,** and **b** three or four times. Point to the sound. (Pause one second.) Say: Get ready. Touch the sound. *The children respond.*

TASK 6 Individual test

Call on different children to identify one or more sounds in task 5.

Story 151

TASK 23 First reading—children read the title and first three sentences

a. You're going to read the first part of this story today.

b. Everybody, touch the title of the story and get ready to read the words in the title the fast way.

c. First word. Check children's responses. (Pause two seconds.) Get ready. Clap. *Bill.*

d. Clap for each remaining word in the title.

e. After the children have read the title, ask: What's this story about? (Signal.) *Bill went fishing.* Yes, **Bill went fishing.**

f. Everybody, get ready to read this story the fast way.

g. First word. Check children's responses. (Pause two seconds.) Get ready. Clap. *Bill.*

h. Clap for the remaining words in the first sentence. Pause at least two seconds between claps.

i. Repeat g and h for the next two sentences. Have the children reread the first three sentences until firm.

TASK 24 Individual children or the group read sentences to complete the first reading

a. I'm going to call on different children to read a sentence. Everybody, follow along and point to the words. If you hear a mistake, raise your hand.

b. Call on a child. Read the next sentence. Do not clap for the words. Let the child read at his own pace, but be sure he reads the sentence correctly.

To correct	Have the child sound out the word. Then return to the beginning of the sentence.

c. Repeat b for most of the remaining sentences in the story. Occasionally have the group read a sentence. When the group is to read, say: Everybody, read the next sentence. (Pause two seconds.) Get ready. Clap for each word in the sentence. Pause at least two seconds between claps.

TASK 25 Second reading—individual children or the group read each sentence; the group answer questions

a. You're going to read the story again. This time I'm going to ask questions.

b. Starting with the first word of the title. Check children's responses. Get ready. Clap as the children read the title. Pause at least two seconds between claps.

c. Call on a child. Read the first sentence. *The child responds.*

d. Repeat b and c in task 24. Present the following comprehension questions to the entire group.

After the children read:	You say:
Bill went fishing.	What's this story about? (Signal.) *Bill went fishing.*
Bill liked to go fishing but he did not get fish.	What did Bill like to do? (Signal.) *He liked to go fishing.* But what happened? (Signal.) *He did not get fish.*
But Bill did not get fish.	How many fish did Bill get? (Signal.) *None.* How many did the big boy get? (Signal.) *Five.* How many did the little boy get? (Signal.) *Nine.*
Then he had a tug on his line.	What happened? (Signal.) *He had a tug on his line.* What's a tug on the line? *The children respond.*
It was an old box.	I wonder if anything is in that old box. We'll find out when we read the next part of the story.

READING VOCABULARY

Do not touch any small letters.

TASK 7   Children read the fast way

a. Get ready to read these words the fast way.

b. Touch the ball for **red.** (Pause three seconds.)   Get ready.

(Signal.) *Red.*

c. Repeat *b* for the remaining words on the page.

TASK 8   Children read the fast way again

a. Get ready to do these words again. Watch where I point.

b. Point to a word. (Pause one second.) Say: Get ready.   (Signal.)

The children respond. Point to the words in this order:
red, rēad, sent, let, went.

c. Repeat *b* until firm.

TASK 9   Individual test

Call on different children to read one word the fast way.

red

went

sent

rēₐd

let

Read the Item 151

TASK 20   Children read item 1

a. Pass out Storybook 3.

b. Open your book to page 34.

c. Point to the title **read the item**. Everybody, touch this title.
Check children's responses.

d. I'll read the title. You point to the words I read. (Pause.)
Get ready. **Read** (pause) **the** (pause) **item**.

e. Your turn to read the title. First word. Check children's responses.
Get ready. Clap for each word as the children read *read the item*.

f. Everybody, say the title. (Pause and signal.) Without looking at the
words, the children say *read the item*. Repeat until firm.

g. You're going to read the item. Touch item 1 and get ready to read.
Check children's responses.

h. First word. Clap for each word as the children read:
If the teacher says "Go," stand up.
Repeat three times or until firm.

i. Everybody, get ready to say item 1 with me. (Pause and signal.)
Without looking at the words, you and the children say: If the
teacher says "Go," (pause one second) stand up.
Repeat four times or until firm.

j. All by yourselves. Say item 1. (Signal.) *If the teacher says "Go,"
stand up.* Repeat four times or until firm.

TASK 21   Children reread item 1 and answer questions

a. Everybody, touch item 1 again. Check children's responses.

b. Read item 1 to yourself. Raise your hand when you know what
you're going to do and when you're going to do it.

c. After the children raise their hands, say: Everybody, what are you
going to do if I say "**Go**"? (Signal.) *Stand up.*

To correct	1. Everybody, read item 1 out loud. Clap as the children read each word.
	2. What are you going to do if I say "**Go**"? (Signal.) *Stand up.*

d. Everybody, when are you going to **stand up**? (Signal.)
If the teacher says "Go."

To correct	1. Everybody, read item 1 out loud. Clap as the children read each word.
	2. When are you going to **stand up**? (Signal.) *If the teacher says "Go."*

e. Repeat *c* and *d* until firm.

TASK 22   Children play the game

a. Everybody, touch item 1. Check children's responses.

b. Read the item to yourself. Raise your hand when you know what
you're going to do and when you're going to do it.

c. After the children raise their hands, say: Let's play the game.
Think about what you're going to do (pause) and when you're going
to do it.

d. Hold out your hand. (Pause.) Get ready. **Go**. (Pause.)
Drop your hand. *(The children stand up immediately.)*

To correct	1. What did I say? (Signal.) *Go.*
	2. What are you supposed to do if I say "**Go**"? (Signal.) *Stand up.*
	3. If the children's responses are not firm, have them read item 1 aloud.
	4. Repeat task 22.

TASK 10   **Children rhyme with an irregular word (to)**

a. Touch the ball for **to.** Everybody, you're going to read this word the fast way. (Pause three seconds.) Get ready. Move your finger quickly along the arrow. *To.* Yes, **to.**

b. Quickly touch the ball for **do.** This word rhymes with **to.** Get ready. Move to **d**, then quickly along the arrow. *Do.* Yes, **do.**

c. Repeat *a* and *b* until firm.

TASK 11   **Children sound out do**

a. Touch the ball for **do.** You're going to sound out this word. Get ready. Quickly touch **d, o** as the children say *dooo.*

b. How do we say the word? (Signal.) *Do.* Yes, **do.**

c. If *a* and *b* are not firm, say: Again. Repeat *a* and *b.*

TASK 12   **Individual test**

Call on different children to do *a* and *b* in task 11.

TASK 13   **Children sound out the word and tell what word**

a. Touch the ball for **there.** Sound it out.

b. Get ready. Touch **th, e, r** as the children say *thththeeerrr.* If sounding out is not firm, repeat *b.*

c. What word? (Signal.) *There.* Yes, **there. There** is my desk.

TASK 14   **Children read the fast way**

Touch the ball for **pet.** Get ready to read this word the fast way. (Pause three seconds.) Get ready. (Signal.) *Pet.*

TASK 15   **Children read the words the fast way**

Have the children read the words on this page the fast way.

TASK 16   **Individual test**

Call on different children to read one word the fast way.

Do not touch any small letters.

to

do

ther_e

pet

151

TASK 15 Children read **tēach** and **tēacher**

a. Touch the ball for **tēach.** You're going to read this word the fast way. (Pause three seconds.) Get ready. Move your finger quickly along the arrow. *Teach.*

b. Return to the ball for **tēach.** Yes, this word is **teach.**

c. Tap under **er** in **tēacher.** So this must be . . . . Touch the ball for **tēacher** and move your finger quickly along the arrow. *Teacher.* Yes, **teacher.**

d. Repeat *b* and *c* until firm.

e. Now you're going to sound out (pause) **teacher.** Get ready. Touch **t, ē, ch, er** as the children say *tēēēcherrr.* Yes, what word? (Signal.) *Teacher.* Yes, **teacher.**

TASK 16 Children sound out the word and tell what word

a. Touch the ball for **tug.** Sound it out.

b. Get ready. Touch **t, u, g** as the children say *tuuug.* If sounding out is not firm, repeat *b.*

c. What word? (Signal.) *Tug.* Yes, **tug.**

TASK 17 Children sound out the word and tell what word

a. Touch the ball for **bill.** Sound it out.

b. Get ready. Touch **b, i,** between the **l**'s as the children say *biiilll.* If sounding out is not firm, repeat *b.*

c. What word? (Signal.) *Bill.* Yes, **bill.**

TASK 18 Children read the words the fast way

a. Now you get to read the words on this page the fast way.

b. Touch the ball for **tēach.** (Pause three seconds.) Get ready. Move your finger quickly along the arrow. *Teach.*

c. Repeat *b* for each word on the page.

TASK 19 Individual test

Call on different children to read one word the fast way.

Do not touch any small letters.

tēach

tēacher

tug

bill

TASK 17   Children sound out the word and tell what word

a. Touch the ball for **did.** Sound it out.
b. Get ready.   Touch **d, i, d** as the children say *diiid.*

If sounding out is not firm, repeat *b.*

c. What word?   (Signal.) *Did.* Yes, **did.**

TASK 18   Children read the fast way

a. Get ready to read these words the fast way.
b. Touch the ball for **the.** (Pause three seconds.) Get ready.

(Signal.) *The.*

c. Repeat *b* for the remaining words on the page.

TASK 19   Children read the fast way again

a. Get ready to do these words again. Watch where I point.
b. Point to a word. (Pause one second.) Say: Get ready.   (Signal.)
The children respond. Point to the words in this order:

then, the, them.

c. Repeat *b* until firm.

TASK 20   Individual test

Call on different children to read one word on the page the fast way.

did

the

then

them

TASK 10 **Children rhyme with nīne and fīne**

a. Touch the ball for **nīne.** **You're going to read this word the fast way.** (Pause three seconds.) **Get ready.** Move your finger quickly along the arrow. *Nine.*

b. Touch the ball for **fīne.** **This word rhymes with** (pause) **nine.** Move to **f,** then quickly along the arrow. *Fine.* **Yes, what word?** (Signal.) *Fine.*

TASK 11 **Children sound out an irregular word (your)**

a. Touch the ball for **your.** **Sound it out.**

b. **Get ready.** Quickly touch each sound as the children say

yyyooouuurrr.

c. **Again.** Repeat *b* until firm.

d. **That's how we** <u>sound out</u> **the word. Here's how we** <u>say</u> **the word.** **Your.** How do we <u>say</u> the word? (Signal.) *Your.*

e. **Now you're going to** <u>sound out</u> **the word. Get ready.** Touch each sound as the children say *yyyooouuurrr.*

f. **Now you're going to say the word. Get ready.** (Signal.) *Your.*

g. **Repeat** *e* **and** *f* **until firm.**

h. **Yes, this word is your. Touch your head.**

i. Call on different children to do *e* and *f.*

TASK 12 **Children identify, then sound out an irregular word (says)**

a. Touch the ball for **says.** **Everybody, you're going to read this word the fast way.** (Pause three seconds.) **Get ready.** Move your finger quickly along the arrow. *Says.* **Yes, says.**

b. **Now you're going to sound out the word. Get ready.** Quickly touch **s, a, y, s** as the children say *sssaaayyysss.*

c. **Again.** Repeat *b.*

d. **How do we say the word?** (Signal.) *Says.*

e. Repeat *b* and *d* until firm.

f. Call on different children to do *b* and *d.*

TASK 13 **Children read the words the fast way**

Have the children read the words on this page the fast way.

TASK 14 **Individual test**

Call on different children to read one word the fast way.

Do not touch any small letters.

Story 121

TASK 21   First reading—children read the story the fast way

Have the children reread any sentences containing words that give them trouble. Keep a list of these words.

a. Pass out Storybook 2.
b. Open your book to page 10.
c. Everybody, touch the title of the story and get ready to read the words in the title the fast way.
d. First word.   Check children's responses. (Pause two seconds.) Get ready.   Clap. *The.*
e. Clap for each remaining word in the title.
f. After the children have read the title, ask: **What's this story about?** (Signal.) *The pet shop.* **Yes, the pet shop.**
g. Everybody, get ready to read this story the fast way.
h. First word.   Check children's responses. (Pause two seconds.) Get ready.   Clap. *A.*
i. Clap for the remaining words in the first sentence. Pause at least two seconds between claps.
j. Repeat *h* and *i* for the next two sentences. Have the children reread the first three sentences until firm.
k. The children are to read the remainder of the story the fast way, stopping at the end of each sentence.
l. After the first reading of the story, print on the board the words that the children missed more than one time. Have the children sound out each word one time and tell what word.
m. After the group's responses are firm, call on individual children to read the words.

TASK 22   Individual test

a. Look at page 10. I'm going to call on different children to read a whole sentence.
b. Call on different children to read a sentence. Do not clap for each word.

TASK 23   Second reading—children read the story the fast way and answer questions

a. You're going to read the story again the fast way and I'll ask questions.
b. Starting with the first word of the title.   Check children's responses. Get ready.   Clap. *The.*
c. Clap for each remaining word. Pause at least two seconds between claps. Pause longer before words that gave the children trouble during the first reading.
d. Ask the comprehension questions below as the children read.

After the children read:	You say:
A girl said to a man, "Let us go to the pet shop."	Who said that? (Signal.) *A girl.* Who was she talking to? (Signal.) *A man.*
The girl said to the man in the pet shop, "I need a dog."	What did she say? (Signal.) *I need a dog.* Who did she say that to? (Signal.) *The man in the pet shop.*
"Let me get that cat."	What kind of cat is he going to get? (Signal.) *A red cat.*
And the girl went home with the red cat.	What did the girl do with the cat? (Signal.) *She went home.*

TASK 24   Picture comprehension

a. What do you think you'll see in the picture?   *The children respond.*
b. Turn the page and look at the picture.
c. Ask these questions:
   1. Why are those hearts all around that girl? *The children respond.* They mean that she loves the cat.
   2. Do you think she'll take good care of that cat? *The children respond.*
   3. What would you do with a red cat?   *The children respond.*

READING VOCABULARY

Do not touch any small letters.

TASK 7   Children read the fast way

a. Get ready to read these words the fast way.

b. Touch the ball for **fill**. (Pause three seconds.)   Get ready. (Signal.)

Fill.

c. Repeat *b* for the remaining words on the page.

TASK 8   Children read the fast way again

a. Get ready to do these words again. Watch where I point.

b. Point to a word. (Pause one second.) Say: Get ready. (Signal.)

The children respond. Point to the words in this order:
līked, brush, hōld, fill.

c. Repeat *b* until firm.

TASK 9   Individual test

Call on different children to read one word the fast way.

fill

brush

hōld

līked

Take-Home 121

READING COMPREHENSION

The children will need pencils.

TASK 25   Children choose the correct words to complete the sentences

a. Pass out Take-Home 121 to each child.

b. Point to the sentences in the box in the reading-comprehension exercise on side 1.

c. Everybody, touch this box on your take-home. Check children's responses.

d. Get ready to read the words in the box the fast way. First word. Check children's responses. Get ready. Clap for each word in the first sentence as the children read *the girl went to a shop*. Pause at least two seconds between claps.

e. Have the children reread the sentence until firm.

f. Get ready to read the next sentence. First word. Check children's responses. Get ready. Clap for each word as the children read *she got a cat*.

g. Have the children reread the sentence until firm.

h. Listen. **The girl went to a shop.** (Pause.) **She got a cat.** Everybody, get ready to tell me the answers. **The girl went to a . . . .** (Signal.) *Shop*. Yes, **shop**. **She got a . . . .** (Signal.) *Cat*. Yes, **cat**.

i. Repeat *h* until firm.

j. Everybody, touch item 1 below the box. Check children's responses. This item tells about the story in the box. Everybody, get ready to read item 1 the fast way. First word. Check children's responses. Get ready. Clap as the children read *the girl went to a . . . .*

k. Touch the word **ship** on the next line. Check children's responses. Did the story say the girl went to a ship? (Signal.) *No*.

To correct	Have the children reread the first sentence in the box. Then repeat the question.

Touch the word **car**. Check children's responses. Did the story say the girl went to a car? (Signal.) *No*.
Touch the word **shop**. Check children's responses. Did the story say the girl went to a shop? (Signal.) *Yes*.

l. Which word is right? (Signal.) *Shop*. Yes, **shop**. Draw a circle around it. Check children's responses.

m. I'll read the sentences in the box. **The girl went to a shop. She got a cat.**

n. Everybody, get ready to read item 2. First word. Check children's responses. Clap as the children read *she got a . . . .*

o. Touch the word **cat** on the next line. Check children's responses. Did the story say she got a cat? (Signal.) *Yes*. Touch the word **dog**. Check children's responses. Did the story say she got a dog? (Signal.) *No*. Touch the word **car**. Check children's responses. Did the story say she got a car? (Signal.) *No*.

p. Which word is right? (Signal.) *Cat*. Yes, **cat**. So what do you do with **cat**? (Signal.) *Draw a circle around it*. Yes, draw a circle around it. Do it. Check children's responses.

PAIR RELATIONS

TASK 26   Children draw a line through the incorrect sentences

a. Point to the sentences below the first picture in the pair-relations exercise on side 2.

b. One of these sentences tells about the picture. Everybody, touch the first sentence. Check children's responses.

c. Reading the fast way.

d. First word. Check children's responses. Get ready. Clap for each word as the children read *that man is mean*.

e. Does that sentence tell about the picture? (Signal.) *No*. So do you draw a line through it? (Signal.) *Yes*. Do it. Check children's responses.

f. Next sentence. First word. Check children's responses. Get ready. Clap for each word as the children read *a girl has a sack*.

g. Does that sentence tell about the picture? (Signal.) *Yes*. So do you draw a line through it? (Signal.) *No*.

h. Next sentence. Repeat *d* and *e* for the remaining sentences.

i. Everybody, you'll do the rest of the boxes later. Remember—draw a line through the sentences that do not tell about the picture.

Lesson 151

ū

u

y

i

SOUNDS

TASK 1   Teaching ȳ as in mȳ

a. Point to ȳ. **My turn.** (Pause.)
Touch ȳ and say: **ȳȳȳ (īīī).**

b. Point to ȳ. **Your turn. When
I touch it, you say it.** (Pause.)
Get ready.   Touch ȳ. *ȳȳȳ.*
Lift your finger.

c. **Again.**   Touch ȳ. *ȳȳȳȳ.*
Lift your finger.

d. Repeat *c* until firm.

TASK 2   Sounds firm-up

a. **Get ready to say the sounds
when I touch them.**

b. Alternate touching ȳ and **u.**
Point to the sound. (Pause one
second.) Say: **Get ready.**
Touch the sound. *The children
respond.*

c. When ȳ and **u** are firm, alternate
touching ȳ, **u, y,** and **i** until all
four sounds are firm.

TASK 3   Individual test

Call on different children to identify ȳ, **u, y,** or **i.**

TASK 4   Teacher introduces cross-out game

a. Use acetate and crayon.

b. **I'll cross out the sounds on this part of the page when you can
tell me every sound.**

c. **Remember—when I touch it, you say it.**

d. Go over the sounds until the children can identify all the sounds
in order.

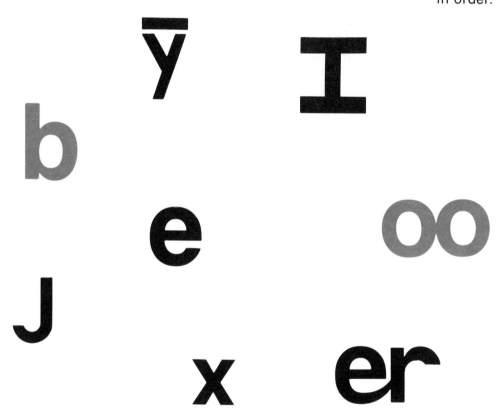

TASK 5   Individual test

Call on different children to identify two or more sounds in task 4.

TASK 6   Teacher crosses out sounds

a. **You told me every sound. Get ready to do it again. This time I'll
cross out each sound when you tell me what it is.**

b. Point to each sound. (Pause.) Say: **Get ready.**   Touch the sound.
The children respond. As you cross out the sound, say:
Goodbye, _____ .

SUMMARY OF INDEPENDENT ACTIVITY

TASK 27   Introduction to independent activity

a. Hold up side 1 of Take-Home 121.
b. Everybody, you're going to finish this take-home on your own.
Tell the children when they will work the remaining items.
Let's go over the things you're going to do.

TASK 28   Sentence copying

a. Point to the dotted sentence in the sentence-copying exercise.
b. You're going to trace the words in this sentence. Then you're going to write the sentence on the other lines.
c. Reading the fast way. First word. Check children's responses.
Get ready. Clap. *The.*
d. Next word. Check children's responses. Get ready. Clap. *Girl.*
e. Repeat *d* for the remaining words.
f. After you finish your take-home, you get to draw a picture about the sentence, **the girl got a cat.** You'll draw your picture on a piece of plain paper.

TASK 29   Cross-out game

Point to the boxed word in the Cross-out Game. Everybody, here's the word you're going to cross out today. What word? (Signal.)
Went. Yes, **went.**

TASK 30   Sound writing

a. Point to the sound-writing exercise on side 2. Here are the sounds you're going to write today. I'll touch the sounds.
You say them.
b. Touch each sound. *The children respond.*
c. Repeat the series until firm.

TASK 31   Pair relations

a. Point to the pair-relations exercise. Remember—you're going to draw a line through the sentences in each box that do not tell about the picture.
b. When the children finish their take-homes, give them sheets of plain paper. Remind them to draw a picture that shows **the girl got a cat.**

END OF LESSON 121

Mastery Test 29 after lesson 150, before lesson 151

a. Get ready to read these words the fast way.

b. (test item) Touch the ball for **jump.** (Pause three seconds.)
   Get ready. (Signal.) *Jump.*

c. (test item) Touch the ball for **fox.** (Pause three seconds.)
   Get ready. (Signal.) *Fox.*

d. (test item) Touch the ball for **broom.** (Pause three seconds.)
   Get ready. (Signal.) *Broom.*

e. (test item) Touch the ball for **start.** (Pause three seconds.)
   Get ready. (Signal.) *Start.*

Total number of test items: **4**

A group is weak if more than one-third of the children missed any of the items on the test.

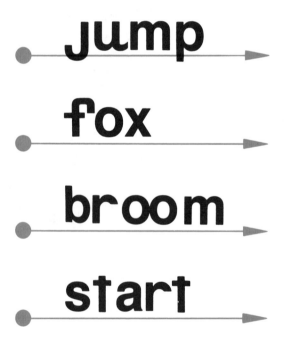

WHAT TO DO

If the group is firm on Mastery Test 29 and was firm on Mastery Test 28:

Present lesson 151 and skip lesson 153. If more than one child missed any of the items on the test, present the firming procedures specified below to those children.

If the group is firm on Mastery Test 29 but was weak on Mastery Test 28:

Present lesson 151 to the group during the next reading period. If more than one child missed any of the items on the test, present the firming procedures specified below to those children.

If the group is weak on Mastery Test 29:

A. Present these firming procedures to the group during the next reading period.
   1. Lesson 147, Reading Vocabulary, pages 243–244, tasks 6 through 15.
   2. Lesson 148, Reading Vocabulary, pages 249–251, tasks 4 through 16.
   3. Lesson 149, Reading Vocabulary, pages 255–256, tasks 5 through 11.
   4. Lesson 150, Reading Vocabulary, pages 261–264, tasks 6 through 24.
B. After presenting the above tasks, again give Mastery Test 29 individually to members of the group who failed the test.
C. If the group is firm (less than one-third of the total group missed any items in the retest), present lesson 151 to the group during the next reading period.
D. If the group is still weak (more than one-third of the total group missed any items on the retest), repeat *A* and *B* during the next reading period.

Lesson 122

SOUNDS

TASK 1 Teaching **b** as in **bag**

a. Point to **b**. **My turn. When I touch it, I'll say it.** (Pause.)
> Touch **b** for an instant, saying: **b.** Do not say **buuh.**

b. Point to **b**. **Your turn. When I touch it, you say it.** (Pause.)
> **Get ready.** Touch **b**. *b.*

c. **Again.** Touch **b**. *b.*
d. Repeat *c* until firm.

TASK 2 Sounds firm-up

a. **Get ready to say the sounds when I touch them.**
b. Alternate touching **b** and **p**. Point to the sound. (Pause one second.)
> Say: **Get ready.** Touch the sound. *The children respond.*
c. When **b** and **p** are firm, alternate touching **d, b, t,** and **p**
> until all four sounds are firm.

TASK 3 Individual test

Call on different children to identify **d, b, t,** or **p.**

TASK 4 Teacher introduces cross-out game

a. Use acetate and crayon.
b. **I'll cross out the sounds on this part of the page when you can tell me every sound.**
c. **Remember—when I touch it, you say it.**
d. Go over the sounds until the children can identify all the sounds in order.

TASK 5 Individual test

Call on different children to identify two or more sounds in task 4.

TASK 6 Teacher crosses out sounds

a. **You told me every sound. Get ready to do it again. This time I'll cross out each sound when you tell me what it is.**
b. Point to each sound. (Pause.) Say: **Get ready.** Touch the sound. *The children respond.* As you cross out the sound, say: **Goodbye, _____ .**

TASK 28   Picture comprehension

a. Everybody, look at the picture.
b. Ask these questions:
 1. What's happening in the picture? *The children respond.*
 The old man is riding the horse.
 2. Does the old man look like he's having fun? *Yes.*
 3. Is the horse having fun? *Yes.*
 4. What would you do if you had a real horse? *The children respond.*

Take-Home 150

SUMMARY OF INDEPENDENT ACTIVITY

TASK 29   Introduction to independent activity

a. Pass out sides 1 and 2 of Take-Home 150 to each child.
b. Everybody, do a good job on your take-home today and I'll give you a bonus take-home.
c. Hold up side 1 of your take-home. You're going to do this take-home on your own. Tell the children when they will work the items. Let's go over some of the things you're going to do.

TASK 30   Reading comprehension

a. Point to the reading-comprehension exercise on side 2.
b. Everybody, get ready to read the sentences in the box the fast way.
c. First word. Check children's responses. Get ready. Clap for each word as the children read the sentences:
 A girl had a horse. She went riding on a horse.
d. Point to items 1 and 2. These items tell about the story in the box. You're going to read each item and circle the right answer.

TASK 31   Sentence copying

a. Point to the dotted sentence in the sentence-copying exercise.
b. You're going to trace the words in this sentence. Then you're going to write the sentence on the other lines.
c. Reading the fast way. First word. Check children's responses. Get ready. Clap for each word.
d. After you finish your take-home, you get to draw a picture about the sentence, **they went riding**. You'll draw your picture on a piece of plain paper. When the children finish their take-homes, give them sheets of plain paper.

TASK 32   Other independent activity: sides 1, 2, 3, 4

Remember to do all the parts of the take-home and to read all the parts carefully. After you draw your picture, I'll give you a bonus take-home.

INDIVIDUAL CHECKOUT: STORYBOOK

TASK 33   3½-minute individual checkout — 4 errors

a. As you are doing your take-home, I'll call on children one at a time to read the **whole story.** Remember, you get two stars if you read the story in less than three and a half minutes and make no more than four errors.
b. Call on a child. Tell the child: Start with the title and read the story carefully the fast way. Go. Time the child. Tell the child any words the child misses. Stop the child as soon as the child makes the fifth error or exceeds the time limit.
c. If the child meets the rate-accuracy criterion, record two stars on your chart for lesson 150. Congratulate the child. Give children who do not earn two stars a chance to read the story again before the next lesson is presented.

133 words/3.5 min = 38 wpm [4 errors]

END OF LESSON 150

Before presenting lesson 151, give Mastery Test 29 to each child.
Do not present lesson 151 to any groups that are not firm on this test.

READING VOCABULARY

Do not touch any small letters.

TASK 7   Children sound out the word and tell what word

a. Touch the ball for **pāint.**   Sound it out.
b. Get ready. Touch **p, ā, n, t** as the children say *pāāānnnt.*
                              If sounding out is not firm, repeat *b.*

c. What word? (Signal.) *Paint.*   Yes, **paint.**

pāint

TASK 8   Children read the fast way

a. Get ready to read these words the fast way.
b. Touch the ball for **men.** (Pause three seconds.)   Get ready.
                                          (Signal.) *Men.*

c. Repeat *b* for the remaining words on the page.

men

TASK 9   Children read the fast way again

a. Get ready to do these words again. Watch where I point.
b. Point to a word. (Pause one second.) Say: Get ready.   (Signal.)
          The children respond. Point to the words in this order:
                                    shots, men, up, pāint.

c. Repeat *b* until firm.

shots

TASK 10   Individual test

Call on different children to read one word the fast way.

up

Story 150

TASK 25   First reading—children read the title and first three sentences

a. Pass out Storybook 3.

b. Open your book to page 31.

c. Everybody, touch the title of the story and get ready to read the words in the title the fast way.

d. First word. Check children's responses. (Pause two seconds.)
Get ready. Clap. *The.*

e. Clap for each remaining word in the title.

f. After the children have read the title, ask: What's this story about?
(Signal.) *The old man finds a horse.*
Yes, **the old man finds a horse.**

g. Everybody, get ready to read this story the fast way.

h. First word. Check children's responses. (Pause two seconds.)
Get ready. Clap. *An.*

i. Clap for the remaining words in the first sentence. Pause at least two seconds between claps.

j. Repeat *h* and *i* for the next two sentences. Have the children reread the first three sentences until firm.

TASK 26   Individual children or the group read sentences to complete the first reading

a. I'm going to call on different children to read a sentence.
Everybody, follow along and point to the words. If you hear a mistake, raise your hand.

b. Call on a child. Read the next sentence. Do not clap for the words. Let the child read at his own pace, but be sure he reads the sentence correctly.

To correct	Have the child sound out the word. Then return to the beginning of the sentence.

c. Repeat *b* for most of the remaining sentences in the story.
Occasionally have the group read a sentence. When the group is to read, say: Everybody, read the next sentence. (Pause two seconds.) Get ready. Clap for each word in the sentence. Pause at least two seconds between claps.

TASK 27   Second reading—individual children or the group read each sentence; the group answer questions

a. You're going to read the story again. This time I'm going to ask questions.

b. Starting with the first word of the title. Check children's responses. Get ready. Clap as the children read the title. Pause at least two seconds between claps.

c. Call on a child. Read the first sentence. *The child responds.*

d. Repeat *b* and *c* in task 26. Present the following comprehension questions to the entire group.

After the children read:	You say:
The old man finds a horse.	What's this story about? (Signal.) *The old man finds a horse.*
"I can not find a man that will ride on me."	What did he say? (Signal.) *I can not find a man that will ride on me.* Where was the old horse? (Signal.) *In a barn.*
"Have you seen a horse that I can ride?"	What did the old man say? (Signal.) *Have you seen a horse that I can ride?*
The old man said, "Old horse, do you like to go for a ride?"	What did he say? (Signal.) *Old horse, do you like to go for a ride?* What do you think the horse will say? *The children respond.* Let's read and find out.
The old horse said, "Yes."	Did the horse want to go for a ride? (Signal.) *Yes.* Everybody, what's the title of this story? (Signal.) *The old man finds a horse.* And what happened in the story? (Signal.) *The old man found a horse.*

TASK 11   Children read the fast way

a. Get ready to read these words the fast way.
b. Touch the ball for **lift.** (Pause three seconds.) Get ready.
(Signal.) *Lift.*

c. Repeat *b* for the remaining words on the page.

TASK 12   Children read the fast way again

a. Get ready to do these words again. Watch where I point.
b. Point to a word. (Pause one second.) Say: Get ready. (Signal.)
The children respond. Point to the words in this order:
with, lots, get, lift.

c. Repeat *b* until firm.

TASK 13   Individual test

Call on different children to read one word the fast way.

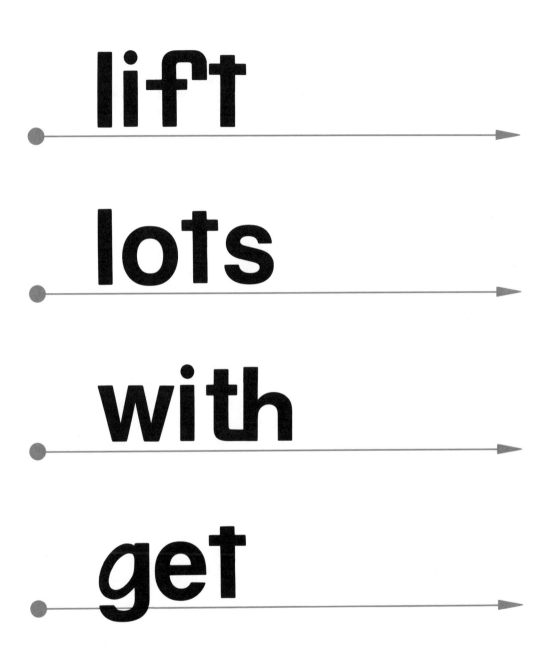

TASK 19 **Children sound out an irregular word (your)**

a. Touch the ball for **your.** Sound it out.

b. Get ready. Quickly touch each sound as the children say

yyyooouuurrr.

c. Again. Repeat *b* until firm.

d. That's how we sound out the word. Here's how we say the word. **Your.** How do we say the word? (Signal.) *Your.*

e. Now you're going to sound out the word. Get ready.
Touch each sound as the children say *yyyooouuurrr.*

f. Now you're going to say the word. Get ready. (Signal.) *Your.*

g. Repeat *e* and *f* until firm.

h. Yes, this word is **your. Your** daddy is a man.

your

TASK 20 **Individual test**

Call on different children to do *e* and *f* in task 19.

TASK 21 **Children identify, then sound out an irregular word (other)**

a. Touch the ball for **other.** Everybody, you're going to read this word the fast way. (Pause three seconds.) Get ready.
Move your finger quickly along the arrow. *Other.* Yes, **other.**

b. Now you're going to sound out the word. Get ready.
Quickly touch **o, th, er** as the children say *ooothhththerrr.*

c. Again. Repeat *b.*

d. How do we say the word? (Signal.) *Other.* Yes, **other.**

e. Repeat *b* and *d* until firm.

other

TASK 22 **Individual test**

Call on different children to do *b* and *d* in task 21.

TASK 23 **Children read the words the fast way**

Have the children read the words on this page the fast way.

TASK 24 **Individual test**

Call on different children to read one word the fast way.

TASK 14   Children identify, then sound out an irregular word (of)

a. Touch the ball for **of.** **Everybody, you're going to read this word the fast way.** (Pause three seconds.) **Get ready.** Move your finger quickly along the arrow. *Of.* **Yes, of.**

b. **Now you're going to sound out the word. Get ready.** Quickly touch **o, f** as the children say *ooofff.*

c. **Again.** Repeat *b.*

d. **How do we say the word?** (Signal.) *Of.* **Yes, of.**

e. Repeat *b* and *d* until firm.

TASK 15   Individual test

Call on different children to do *b* and *d* in task 14.

TASK 16   Children read the fast way

a. **Get ready to read these words the fast way.**

b. Touch the ball for **then.** (Pause three seconds.) **Get ready.** (Signal.) *Then.*

c. Repeat *b* for the remaining words on the page.

TASK 17   Children read the fast way again

a. **Get ready to do these words again. Watch where I point.**

b. Point to a word. (Pause one second.) Say: **Get ready.** (Signal.) *The children respond.* Point to the words in this order: **hēre, then, of, there.**

c. Repeat *b* until firm.

TASK 18   Individual test

Call on different children to read one word the fast way.

Do not touch any small letters.

TASK 15 Children read a word beginning with two consonants (stand)

a. Cover **s.** Run your finger under **tand.** You're going to sound out this part. Get ready. Touch **t, a, n, d** as the children say *taaannnd.*

b. Say it fast. (Signal.) *Tand.* Yes, this part is **tand.**

c. Uncover **s.** Point to **s.** You're going to say this first. Move your finger quickly under **tand.** Then you're going to say (pause) **tand.**

d. Point to **s.** What are you going to say first? (Signal.) *sss.* What are you going to say next? (Signal.) *Tand.*

e. Repeat **d** until firm.

f. Touch the ball for **stand.** Get ready. Move to **s,** then quickly along the arrow. *Ssstand.*

g. Say it fast. (Signal.) *Stand.* Yes, what word? (Signal.) *Stand.* Yes, **stand.** Good reading.

h. Again. Repeat *f* and *g* until firm.

i. Now you're going to sound out (pause) **stand.** Get ready. Touch **s, t, a, n, d** as the children say *ssstaaannnd.* What word? (Signal.) *Stand.* Yes, **stand.**

stand

TASK 16 Children sound out an irregular word (barn)

a. Touch the ball for **barn.** Sound it out.

b. Get ready. Quickly touch each sound as the children say *baaarrrnnn.*

c. Again. Repeat *b* until firm.

d. That's how we <u>sound out</u> the word. Here's how we <u>say</u> the word. **Barn.** How do we <u>say</u> the word? (Signal.) *Barn.*

e. Now you're going to <u>sound out</u> the word. Get ready. Touch each sound as the children say *baaarrrnnn.*

f. Now you're going to say the word. Get ready. (Signal.) *Barn.*

g. Repeat *e* and *f* until firm.

h. Yes, this word is **barn.** The horse is in the **barn.**

barn

TASK 17 Individual test

Call on different children to do *e* and *f* in task 16.

TASK 18 Children read the words the fast way

Have the children read the words on this page the fast way.

Story 122

TASK 19 First reading—children read the story the fast way

Have the children reread any sentences containing words that give them trouble. Keep a list of these words.

a. Pass out Storybook 2.
b. Open your book to page 13.
c. Everybody, touch the title of the story and get ready to read the words in the title the fast way.

d. First word. Check children's responses. (Pause two seconds.)
Get ready. Clap. *The.*

e. Clap for each remaining word in the title.
f. After the children have read the title, ask: What's this story about?
(Signal.) *The cow on the road.* Yes, **the cow on the road.**
g. Everybody, get ready to read this story the fast way.
h. First word. Check children's responses. (Pause two seconds.)
Get ready.   Clap. *Lots.*

i. Clap for the remaining words in the first sentence. Pause at least two seconds between claps.
j. Repeat *h* and *i* for the next two sentences. Have the children reread the first three sentences until firm.
k. The children are to read the remainder of the story the fast way, stopping at the end of each sentence.
l. After the first reading of the story, print on the board the words that the children missed more than one time. Have the children sound out each word one time and tell what word.
m. After the group's responses are firm, call on individual children to read the words.

TASK 20 Individual test

a. Turn back to page 13. I'm going to call on different children to read a whole sentence.
b. Call on different children to read a sentence. Do not clap for each word.

TASK 21 Second reading—children read the story the fast way and answer questions

a. You're going to read the story again the fast way and I'll ask questions.
b. Starting with the first word of the title.   Check children's responses. Get ready. Clap. *The.*
c. Clap for each remaining word. Pause at least two seconds between claps. Pause longer before words that gave the children trouble during the first reading.
d. Ask the comprehension questions below as the children read.

After the children read:	You say:
The cow on the road.	What's this story about? (Signal.) *The cow on the road.*
Lots of men went in a little car.	Who went in the little car? (Signal.) *Lots of men.*
The men said, "We will lift this cow."	What did they say? (Signal.) *We will lift this cow.* Do you think they'll lift her? *The children respond.* Let's read and find out.
The men did not lift the cow.	Did they lift her? (Signal.) *No.*
"I can lift me."	What did the cow say? (Signal.) *I can lift me.*
So the men sat on the road and the cow went home in the car.	What happened? (Signal.) *The men sat on the road and the cow went home in the car.*

TASK 22 Picture comprehension

a. Everybody, look at the picture.
b. Ask these questions:
1. Do those men look happy? *No.*
2. Why couldn't they lift the cow? *The children respond.* *The cow was too fat.*
3. Do you think you could lift the cow? *The children respond.*

150

TASK 9 Children identify, then sound out an irregular word (talked)

a. Touch the ball for **talked.** Everybody, you're going to read this word the fast way. (Pause three seconds.) Get ready. Move your finger quickly along the arrow. *Talked.* Yes, **talked.**

b. Now you're going to sound out the word. Get ready. Quickly touch **t, a, l, k, d** as the children say *taaalllkd.*

c. Again. Repeat *b.*

d. How do we say the word? (Signal.) *Talked.* Yes, **talked.**

e. Repeat *b* and *d* until firm.

TASK 10 Individual test

Call on different children to do *b* and *d* in task 9.

TASK 11 Children sound out an irregular word (says)

a. Touch the ball for **says.** Sound it out.

b. Get ready. Quickly touch each sound as the children say *sssaaayyysss.*

c. Again. Repeat *b* until firm.

d. That's how we <u>sound out</u> the word. Here's how we <u>say</u> the word. **Says.** How do we <u>say</u> the word? (Signal.) *Says.*

e. Now you're going to <u>sound out</u> the word. Get ready. Touch each sound as the children say *sssaaayyysss.*

f. Now you're going to say the word. Get ready. (Signal.) *Says.*

g. Repeat *e* and *f* until firm.

h. Yes, this word is **says.** If the teacher **says** "Go," hold up a hand.

TASK 12 Individual test

Call on different children to do *e* and *f* in task 11.

TASK 13 Children sound out the word and tell what word

a. Touch the ball for **hōrse.** Sound it out.

b. Get ready. Touch **h, ō, r, s** as the children say *hōōōrrrsss.* If sounding out is not firm, repeat *b.*

c. What word? (Signal.) *Horse.* Yes, **horse.**

TASK 14 Children read the words the fast way

Have the children read the words on this page the fast way.

Do not touch any small letters.

Take-Home 122

READING COMPREHENSION
The children will need pencils.

TASK 23   Children choose the correct words to complete the sentences

a. Pass out Take-Home 122 to each child.

b. Point to the sentences in the box in the reading-comprehension exercise on side 1.

c. Everybody, touch this box on your take-home. Check children's responses.

d. Get ready to read the words in the box the fast way. First word. Check children's responses. Get ready. Clap for each word in the first sentence as the children read *the cow was on the road.* Pause at least two seconds between claps.

e. Have the children reread the sentence until firm.

f. Get ready to read the next sentence. First word. Check children's responses. Get ready. Clap for each word as the children read *the men got mad.*

g. Have the children reread the sentence until firm.

h. Listen. **The cow was on the road.** (Pause.) **The men got mad.** Everybody, get ready to tell me the answers. The cow was on the . . . . (Signal.) *Road.* Yes, **road.** The men got . . . . (Signal.) *Mad.* Yes, **mad.**

i. Repeat *h* until firm.

j. Everybody, touch item 1 below the box. Check children's responses. This item tells about the story in the box. Everybody, get ready to read item 1 the fast way. First word. Check children's responses. Get ready. Clap as the children read *the cow was on the . . . .*

k. Touch the word **car** on the next line. Check children's responses. Did the story say the cow was on the car? (Signal.) *No.*

To correct	Have the children reread the first sentence in the box. Then repeat the question.

Touch the word **rōad.** Check children's responses. Did the story say the cow was on the road? (Signal.) *Yes.* Touch the word **farm.** Check children's responses. Did the story say the cow was on the farm? (Signal.) *No.*

l. Which word is right? (Signal.) *Road.* Yes, **road.** Draw a circle around it. Check children's responses.

m. I'll read the sentences in the box. **The cow was on the road. The men got mad.**

n. Everybody, get ready to read item 2. First word. Check children's responses. Clap as the children read *the men got . . . .*

o. Touch the word **sad** on the next line. Check children's responses. Did the story say the men got sad? (Signal.) *No.* Touch the word **māde.** Check children's responses. Did the story say the men got made? (Signal.) *No.* Touch the word **mad.** Check children's responses. Did the story say the men got mad? (Signal.) *Yes.*

p. Which word is right? (Signal.) *Mad.* Yes, **mad.** So what do you do with **mad?** (Signal.) *Draw a circle around it.* Yes, draw a circle around it. Do it. Check children's responses.

READING VOCABULARY

Do not touch any small letters.

TASK 6   Children read the fast way

a. Get ready to read these words the fast way.

b. Touch the ball for **tēacher.** (Pause three seconds.) Get ready.
(Signal.) *Teacher.*

c. Repeat *b* for the remaining words on the page.

TASK 7   Children read the fast way again

a. Get ready to do these words again. Watch where I point.

b. Point to a word. (Pause one second.) Say: Get ready.   (Signal.)
The children respond. Point to the words in this order:
rīding, get, sēēn, tēacher, got.

c. Repeat *b* until firm.

TASK 8   Individual test

Call on different children to read one word the fast way.

tēacher

got

get

sēēn

rīding

SUMMARY OF INDEPENDENT ACTIVITY

TASK 24   Introduction to independent activity

a. Hold up side 1 of Take-Home 122.

b. Everybody, you're going to finish this take-home on your own.
Tell the children when they will work the remaining items.
Let's go over the things you're going to do.

TASK 25   Sentence copying

a. Point to the dotted sentence in the sentence-copying exercise.

b. You're going to trace the words in this sentence. Then you're
going to write the sentence on the other lines.

c. Reading the fast way. First word. Check children's responses.
Get ready. Clap. *The.*

d. Next word. Check children's responses. Get ready. Clap. *Cow.*

e. Repeat *d* for the remaining words.

f. After you finish your take-home, you get to draw a picture about
the sentence, **the cow sat in a car.** You'll draw your picture
on a piece of plain paper.

TASK 26   Cross-out game

Point to the boxed word in the Cross-out Game. Everybody, here's
the word you're going to cross out today. What word?
(Signal.) *Pet.* Yes, **pet.**

TASK 27   Sound writing

a. Point to the sound-writing exercise on side 2. Here are the
sounds you're going to write today. I'll touch the sounds.
You say them.

b. Touch each sound. *The children respond.*

c. Repeat the series until firm.

TASK 28   Pair relations

a. Point to the pair-relations exercise. Remember—you're going to
draw a line through the sentences in each box that do not
tell about the picture.

b. When the children finish their take-homes, give them sheets of
plain paper. Remind them to draw a picture that shows
the cow sat in a car.

END OF LESSON 122

Lesson 150

SOUNDS

TASK 1 Teaching ȳ as in mȳ

a. Point to ȳ. **My turn.** (Pause.) Touch ȳ and say: **ȳȳȳ(īīī).**
b. Point to ȳ. **Your turn. When I touch it, you say it.** (Pause.)
   Get ready. Touch ȳ. _ȳȳȳ._ Lift your finger.
c. **Again.** Touch ȳ. _ȳȳȳȳ._ Lift your finger.
d. Repeat c until firm.

TASK 2 Sounds firm-up

a. **Get ready to say the sounds when I touch them.**
b. Alternate touching ȳ and **j.** Point to the sound. (Pause one second.)
   Say: **Get ready.** Touch the sound. _The children respond._
c. When ȳ and **j** are firm, alternate touching ȳ, **j, e,** and **y** until all four sounds are firm.

TASK 3 Individual test

Call on different children to identify ȳ, **j, e,** or **y.**

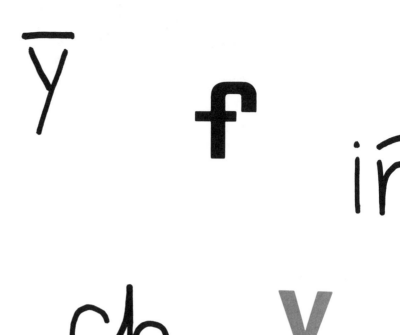

TASK 4 Sounds firm-up

a. Point to ȳ. **When I touch the sound, you say it.**
b. (Pause.) **Get ready.** Touch ȳ. _ȳȳȳ._
c. **Again.** Repeat b until firm.
d. **Get ready to say all the sounds when I touch them.**
e. Alternate touching ȳ, **f, ing, ch, v, x, oo,** and **er** three or four times. Point to the sound. (Pause one second.) Say: **Get ready.** Touch the sound. _The children respond._

TASK 5 Individual test

Call on different children to identify one or more sounds in task 4.

260

Lesson 123

SOUNDS

TASK 1   Teacher introduces cross-out game

a. Use acetate and crayon.
b. I'll cross out the sounds on this part of the page when you can tell me every sound.

c. Remember—when I touch it, you say it.
d. Go over the sounds until the children can identify all the sounds in order.

TASK 2   Individual test

Call on different children to identify two or more sounds in task 1.

g   h

b   t

b

TASK 3   Teacher crosses out sounds

a. You told me every sound. Get ready to do it again. This time I'll cross out each sound when you tell me what it is.
b. Point to each sound. (Pause.) Say: Get ready. Touch the sound.
The children respond. As you cross out the sound, say:
Goodbye, _____ .

b   r

ch

p   d

v

TASK 4   Sounds firm-up

a. Point to **b.** When I touch the sound, you say it.
b. (Pause.) Get ready. Touch **b.** *b.*
c. Again. Repeat *b* until firm.
d. Get ready to say all the sounds when I touch them.
e. Alternate touching **r, ch, b, p, d, v, e,** and **n** three or four times. Point to the sound.
(Pause one second.) Say:
Get ready. Touch the sound.
The children respond.

e

n

TASK 5   Individual test

Call on different children to identify one or more sounds in task 4.

TASK 21   Picture comprehension

a. What do you think you'll see in the picture? *The children respond.*
b. Turn the page and look at the picture.
c. Ask these questions:
   1. Is that an old car? (Signal.) *Yes.*
   2. What are those men doing? *The children respond.*
   3. Do you think it would be fun to sit in an old car like that? *The children respond.*

Take-Home 149

SUMMARY OF INDEPENDENT ACTIVITY

TASK 22   Introduction to independent activity

a. Pass out Take-Home 149 to each child.
b. Everybody, you're going to do this take-home on your own. Tell the children when they will work the items. Let's go over the things you're going to do.

TASK 23   Story items

a. Hold up side 1 of your take-home and point to the story-items exercise.
b. Everybody, here are items about the story we read today.
c. Think about what happened in the story and circle the right answer for each item.

TASK 24   Picture comprehension

a. Point to the pictures in the picture-comprehension exercise. Everybody, you're going to look at the picture. Then you're going to read each item and write the missing word.
b. Remember—the first sound of each missing word is already written in the blank.

TASK 25   Reading comprehension

a. Point to the reading-comprehension exercise on side 2.
b. Everybody, get ready to read the sentences in the box the fast way.
c. First word. Check children's responses. Get ready. Clap for each word as the children read the sentences: *A girl went riding in a car. She went to a farm.*
d. Point to items 1 and 2. These items tell about the story in the box. You're going to read each item and circle the right answer.

TASK 26   Sound writing

a. Point to the sound-writing exercise. Here are the sounds you're going to write today. I'll touch the sounds. You say them.
b. Touch each sound. *The children respond.*
c. Repeat the series until firm.

TASK 27   Sentence copying

a. Point to the dotted sentence in the sentence-copying exercise.
b. You're going to trace the words in this sentence. Then you're going to write the sentence on the other lines.
c. Reading the fast way. First word. Check children's responses. Get ready. Clap for each word.
d. After you finish your take-home, you get to draw a picture about the sentence, **the car did not start**. You'll draw your picture on a piece of plain paper. When the children finish their take-homes give them sheets of plain paper.

END OF LESSON 149

READING VOCABULARY

Do not touch any small letters.

TASK 6   Children read the fast way

a. Get ready to read these words the fast way.

b. Touch the ball for **there.** (Pause three seconds.) Get ready.

(Signal.) *There.*

c. Repeat *b* for the remaining words on the page.

TASK 7   Children read the fast way again.

a. Get ready to do these words again. Watch where I point.

b. Point to a word. (Pause one second.) Say: Get ready. (Signal.)

The children respond. Point to the words in this order:

then, there, this, the.

c. Repeat *b* until firm.

TASK 8   Individual test

Call on different children to read one word the fast way.

ther e

then

the

this

Story 149

TASK 18 First reading—children read the title and first three sentences

a. Pass out Storybook 3.

b. Open your book to page 28.

c. Everybody, touch the title of the story and get ready to read the words in the title the fast way.

d. First word. Check children's responses. (Pause two seconds.)

Get ready. Clap. *Will.*

e. Clap for each remaining word in the title.

f. After the children have read the title, ask: What's this story about? (Signal.) *Will the old car start?* Yes, **will the old car start.**

g. Everybody, get ready to read this story the fast way.

h. First word. Check children's responses. (Pause two seconds.)

Get ready. Clap. *A.*

i. Clap for the remaining words in the first sentence. Pause at least two seconds between claps.

j. Repeat *h* and *i* for the next two sentences. Have the children reread the first three sentences until firm.

TASK 19 Individual children or the group read sentences to complete the first reading

a. I'm going to call on different children to read a sentence. Everybody, follow along and point to the words. If you hear a mistake, raise your hand.

b. Call on a child. Read the next sentence. Do not clap for the words. Let the child read at his own pace, but be sure he reads the sentence correctly.

To correct	Have the child sound out the word. Then return to the beginning of the sentence.

c. Repeat *b* for most of the remaining sentences in the story. Occasionally have the group read a sentence. When the group is to read, say: Everybody, read the next sentence. (Pause two seconds.) Get ready. Clap for each word in the sentence. Pause at least two seconds between claps.

TASK 20 Second reading—individual children or the group read each sentence; the group answer questions

a. You're going to read the story again. This time I'm going to ask questions.

b. Starting with the first word of the title. Check children's responses. Get ready. Clap as the children read the title. Pause at least two seconds between claps.

c. Call on a child. Read the first sentence. *The child responds.*

d. Repeat *b* and *c* in task 19. Present the following comprehension questions to the entire group.

After the children read:	You say:
Will the old car start?	What are you going to find out in this story? (Signal.) *Will the old car start?*
The old car did not start.	What was wrong with the old car? (Signal.) *It did not start.*
"Rats do not have cars."	What did the rat say? (Signal.) *Rats do not have cars.* What did the man want the rat to do? (Signal.) *Start his car.*
"I can but I will not."	What did the big man say? (Signal.) *I can but I will not.* What did he say he will not do? (Signal.) *Start the car.*
"I never start cars if I am sitting."	What did the big man say? (Signal.) *I never start cars if I am sitting.*
So the big man got in the car and made the car start.	What happened? (Signal.) *The big man got in the car and made the car start.*
"So I will keep sitting in it."	Where is the big man going to keep sitting? *The children respond.* Yes, in the old car. Why does he want to sit there? *The children respond.* Yes, he likes the old car.

TASK 9   Children sound out the word and tell what word

a. Touch the ball for **chicks.**   Sound it out.

b. Get ready.   Touch **ch, i, c, s** as the children say *chiiicsss.*

If sounding out is not firm, repeat *b.*

c. What word?   (Signal.) *Chicks.*   Yes, **chicks.**

TASK 10   Children read the fast way

a. Get ready to read these words the fast way.

b. Touch the ball for **pet.** (Pause three seconds.)   Get ready.

(Signal.) *Pet.*

c. Repeat *b* for the remaining words on the page.

TASK 11   Children read the fast way again

a. Get ready to do these words again. Watch where I point.

b. Point to a word. (Pause one second.) Say: Get ready.   (Signal.)
The children respond. Point to the words in this order:
pāint, pet, sent, pig.

c. Repeat *b* until firm.

TASK 12   Individual test

Call on different children to read one word on the page the fast way.

Do not touch any small letters.

chicks

pet

sent

pig

pāint

TASK 12   Children sound out an irregular word (tart)

a. Touch the ball for **tart.** Sound it out.
b. Get ready.   Quickly touch each sound as the children say *taaarrrt.*
c. Again.   Repeat *b* until firm.
d. That's how we <u>sound out</u> the word. Here's how we <u>say</u> the word.
    Tart. How do we <u>say</u> the word?   (Signal.) *Tart.*
e. Now you're going to <u>sound out</u> the word. Get ready.
    Touch each sound as the children say *taaarrrt.*
f. Now you're going to say the word. Get ready.   (Signal.) *Tart.*
g. Repeat *e* and *f* until firm.
h. Yes, this word is **tart.**

tart

TASK 13   Individual test

Call on different children to do *e* and *f* in task 12.

TASK 14   Children rhyme with irregular word (tart)

a. Touch the ball for **tart.** Everybody, you're going to read this
   word the fast way. Get ready.   (Signal.) *Tart.*
b. Touch the ball for **start.** This word rhymes with   (pause) **tart.**
   Get ready.   Move to **s,** then quickly along the arrow. *Start.*
c. Repeat *a* and *b* until firm.

start

TASK 15   Individual test

Call on different children to do *e* and *f* in task 14.

TASK 16   Children read the words the fast way

Have the children read the words on this page the fast way.

TASK 17   Individual test

Call on different children to read one word the fast way.

TASK 13 Children sound out an irregular word (park)

a. Touch the ball for **park.** Sound it out.
b. Get ready. Quickly touch each sound as the children say *paaarrrk.*
c. Again. Repeat *b* until firm.
d. That's how we <u>sound out</u> the word. Here's how we <u>say</u> the word.
          Park. How do we <u>say</u> the word? (Signal.) *Park.*
e. Now you're going to <u>sound out</u> the word. Get ready.
          Touch each sound as the children say *paaarrrk.*
f. Now you're going to say the word. Get ready. (Signal.) *Park.*
g. Repeat *e* and *f* until firm.
h. Yes, this word is **park.** There are swings in that **park.**
i. Call on different children to do *e* and *f.*

TASK 14 Children sound out the word and tell what word

a. Touch the ball for **bug.** Sound it out.
b. Get ready. Touch **b, u, g** as the children say *buuug.*
          If sounding out is not firm, repeat *b.*
c. What word? (Signal.) *Bug.* Yes, **bug.**

TASK 15 Children sound out the word and tell what word

Repeat the procedures in task 14 for **duck.**

TASK 16 Children sound out an irregular word (girl)

a. Touch the ball for **girl.** Sound it out.
b. Get ready. Quickly touch each sound as the children say *giiirrrlll.*
c. Again. Repeat *b* until firm.
d. That's how we <u>sound out</u> the word. Here's how we <u>say</u> the word
          Girl. How do we <u>say</u> the word? (Signal.) *Girl.*
e. Now you're going to <u>sound out</u> the word. Get ready.
          Touch each sound as the children say *giiirrrlll.*
f. Now you're going to say the word. Get ready. (Signal.) *Girl.*
g. Repeat *e* and *f* until firm.
h. Yes, this word is **girl.** The little **girl** has black hair.
i. Call on different children to do *e* and *f.*

TASK 17 Children read the words the fast way

Have children read the words on this page the fast way.

Do not touch any small letters.

park

bug

duck

girl

149

TASK 10   Children read bring and bringing

a. Cover **b.** Point to **ring.** You're going to read this part of the word the fast way. (Pause three seconds.) **Get ready.** (Signal.) *Ring.* Yes, **ring.**

b. Uncover **b.** Point to **b.** You're going to say this first. Move your finger quickly under **ring.** Then you're going to say (pause) **ring.**

c. Point to **b.** What are you going to say first? (Signal.) *b.* What are you going to say next? (Signal.) *Ring.*

d. Repeat *c* until firm.

e. Touch the ball for **bring.** **Get ready.** Move to **b,** then quickly along the arrow. *Bring.*

f. **Say it fast.** (Signal.) *Bring.* Yes, what word? (Signal.) *Bring.* Yes, **bring.** Good reading.

g. **Again.** Repeat *e* and *f* until firm.

h. Return to the ball for **bring.** Yes, this word is **bring.**

i. Touch the ball for **bringing.** So this must be **bring** . . . . Touch **ing.** *Ing.* What word? (Signal.) *Bringing.* Yes, **bringing.**

j. **Again.** Repeat *h* and *i* until firm.

k. Touch the ball for **bring.** This word is **bring.** Touch the ball for **bringing.** So this must be . . . . Quickly run your finger under **bring** and tap **ing.** *Bringing.* Yes, **bringing.**

l. **Again.** Repeat *k* until firm.

m. **Now you're going to sound out** (pause) **bringing.** Get ready. Touch **b, r, ing, ing** as the children say *brrriiingiiing.* Yes, what word? (Signal.) *Bringing.* Yes, **bringing.**

TASK 11   Children read tēach and tēacher

a. Touch the ball for **tēach.** You're going to read this word the fast way. (Pause three seconds.) **Get ready.** Move your finger quickly along the arrow. *Teach.*

b. Return to the ball for **tēach.** Yes, this word is **teach.**

c. Touch the ball for **tēacher.** So this must be **teach** . . . . Touch **er.** *Er.* What word? (Signal.) *Teacher.* Yes, **teacher.**

d. **Again.** Repeat *b* and *c* until firm.

e. Touch the ball for **tēach.** This word is **teach.**

f. Touch the ball for **tēacher.** So this must be . . . . Quickly run your finger under **tēach** and tap **er.** *Teacher.* Yes, **teacher.**

g. **Again.** Repeat *e* and *f* until firm.

h. **Now you're going to sound out** (pause) **teacher.** Get ready. Touch **t, ē, ch, er** as the children say *tēēēcherr.* Yes, what word? (Signal.) *Teacher.* Yes, **teacher.**

Do not touch any small letters.

bring

bringing

tēach

tēacher

Story 123

TASK 18 First reading—children read the story the fast way

Have the children reread any sentences containing words that give them trouble. Keep a list of these words.

a. Pass out Storybook 2.
b. Open your book to page 16.
c. Everybody, touch the title of the story and get ready to read the words in the title the fast way.
d. First word. Check children's responses. (Pause two seconds.) Get ready. Clap. *A.*
e. Clap for each remaining word in the title.
f. After the children have read the title, ask: What's this story about? (Signal.) *A girl and a goat.* Yes, **a girl and a goat.**
g. Everybody, get ready to read this story the fast way.
h. First word. Check children's responses. (Pause two seconds.) Get ready. Clap. *A.*
i. Clap for the remaining words in the first sentence. Pause at least two seconds between claps.
j. Repeat *h* and *i* for the next two sentences. Have the children reread the first three sentences until firm.
k. The children are to read the remainder of the story the fast way, stopping at the end of each sentence.
l. After the first reading of the story, print on the board the words that the children missed more than one time. Have the children sound out each word one time and tell what word.
m. After the group's responses are firm, call on individual children to read the words.

TASK 19 Individual test

a. Look at page 16. I'm going to call on different children to read a whole sentence.

b. Call on different children to read a sentence. Do not clap for each word.

TASK 20 Second reading—children read the story the fast way and answer questions

a. You're going to read the story again the fast way and I'll ask questions.

b. Starting with the first word of the title. Check children's responses. Get ready. Clap. *A.*

c. Clap for each remaining word. Pause at least two seconds between claps. Pause longer before words that gave the children trouble during the first reading.

d. Ask the comprehension questions below as the children read.

After the children read:	You say:
A girl and a goat.	What's this story about? (Signal.) *A girl and a goat.*
She met a goat.	Who did she meet? (Signal.) *A goat.* Where was she going? (Signal.) *To a farm.*
"We will pet a pig."	What did she say? (Signal.) *We will pet a pig.*
"I do not pet pigs."	What did the goat say? (Signal.) *I do not pet pigs.*
"I will go to the park and pet a duck."	What did the goat say? (Signal.) *I will go to the park and pet a duck.* Is the goat going to the farm? (Signal.) *No.* Where's the goat going? (Signal.) *To the park.*
And the girl went to the farm to pet a pig.	What did the goat do? (Signal.) *The goat went to the park to pet a duck.* What did the girl do? (Signal.) *She went to the farm to pet a pig.*

READING VOCABULARY

TASK 5   Children sound out an irregular word (says)

a. Touch the ball for **says.** Sound it out.
b. Get ready. Quickly touch each sound as the children say
sssaaayyysss.

To correct	If the children do not say the sounds you touch **1.** Say: **You've got to say the sounds I touch.** **2.** Repeat *a* and *b* until firm.

c. Again. Repeat *b* until firm.
d. That's how we <u>sound out</u> the word. Here's how we <u>say</u> the word.
Says. How do we <u>say</u> the word? (Signal.) *Says.*
e. Now you're going to <u>sound out</u> the word. Get ready.
Touch each sound as the children say *sssaaayyysss.*
f. Now you're going to say the word. Get ready. (Signal.) *Says.*
g. Repeat *e* and *f* until firm.
h. Yes, this word is **says.** When the teacher **says** "Go," stand up.

TASK 6   Individual test

Call on different children to do *e* and *f* in task 5.

TASK 7   Children read the fast way

a. Get ready to read these words the fast way.
b. Touch the ball for **fill.** (Pause three seconds.) Get ready.
(Signal.) *Fill.*
c. Repeat *b* for the remaining words on the page.

TASK 8   Children read the fast way again

a. Get ready to do these words again. Watch where I point.
b. Point to a word. (Pause one second.) Say: Get ready. (Signal.)
The children respond. Point to the words in this order:
jump, fill, never, stop.
c. Repeat *b* until firm.

TASK 9   Individual test

Call on different children to read one word on the page the fast way.

says

fill

stop

never

jump

TASK 21   Picture comprehension

a. What do you think you'll see in the picture? *The children respond.*

b. Turn the page and look at the picture.

c. *Ask these questions:*

   1. Where is the girl? *The children respond.*   On a farm.

   2. What is she doing? *The children respond.*   Petting a pig.

   3. Did you ever pet a pig? *The children respond.*

Take-Home 123

READING COMPREHENSION

The children will need pencils.

TASK 22   Children choose the correct words to complete the sentences

a. Pass out Take-Home 123 to each child.

b. Point to the sentences in the box in the reading-comprehension exercise on side 1.

c. Everybody, touch this box on your take-home.
Check children's responses.

d. Get ready to read the words in the box the fast way. First word.
Check children's responses.   Get ready. Clap for each word in the first sentence as the children read *the goat went to the park.*
Pause at least two seconds between claps.

e. Have the children reread the sentence until firm.

f. Get ready to read the next sentence. First word. Check children's responses.   Get ready. Clap for each word as the children read *the girl went to the farm.*

g. Have the children reread the sentence until firm.

h. Listen. **The goat went to the park.** (Pause.)   **The girl went to the farm.** Everybody, get ready to tell me the answers.
The goat went . . . . (Signal.) *To the park.*   Yes, **to the park.**
The girl went to the . . . . (Signal.) *Farm.*   Yes, **farm.**

i. Repeat *h* until firm.

j. Everybody, touch item 1 below the box. Check children's responses.
This item tells about the story in the box.
Everybody, get ready to read item 1 the fast way.
First word. Check children's responses.
Get ready. Clap as the children read *the goat went . . . .*

k. Touch the words **in a car** on the next line. Check children's responses.   Did the story say the goat went in a car? (Signal.) *No.*

To correct	Have the children reread the first sentence in the box. Then repeat the question.

Touch the words **in the rain.** Check children's responses.
Did the story say the goat went in the rain? (Signal.) *No.*
Touch the words **to the park.** Check children's responses.
Did the story say the goat went to the park? (Signal.) *Yes.*

l. What words are right? (Signal.) *To the park.*   Yes, **to the park.**
Draw a circle around them. Check children's responses.

m. I'll read the sentences in the box. **The goat went to the park.**
The girl went to the farm.

n. Everybody, get ready to read item 2. First word. Check children's responses. Clap as the children read *the girl went to the . . . .*

o. Touch the word **car** on the next line. Check children's responses.
Did the story say the girl went to the car? (Signal.) *No.*
Touch the word **farm.** Check children's responses.
Did the story say the girl went to the farm? (Signal.) *Yes.*
Touch the word **park.** Check children's responses.
Did the story say the girl went to the park? (Signal.) *No.*

p. Which word is right? (Signal.) *Farm.*   Yes, **farm.** So what do you do with **farm**? (Signal.) *Draw a circle around it.*
Yes, draw a circle around it. Do it.
Check children's responses.

Lesson 149

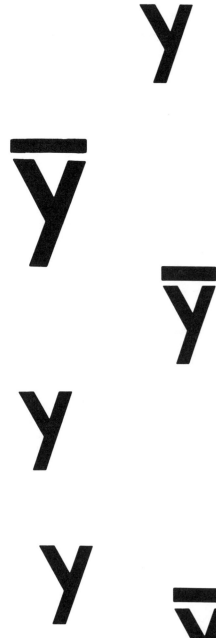

SOUNDS

TASK 1 Teacher firms up **y** as in **yes**
a. Point to **y**. Everybody, get ready to tell me this sound. Get ready.
   Touch y. *yyy.*
b. Point to **ȳ**. Everybody, look at the line over this sound. This is not **yyy**. Is it **yyy**? (Signal.) *No.*
c. Point to each sound and ask: Is this **yyy**? *The children respond.*
d. Repeat *c* until firm.

TASK 2 Teaching **ȳ** as in **mȳ**; children discriminate **y—ȳ**
a. Point to the first **ȳ**. Everybody, this is **ȳȳȳ** (**īīī**).
b. When I touch it, you say it. (Pause.) Get ready. Touch **ȳ**. *ȳȳȳ.*
c. Again. Touch **ȳ**. *ȳȳȳ.*
d. Repeat *c* until firm.
e. Get ready to do all these sounds. When I touch the sound, you say it. Alternate touching the sounds. Before touching each **ȳ**, trace the line and say: Remember—this is not **yyy**.
f. Repeat *e* until all the sounds are firm.

TASK 3 Sounds firm-up
a. Point to **ȳ**. When I touch the sound, you say it.
b. (Pause.) Get ready. Touch **ȳ**. *ȳȳȳ.*
c. Again. Repeat *b* until firm.
d. Get ready to say all the sounds when I touch them.
e. Alternate touching **ȳ**, **y**, **ī**, and **I** three or four times. Point to the sound. (Pause one second.) Say: Get ready. Touch the sound.
   The children respond.

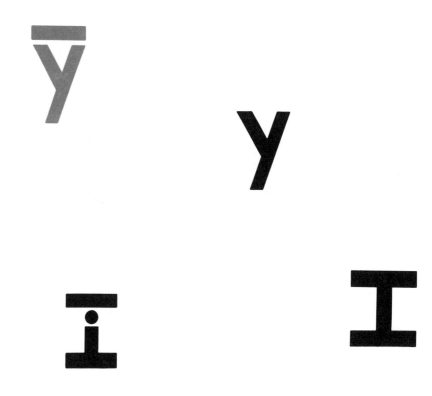

TASK 4 Individual test
Call on different children to identify one or more sounds in task 3.

SUMMARY OF INDEPENDENT ACTIVITY

TASK 23 Introduction to independent activity

a. Hold up side 1 of Take-Home 123.

b. Everybody, you're going to finish this take-home on your own.
Tell the children when they will work the remaining items.
Let's go over the things you're going to do.

TASK 24 Sentence copying

a. Point to the dotted sentence in the sentence-copying exercise.

b. You're going to trace the words in this sentence. Then you're going
to write the sentence on the other lines.

c. Reading the fast way. First word. Check children's responses.
Get ready. Clap. *It.*

d. Next word. Check children's responses. Get ready. Clap. *Is.*

e. Repeat *d* for the remaining words.

f. After you finish your take-home, you get to draw a picture about
the sentence, **it is fun to pet pigs**. You'll draw your picture on
a piece of plain paper.

TASK 25 Cross-out game

Point to the boxed word in the Cross-out Game. Everybody, here's
the word you're going to cross out today. What word? (Signal.)
Roads. Yes, **roads.**

TASK 26 Sound writing

a. Point to the sound-writing exercise on side 2. Here are the sounds
you're going to write today. I'll touch the sounds. You say them.

b. Touch each sound. *The children respond.*

c. Repeat the series until firm.

TASK 27 Pair relations

a. Point to the pair-relations exercise. Remember—you're going to
draw a line through the sentences in each box that do not tell
about the picture.

b. When the children finish their take-homes, give them sheets of plain
paper. Remind them to draw a picture that shows **it is fun
to pet pigs.**

END OF LESSON 123

TASK 20 Picture comprehension

a. Everybody, look at the picture.
b. Ask these questions:
1. What's happening in the picture? *The children respond.*
The girl is jumping into the pool.
2. Does that look like fun to you? *The children respond.*
3. What would you do if you had your own swimming pool?
The children respond.

Take-Home 148

SUMMARY OF INDEPENDENT ACTIVITY

TASK 21 Introduction to independent activity

a. Pass out Take-Home 148 to each child.
b. Everybody, you're going to do this take-home on your own.
Tell the children when they will work the items.
Let's go over the things you're going to do.

TASK 22 Story items

a. Hold up side 1 of your take-home and point to the story-items
exercise.
b. Everybody, here are items about the story we read today.
c. Think about what happened in the story and circle the right
answer for each item.

TASK 23 Picture comprehension

a. Point to the pictures in the picture-comprehension exercise.
Everybody, you're going to look at the picture. Then you're going
to read each item and write the missing word.
b. Remember—the first sound of each missing word is already
written in the blank.

TASK 24 Reading comprehension

a. Point to the reading-comprehension exercise on side 2.
b. Everybody, get ready to read the sentences in the box the fast way.
c. First word. Check children's responses. Get ready. Clap for each
word as the children read the sentences:
The man had a pet cow. He talked to the cow.
d. Point to items 1 and 2. These items tell about the story in the
box. You're going to read each item and circle the right answer.

TASK 25 Sound writing

a. Point to the sound-writing exercise. Here are the sounds you're
going to write today. I'll touch the sounds. You say them.
b. Touch each sound. *The children respond.*
c. Repeat the series until firm.

TASK 26 Sentence copying

a. Point to the dotted sentence in the sentence-copying exercise.
b. You're going to trace the words in this sentence. Then you're
going to write the sentence on the other lines.
c. Reading the fast way. First word. Check children's responses.
Get ready. Clap for each word.
d. After you finish your take-home, you get to draw a picture about
the sentence, **shē went to the moon**. You'll draw your picture
on a piece of plain paper. When the children finish their
take-homes, give them sheets of plain paper.

END OF LESSON 148

Lesson 124

SOUNDS

TASK 1 Teaching ing as in sing

a. Point to **ing**. Here's a new sound.
b. My turn. (Pause.) Touch **ing** and say: iiing.
c. Again. Touch **ing** for a longer time. iiiing. Lift your finger.
d. Point to **ing**. Your turn. When I touch it, you say it. (Pause.)
Get ready. Touch **ing**. *iiing.* Lift your finger.
e. Again. Touch **ing**. *iiiiing.* Lift your finger.
f. Repeat *e* until firm.

TASK 2 Individual test

Call on different children to identify **ing.**

TASK 3 Sounds firm-up

a. Get ready to say the sounds when I touch them.
b. Alternate touching **n** and **ing**. Point to the sound. (Pause one second.) Say: Get ready. Touch the sound. *The children respond.*
c. When **n** and **ing** are firm, alternate touching **ing, g, n,** and **i** until all four sounds are firm.

TASK 4 Individual test

Call on different children to identify **ing, g, n,** or **i.**

TASK 5 Sounds firm-up

a. Point to **ing**. When I touch the sound, you say it.
b. (Pause.) Get ready. Touch **ing**. *ing.*
c. Again. Repeat *b* until firm.
d. Get ready to say all the sounds when I touch them.
e. Alternate touching **l, u, ch, b, e, h, p,** and **ing** three or four times. Point to the sound. (Pause one second.) Say: Get ready. Touch the sound. *The children respond.*

TASK 6 Individual test

Call on different children to identify one or more sounds in task 5.

Story 148

TASK 17 First reading—children read the title and first three sentences

a. Pass out Storybook 3.

b. Open your book to page 25.

c. Everybody, touch the title of the story and get ready to read the words in the title the fast way.

d. First word. Check children's responses. (Pause two seconds.) **Get ready.** Clap. *Finding.*

e. Clap for each remaining word in the title.

f. After the children have read the title, ask: **What's this story about?** (Signal.) *Finding some fun on the moon.* **Yes, finding some fun on the moon.**

g. Everybody, get ready to read this story the fast way.

h. First word. Check children's responses. (Pause two seconds.) **Get ready.** Clap. *Some.*

i. Clap for the remaining words in the first sentence. Pause at least two seconds between claps.

j. Repeat *h* and *i* for the next two sentences. Have the children reread the first three sentences until firm.

TASK 18 Individual children or the group read sentences to complete the first reading

a. I'm going to call on different children to read a sentence. Everybody, follow along and point to the words. If you hear a mistake, raise your hand.

b. Call on a child. **Read the next sentence.** Do not clap for the words. Let the child read at his own pace, but be sure he reads the sentence correctly.

To correct	Have the child sound out the word. Then return to the beginning of the sentence.

c. Repeat *b* for most of the remaining sentences in the story. Occasionally have the group read a sentence. When the group is to read, say: **Everybody, read the next sentence.** (Pause two seconds.) **Get ready.** Clap for each word in the sentence. Pause at least two seconds between claps.

TASK 19 Second reading—individual children or the group read each sentence; the group answer questions

a. You're going to read the story again. This time I'm going to ask questions.

b. Starting with the first word of the title. Check children's responses. **Get ready.** Clap as the children read the title. Pause at least two seconds between claps.

c. Call on a child. **Read the first sentence.** *The child responds.*

d. Repeat *b* and *c* in task 18. Present the following comprehension questions to the entire group.

After the children read:	You say:
Finding some fun on the moon	**What's this story about?** (Signal.) *Finding some fun on the moon.*
A girl said, "I will find some fun."	**What did she say?** (Signal.) *I will find some fun.* **Where was she?** (Signal.) *On the moon.* **How did the girls get to the moon?** (Signal.) *In a moon ship.*
"Come with me."	**What did the cow say?** (Signal.) *We have lots of fun. Come with me.* **I wonder what kind of fun they have. Let's read and find out.**
She jumped into the pool.	**What did the cow do?** (Signal.) *She jumped into the pool.* **How do they have fun on the moon?** (Signal.) *Jumping into the pool.*
The girl did not tell the other girls that she went swimming with a moon cow.	**I wonder why she didn't tell the other girls about the pool.** *The children respond.*

READING VOCABULARY

Do not touch any small letters.

TASK 7   Children read the fast way

a. Get ready to read these words the fast way.

b. Touch the ball for **bug**. (Pause three seconds.) Get ready.

(Signal.) *Bug.*

c. Repeat *b* for the remaining words on the page.

TASK 8   Children read the fast way again

a. Get ready to do these words again. Watch where I point.

b. Point to a word. (Pause one second.) Say: Get ready. (Signal.)
The children respond. Point to the words in this order:
nōse, gō, gōing, his, bug.

c. Repeat *b* until firm.

TASK 9   Individual test

Call on different children to read one word the fast way.

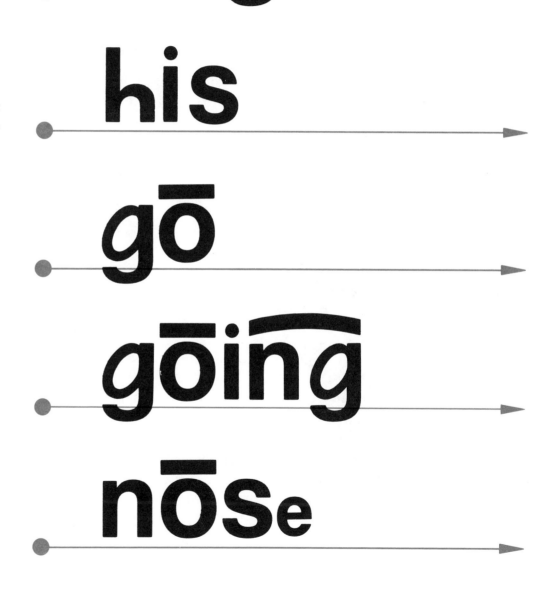

TASK 12   Children sound out an irregular word (some)

a. Touch the ball for **some.** Sound it out.
b. Get ready.   Quickly touch each sound as the children say

sssooommmeee.

To correct	If the children do not say the sounds you touch
	1. Say: **You've got to say the sounds I touch.**
	2. Repeat *a* and *b* until firm.

c. Again.   Repeat *b* until firm.
d. That's how we <u>sound out</u> the word. Here's how we <u>say</u> the word.
Some. How do we <u>say</u> the word?   (Signal.) *Some.*
e. Now you're going to <u>sound out</u> the word. Get ready.
Touch each sound as the children say *sssooommmeee.*
f. Now you're going to say the word. Get ready.   (Signal.) *Some.*
g. Repeat *e* and *f* until firm.
h. Yes, this word is **some.** Would you like to eat **some** cake?

TASK 13   Individual test

Call on different children to do *e* and *f* in task 12.

TASK 14   Children sound out the word and tell what word

a. Touch the ball for **jumped.** Sound it out.
b. Get ready.   Touch **j, u, m, p, d** as the children say *juuummmpd.*
If sounding out is not firm, repeat *b.*
c. What word?   (Signal.) *Jumped.* Yes, **jumped.**

TASK 15   Children read the words the fast way

a. Now you get to read the words on this page the fast way.
b. Touch the ball for **some.** (Pause three seconds.) Get ready.
Move your finger quickly along the arrow. *Some.*
c. Repeat *b* for **jumped.**

TASK 16   Individual test

Call on different children to read one word the fast way.

Do not touch any small letters.

TASK 10   Children identify, then sound out an irregular word (of)

a. Touch the ball for **of.** Everybody, you're going to read this word the fast way. (Pause three seconds.) Get ready. Move your finger quickly along the arrow. *Of.* Yes, **of.**

b. Now you're going to sound out the word. Get ready. Quickly touch **o, f** as the children say *ooofff.*

c. Again. Repeat *b.*

d. How do we say the word? (Signal.) *Of.* Yes, **of.**

e. Repeat *b* and *d* until firm.

TASK 11   Individual test

Call on different children to do *b* and *d* in task 10.

TASK 12   Children read the fast way

a. Get ready to read these words the fast way.

b. Touch the ball for **pāint.** (Pause three seconds.) Get ready. (Signal.) *Paint.*

c. Repeat *b* for **get.**

TASK 13   Children read the fast way again

a. Get ready to do these words again. Watch where I point.

b. Point to a word. (Pause one second.) Say: Get ready. (Signal.) *The children respond.* Point to the words in this order: **get, of, pāint.**

c. Repeat *b* until firm.

TASK 14   Individual test

Call on different children to read one word the fast way.

Do not touch any small letters.

TASK 8 Children rhyme with moon

a. Touch the ball for **moon.** You're going to read this word the
fast way. (Pause three seconds.) Get ready.
Move your finger quickly along the arrow. *Moon.*
b. Touch the ball for **soon.** This word rhymes with (pause) **moon.**
Move to **s,** then quickly along the arrow. *Soon.*
Yes, what word? (Signal.) *Soon.*

**TASK 9 Children read a word beginning with two consonants
(broke)**

a. Cover **b.** Run your finger under **rōke.** You're going to sound out
this part. Get ready. Touch **r, ō, k** as the children say *rrrōōōk.*
b. Say it fast. (Signal.) *Rōke.* Yes, this part is **rōke.**
c. Uncover **b.** Point to **b.** You're going to say this first.
Move your finger quickly under **rōke.** Then you're going to say
(pause) **rōke.**
d. Point to **b.** What are you going to say first? (Signal.) *b.*
What are you going to say next? (Signal.) *Rōke.*
e. Repeat *d* until firm.
f. Touch the ball for **brōke.** Get ready. Move to **b,** then quickly
along the arrow. *Broke.*
g. Say it fast. (Signal.) *Broke.* Yes, what word? (Signal.) *Broke.*
Yes, **broke.** Good reading.
h. Again. Repeat *f* and *g* until firm.
i. Now you're going to sound out (pause) **broke.** Get ready.
Touch **b, r, ō, k** as the children say *brrrōōōk.*
What word? (Signal.) *Broke.* Yes, **broke.**

TASK 10 Children read the words the fast way

Have the children read the words on this page the fast way.

TASK 11 Individual test

Call on different children to read one word the fast way.

Do not touch any small letters.

moon

soon

brōke

124

Do not touch any small letters.

TASK 15 **Children read kiss and kissed**

a. Touch the ball for **kiss.** You're going to read this word the fast way. (Pause three seconds.) Get ready. Move your finger quickly along the arrow. *Kiss.*

b. Return to the ball for **kiss.** Yes, this word is **kiss.**

c. Touch the ball for **kissed.** So this must be **kiss** . . . . Touch **d.** *d.* What word? (Signal.) *Kissed.* Yes, **kissed.**

d. Again. Repeat *b* and *c* until firm.

e. Touch the ball for **kiss.** This word is **kiss.**

f. Touch the ball for **kissed.** So this must be . . . . Quickly run your finger under **kiss** and tap **d.** *Kissed.* Yes, **kissed.**

g. Again. Repeat *e* and *f* until firm.

h. Now you're going to sound out (pause) **kissed.** Get ready. Touch **k, i,** between the **s**'s, **d** as the children say *kiiisssd.* Yes, what word? (Signal.) *Kissed.* Yes, **kissed.**

kiss

kissed

READING VOCABULARY

TASK 4   Children read a word beginning with two consonants (swimming)

a. Cover **s**. Run your finger under **wimming**. You're going to sound out this part. Get ready. Touch **w, i**, between the **m**'s, **ing** as the children say *wwwiiimmmiiing*.

b. Say it fast. (Signal.) *Wimming*. Yes, this part is **wimming**.

c. Uncover **s**. Point to **s**. You're going to say this first. Move your finger quickly under **wimming**. Then you're going to say (pause) **wimming**.

d. Point to **s**. What are you going to say first? (Signal.) *sss*. What are you going to say next? (Signal.) *Wimming*.

e. Repeat *d* until firm.

f. Touch the ball for **swimming**. Get ready. Move to **s**, then quickly along the arrow. *Ssswimming*.

g. Say it fast. (Signal.) *Swimming*. Yes, what word? (Signal.) *Swimming*. Yes, **swimming**. Good reading.

h. Again. Repeat *f* and *g* until firm.

i. Now you're going to sound out (pause) **swimming**. Get ready. Touch **s, w, i**, between the **m**'s, **ing** as the children say *ssswwwiiimmmiiing*. What word? (Signal.) *Swimming*. Yes, **swimming**.

TASK 5   Children read the fast way

a. Get ready to read these words the fast way.

b. Touch the ball for **jumps**. (Pause three seconds.) Get ready. (Signal.) *Jumps*.

c. Repeat *b* for the remaining words on the page.

TASK 6   Children read the fast way again

a. Get ready to do these words again. Watch where I point.

b. Point to a word. (Pause one second.) Say: Get ready. (Signal.) *The children respond.* Point to the words in this order: **jumps, pool, men.**

c. Repeat *b* until firm.

TASK 7   Individual test

Call on different children to read one word on the page the fast way.

swimming

jumps

men

pool

124

TASK 16 Children read the fast way

a. Get ready to read these words the fast way.

b. Touch the ball for **there.** (Pause three seconds.) Get ready.

(Signal.) *There.*

c. Repeat *b* for the remaining words on the page.

TASK 17 Children read the fast way again

a. Get ready to do these words again. Watch where I point.

b. Point to a word. (Pause one second.) Say: Get ready. (Signal.)
The children respond. Point to the words in this order:
them, this, there, thōse.

c. Repeat *b* until firm.

TASK 18 Individual test

Call on different children to read one word the fast way.

Do not touch any small letters.

there

them

thōse

this

Lesson 148

SOUNDS

TASK 1   Teacher and children play the sounds game

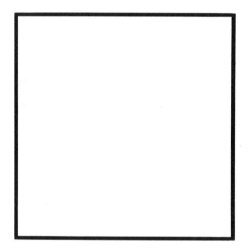

a. Use acetate and crayon. Write the sounds in the symbol box. Keep score in the score box.

b. I'm smart. I bet I can beat you in a game.

c. Here's the rule. When I touch a sound, you say it.

d. Play the game.
Make one symbol at a time in the symbol box. Use the symbols **ī, ing, b,** and **j.** Make each symbol quickly. (Pause.) Touch the symbol. Play the game for about two minutes.
Then ask: Who won? Draw a mouth on the face in the score box.

TASK 2   Child plays teacher

a. Use acetate and crayon.

b. [Child's name] is going to be the teacher.

c. [He or She] is going to touch the sounds. When [he or she] touches a sound, you say it.

d. The child points to and touches the sounds. You circle any sound that is not firm.

e. After the child has completed the page, present all the circled sounds to the children.

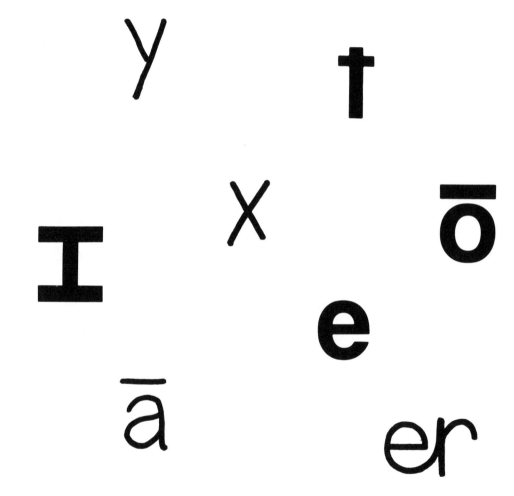

TASK 3   Individual test

Call on different children. If you can say the sound when I call your name, you may cross it out.

Story 124

TASK 19 First reading—children read the story the fast way

Have the children reread any sentences containing words that give them trouble. Keep a list of these words.

a. Pass out Storybook 2.
b. Open your book to page 19.
c. Everybody, touch the title of the story and get ready to read the words in the title the fast way.
d. First word. Check children's responses. (Pause two seconds.) Get ready. Clap. *Paint.*
e. Clap for each remaining word in the title.
f. After the children have read the title, ask: What's this story about? (Signal.) *Paint that nose.* Yes, **paint that nose.**
g. Everybody, get ready to read this story the fast way.
h. First word. Check children's responses. (Pause two seconds.) Get ready. Clap. *A.*
i. Clap for the remaining words in the first sentence. Pause at least two seconds between claps.
j. Repeat *h* and *i* for the next two sentences. Have the children reread the first three sentences until firm.
k. The children are to read the remainder of the story the fast way, stopping at the end of each sentence.
l. After the first reading of the story, print on the board the words that the children missed more than one time. Have the children sound out each word one time and tell what word.
m. After the group's responses are firm, call on individual children to read the words.

TASK 20 Individual test

a. Turn back to page 19. I'm going to call on different children to read a whole sentence.
b. Call on different children to read a sentence. Do not clap for each word.

TASK 21 Second reading—children read the story the fast way and answer questions

a. You're going to read the story again the fast way and I'll ask questions.
b. Starting with the first word of the title. Check children's responses. Get ready. Clap. *Paint.*
c. Clap for each remaining word. Pause at least two seconds between claps. Pause longer before words that gave the children trouble during the first reading.
d. Ask the comprehension questions below as the children read.

After the children read:	You say:
Paint that nose.	What's this story about? (Signal.) *Paint that nose.*
The fat dog had a red nose.	What did the fat dog have? (Signal.) *A red nose.*
The little dog had a red nose.	What did the little dog have? (Signal.) *A red nose.*
The little dog said, "I wish I did not have a red nose."	What did the little dog say? (Signal.) *I wish I did not have a red nose.*
He said, "Paint that nose."	What did the fat dog say? (Signal.) *Paint that nose.* Who said that? (Signal.) *The fat dog.*
Now the fat dog has paint on his ear.	Where does the fat dog have paint? (Signal.) *On his ear.* How did it get there? *The children respond.* The little dog kissed his ear.

TASK 22 Picture comprehension

a. Everybody, look at the picture.
b. Ask these questions:
1. What is that little dog doing? *The children respond.* He's kissing the fat dog on the ear. I bet he'll leave a big mark on that fat dog's ear.
2. Did you ever paint your nose? *The children respond.*

TASK 24   Picture comprehension

a. What do you think you'll see in the picture?   *The children respond.*
b. Turn the page and look at the picture.
c. Ask these questions:
  1. Why does Ann look so surprised?   *The children respond.*
                           Because the cat is talking.
  2. What's the cat saying?   *The children respond.* Yes, **I will not
     go with you.** I bet it would be a lot of fun to have a talking cat.

Take-Home 147

STORY ITEMS

The children will need pencils.

TASK 25   Children complete sentences and answer story questions

a. Pass out Take-Home 147 to each child.
b. Point to the story-items exercise on side 1. These items are about
                           the story you just read.
c. Point to the blank in item 1. Something is missing. When you get
     to this blank, say "**Blank.**" What will you say?   (Signal.) *Blank.*
d. Everybody, get ready to read item 1. Get ready.   Clap for each
                           word as the children read
     the girl said, "cats can not blank." Repeat until firm.
e. What goes in the blank?   (Signal.) *Talk.* Yes, **talk**.
 f. Everybody, read item 2 and when you come to a blank, say
     "**Blank.**" Get ready.   Clap for each word as the children read
                           ann said, "can I have that blank?" Repeat until firm.
g. What goes in the blank?   (Signal.) *Cat.* Yes, **cat**.
h. Everybody, read item 3 and when you come to a blank, say
     "**Blank.**" Get ready.   Clap for each word as the children read
                           the blank said, "I will not go with you." Repeat until firm.
 i. What goes in the blank?   (Signal.) *Cat.* Yes, **cat**.
 j. Everybody, read item 4 and when you come to a blank, say
     "**Blank.**" Get ready.   Clap for each word as the children read
                           ann said, "I will leave this blank." Repeat until firm.
k. What goes in the blank?   (Signal.) *Park.* Yes, **park**.
 l. Now, everybody, read each item to yourself and circle the right
                           answer. Check children's responses.

SUMMARY OF INDEPENDENT ACTIVITY

TASK 26   Introduction to independent activity

Hold up Take-Home 147. Everybody, you're going to finish this
     take-home on your own.   Tell the children when they will work the
                           remaining items. Let's go over the things you're going to do.

TASK 27   Picture comprehension

a. Point to the pictures on side 1. Everybody, you're going to look
                           at the picture. Then you're going to read each item and write the
                                                    missing word.
b. Remember—the first sound of each missing word is already
                                                    written in the blank.

TASK 28   Reading comprehension

a. Point to the reading-comprehension exercise on side 2.
b. Everybody, get ready to read the sentences in the box the fast way.
c. First word.   Check children's responses. Get ready.   Clap for each
                           word as the children read the sentences:
                           The man liked to swim. So he jumped into the lake.
d. Point to items 1 and 2. These items tell about the story in the
                           box. You're going to read each item and circle the right answer.

TASK 29   Sound writing

a. Point to the sound-writing exercise. Here are the sounds you're
                           going to write today. I'll touch the sounds. You say them.
b. Touch each sound. *The children respond.* Repeat until firm.

TASK 30   Sentence copying

a. Point to the dotted sentence in the sentence-copying exercise.
b. You're going to trace the words in this sentence. Then you're going
                           to write the sentence on the other lines.
c. Reading the fast way. First word.   Check children's responses.
                           Get ready.   Clap for each word.
d. After you finish your take-home, you get to draw a picture about
                           the sentence, **cats do not talk.** You'll draw your picture on a
     piece of plain paper.   When the children finish their take-homes,
                           give them sheets of plain paper.

END OF LESSON 147

Take-Home 124

CROSS-OUT GAME

The children will need pencils.

TASK 23 Children cross out **red** and circle **nōse**

---

a. Pass out Take-Home 124 to each child.

b. Hold up side 1 of your take-home and point to the Cross-out Game.

c. Everybody, here's a new Cross-out Game. The words in the box show what you're going to do. Point to the word **red**. Look at the word **red**. It's crossed out. So you're going to cross out every word **red**.

d. Point to the word **nōse**. Look at the word **nose**. It's circled. So you're going to circle every word **nose**.

e. Everybody, touch a word that you're going to cross out. Check children's responses.

f. Touch a word that you're going to circle. Check children's responses.

g. Everybody, circle every word **nose** and cross out every word **red**. Check children's responses.

SUMMARY OF INDEPENDENT ACTIVITY

TASK 24 Introduction to independent activity

a. Hold up side 1 of Take-Home 124.

b. Everybody, you're going to finish this take-home on your own. Tell the children when they will work the remaining items. Let's go over the things you're going to do.

TASK 25 Sentence copying

a. Point to the dotted sentence in the sentence-copying exercise.

b. You're going to trace the words in this sentence. Then you're going to write the sentence on the other lines.

c. Reading the fast way. First word. Check children's responses. Get ready. Clap. *He.*

d. Next word. Check children's responses. Get ready. Clap. *Had.*

e. Repeat *d* for the remaining words.

f. After you finish your take-home, you get to draw a picture about the sentence, **hē had a red nōse.** You'll draw your picture on a piece of plain paper.

TASK 26 Reading comprehension

---

a. Point to the boxed sentences in the reading-comprehension exercise.

b. Everybody, get ready to read the sentences the fast way.

c. First word. Check children's responses. Get ready. Clap for each word as the children read *the little dog had a red nose.*

d. Have the children reread the sentence until firm.

e. Get ready to read the next sentence. Repeat *c* and *d* for **hē was mad.**

f. Point to items 1 and 2. These items tell about the story in the box. You're going to read each item and circle the right answer.

TASK 27 Sound writing

a. Point to the sound-writing exercise on side 2. Here are the sounds you're going to write today. I'll touch the sounds. You say them.

b. Touch each sound. *The children respond.*

c. Repeat the series until firm.

TASK 28 Pair relations

a. Point to the pair-relations exercise. Remember—you're going to draw a line through the sentences in each box that do not tell about the picture.

b. When the children finish their take-homes, give them sheets of plain paper. Remind them to draw a picture that shows **hē had a red nose.**

END OF LESSON 124

Story 147

TASK 21 First reading—children read the title and first three sentences

a. Pass out Storybook 3.

b. Open your book to page 22. Now you're going to finish the story about the girl and the talking cat.

c. Everybody, touch the title of the story and get ready to read the words in the title the fast way.

d. First word. Check children's responses. (Pause two seconds.) Get ready. Clap. *The.*

e. Clap for each remaining word in the title.

f. After the children have read the title, ask: What's this story about? (Signal.) *The cat that talked.* Yes, **the cat that talked**.

g. Everybody, get ready to read this story the fast way.

h. First word. Check children's responses. (Pause two seconds.) Get ready. Clap. *A.*

i. Clap for the remaining words in the first sentence. Pause at least two seconds between claps.

j. Repeat h and i for the next two sentences. Have the children reread the first three sentences until firm.

TASK 22 Individual children or the group read sentences to complete the first reading

a. I'm going to call on different children to read a sentence. Everybody, follow along and point to the words. If you hear a mistake, raise your hand.

b. Call on a child. Read the next sentence. Do not clap for the words. Let the child read at his own pace, but be sure he reads the sentence correctly.

To correct	Have the child sound out the word. Then return to the beginning of the sentence.

c. Repeat b for most of the remaining sentences in the story. Occasionally have the group read a sentence. When the group is to read, say: Everybody, read the next sentence. (Pause two seconds.) Get ready. Clap for each word in the sentence. Pause at least two seconds between claps.

TASK 23 Second reading—individual children or the group read each sentence; the group answer questions

a. You're going to read the story again. This time I'm going to ask questions.

b. Starting with the first word of the title. Check children's responses. Get ready. Clap as the children read the title. Pause at least two seconds between claps.

c. Call on a child. Read the first sentence. *The child responds.*

d. Repeat b and c in task 22. Present the following comprehension questions to the entire group.

After the children read:	You say:
"Cats can not talk."	What did the girl say? (Signal.) *Cats can not talk.* Where were the girl and the cat? (Signal.) *In the park.* Do you remember what the cat said to her? (Signal.) *I can talk to you.*
The girl gave the cat a big hug.	How do you give a cat a big hug? *The children respond.*
The cat said, "I never had a cat that talked either."	What did the cat say? (Signal.) *I never had a cat that talked either.* That's silly.
She went up to the girl and said, "Can I have that cat?"	What did she say? (Signal.) *Can I have that cat?* Who said that? (Signal.) *Ann.* What do you think will happen? *The children respond.*
The cat said, "I will not go with you."	What did the cat say? (Signal.) *I will not go with you.* What do you think Ann will do now? *The children respond.*
"I will leave this park."	What did Ann say? *The children respond.* I'll bet Ann was surprised to hear that cat talk.
And she did.	What did she do? (Signal.) *She left the park.*

Lesson 125

SOUNDS

TASK 1   Teaching **ing** as in **sing**

a. Point to **ing.** My turn.   (Pause.)
Touch **ing** and say: iiing.
b. Point to **ing.** Your turn. When
I touch it, you say it.   (Pause.)
Get ready.   Touch **ing.** iiing.
Lift your finger.
c. Again.   Touch **ing.** iiiing.
Lift your finger.
d. Repeat c until firm.

TASK 2   Sounds firm-up

a. Get ready to say the sounds
when I touch them.
b. Alternate touching **b** and **ing.**
Point to the sound. (Pause one
second.) Say: Get ready.   Touch
the sound. *The children respond.*
c. When **b** and **ing** are firm, alternate
touching **b, i, ing,** and **n** until all
four sounds are firm.

TASK 3   Individual test

Call on different children to identify
b, i, ing, or **n.**

TASK 4   Teacher introduces cross-out game

a. Use acetate and crayon.
b. I'll cross out the sounds on this part of the page when you can tell
me every sound.
c. Remember—when I touch it, you say it.
d. Go over the sounds until the children can identify all the sounds
in order.

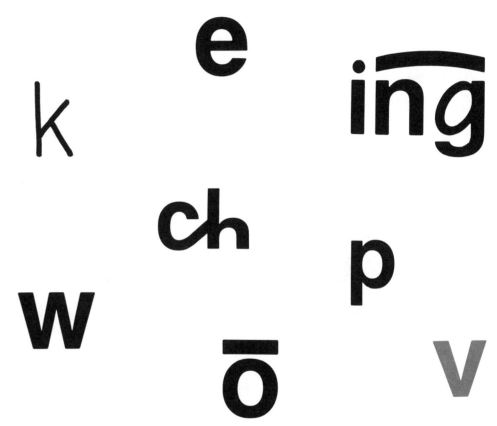

TASK 5   Individual test

Call on different children to identify two or more sounds in task 4.

TASK 6   Teacher crosses out sounds

a. You told me every sound. Get ready to do it again. This time I'll
cross out each sound when you tell me what it is.
b. Point to each sound. (Pause.) Say: Get ready.   Touch the sound.
The children respond. As you cross out the sound, say:
Goodbye, _____.

TASK 16   Children read a word beginning with two consonants (stōre)

Do not touch any small letters.

a. Cover **s.** Point to **tōre.** You're going to read this part of the word the fast way. (Pause three seconds.) Get ready. (Signal.) *Tōre.* Yes, **tōre.**

b. Uncover **s.** Point to **s.** You're going to say this first. Move your finger quickly under **s.** Then you're going to say (pause) **tōre.**

c. Point to **s.** What are you going to say first? (Signal.) *sss.* What are you going to say next? (Signal.) *Tōre.*

d. Repeat *c* until firm.

e. Touch the ball for **stōre.** Remember, first you say **sss;** then you say **tōre.** Get ready. Move to **s,** then quickly along the arrow. *Ssstōre.*

f. Say it fast. (Signal.) *Store.* Yes, what word? (Signal.) *Store.* Yes, **store.** Good reading.

g. Again. Repeat *e* and *f* until firm.

h. Now you're going to sound out (pause) **store.** Get ready. Touch **s, t, ō, r** as the children say *ssstōōōrrr.* What word? (Signal.) *Store.* Yes, **store.**

stōre

TASK 17   Children identify, then sound out an irregular word (walked)

a. Touch the ball for **walked.** Everybody, you're going to read this word the fast way. (Pause three seconds.) Get ready. Move your finger quickly along the arrow. *Walked.* Yes, **walked.**

b. Now you're going to sound out the word. Get ready. Quickly touch **w, a, l, k, d** as the children say *wwwaaalllkd.*

c. Again. Repeat *b.*

d. How do we say the word? (Signal.) *Walked.* Yes, **walked.**

e. Repeat *b* and *d* until firm.

walked

TASK 18   Individual test—Have children do *b* and *d* in task 17.

TASK 19   Children read the words the fast way

Have the children read the words on this page the fast way.

TASK 20   Individual test—Have children read one word the fast way.

READING VOCABULARY

Do not touch any small letters.

TASK 7   Children read the fast way

a. Get ready to read these words the fast way.

b. Touch the ball for **gōing.** (Pause three seconds.) Get ready.

(Signal.) *Going.*

c. Repeat *b* for the remaining words on the page.

TASK 8   Children read the fast way again

a. Get ready to do these words again. Watch where I point.

b. Point to a word. (Pause one second.) Say: Get ready. (Signal.)

The children respond. Point to the words in this order:

bug, ēating, tāke, gōing.

c. Repeat *b* until firm.

TASK 9   Individual test

Call on different children to read one word the fast way.

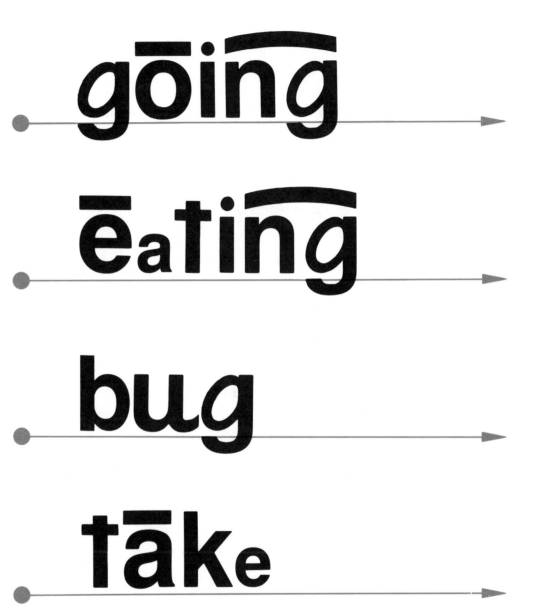

TASK 9 Children identify, then sound out an irregular word (loved)

a. Touch the ball for **loved.** Everybody, you're going to read this word the fast way. (Pause three seconds.) Get ready. Move your finger quickly along the arrow. *Loved.* Yes, **loved.**

b. Now you're going to sound out the word. Get ready. Quickly touch **l, o, v, e, d** as the children say *Lllooovvveeed.*

c. Again. Repeat *b.*

d. How do we say the word? (Signal.) *Loved.* Yes, **loved.**

e. Repeat *b* and *d* until firm.

TASK 10 Individual test

Call on different children to do *b* and *d* in task 9.

TASK 11 Children sound out the word and tell what word

a. Touch the ball for **jump.** Sound it out.

b. Get ready. Touch **j, u, m, p** as the children say *juuummmp.* If sounding out is not firm, repeat *b.*

c. What word? (Signal.) *Jump.* Yes, **jump.**

TASK 12 Children sound out the word and tell what word

Repeat the procedures in task 11 for **tōre.**

TASK 13 Children sound out the word and tell what word

Repeat the procedures in task 11 for **pool.**

TASK 14 Children read the words the fast way

a. Now you get to read the words on this page the fast way.

b. Touch the ball for **loved.** (Pause three seconds.) Get ready. Move your finger quickly along the arrow. *Loved.*

c. Repeat *b* for each word on the page.

TASK 15 Individual test

Call on different children to read one word the fast way.

Do not touch any small letters.

loved

jump

tōre

pool

TASK 10 Children read a word beginning with two consonants (slēēp)

a. Cover **s.** Run your finger under **lēēp.** You're going to sound out this part. Get ready. Touch **l,** between the **ē**'s, **p** as the children say *lllēēēp.*

b. Say it fast. (Signal.) *Lēēp.* Yes, this part is **lēēp.**

c. Uncover **s.** Point to **s.** You're going to say this first. Move your finger quickly under **lēēp.** Then you're going to say (pause) **lēēp.**

d. Point to **s.** What are you going to say first? (Signal.) *sss.* What are you going to say next? (Signal.) *Lēēp.*

e. Repeat *d* until firm.

f. Touch the ball for **slēēp.** Remember—first you say **sss;** then you say **lēēp.** Get ready. Move to **s,** then quickly along the arrow. *Ssslēēp.*

g. Say it fast. (Signal.) *Sleep.* Yes, what word? (Signal.) *Sleep.* Yes, **sleep.** Good reading.

h. Again. Repeat *f* and *g* until firm.

i. Now you're going to sound out (pause) **sleep.** Get ready. Touch **s, l,** between the **ē**'s, **p** as the children say *ssslllēēēp.* What word? (Signal.) *Sleep.* Yes, **sleep.**

TASK 11 Children read the fast way

a. Get ready to read these words the fast way.

b. Touch the ball for **that.** (Pause three seconds.) Get ready. (Signal.) *That.*

c. Repeat *b* for the remaining words on the page.

TASK 12 Children read the fast way again

a. Get ready to do these words again. Watch where I point.

b. Point to a word. (Pause one second.) Say: Get ready. (Signal.) *The children respond.* Point to the words in this order: **that, there, hat, hēre.**

c. Repeat *b* until firm.

TASK 13 Individual test

Call on different children to read one word on the page the fast way.

Do not touch any small letters.

slēēp

that

hat

thᵉre

hērᵉ

READING VOCABULARY

Do not touch any small letters.

TASK 6 Children read the fast way

a. Get ready to read these words the fast way.

b. Touch the ball for **them.** (Pause three seconds.) Get ready.
(Signal.) *Them.*

c. Repeat *b* for the remaining words on the page.

TASK 7 Children read the fast way again

a. Get ready to do these words again. Watch where I point.

b. Point to a word. (Pause one second.) Say: Get ready. (Signal.)
The children respond. Point to the words in this order:
never, they, must, them, ēither.

c. Repeat *b* until firm.

TASK 8 Individual test

Call on different children to read one word the fast way.

them

they

ēither

never

must

TASK 14   Children read the fast way

a. Get ready to read these words the fast way.

b. Touch the ball for **his.** (Pause three seconds.) Get ready.

(Signal.) *His.*

c. Repeat *b* for the remaining words on the page.

TASK 15   Children read the fast way again

a. Get ready to do these words again. Watch where I point.

b. Point to a word. (Pause one second.) Say: Get ready. (Signal.)
The children respond. Point to the words in this order:
his, give, ēach, let.

c. Repeat *b* until firm.

TASK 16   Individual test

Call on different children to read one word the fast way.

Do not touch any small letters.

his

let

ēach

give

Lesson 147

SOUNDS

TASK 1 Teaching **j** as in **jump**

a. Point to **j**. My turn. When I touch it, I'll say it. (Pause.)
Touch **j** for an instant, saying: *j.* Do not say **juuh**.

b. Point to **j**. Your turn. When I touch it, you say it. (Pause.)
Get ready. Touch **j**. *j.*

c. Again. Touch **j**. *j.*

d. Repeat *c* until firm.

TASK 2 Sounds firm-up

a. Get ready to say the sounds when I touch them.

b. Alternate touching **j** and **y**. Point to the sound. (Pause one second.)
Say: Get ready. Touch the sound. *The children respond.*

c. When **j** and **y** are firm, alternate touching **j**, **y**, **g**, and **ch** until all four sounds are firm.

TASK 4 Sounds firm-up

a. Point to **j**. When I touch the sound, you say it.

b. (Pause.) Get ready. Touch **j**. *j.*

c. Again. Repeat *b* until firm.

d. Get ready to say all the sounds when I touch them.

e. Alternate touching **j**, **x**, **oo**, **er**, **ī**, **i**, **e**, and **u** three or four times. Point to the sound. (Pause one second.) Say: Get ready. Touch the sound. *The children respond.*

TASK 3 Individual test

Call on different children to identify **j**, **y**, **g**, or **ch**.

TASK 5 Individual test

Call on different children to identify one or more sounds in task 4.

Story 125

TASK 17 First reading—children read the story the fast way

Have the children reread any sentences containing words that give them trouble. Keep a list of these words.

a. Pass out Storybook 2.

b. Open your book to page 22.

c. Everybody, touch the title of the story and get ready to read the words in the title the fast way.

d. First word. Check children's responses. (Pause two seconds.)
Get ready. Clap. *The.*

e. Clap for each remaining word in the title.

f. After the children have read the title, ask: What's this story about?
(Signal.) *The red hat.* Yes, **the red hat.**

g. Everybody, get ready to read this story the fast way.

h. First word. Check children's responses. (Pause two seconds.)
Get ready. Clap. *The.*

i. Clap for the remaining words in the first sentence. Pause at least two seconds between claps.

j. Repeat *h* and *i* for the next two sentences. Have the children reread the first three sentences until firm.

k. The children are to read the remainder of the story the fast way, stopping at the end of each sentence.

l. After the first reading of the story, print on the board the words that the children missed more than one time. Have the children sound out each word one time and tell what word.

m. After the group's responses are firm, call on individual children to read the words.

TASK 18 Individual test

a. Look at page 22. I'm going to call on different children to read a whole sentence.

b. Call on different children to read a sentence. Do not clap for each word.

TASK 19 Second reading—children read the story the fast way and answer questions

a. You're going to read the story again the fast way and I'll ask questions.

b. Starting with the first word of the title. Check children's responses. Get ready. Clap. *The.*

c. Clap for each remaining word. Pause at least two seconds between claps. Pause longer before words that gave the children trouble during the first reading.

d. Ask the comprehension questions below as the children read.

After the children read:	You say:
The red hat.	What's this story about? (Signal.) *The red hat.*
The fish had a car and no hat.	What did the fish have? (Signal.) *A car and no hat.*
"I need a red hat."	What did she say? (Signal.) *I need a red hat.*
The fish said, "Can I have that red hat?"	What did she say? (Signal.) *Can I have that red hat?* Do you think the cow will let her have the hat? *The children respond.* Let's read and find out.
The cow said, "No."	Did the cow want to give the red hat to the fish? (Signal.) *No.*
So the fish got a red hat and the cow got a car.	What did the fish get? (Signal.) *A red hat.* What did the cow get? (Signal.) *A car.* Do you think they're both happy now? *The children respond.*

TASK 20 Picture comprehension

a. What do you think you'll see in the picture? *The children respond.*

b. Turn the page and look at the picture.

c. Ask these questions:
1. What is that fish wearing? *A red hat.*
2. What's the cow doing? *Driving a car.*
3. What would you do if you had a car? *The children respond.*
4. Would you trade it for a red hat? *The children respond.*

READING COMPREHENSION

TASK 25 Children choose the correct words to fill in the blanks

a. Point to the reading-comprehension exercise on side 2.

b. Everybody, get ready to read the sentences in the box the fast way.

c. Get ready. Clap for each word as the children read:
She had a dog. The dog did not talk. Repeat until firm.

d. Listen. **She had a dog.** (Pause.) **The dog did not talk**.

e. Everybody, get ready to tell me the answer. Listen. **She had a**
(pause) **something**. Tell me what that something was. She had
a . . . . (Signal.) *Dog.* Yes, **dog.** She had a dog.

f. Listen. **She had a dog. The** (pause) **something did not talk**.
The . . . . (Signal.) *Dog.* Yes, **dog.** The dog did not talk.

g. Repeat *b* through *f* until firm.

h. Everybody, get ready to read the sentences in the box the fast way
again. Get ready. Clap for each word as the children read:
She had a dog. The dog did not talk.

i. Everybody, read item 1 to yourself and touch the word that goes in
the blank. Check children's responses.

j. What word goes in the blank? (Signal.) *Dog.*

k. Everybody, circle the word **dog** under item 1. Check children's
responses.

l. Everybody, read item 2 to yourself and touch the word that goes
in the blank. Check children's responses.

m. What word goes in the blank? (Signal.) *Dog.*

n. Circle the word **dog** under item 2. Check children's responses.

SUMMARY OF INDEPENDENT ACTIVITY

TASK 26 Introduction to independent activity

a. Hold up Take-Home 146.

b. Everybody, you're going to finish this take-home on your own.
Tell the children when they will work the remaining items.
Let's go over the things you're going to do.

TASK 27 Sound writing

a. Point to the sound-writing exercise on side 2. Here are the sounds
you're going to write today. I'll touch the sounds. You say them.

b. Touch each sound. *The children respond.*

c. Repeat the series until firm.

TASK 28 Sentence copying

a. Point to the dotted sentence in the sentence-copying exercise.

b. You're going to trace the words in this sentence. Then you're going
to write the sentence on the other lines.

c. Reading the fast way. First word. Check children's responses.
Get ready. Clap for each word.

d. After you finish your take-home, you get to draw a picture about
the sentence, **I can talk to you**. You'll draw your picture on a
piece of plain paper. When the children finish their take-homes,
give them sheets of plain paper.

END OF LESSON 146

Take-Home 125

CROSS-OUT GAME
The children will need pencils.

TASK 21 Children cross out **do** and circle **nō**.

a. Pass out sides 1 and 2 of Take-Home 125 to each child.

b. Everybody, do a good job on your take-home today and I'll give you a bonus take-home.

c. Hold up side 1 of your take-home and point to the Cross-out Game.

d. Everybody, here's the new Cross-out Game. The words in the box show what you're going to do. Point to the word **do**. Look at the word **do**. It's crossed out. So you're going to cross out every word **do**.

e. Point to the word **nō**. Look at the word **no**. It's circled. So you're going to circle every word **no**.

f. Everybody, touch a word that you're going to cross out. Check children's responses.

g. Touch a word that you're going to circle. Check children's responses.

h. Everybody, circle every word **no** and cross out every word **do**. Check children's responses.

SUMMARY OF INDEPENDENT ACTIVITY

TASK 22 Sentence copying

a. Hold up side 1 of Take-Home 125.

b. Point to the dotted sentence in the sentence-copying exercise.

c. You're going to trace the words in this sentence. Then you're going to write the sentence on the other lines.

d. Reading the fast way. First word. Check children's responses. Get ready. Clap. *She.*

e. Next word. Check children's responses. Get ready. Clap. *Got.*

f. Repeat e for the remaining words.

g. After you finish your take-home, you get to draw a picture about the sentence, **she got a red hat.** You'll draw your picture on a piece of plain paper.

TASK 23 Reading comprehension

a. Point to the boxed sentences in the reading-comprehension exercise.

b. Everybody, get ready to read the sentences the fast way.

c. First word. Check children's responses. Get ready. Clap for each word as the children read *the fish got a hat.*

d. Have the children reread the sentence until firm.

e. Get ready to read the next sentence. Repeat c and d for **the cow got a car.**

f. Point to items 1 and 2. These items tell about the story in the box. You're going to read each item and circle the right answer.

TASK 24 Other independent activity: sides 1, 2, 3, 4

Remember to do all the parts of the take-home and to read all the parts carefully. After you draw your picture, I'll give you a bonus take-home.

INDIVIDUAL CHECKOUT: STORYBOOK

TASK 25 3-minute individual checkout — whole story

a. As you are doing your take-home, I'll call on children one at a time to read the **whole story.** Remember, you get two stars if you read the story in less than three minutes and make no more than three errors.

b. Call on a child. Tell the child: Start with the title and read the story carefully the fast way. Go. Time the child. Tell the child any words the child misses. Stop the child as soon as the child makes the fourth error or exceeds the time limit.

c. If the child meets the rate-accuracy criterion, record two stars on your chart for lesson 125. Congratulate the child. Give children who do not earn two stars a chance to read the story again before the next lesson is presented.

89 words/3 min = 30 wpm [3 errors]

END OF LESSON 125

Before presenting lesson 126, give Mastery Test 24 to each child.
Do not present lesson 126 to any groups that are not firm on this test.

TASK 22 Picture comprehension

a. Everybody, look at the picture.

b. Ask these questions:

1. Where are the girl and the cat in this picture? *The children respond.* In the park.

2. How do you know they're in the park? *The children respond.*

3. Why does that girl look so surprised? *The children respond.* The cat is talking to her.

4. What is the cat saying to the girl? *The children respond.* Yes, I can talk to you.

5. What would you do with a talking cat? *The children respond.*

Take-Home 146

STORY ITEMS

The children will need pencils.

TASK 23 Children complete sentences and answer story questions

a. Pass out Take-Home 146 to each child.

b. Point to the story-items exercise on side 1. These items are about the story you just read.

c. Point to the blank in item 1. Something is missing. When you get to this blank, say "**Blank**." What will you say? (Signal.) *Blank.*

d. Everybody, get ready to read item 1. Get ready. Clap for each word as the children read *a girl went to the shop with her blank.* Repeat until firm.

e. What goes in the blank? (Signal.) *Cat.* Yes, **cat.**

f. Everybody, read item 2. Get ready. Clap for each word as the children read *then they went to the blank.* Repeat until firm.

g. What's the answer? (Signal.) *Park.*

h. Everybody, read item 3 and when you come to a blank, say "**Blank**." Get ready. Clap for each word as the children read: *she said, "you can not blank to me."* Repeat until firm.

i. What goes in the blank? (Signal.) *Talk.* Yes, **talk.**

j. Everybody, read item 4. Get ready. Clap for each word as the children read *did the cat talk?* Repeat until firm.

k. What's the answer? (Signal.) *Yes.*

l. Now, everybody, read each item to yourself and circle the right answer. Check children's responses.

PICTURE COMPREHENSION

TASK 24 Children look at the picture and complete the missing word

Refer to sounds, not letter names, in missing words.

a. Point to the first picture in the picture-comprehension exercise.

b. Everybody, touch this picture. Check children's responses.

c. Tell me what you see in this picture. Accept reasonable responses.

d. Point to the sound in the blank in item 1. Something is missing. When you get to this, say "**Blank**." What will you say? (Signal.) *Blank.*

e. Everybody, get ready to read item 1.

f. Get ready. Clap for each word as the children read *the blank is sitting.* Repeat until firm.

g. Look at the picture and get ready to tell me who is sitting. (Pause.) Who is sitting? (Signal.) *Cat.* Yes, **cat.**

h. I'll say the sounds in the word **cat.** c (pause) **aaa** (pause) **t.** Again. c (pause) **aaa** (pause) **t.**

i. Your turn. Say the sounds in **cat.** Get ready. Signal for each sound as the children say c (pause) *aaa* (pause) *t.* Repeat until firm.

j. Look at the blank in item 1. The **c** is already written in the blank. So what sounds are you going to write next? Signal for each sound as the children say *aaa* (pause) *t.* The children are not to write the sounds now.

k. Repeat *i* and *j* until firm.

l. Now write the missing word in the blank. Remember—the **c** is already written. Check children's responses.

m. Repeat *e* through *l* for item 2.

n. Repeat *b* through *m* for the second picture.

Mastery Test 24   after lesson 125, before lesson 126

a. Get ready to read this story the fast way.
b. **(test item)** First word. (Pause two seconds.) Get ready. Clap. *A.*
c. **(12 test items)** Clap one time for each remaining word in the story. Pause two seconds between claps.

Total number of test items: **13**

A group is weak if more than one-third of the children missed two or more words on the test.

WHAT TO DO

If the group is firm on Mastery Test 24 and was firm on Mastery Test 23:

Skip lesson 126 and present lesson 127 to the group during the next reading period. If more than one child missed two or more words on the test, present the firming procedures specified in the next column to those children.

If the group is firm on Mastery Test 24 but was weak on Mastery Test 23:

Present lesson 126 to the group during the next reading period. If more than one child missed two or more words on the test, present the firming procedures specified below to those children.

If the group is weak on Mastery Test 24:

A. Present these firming procedures to the group during the next reading period. Present each story until the children make no more than three mistakes. Then proceed to the next story.
  1. Lesson 123, Story, page 96, tasks 18, 19.
  2. Lesson 124, Story, page 104, tasks 19, 20.
  3. Lesson 125, Story, page 110, tasks 17, 18.
B. After presenting the above tasks, again give Mastery Test 24 individually to members of the group who failed the test.
C. If the group is firm (less than one-third of the total group missed two or more words in the story on the retest), present lesson 126 to the group during the next reading period.
D. If the group is still weak (more than one-third of the total group missed two or more words in the story on the retest), repeat *A* and *B* during the next reading period.

a man on a farm

has lots of cars.

hē has ōld cars.

Story 146

TASK 19 First reading—children read the title and first three sentences

a. Pass out Storybook 3.

b. Open your book to page 20. You're going to read the first part of this story today.

c. Everybody, touch the title of the story and get ready to read the words in the title the fast way.

d. First word. Check children's responses. (Pause two seconds.) Get ready. Clap. *The.*

e. Clap for each remaining word in the title.

f. After the children have read the title, ask: What's this story about? (Signal.) *The cat that talked.* Yes, **the cat that talked.**

g. Everybody, get ready to read this story the fast way.

h. First word. Check children's responses. (Pause two seconds.) Get ready. Clap. *A.*

i. Clap for the remaining words in the first sentence. Pause at least two seconds between claps.

j. Repeat *h* and *i* for the next two sentences. Have the children reread the first three sentences until firm.

TASK 20 Individual children or the group read sentences to complete the first reading

a. I'm going to call on different children to read a sentence. Everybody, follow along and point to the words. If you hear a mistake, raise your hand.

b. Call on a child. Read the next sentence. Do not clap for the words. Let the child read at his own pace, but be sure he reads the sentence correctly.

To correct	Have the child sound out the word. Then return to the beginning of the sentence.

c. Repeat *b* for most of the remaining sentences in the story. Occasionally have the group read a sentence. When the group is to read, say: Everybody, read the next sentence. (Pause two seconds.) Get ready. Clap for each word in the sentence. Pause at least two seconds between claps.

TASK 21 Second reading—individual children or the group read each sentence; the group answer questions

a. You're going to read the story again. This time I'm going to ask questions.

b. Starting with the first word of the title. Check children's responses. Get ready. Clap as the children read the title. Pause at least two seconds between claps.

c. Call on a child. Read the first sentence. *The child responds.*

d. Repeat *b* and *c* in task 20. Present the following comprehension questions to the entire group.

After the children read:	You say:
The cat that talked.	What's this story about? (Signal.) *The cat that talked.*
She went to the shop with her cat.	What did she do? (Signal.) *She went to the shop with her cat.*
She went to the park with her cat.	Name two things she did with her cat. (Signal.) *She went to the shop and to the park with her cat.*
"But you can not talk to me and that makes me sad."	Why was the girl sad? (Signal.) *Because the cat couldn't talk to her.*
The cat said, "I can talk to you."	What did the cat say? (Signal.) *I can talk to you.* That cat talked to her. I wonder what will happen next. We'll find out when we read the next part of the story.

Lesson 126

Groups that are firm on Mastery Tests 23 and 24 should skip this lesson and do lesson 127 today.

SOUNDS

TASK 1 Teacher introduces cross-out game

a. Use acetate and crayon.

b. I'll cross out the sounds on this page when you can tell me every sound.

c. Remember—when I touch it, you say it.
d. Go over the sounds until they can identify all the sounds in order.

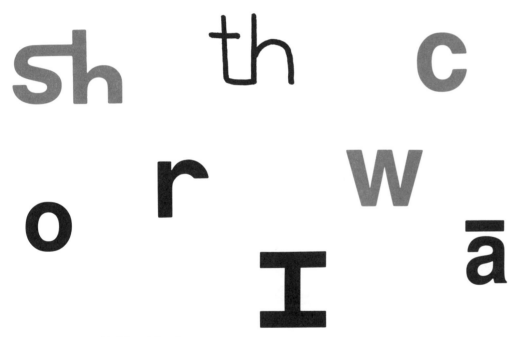

TASK 2 Individual test

Call on different children to identify two or more sounds in task 1.

TASK 3 Teacher crosses out sounds

a. You told me every sound. Get ready to do it again. This time I'll cross out each sound when you tell me what it is.
b. Point to each sound. (Pause.) Say: Get ready. Touch the sound. *The children respond.* As you cross out the sound, say: Goodbye, _____ .

TASK 4 Teacher and children play the sounds game

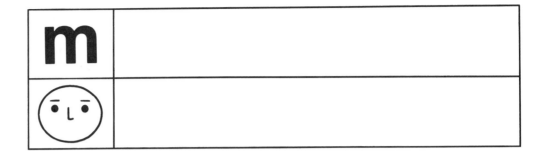

a. Use acetate and crayon. Write the sounds in the symbol box. Keep score in the score box.

b. I'm smart. I bet I can beat you in a game.

c. Here's the rule. When I touch a sound, you say it.
d. Play the game.
Make one symbol at a time in the symbol box. Use the symbols **b, ing, e** and **ch.**
Make each symbol quickly. (Pause.) Touch the symbol.
Play the game for about two minutes.
Then ask: Who won? Draw a mouth on the face in the score box.

TASK 16 Children identify, then sound out an irregular word

a. Touch the ball for **walked.** Everybody, you're going to read this word the fast way. (Pause three seconds.) Get ready. Move your finger quickly along the arrow. *Walked.* Yes, **walked.**

b. Now you're going to sound out the word. Get ready. Quickly touch **w, a, l, k, d** as the children say *wwwaaalllkd.*

c. Again. Repeat *b.*

d. How do we say the word? (Signal.) *Walked.* Yes, **walked.**

e. Repeat *b* and *d* until firm.

f. Call on different children to do *b* and *d.*

Do not touch any small letters.

walked

TASK 17 Children read rush, brush, and brushed

a. Cover **b.** Point to **rush.** You're going to read this part of the word the fast way. (Pause three seconds.) Get ready. (Signal.) *Rush.* Yes, **rush.**

b. Uncover **b.** Point to **b.** You're going to say this first. Move your finger quickly under **rush.** Then you're going to say (pause) **rush.**

c. Point to **b.** What are you going to say first? (Signal.) *b.* What are you going to say next? (Signal.) *Rush.*

d. Repeat *c* until firm.

e. Touch the ball for **brush.** Get ready. Move to **b,** then quickly along the arrow. *Brush.*

f. Say it fast. (Signal.) *Brush.* Yes, what word? (Signal.) *Brush.* Yes, **brush.** Good reading.

g. Again. Repeat *e* and *f* until firm.

h. Return to the ball for **brush.** Yes, this word is **brush.**

i. Touch the ball for **brushed.** So this must be **brush** . . . . Touch **d.** *d.* What word? (Signal.) *Brushed.* Yes, **brushed.**

j. Again. Repeat *h* and *i* until firm.

k. Touch the ball for **brush.** This word is **brush.** Touch the ball for **brushed.** So this must be . . . . Quickly run your finger under **brush** and tap **d.** *Brushed.* Yes, **brushed.**

l. Again. Repeat *k* until firm.

m. Now you're going to sound out (pause) **brushed.** Get ready. Touch **b, r, u, sh, d** as the children say *brrruuushshshd.* Yes, what word? (Signal.) *Brushed.* Yes, **brushed.**

brush

brushed

TASK 18 Children read the words the fast way

Have the children read the words the fast way.

READING VOCABULARY

TASK 5   Children sound out the word and tell what word

a. Touch the ball for **bē.** Sound it out.
b. Get ready. Touch **b, ē** as the children say *bēēē.*
                    If sounding out is not firm, repeat *b.*
c. What word? (Signal.) *Be.*   Yes, **be.**

TASK 6   Children sound out the word and tell what word

a. Touch the ball for **big.** Sound it out.
b. Get ready. Touch **b, i, g** as the children say *biiig.*
                    If sounding out is not firm, repeat *b.*
c. What word? (Signal.) *Big.*   Yes, **big.**

TASK 7   Children sound out the word and tell what word

Repeat the procedures in task 6 for **getting.**

TASK 8   Children sound out the word and tell what word

Repeat the procedures in task 6 for **bed.**

TASK 9   Children sound out the word and tell what word

Repeat the procedures in task 6 for **bit.**

TASK 10   Children read the words the fast way

a. Now you get to read the words on this page the fast way.
b. Touch the ball for **bē.** (Pause three seconds.) Get ready.
                    Move your finger quickly along the arrow. *Be.*
c. Repeat *b* for each word on the page.

TASK 11   Individual test

Call on different children to read one word the fast way.

TASK 10   Children identify, then sound out an irregular word (talked)

a. Touch the ball for **talked.** Everybody, you're going to read this word the fast way. (Pause three seconds.) Get ready. Move your finger quickly along the arrow. *Talked.* Yes, **talked.**

b. Now you're going to sound out the word. Get ready. Quickly touch **t, a, l, k, d** as the children say *taaalllkd.*

c. Again. Repeat *b.*

d. How do we say the word? (Signal.) *Talked.* Yes, **talked.**

e. Repeat *b* and *d* until firm.

TASK 11   Individual test

Call on different children to do *b* and *d* in task 10.

TASK 12   Children identify, then sound out an irregular word (was)

a. Touch the ball for **was.** Everybody, you're going to read this word the fast way. (Pause three seconds.) Get ready. Move your finger quickly along the arrow. *Was.* Yes, **was.**

b. Now you're going to sound out the word. Get ready. Quickly touch **w, a, s** as the children say *wwwaaasss.*

c. Again. Repeat *b.*

d. How do we say the word? (Signal.) *Was.* Yes, **was.**

e. Repeat *b* and *d* until firm.

TASK 13   Individual test

Call on different children to do *b* and *d* in task 12.

TASK 14   Children sound out the word and tell what word

a. Touch the ball for **dāy.** Sound it out.

b. Get ready. Touch **d, ā, y** as the children say *dāāāyyy.* If sounding out is not firm, repeat *b.*

c. What word? (Signal.) *Day.* Yes, **day.**

TASK 15   Children read the words the fast way

Have the children read the words the fast way.

Do not touch any small letters.

TASK 12 Children read the fast way

a. Get ready to read these words the fast way.

b. Touch the ball for **ēating.** (Pause three seconds.) Get ready.
(Signal.) *Eating.*

c. Repeat *b* for the remaining words on the page.

TASK 13 Children read the fast way again

a. Get ready to do these words again. Watch where I point.

b. Point to a word. (Pause one second.) Say: Get ready. (Signal.)
The children respond. Point to the words in this order:
dog, slēēp, ēating, hit, bugs.

c. Repeat *b* until firm.

TASK 14 Individual test

Call on different children to read one word the fast way.

Do not touch any small letters.

READING VOCABULARY

TASK 7   Children read the fast way

a. Get ready to read these words the fast way.
b. Touch the ball for **shop.** (Pause three seconds.) Get ready.
(Signal.) *Shop.*

c. Repeat *b* for the remaining words on the page.

TASK 8   Children read the fast way again

a. Get ready to do these words again. Watch where I point.
b. Point to a word. (Pause one second.) Say: Get ready. (Signal.)
The children respond. Point to the words in this order:
shop, hop, never, soon, must.

c. Repeat *b* until firm.

TASK 9   Individual test

Call on different children to read one word the fast way.

shop

soon

must

never

hop

Story 126

TASK 15   First reading—children read the story the fast way

Have the children reread any sentences containing words that give them trouble. Keep a list of these words.

a. Pass out Storybook 2.
b. Open your book to page 25.
c. Everybody, touch the title of the story and get ready to read the words in the title the fast way.
d. First word. Check children's responses. (Pause two seconds.) Get ready. Clap. *A.*
e. Clap for each remaining word in the title.
f. After the children have read the title ask: What's this story about? (Signal.) *A bug and a dog.* Yes, **a bug and a dog**.
g. Everybody, get ready to read this story the fast way.
h. First word. Check children's responses. (Pause two seconds.) Get ready. Clap. *A.*
i. Clap for the remaining words in the first sentence. Pause at least two seconds between claps.
j. Repeat *h* and *i* for the next two sentences. Have the children reread the first three sentences until firm.
k. The children are to read the remainder of the story the fast way, stopping at the end of each sentence.
l. After the first reading of the story, print on the board the words that the children missed more than one time. Have the children sound out each word one time and tell what word.
m. After the group's responses are firm, call on individual children to read the words.

TASK 16   Individual test

a. Turn back to page 25. I'm going to call on different children to read a whole sentence.
b. Call on different children to read a sentence. Do not clap for each word.

TASK 17   Second reading—children read the story the fast way and answer questions

a. You're going to read the story again the fast way and I'll ask questions.
b. Starting with the first word of the title. Check children's responses. Get ready. Clap. *A.*
c. Clap for each remaining word. Pause at least two seconds between claps. Pause longer before words that gave the children trouble during the first reading.
d. Ask the comprehension questions below as the children read.

After the children read:	You say:
A bug and a dog.	What's this story about? (Signal.) *A bug and a dog.*
The dog said, "That bug is so little I can not see him on the log."	What did the dog say? (Signal.) *That bug is so little I can not see him on the log.*
The bug said, "I will eat this log."	What did the bug say? (Signal.) *I will eat this log.*
He bit and bit and bit at the log.	What did the bug do? (Signal.) *He bit and bit and bit at the log.*
The dog said, "That bug can eat logs as well as a big bug can."	What did the dog say? (Signal). *That bug can eat logs as well as a big bug can.*

TASK 18   Picture comprehension

a. Everybody, look at the picture.
b. Ask these questions:
   1. Is that a big bug? (Signal.) *No.*
   2. What's that little bug doing with the log? *The children respond.* He is eating it.
   3. Do you think a little bug can eat a log? *The children respond.*

Lesson 146

Groups that are firm on Mastery Tests 27 and 28 should skip this lesson and do lesson 147 today.

SOUNDS

TASK 1   Teaching j as in jump

a. Point to **j.** My turn. When I touch it, I'll say it. (Pause.)
Touch **j** for an instant, saying: j. Do not say **juuh.**

b. Point to **j.** Your turn. When I touch it, you say it. (Pause.)
Get ready. Touch **j.** *j.*

c. Again. Touch **j.** *j.*

d. Repeat *c* until firm.

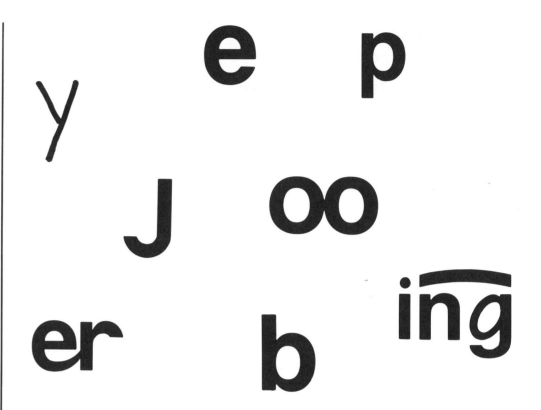

TASK 2   Sounds firm-up

a. Get ready to say the sounds when I touch them.

b. Alternate touching **j** and **ch.** Point to the sound. (Pause one second.)
Say: Get ready. Touch the sound. *The children respond.*

c. When **j** and **ch** are firm, alternate touching **j, ch, g,** and **x** until all four sounds are firm.

TASK 3   Individual test

Call on different children to identify **j, ch, g,** or **x.**

TASK 4   Teacher introduces cross-out game

a. Use acetate and crayon.

b. I'll cross out the sounds on this part of the page when you can tell me every sound.

c. Remember—when I touch it, you say it.

d. Go over the sounds until the children can identify all the sounds in order.

TASK 5   Individual test

Call on different children to identify two or more sounds in task 4.

TASK 6   Teacher crosses out sounds

a. You told me every sound. Get ready to do it again. This time I'll cross out each sound when you tell me what it is.

b. Point to each sound. (Pause.) Say: Get ready. Touch the sound. *The children respond.* As you cross out the sound, say:
Goodbye, _____.

235

Take-Home 126

PAIR RELATIONS
The children will need pencils.

TASK 19   Children draw a line from the word to the correct picture

a. Pass out Take-Home 126 to each child.

b. Point to the first set in the pair-relations exercise on side 2
(duck, nōse, ēar).

c. Everybody, here's a new Matching Game. In this game you match
pictures with the words that tell about the picture.

d. Everybody, touch the first word. Check children's responses.

e. Get ready to read that word the fast way. (Pause.) Get ready.
Clap. *Duck.*   Yes, **duck.**

f. Everybody, touch the picture that shows a duck.
Check children's responses.

g. You're going to draw a line from the word **duck** to the picture that
shows a duck.

h. Read the word and draw the line. Check children's responses.

i. Everybody, touch the next word. Check children's responses.

j. Get ready to read that word the fast way. (Pause.) Get ready.
Clap. *Nose.*   Yes, **nose.**

k. Everybody, touch the picture that shows a nose.
Check children's responses.

l. You're going to draw a line from the word **nose** to the picture that
shows a nose.

m. Read the word and draw the line. Check children's responses.

n. Repeat *i* through *m* for the word **ēar.**

o. You'll finish drawing lines to the right pictures later.

SUMMARY OF INDEPENDENT ACTIVITY

TASK 20   Introduction to independent activity

a. Hold up side 1 of Take-Home 126.

b. Everybody, you're going to finish this take-home on your own.
Tell the children when they will work the remaining items.
Let's go over the things you're going to do.

TASK 21   Sentence copying

a. Point to the dotted sentence in the sentence-copying exercise.

b. You're going to trace the words in this sentence. Then you're
going to write the sentence on the other lines.

c. Reading the fast way. First word. Check children's responses.
Get ready. Clap. *The.*

d. Next word. Check children's responses. Get ready. Clap. *Bug.*

e. Repeat *d* for the remaining words.

f. After you finish your take-home, you get to draw a picture about
the sentence, **the bug bit the log.** You'll draw your picture on
a piece of plain paper.

TASK 22   Cross-out game

a. Point to the boxed words in the Cross-out Game. Everybody, what
word are you going to circle? (Signal.) *So.*   Yes, **so.**

b. What word are you going to cross out? (Signal.) *On.*   Yes, **on.**

TASK 23   Reading comprehension

a. Point to the boxed sentences in the reading-comprehension exercise.

b. Everybody, get ready to read the sentences the fast way.

c. First word. Check children's responses. Get ready. Clap for
each word as the children read *the bug got mad.*

d. Have the children reread the sentence until firm.

e. Get ready to read the next sentence. Do *c* and *d* for **sō shē bit a log.**

f. Point to items 1 and 2. These items tell about the story in the
box. You're going to read each item and circle the right answer.

TASK 24   Sound writing

a. Point to the sound-writing exercise on side 2. Here are the sounds
you're going to write today. I'll touch the sounds. You say them.

b. Touch each sound. *The children respond.*

c. Repeat the series until firm.

TASK 25   Pair relations

a. Point to the pair-relations exercise. You're going to read each word.
Then draw a line from the word to the right picture.

b. When the children finish their take-homes, give them sheets of paper.
Remind them to draw a picture that shows **the bug bit the log.**

END OF LESSON 126

Mastery Test 28   after lesson 145, before lesson 146

Read this story the fast way. Do not clap for the words. Let the child read at his own pace.

Total number of test items: **21**

A group is weak if more than one-third of the children missed two or more words on the test.

WHAT TO DO

If the group is firm on Mastery Test 28 and was firm on Mastery Test 27:

Skip lesson 146 and present lesson 147 to the group during the next reading period. If more than one child missed two or more words on the test, present the firming procedures specified in the next column to those children.

If the group is firm on Mastery Test 28 but was weak on Mastery Test 27:

Present lesson 146 to the group during the next reading period. If more than one child missed two or more words on the test, present the firming procedures specified below to those children.

If the group is weak on Mastery Test 28:

A. Present these firming procedures to the group during the next reading period. Present each story until the children make no more than three mistakes. Then proceed to the next story.
   1. Lesson 143, Story, page 219, tasks 18, 19.
   2. Lesson 144, Story, page 224, tasks 16, 17.
   3. Lesson 145, Story, page 231, tasks 21, 22.
B. After presenting the above tasks, again give Mastery Test 28 individually to members of the group who failed the test.
C. If the group is firm (less than one-third of the total group missed two or more words in the story on the retest), present lesson 146 to the group during the next reading period.
D. If the group is still weak (more than one-third of the total group missed two or more words in the story on the retest), repeat A and B during the next reading period.

a boy and his mother went

to a toy shop. they went

to get toys. the boy said,

"I like toys."

Lesson 127

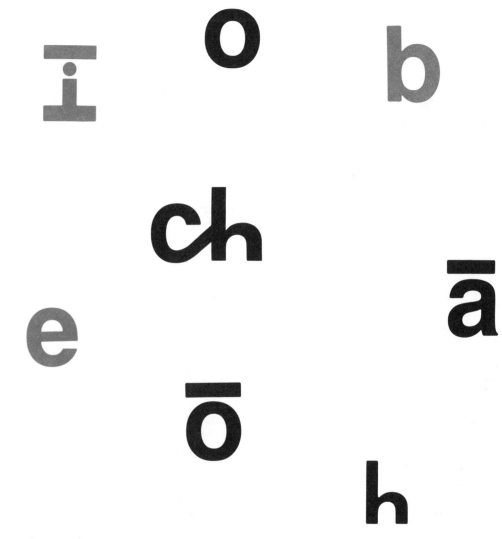

SOUNDS

TASK 1   Teaching ī as in īce

a. Point to ī. Here's a new sound.

b. My turn. (Pause.) Touch ī and
say: īīī.

c. Again. Touch ī for a longer time.
īīīīī. Lift your finger.

d. Point to ī. Your turn. When I
touch it, you say it. (Pause.)
Get ready. Touch. ī. īīī.
Lift your finger.

e. Again. Touch ī. īīīīīī.
Lift your finger.

f. Repeat e until firm.

TASK 2   Individual test

Call on different children to identify ī.

TASK 3   Sounds firm-up

a. Get ready to say the sounds
when I touch them.

b. Alternate touching i and ī. Point
to the sound. (Pause one second.)
Say: Get ready. Touch the
sound. *The children respond.*

c. When i and ī are firm, alternate
touching ī, i, I, and **ing** until all
four sounds are firm.

TASK 4   Individual test

Call on different children to identify
ī, i, I, or **ing**.

TASK 5   Sounds firm-up

a. Point to ī. When I touch the sound, you say it.

b. (Pause.) Get ready. Touch ī. īīī.

c. Again. Repeat b until firm.

d. Get ready to say all the sounds when I touch them.

e. Alternate touching **o, b, ch, e, ō, ī, ā,** and **h** three or four times.
Point to the sound. (Pause one second.)
Say: Get ready. Touch the sound. *The children respond.*

TASK 6   Individual test

Call on different children to identify one or more sounds in task 5.

READING COMPREHENSION

TASK 27 Children choose the correct words to fill in the blanks

a. Point to the reading-comprehension exercise on side 2.

b. Everybody, get ready to read the sentences in the box the fast way.

c. Get ready. Clap for each word as the children read:
He liked to eat. So he ate beans and cake. Repeat until firm.

d. Listen. **He liked to eat.** (Pause.) **So he ate beans and cake.**

e. Everybody, get ready to tell me the answer. Listen. **He** (pause) **something to eat.** Tell me what that something was. He . . . .
(Signal.) *Liked.* Yes, **liked.** He liked to eat.

f. Listen. **He liked to eat. So he ate beans and something.** So he ate beans and . . . . (Signal.) *Cake.* Yes, **cake.**

g. Repeat *b* through *f* until firm.

h. Everybody, get ready to read the sentences in the box the fast way again. Get ready. Clap for each word as the children read:
He liked to eat. So he ate beans and cake.

i. Everybody, read item 1 to yourself and touch the word that goes in the blank. Check children's responses.

j What word goes in the blank? (Signal.) *Liked.*

k Everybody, circle the word **liked** under item 1. Check children's responses.

l. Everybody, read item 2 to yourself and touch the word that goes in the blank. Check children's responses.

m. What word goes in the blank? (Signal.) *Cake.*

n. Circle the word **cāke** under item 2. Check children's responses.

SUMMARY OF INDEPENDENT ACTIVITY

TASK 28 Introduction to independent activity

a. Hold up Take-Home 145.

b. You're going to finish this take-home on your own.
Tell the children when they will work the remaining items.
Let's go over the things you're going to do.

TASK 29 Sound writing

a. Point to the sound-writing exercise on side 2. Here are the sounds you're going to write today. I'll touch the sounds. You say them.

b. Touch each sound. *The children respond.*

c. Repeat the series until firm.

TASK 30 Sentence copying

a. Point to the dotted sentence in the sentence-copying exercise.

b. You're going to trace the words in this sentence. Then you're going to write the sentence on the other lines.

c. Reading the fast way. First word. Check children's responses.
Get ready. Clap for each word.

d. After you finish your take-home, you get to draw a picture about the sentence, "**I bite,**" **a bug said.** You'll draw your picture on a piece of plain paper. When the children finish their take-homes, give them sheets of plain paper.

INDIVIDUAL CHECKOUT: STORYBOOK

TASK 31 3-minute individual checkout

a As you are doing your take-home, I'll call on children one at a time to read the **whole story.** Remember, you get two stars if you read the story in less than three minutes and make no more than three errors.

b. Call on a child. Tell the child: Start with the title and read the story carefully the fast way. Go. Time the child. Tell the child any words the child misses. Stop the child as soon as the child makes the fourth error or exceeds the time limit.

c. If the child meets the rate-accuracy criterion, record two stars on your chart for lesson 145. Congratulate the child. Give children who do not earn two stars a chance to read the story again before the next lesson is presented.

107 words/3 min = 36 wpm [3 errors]

TASK 32: Bonus take-home: sides 3 and 4

After the children have completed their take-home exercises, give them sides 3 and 4 of Take-Home 145. Tell them they may keep the stories and read them.

END OF LESSON 145

Before presenting lesson 146, give Mastery Test 28 to each child.
Do not present lesson 146 to any groups that are not firm on this test.

READING VOCABULARY

Do not touch any small letters.

TASK 7   Children read the fast way

a. Get ready to read these words the fast way.

b. Touch the ball for **slēēping.** (Pause three seconds.) Get ready.
(Signal.) *Sleeping.* Yes, **sleeping.**

c. Repeat *b* for the remaining words on the page.

TASK 8   Children read the fast way again

a. Get ready to do these words again. Watch where I point.

b. Point to a word. (Pause one second.) Say: Get ready. (Signal.)
The children respond. Point to the words in this order:
fishing, nōse, then, slēēping, lēaf.

c. Repeat *b* until firm.

TASK 9   Individual test

Call on different children to read one word the fast way.

slēēping

fishing

lēaf

nōse

then

TASK 24   Picture comprehension

a. Everybody, look at the picture.
b. Ask these questions:
   1. What's the pig doing? *The children respond.* Biting his leg.
   2. Why is the bug laughing? *The children respond.*
                              Yes, she tricked the pig. That bug is pretty smart.

Take-Home 145

STORY ITEMS
The children will need pencils.

TASK 25   Children complete sentences and answer story questions

a. Pass out sides 1 and 2 of Take-Home 145 to each child.
b. Everybody, do a good job on your take-home today and I'll give you
                                          a bonus take-home.
c. Hold up side 1 of your take-home. Point to the story-items exercise
         on side 1. These items are about the story you just read.
d. Point to the blank in item 1. Something is missing. When you get
         to this blank, say "**Blank**." What will you say? (Signal.) *Blank.*
e. Everybody, get ready to read item 1. Get ready. Clap for each
         word as the children read *a bug and a blank met on a road.*
                                          Repeat until firm.
f. What goes in the blank? (Signal.) *Pig.* Yes, **pig.**
g. Everybody, read item 2 and when you come to a blank, say
         "**Blank**." Get ready. Clap for each word as the children read
                  the bug bit a blank. Repeat until firm.
h. What goes in the blank? (Signal.) *Log.* Yes, **log.**
i. Everybody, read item 3 and when you come to a blank, say
         "**Blank**." Get ready. Clap for each word as the children read
                  the pig bit blank. Repeat until firm.
j. What goes in the blank? (Signal.) *His leg.* Yes, **his leg.**
k. Everybody, read item 4. Get ready. Clap for each word as the
                  children read *did the pig bite better?*
l. What's the answer? (Signal.) *Yes.*
m. Now, everybody, read each item to yourself and circle the right
                  answer. Check children's responses.

PICTURE COMPREHENSION

TASK 26   Children look at the picture and complete the missing word

Refer to sounds, not letter names, in missing words.

a. Point to the first picture in the picture-comprehension exercise.
b. Everybody, touch this picture. Check children's responses.
c. Tell me what you see in this picture. Accept reasonable responses.
d. Point to the sound in the blank at the beginning of item 1.
         Something is missing. When you get to this, say "**Blank**." What will
                              you say? (Signal.) *Blank.*
e. Everybody, get ready to read item 1.
f. Get ready. Clap for each word as the children read *blank has a cat.*
                              Repeat until firm.
g. Look at the picture and get ready to tell me who has a cat. (Pause.)
                  Who has a cat? (Signal.) *She.* Yes, **she.**
h. I'll say the sounds in the word **she. shshsh** (pause) $\bar{e}\bar{e}\bar{e}$. Again.
                              shshsh (pause) $\bar{e}\bar{e}\bar{e}$.
i. Your turn. Say the sounds in **she.** Get ready. Signal for each
         sound as the children say *shshsh* (pause) $\bar{e}\bar{e}\bar{e}$. Repeat until firm.
j. Look at the blank in item 1. The **shshsh** is already written in the
                  blank. So what sound are you going to write next?
         Signal as the children say $\bar{e}\bar{e}\bar{e}$. The children are not to write the
                              sounds now.
k. Repeat *i* and *j* until firm.
l. Now write the missing word in the blank. Remember—the
         shshsh is already written. Check children's responses.
m. Repeat *e* through *l* for item 2.
n. Repeat *b* through *m* for the second picture.

TASK 10 Children read a word beginning with two consonants (**slam**)

a. Cover **s.** Run your finger under **lam.** You're going to sound out this part. Get ready. Touch **l, a, m** as the children say *lllaaammm.*

b. Say it fast. (Signal.) *Lam.* Yes, this part is **lam.**

c. Uncover **s.** Point to **s.** You're going to say this first. Move your finger quickly under **lam.** Then you're going to say (pause) **lam.**

d. Point to **s.** What are you going to say first? (Signal.) *sss.* What are you going to say next? (Signal.) *Lam.*

e. Repeat *d* until firm.

f. Touch the ball for **slam.** Remember—first you say **sss**; then you say **lam.** Get ready. Move to **s,** then quickly along the arrow. *Ssslam.*

g. Say it fast. (Signal.) *Slam.* Yes, what word? (Signal.) *Slam.* Yes, **slam.** Good reading.

h. Again. Repeat *f* and *g* until firm.

i. Now you're going to sound out (pause) **slam.** Get ready. Touch **s, l, a, m** as the children say *ssslllaaammm.* What word? (Signal.) *Slam.* Yes, **slam.**

slam

TASK 11 Children sound out the word and tell what word

a. Touch the ball for **let's.** Sound it out.

b. Get ready. Touch **l, e, t, s** as the children say *llleeetsss.* If sounding out is not firm, repeat *b.*

c. What word? (Signal.) *Let's.* Yes, **let's.**

let's

TASK 12 Children sound out the word and tell what word

Repeat the procedures in task 11 for **but.**

but

TASK 13 Children read the words the fast way

a. Now you get to read the words on this page the fast way.

b. Touch the ball for **slam.** (Pause three seconds.) Get ready. Move your finger quickly along the arrow. *Slam.*

c. Repeat *b* for each word on the page.

TASK 14 Individual test

Call on different children to read one word the fast way.

Story 145

TASK 21 First reading—children read the title and first three sentences

a. Pass out Storybook 3.

b. Open your book to page 17.

c. Everybody, touch the title of the story and get ready to read the words in the title the fast way.

d. First word. Check children's responses. (Pause two seconds.) Get ready. Clap. *The.*

e. Clap for each remaining word in the title.

f. After the children have read the title, ask: What's this story about? (Signal.) *The pig that bit his leg.* Yes, **the pig that bit his leg**.

g. Everybody, get ready to read this story the fast way.

h. First word. Check children's responses. (Pause two seconds.) Get ready. Clap. *A.*

i. Clap for the remaining words in the first sentence. Pause at least two seconds between claps.

j. Repeat *h* and *i* for the next two sentences. Have the children reread the first three sentences until firm.

TASK 22 Individual children or the group read sentences to complete the first reading

a. I'm going to call on different children to read a sentence. Everybody, follow along and point to the words. If you hear a mistake, raise your hand.

b. Call on a child. Read the next sentence. Do not clap for the words. Let the child read at his own pace, but be sure he reads the sentence correctly.

To correct	Have the child sound out the word. Then return to the beginning of the sentence.

c. Repeat *b* for most of the remaining sentences in the story. Occasionally have the group read a sentence. When the group is to read, say: Everybody, read the next sentence. (Pause two seconds.) Get ready. Clap for each word in the sentence. Pause at least two seconds between claps.

TASK 23 Second reading—individual children or the group read each sentence; the group answer questions

a. You're going to read the story again. This time I'm going to ask questions.

b. Starting with the first word of the title. Check children's responses. Get ready. Clap as the children read the title. Pause at least two seconds between claps.

c. Call on a child. Read the first sentence. *The child responds.*

d. Repeat *b* and *c* in task 22. Present the following comprehension questions to the entire group.

After the children read:	You say:
The pig that bit his leg.	What's this story about? (Signal.) *The pig that bit his leg.*
The pig said, "I can walk better than you."	What did the pig say? (Signal.) *I can walk better than you.* Who is he talking to? (Signal.) *A bug.*
Then she bit a log.	What did she do? (Signal.) *She bit a log.* I wonder if the pig can do that.
The pig went bite, bite, bite, and ate the log.	What did the pig do? (Signal.) *He went bite, bite, bite, and ate the log.* Who is better at eating logs? (Signal.) *The pig.*
The pig said, "I can do better than that."	What did the pig say? (Signal.) *I can do better than that.*
The pig gave his leg a big bite.	What did the pig do? (Signal.) *He gave his leg a big bite.* Whose leg did he bite? (Signal.) *His own leg.*
The bug said, "You bite pigs better than me."	What did the bug say? (Signal.) *You bite pigs better than me.* Who bites pigs better, the pig or the bug? (Signal.) *The pig.* Who is smarter? (Signal.) *The bug.* Why? *The children respond.*

TASK 15   Children read a word beginning with two consonants (slip)

a. Cover **s**. Point to **lip**. You're going to read this part of the word the fast way. (Pause three seconds.) Get ready. (Signal.) *Lip.* Yes, **lip**.

b. Uncover **s**. Point to **s**. You're going to say this first. Move your finger quickly under **lip**. Then you're going to say (pause) **lip**.

c. Point to **s**. What are you going to say first? (Signal.) *sss.* What are you going to say next? (Signal.) *Lip.*

d. Repeat *c* until firm.

e. Touch the ball for **slip**. Remember—first you say **sss**; then you say **lip**. Get ready. Move to **s**, then quickly along the arrow. *Ssslip.*

f. Say it fast. (Signal.) *Slip.* Yes, what word? (Signal.) *Slip.* Yes, **slip**. Good reading.

g. Again. Repeat *e* and *f* until firm.

h. Now you're going to sound out (pause) **slip**. Get ready. **s, l, i, p** as the children say *sssllliiip.* What word? (Signal.) *Slip.* Yes, **slip**.

slip

TASK 16   Children identify, then sound out an irregular word (to)

a. Touch the ball for **to**. Everybody, you're going to read this word the fast way. (Pause three seconds.) Get ready. Move your finger quickly along the arrow. *To.* Yes, **to**.

b. Now you're going to sound out the word. Get ready. Quickly touch **t, o** as the children say *tooo.*

c. Again. Repeat *b.*

d. How do we say the word? (Signal.) *To.* Yes, **to**.

e. Repeat *b* and *d* until firm.

to

TASK 17   Individual test—Have children do *b* and *d* in task 16.

TASK 18   Children read the words the fast way

Now you get to read the words on this page the fast way.

b. Touch the ball for **slip**. (Pause three seconds.) Get ready. Move your finger quickly along the arrow. *Slip.* Yes, **slip.**

c. Repeat *b* for **to**.

TASK 19   Individual test—Have children read one word the fast way.

145

TASK 18   Children read the fast way

a. Get ready to read these words the fast way.
b. Touch the ball for **met.** (Pause three seconds.) Get ready.
(Signal.) *Met.*

c. Repeat *b* for the remaining words on the page.

TASK 19   Children read the fast way again

a. Get ready to do these words again. Watch where I point.
b. Point to a word. (Pause one second.) Say: Get ready.   (Signal.)
The children respond. Point to the words in this order:
met, let, then, ship, than.

c. Repeat *b* until firm.

TASK 20   Individual test

Call on different children to read one word the fast way.

met

then

ship

let

than

Story 127

TASK 20   First reading—children read the story the fast way

Have the children reread any sentences containing words that give
them trouble. Keep a list of these words.

a. Pass out Storybook 2.
b. Open your book to page 28.
c. Everybody, touch the title of the story and get ready to read the
words in the title the fast way.
d. First word. Check children's responses. (Pause two seconds.)
Get ready. Clap. *The.*
e. Clap for the remaining word in the title.
f. After the children have read the title, ask: What's this story about?
(Signal.) *The bugs.* Yes, **the bugs.**
g. Everybody, get ready to read this story the fast way.
h. First word. Check children's responses. (Pause two seconds.)
Get ready. Clap. *A.*
i. Clap for the remaining words in the first sentence. Pause at least
two seconds between claps.
j. Repeat *h* and *i* for the next two sentences. Have the children reread
the first three sentences until firm.
k. The children are to read the remainder of the story the fast way,
stopping at the end of each sentence.
l. After the first reading of the story, print on the board the words that
the children missed more than one time. Have the children
sound out each word one time and tell what word.
m. After the group's responses are firm, call on individual children
to read the words.

TASK 21   Individual test

a. Look at page 28. I'm going to call on different children to read
a whole sentence.
b. Call on different children to read a sentence. Do not clap for
each word.

TASK 22   Second reading—children read the story the fast way and answer questions

a. You're going to read the story again the fast way and I'll ask
questions.
b. Starting with the first word of the title. Check children's
responses. Get ready. Clap. *The.*
c. Clap for each remaining word. Pause at least two seconds between
claps. Pause longer before words that gave the children trouble
during the first reading.
d. Ask the comprehension questions below as the children read.

After the children read:	You say:
The bugs.	What's this story about? (Signal.) *The bugs.*
The big bug said, "Let's go eat."	Did the big bug want to eat? (Signal.) *Yes.*
So the big bug ate a leaf and a nut and a rock.	What did the big bug eat? (Signal.) *A leaf, a nut, and a rock.*
So the little bug ate a leaf and a nut and a rock.	What did the little bug eat? (Signal.) *A leaf, a nut, and a rock.*
She ate the log.	Did she eat the log? (Signal.) *Yes.*
Then she ate ten more logs.	Then what did she eat? (Signal.) *Ten more logs.*
The little bug said, "Now let's eat more."	What did the little bug say? (Signal.) *Now let's eat more.*

TASK 23   Picture comprehension

a. What do you think you'll see in the picture? *The children respond.*
b. Look at the picture.
c. Ask these questions:
   1. What is the little bug eating? *The children respond.* A log.
   2. Do you think the big bug is surprised to see what the little bug
   can eat? *The children respond.*

TASK 12   Children read the fast way

Touch the ball for **moon.** Get ready to read this word the fast way.
(Pause three seconds.) Get ready. (Signal.) *Moon.*

Do not touch any small letters.

moon

TASK 13   Children sound out the word and tell what word

a. Touch the ball for **chip.** Sound it out.
b. Get ready. Touch **ch, i, p** as the children say *chiiip.*
If sounding out is not firm, repeat *b.*
c. What word? (Signal.) *Chip.* Yes, **chip.**

chip

TASK 14   Children sound out the word and tell what word

a. Touch the ball for **better.** Sound it out.
b. Get ready. Touch **b, e,** between the **t**'s, **er** as the children say
beeeterrr. If sounding out is not firm, repeat *b.*
c. What word? (Signal.) *Better.* Yes, **better.**

better

TASK 15   Children sound out the word and tell what word

a. Touch the ball for **p̄ile.** Sound it out.
b. Get ready. Touch **p, ̄i, l** as the children say *p̄iiilll.*
If sounding out is not firm, repeat *b.*
c. What word? (Signal.) *Pile.* Yes, **pile.**

p̄ile

TASK 16   Children read the words the fast way

a. Now you get to read the words on this page the fast way.
b. Touch the ball for **moon.** (Pause three seconds.) Get ready.
Move your finger quickly along the arrow. *Moon.*
c. Repeat *b* for each word on the page.

TASK 17   Individual test

Call on different children to read one word the fast way.

Take-Home 127

PAIR RELATIONS
The children will need pencils.

TASK 24   Children draw a line from the word to the correct picture

a. Pass out Take-Home 127 to each child.
b. Point to the first set in the pair-relations exercise on side 2
(dog, gāte, rōad).
c. Everybody, here's the new Matching Game. In this game you match pictures with the words that tell about the picture.
d. Everybody, touch the first word.   Check children's responses.
e. Get ready to read that word the fast way. (Pause.) Get ready.
Clap. *Dog.* Yes, **dog.**
f. Everybody, touch the picture that shows a dog.
Check children's responses.
g. You're going to draw a line from the word **dog** to the picture that shows a dog.
h. Read the word and draw the line.   Check children's responses.
i. Everybody, touch the next word.   Check children's responses.
j. Get ready to read that word the fast way. (Pause.) Get ready.
Clap. *Gate.* Yes, **gate.**
k. Everybody, touch the picture that shows a gate.
Check children's responses.
l. You're going to draw a line from the word **gate** to the picture that shows a gate.
m. Read the word and draw the line.   Check children's responses.
n. Repeat *i* through *m* for the word **rōad.**
o. You'll finish drawing lines to the right pictures later.

SUMMARY OF INDEPENDENT ACTIVITY

TASK 25   Introduction to independent activity

a. Hold up side 1 of Take-Home 127.
b. Everybody, you're going to finish this take-home on your own.
Tell the children when they will work the remaining items.
Let's go over the things you're going to do.

TASK 26   Sentence copying

a. Point to the dotted sentence in the sentence-copying exercise.
b. You're going to trace the words in this sentence. Then you're going to write the sentence on the other lines.
c. Reading the fast way. First word.   Check children's responses.
Get ready. Clap. *She.*
d. Next word.   Check children's responses.   Get ready.   Clap. *Ate.*
e. Repeat *d* for the remaining words.
f. After you finish your take-home, you get to draw a picture about the sentence, **shē āte the log.** You'll draw your picture on a piece of plain paper.

TASK 27   Cross-out game

a. Point to the boxed words in the Cross-out Game. Everybody, what word are you going to circle? (Signal.) *Bug.* Yes, bug.
b. What word are you going to cross out? (Signal.) *Big.* Yes, big.

TASK 28   Reading comprehension

a. Point to the boxed sentences in the reading-comprehension exercise.
b. Everybody, get ready to read the sentences the fast way.
c. First word. Check children's responses. Get ready. Clap for each word as the children read *a big bug met a little bug.*
d. Have the children reread the sentence until firm.
e. Get ready to read the next sentence.
Repeat *c* and *d* for **hē said, "let's gō ēat."**
f. Point to items 1 and 2. These items tell about the story in the box.
You're going to read each item and circle the right answer.

TASK 29   Sound writing

a. Point to the sound-writing exercise on side 2. Here are the sounds you're going to write today. I'll touch the sounds. You say them.
b. Touch each sound. *The children respond.* Repeat until firm.

TASK 30   Pair relations

a. Point to the pair-relations exercise. You're going to read each word. Then draw a line from the word to the right picture.
b. When the children finish their take-homes, give them sheets of plain paper. Remind them to draw a picture that shows **shē āte the log.**

END OF LESSON 127

READING VOCABULARY

Do not touch any small letters.

TASK 7 Children read walk and walked

a. Touch the ball for **walk.** You're going to read this word the fast way. (Pause three seconds.) Get ready. Move your finger quickly along the arrow. *Walk.*

b. Return to the ball for **walk.** Yes, this word is **walk.**

c. Touch the ball for **walked.** So this must be **walk** . . . . Touch **d.** *d.* What word? (Signal.) *Walked.* Yes, **walked.**

d. Again. Repeat *b* and *c* until firm.

e. Touch the ball for **walk.** This word is **walk.**

f. Touch the ball for **walked.** So this must be. . . . Quickly run your finger under **walk** and tap **d.** *Walked.* Yes, **walked.**

g. Again. Repeat *e* and *f* until firm.

h. Now you're going to sound out (pause) **walked.** Get ready. Touch **w, a, l, k, d** as the children say *wwwaaalllkd.*

i. How do we say the word? (Signal.) *Walked.* Yes, **walked.**

TASK 8 Children identify, then sound out an irregular word (talked)

a. Touch the ball for **talked.** Everybody, you're going to read this word the fast way. (Pause three seconds.) Get ready. Move your finger quickly along the arrow. *Talked.* Yes, **talked.**

b. Now you're going to sound out the word. Get ready. Quickly touch **t, a, l, k, d** as the children say *taaalllkd.*

c. Again. Repeat *b.*

d. How do we say the word? (Signal.) *Talked.* Yes, **talked.**

e. Repeat *b* and *d* until firm.

TASK 9 Children identify, then sound out an irregular word (loved)

a. Touch the ball for **loved.** Everybody, you're going to read this word the fast way. (Pause three seconds.) Get ready. Move your finger quickly along the arrow. *Loved.* Yes, **loved.**

b. Now you're going to sound out the word. Get ready. Quickly touch **l, o, v, e, d** as the children say *lllooovvveeed.*

c. Again. Repeat *b.*

d. How do we say the word? (Signal.) *Loved.* Yes, **loved.**

e. Repeat *b* and *d* until firm.

walk

walked

talked

loved

TASK 10 Children read the words the fast way

Have the children read the words on this page the fast way.

TASK 11 Individual test

Call on different children to read one word the fast way.

Lesson 128

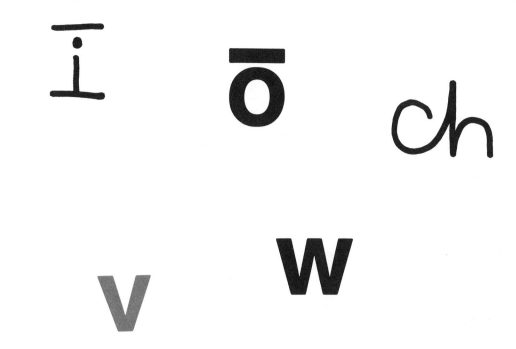

SOUNDS

TASK 1   Teaching ī as in īce

a. Point to ī. My turn. (Pause.)
Touch ī and say: īīī.
b. Point to ī. Your turn. When
I touch it, you say it. (Pause.)
Get ready. Touch ī. īīī.
Lift your finger.
c. Again. Touch ī. īīīī. Lift your finger.
d. Repeat *c* until firm.

TASK 2   Sounds firm-up

a. Get ready to say the sounds
when I touch them.
b. Alternate touching ī and **e.** Point
to the sound. (Pause one second.)
Say: Get ready. Touch the
sound. *The children respond.*
c. When ī and **e** are firm, alternate
touching **e,** ī**, i,** and **ing** until all
four sounds are firm.

TASK 3   Individual test

Call on different children to identify **e,** ī**, i,** or **ing.**

TASK 4   Sounds firm-up

a. Point to ī. When I touch the
sound, you say it.
b. (Pause.) Get ready. Touch ī. īīī.
c. Again. Repeat *b* until firm.
d. Get ready to say all the sounds
when I touch them.
e. Alternate touching ī, ō**, ch, v, w,
k, p,** and **b** three or four times.
Point to the sound.
(Pause one second.) Say:
Get ready. Touch the sound.
The children respond.

TASK 5   Individual test

Call on different children to identify
one or more sounds in task 4.

Lesson 145

J

g

sh

ch

SOUNDS

TASK 1   Teaching **j** as in **jump**

a. Point to **j**. Here's a new sound.
   It's a quick sound.
b. My turn.   (Pause.) Touch **j** for
   an instant, saying: j.
   Do not say **juuh**.
c. Again.   Touch **j** and say: j.
d. Point to **j**. Your turn. When I
   touch it, you say it.   (Pause.)
   Get ready.   Touch **j**. *j*.
e. Again.   Touch **j**. *j*.
f. Repeat *e* until firm.

TASK 2   Individual test

Call on different children to identify **j**.

TASK 3   Sounds firm-up

a. Get ready to say the sounds when I touch them.
b. Alternate touching **j** and **g**. Point to the sound. (Pause one second.)
   Say: Get ready.   Touch the sound. *The children respond.*
c. When **j** and **g** are firm, alternate touching **j**, **g**, **sh**, and **ch** until all
   four sounds are firm.

TASK 4   Individual test

Call on different children to identify **j**, **g**, **sh**, or **ch**.

TASK 5   Sounds firm-up

a. Point to **j**. When I touch the sound, you say it.
b. (Pause.) Get ready.   Touch **j**. *j*.
c. Again.   Repeat *b* until firm.
d. Get ready to say all the sounds when I touch them.
e. Alternate touching **oo, y, j, er, ī, c, x,** and **ō** three or four times.
   Point to the sound. (Pause one second.) Say: Get ready.
   Touch the sound. *The children respond.*

J   oo   y

ī

er   c

x   ō

TASK 6   Individual test

Call on different children to identify one or more sounds in task 5.

227

READING VOCABULARY

Do not touch any small letters.

TASK 6 Children sound out the word and tell what word

a. Touch the ball for **pond**. **Sound it out.**
b. **Get ready.** Touch **p, o, n, d** as the children say *pooonnnd.*
                                 If sounding out is not firm, repeat b.
c. **What word?** (Signal.) *Pond.* **Yes, pond.**

TASK 7 Children sound out the word and tell what word

a. Touch the ball for **back**. **Sound it out.**
b. **Get ready.** Touch **b, a, c** as the children say *baaac.*
                                 If sounding out is not firm, repeat b.
c. **What word?** (Signal.) *Back.* **Yes, back.**

TASK 8 Children sound out the word and tell what word

a. Touch the ball for **bed**. **Sound it out.**
b. **Get ready.** Touch **b, e, d** as the children say *beeed.*
                                 If sounding out is not firm, repeat b.
c. **What word?** (Signal.) *Bed.* **Yes, bed.**

TASK 9 Children sound out the word and tell what word

a. Touch the ball for **bus**. **Sound it out.**
b. **Get ready.** Touch **b, u, s** as the children say *buuusss.*
                                 If sounding out is not firm, repeat b.
c. **What word?** (Signal.) *Bus.* **Yes, bus.**

TASK 10 Children read the words the fast way

a. **Now you get to read the words on this page the fast way.**
b. Touch the ball for **pond**. (Pause three seconds.) **Get ready.**
                      Move your finger quickly along the arrow. *Pond.*
c. Repeat *b* for each word on the page.

TASK 11 Individual test

Call on different children to read one word the fast way.

READING COMPREHENSION

TASK 22   Children choose the correct words to fill in the blanks

a. Point to the reading-comprehension exercise on side 2.
b. Everybody, get ready to read the sentences in the box the fast way.
c. Get ready.   Clap for each word as the children read:
> A little bug bit a big bug. The little bug was mad.
> Repeat until firm.

d. Listen. **A little bug bit a big bug**.   (Pause.)   **The little bug was mad**.

e. Everybody, get ready to tell me the answer. Listen. **A little** (pause) **something bit a big bug**. Tell me what that something was. A little . . . . (Signal.) *Bug.* Yes, **bug**. A little bug bit a big bug.

f. Listen. **A little bug bit a big bug. The little bug was** (pause) **something**. The little bug was . . . . (Signal.) *Mad.* Yes, **mad**.

g. Repeat *b* through *f* until firm.
h. Everybody, get ready to read the sentences in the box the fast way again. Get ready.   Clap for each word as the children read:
> A little bug bit a big bug. The little bug was mad.

i. Everybody, read item 1 to yourself and touch the word that goes in the blank.   Check children's responses.
j. What word goes in the blank? (Signal.) *Bug.*
k. Everybody, circle the word **bug** under item 1.
Check children's responses.
l. Everybody, read item 2 to yourself and touch the word that goes in the blank.   Check children's responses.
m. What word goes in the blank? (Signal.) *Mad.*
n. Circle the word **mad** under item 2.   Check children's responses.

SUMMARY OF INDEPENDENT ACTIVITY

TASK 23   Introduction to independent activity

a. Hold up Take-Home 144.
b. Everybody, you're going to finish this take-home on your own.
Tell the children when they will work the remaining items.
Let's go over the things you're going to do.

TASK 24   Sound writing

a. Point to the sound-writing exercise on side 2. Here are the sounds you're going to write today. I'll touch the sounds. You say them.
b. Touch each sound. *The children respond.*
c. Repeat the series until firm.

TASK 25   Sentence copying

a. Point to the dotted sentence in the sentence-copying exercise.
b. You're going to trace the words in this sentence. Then you're going to write the sentence on the other lines.
c. Reading the fast way. First word. Check children's responses.
Get ready.   Clap for each word.
d. After you finish your take-home, you get to draw a picture about the sentence, **hē sat on the shōre**. You'll draw your picture on a piece of plain paper.   When the children finish their take-homes, give them sheets of plain paper.

END OF LESSON 144

TASK 12   Children sound out an irregular word (walk)

a. Touch the ball for **walk.** Sound it out.
b. Get ready.   Quickly touch each sound as the children say *wwwaaalllk.*
c. Again.   Repeat *b* until firm.
d. That's how we sound out the word. Here's how we say the word.
           Walk. How do we say the word?   (Signal.) *Walk.*
e. Now you're going to sound out the word. Get ready.
           Touch each sound as the children say *wwwaaalllk.*
f. Now you're going to say the word. Get ready.   (Signal.) *Walk.*
g. Repeat *e* and *f* until firm.

walk

TASK 13   Children rhyme with an irregular word (walk)

a. Touch the ball for **walk.** Everybody, you're going to read this word
                    the fast way. Get ready.   (Signal.) *Walk.*
b. Touch the ball for **talk.** This word rhymes with   (pause) **walk.**
            Get ready.   Move to **t,** then quickly along the arrow. *Talk.*
c. Repeat *a* and *b* until firm.

TASK 14   Children sound out talk

Have the children sound out **talk.** *Taaalllk.* How do we say the word?
                    (Signal.) *Talk.* Yes, **talk.** A baby can not **talk.**

talk

TASK 15   Children read the words the fast way

a. Now you get to read the words on this page the fast way.
b. Touch the ball for **talk.** (Pause three seconds.) Get ready.
                    Move your finger quickly along the arrow. *Talk.*
c. Repeat *b* for **walk.**

TASK 16   Individual test

Call on different children to read one word the fast way.

TASK 19 **Picture comprehension**

a. What do you think you'll see in the picture? *The children respond.*
b. Turn the page and look at the picture.
c. Ask these questions:
    1. What's happening in the picture? *The children respond.*
                          The bug is giving the eagle a dime.
    2. Would you give the eagle a dime? *The children respond.*

Take-Home 144

STORY ITEMS

The children will need pencils.

TASK 20 **Children complete sentences and answer story questions**

a. Pass out Take-Home 144 to each child.
b. Point to the story-items exercise on side 1. These items are about the story you just read.
c. Point to the blank in item 1. Something is missing. When you get to this blank, say "**Blank.**" What will you say? (Signal.) *Blank.*
d. Everybody, get ready to read item 1. Get ready. Clap for each word as the children read *a big blank came and sat on the shore.* Repeat until firm.
e. What goes in the blank? (Signal.) *Eagle.* Yes, **eagle.**
f. Everybody, read item 2 and when you come to a blank, say "**Blank.**"
g. Get ready. Clap for each word as the children read: *the eagle said, "give me a blank."* Repeat until firm.
h. What goes in the blank? (Signal.) *Dime.* Yes, **dime.**
i. Everybody, read item 3. Get ready. Clap for each word as the children read *did the bug give the eagle a dime?* Repeat until firm.
j. What's the answer? (Signal.) *Yes.*
k. Everybody, get ready to read item 4. Get ready. Clap for each word as the children read *did the bug go to the other side?* What's the answer? (Signal.) *Yes.*
l. Now, everybody, read each item to yourself and circle the right answer. Check children's responses.

PICTURE COMPREHENSION

TASK 21 **Children look at the picture and complete the missing word**

Refer to sounds, not letter names, in missing words.

a. Point to the first picture in the picture-comprehension exercise.
b. Everybody, touch this picture. Check children's responses.
c. Tell me what you see in this picture. Accept reasonable responses.
d. Point to the sound in the blank in item 1. Something is missing. When you get to this, say "**Blank.**" What will you say? (Signal.) *Blank.*
e. Everybody, get ready to read item 1.
f. Get ready. Clap for each word as the children read *the blank is fat.* Repeat until firm.
g. Look at the picture and get ready to tell me what is fat. (Pause.) The . . . (Signal.) *man* . . . is fat. Yes, **man.**
h. I'll say the sounds in the word **man. mmm** (pause) **aaa** (pause) **nnn.**
i. Your turn. Say the sounds in **man.** Get ready. Signal for each sound as the children say *mmm* (pause) *aaa* (pause) *nnn.* Repeat until firm.
j. Look at the blank in item 1. The **mmm** is already written in the blank. So what sounds are you going to write next? Signal for each sound as the children say *aaa* (pause) *nnn.* The children are not to write the sounds now.
k. Repeat *i* and *j* until firm.
l. Now write the missing word in the blank. Remember—the **mmm** is already written. Check children's responses.
m. Repeat *e* through *l* for item 2.
n. Repeat *b* through *m* for the second picture.

TASK 17 **Children read the fast way**

a. Get ready to read these words the fast way.

b. Touch the ball for **get.** (Pause three seconds.) Get ready.
(Signal.) *Get.*

c. Repeat *b* for the remaining words on the page.

TASK 18 **Children read the fast way again**

a. Get ready to do these words again. Watch where I point.

b. Point to a word. (Pause one second.) Say: Get ready. (Signal.)
The children respond. Point to the words in this order:
bit, down, get.

c. Repeat *b* until firm.

TASK 19 **Individual test**

Call on different children to read one word the fast way.

get

bit

down

Story 144

TASK 16 First reading—children read the title and first three sentences

a. Pass out Storybook 3.

b. Open your book to page 14. Now you're going to finish the story about the bug that wanted to get to the other side of the lake.

c. Everybody, touch the title of the story and get ready to read the words in the title the fast way.

d. First word. Check children's responses. (Pause two seconds.) Get ready. Clap. *The.*

e. Clap for each remaining word in the title.

f. After the children have read the title, ask: What's this story about? (Signal.) *The other side of the lake.* Yes, **the other side of the lake.**

g. Everybody, get ready to read this story the fast way.

h. First word. Check children's responses. (Pause two seconds.) Get ready. Clap. *A.*

i. Clap for the remaining words in the first sentence. Pause at least two seconds between claps.

j. Repeat *h* and *i* for the next two sentences. Have the children reread the first three sentences until firm.

TASK 17 Individual children or the group read sentences to complete the first reading

a. I'm going to call on different children to read a sentence. Everybody, follow along and point to the words. If you hear a mistake, raise your hand.

b. Call on a child. Read the next sentence. Do not clap for the words. Let the child read at his own pace, but be sure he reads the sentence correctly.

To correct	Have the child sound out the word. Then return to the beginning of the sentence.

c. Repeat *b* for most of the remaining sentences in the story. Occasionally have the group read a sentence. When the group is to read, say: Everybody, read the next sentence. (Pause two seconds.) Get ready. Clap for each word in the sentence. Pause at least two seconds between claps.

TASK 18 Second reading—individual children or the group read each sentence; the group answer questions

a. You're going to read the story again. This time I'm going to ask questions.

b. Starting with the first word of the title. Check children's responses. Get ready. Clap as the children read the title. Pause at least two seconds between claps.

c. Call on a child. Read the first sentence. *The child responds.*

d. Repeat *b* and *c* in task 17. Present the following comprehension questions to the entire group.

After the children read:	You say:
Then a big eagle came and sat down on the shore.	What happened? (Signal.) *A big eagle came and sat down on the shore.* Do you think the eagle can help the bug get to the other side? *The children respond.* How? *The children respond.* Let's read and find out.
"Give me a dime and I will take you to the other side."	What did the eagle say? (Signal.) *Give me a dime and I will take you to the other side.* Do you think the bug will do that? *The children respond.* Let's read and find out.
So the bug gave the eagle a dime and got on the eagle.	Did the bug give the eagle a dime? (Signal.) *Yes.* Then what did the bug do? (Signal.) *He got on the eagle.*
They went over the lake.	Did the bug get to the other side of the lake? (Signal.) *Yes.* How? *The children respond.* Yes, the eagle took him over.

Story 128

TASK 20 First reading—children read the story the fast way

Have the children reread any sentences containing words that give them trouble. Keep a list of these words.

a. Pass out Storybook 2.
b. Open your book to page 31.
c. Everybody, touch the title of the story and get ready to read the words in the title the fast way.
d. First word. Check children's responses. (Pause two seconds.) Get ready. Clap. *The*
e. Clap for each remaining word in the title.
f. After the children have read the title, ask: What's this story about? (Signal.) *The bug bus.* Yes, the bug bus.
g. Everybody, get ready to read this story the fast way.
h. First word. Check children's responses. (Pause two seconds.) Get ready. Clap. *A.*
i. Clap for the remaining words in the first sentence. Pause at least two seconds between claps.
j. Repeat h and i for the next two sentences. Have the children reread the first three sentences until firm.
k. The children are to read the remainder of the story the fast way, stopping at the end of each sentence.
l. After the first reading of the story, print on the board the words that the children missed more than one time. Have the children sound out each word one time and tell what word.
m. After the group's responses are firm, call on individual children to read the words.

TASK 21 Individual test

a. Turn back to page 31. I'm going to call on different children to read a whole sentence.
b. Call on different children to read a sentence. Do not clap for each word.

TASK 22 Second reading—children read the story the fast way and answer questions

a. You're going to read the story again the fast way and I'll ask questions.
b. Starting with the first word of the title. Check children's responses. Get ready. Clap. *The.*
c. Clap for each remaining word. Pause at least two seconds between claps. Pause longer before words that gave the children trouble during the first reading.
d. Ask the comprehension questions below as the children read.

After the children read:	You say:
The bug bus.	What's this story about? (Signal.) *The bug bus.*
A little bug sat on the back of a big dog.	What did the little bug do? (Signal.) *Sat on the back of a big dog.*
"I am not a bus."	What did the dog say? (Signal.) *I am not a bus.*
She went to sleep.	Did the bug get down? (Signal.) *No.* What did she do? (Signal). *She went to sleep.*
The dog said, "I am not a bed."	What did the dog say? (Signal.) *I am not a bed.* Do you think the bug will get down? *The children respond.* Let's read and find out.
The dog ran to the pond and went in.	What did the dog do? (Signal). *The dog ran to the pond and went in.*
"Take me back to the sand."	What did the bug say? (Signal.) *Take me back to the sand.*
"No," the dog said.	Did the dog go back to the sand? (Signal.) *No.*
Ten bugs came and got on the dog.	What happened? (Signal.) *Ten bugs came and got on the dog.*
The dog said, "I feel like a bug bus."	What did the dog say? (Signal.) *I feel like a bug bus.*

144

TASK 9   Children read a word beginning with two consonants

a. Cover **b.** Point to **room.** You're going to read this part of the word the fast way. (Pause three seconds.) Get ready. (Signal.) *Room.* Yes, **room.**

b. Uncover **b.** Point to **b.** You're going to say this first. Move your finger quickly under **b.** Then you're going to say (pause) **room.**

c. Point to **b.** What are you going to say first? (Signal.) *b.* What are you going to say next? (Signal.) *Room.* Repeat until firm.

d. Touch the ball for **broom.** Remember, first you say **b**; then you say **room.** Get ready. Move to **b,** then quickly along the arrow. *Broom.*

e. Say it fast. (Signal.) *Broom.* Yes, what word? (Signal.) *Broom.* Yes, **broom.** Good reading.

f. Again. Repeat *d* and *e* until firm.

g. Now you're going to sound out (pause) **broom.** Get ready. Touch **b, r, oo, m** as the children say *brrroooommm.* What word? (Signal.) *Broom.* Yes, **broom.**

TASK 10   Children sound out the word and tell what word

a. Touch the ball for **dīme.** Sound it out.

b. Get ready. Touch **d, ī, m** as the children say *dīīīmmm.*

c. What word? (Signal.) *Dime.* Yes, **dime.**

TASK 11   Children sound out the word and tell what word

Repeat the procedures in task 10 for **chōre.**

TASK 12   Children identify, then sound out an irregular word (you)

a. Touch the ball for **you.** Everybody, you're going to read this word the fast way. (Pause three seconds.) Get ready. Move your finger quickly along the arrow. *You.* Yes, **you.**

b. Now you're going to sound out the word. Get ready. Quickly touch **y, o, u** as the children say *yyyooouuu.* Repeat until firm.

c. How do we say the word? (Signal.) *You.* Yes, **you.**

d. Repeat *b* and *c* until firm.

TASK 13   Individual test—Have children do *b* and *c* in task 12.

TASK 14   Children read the words the fast way

Have the children read the words on this page the fast way.

TASK 15   Individual test—Have children read one word the fast way.

Do not touch any small letters.

TASK 23   Picture comprehension

a. Everybody, look at the picture.
b. Ask these questions:
   1. What are those little bugs doing? *The children respond.*
                      They're riding on a bug bus.
   2. Does the dog like having the bugs on his back? *No.*

Take-Home 128

SUMMARY OF INDEPENDENT ACTIVITY

TASK 24   Introduction to independent activity

a. Pass out Take-Home 128 to each child.
b. Everybody, you're going to do this take-home on your own.
                   Tell the children when they will work the items.
                   Let's go over the things you're going to do.

TASK 25   Sentence copying

a. Hold up side 1 of your take-home and point to the dotted sentence in the sentence-copying exercise.
b. You're going to trace the words in this sentence. Then you're going to write the sentence on the other lines.
c. Reading the fast way. First word. Check children's responses.
                      Get ready. Clap. *The.*
d. Next word. Check children's responses. Get ready. Clap. *Bug.*
e. Repeat *d* for the remaining words.
f. After you finish your take-home, you get to draw a picture about the sentence, **the bug was on a dog.** You'll draw your picture on a piece of plain paper.

TASK 26   Cross-out game

a. Point to the boxed words in the Cross-out Game. Everybody, what word are you going to circle? (Signal.) *Pet.* Yes, pet.
b. What word are you going to cross out? (Signal.) *Get.* Yes, **get.**

TASK 27   Reading comprehension

a. Point to the boxed sentences in the reading-comprehension exercise.
b. Everybody, get ready to read the sentences the fast way.
c. First word. Check children's responses. Get ready. Clap for each word as the children read *the dog said, "I am a dog."*
d. Have the children reread the sentence until firm.
e. Get ready to read the next sentence.
                      Repeat *c* and *d* for "**I am not a bus.**"
f. Point to items 1 and 2. These items tell about the story in the box. You're going to read each item and circle the right answer.

TASK 28   Sound writing

a. Point to the sound-writing exercise on side 2. Here are the sounds you're going to write today. I'll touch the sounds.
                      You say them.
b. Touch each sound. *The children respond.*
c. Repeat the series until firm.

TASK 29   Pair relations

a. Point to the pair-relations exercise. You're going to read each word. Then draw a line from the word to the right picture.
b. When the children finish their take-homes, give them sheets of plain paper. Remind them to draw a picture that shows **the bug was on a dog.**

END OF LESSON 128

READING VOCABULARY

Do not touch any small letters.

TASK 6   Children read the fast way

a. Get ready to read these words the fast way.

b. Touch the ball for **room.** (Pause three seconds.)   Get ready.
(Signal.) *Room.*

c. Repeat *b* for the remaining words on the page.

TASK 7   Children read the fast way again

a. Get ready to do these words again. Watch where I point.

b. Point to a word. (Pause one second.) Say: Get ready.   (Signal.)
The children respond. Point to the words in this order:
room, shōre, ēagle, sitting, yes.

c. Repeat *b* until firm.

TASK 8   Individual test

Call on different children to read one word the fast way.

room

sitting

yes

shōre

ēagle

Lesson 129

SOUNDS

TASK 1 Child plays teacher

a. Use acetate and crayon.
b. [Child's name] is going to be the teacher.
c. He is going to touch the sounds. When he touches a sound, you say it.

d. The child points to and touches the sounds. You circle any sound that is not firm.

e. After the child has completed the page, present all the circled sounds to the children.

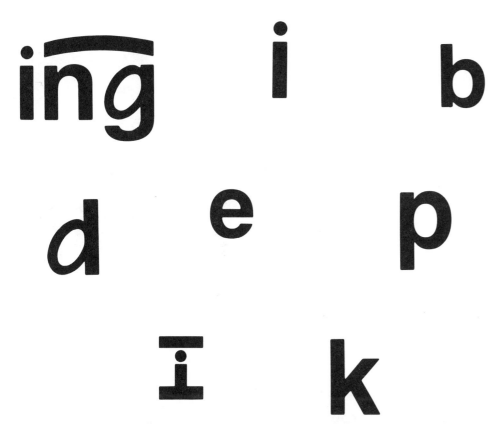

TASK 2 Individual test

Call on different children. If you can say the sound when I call your name, you may cross it out.

TASK 3 Sounds firm-up

a. Point to I. When I touch the sound, you say it.
b. (Pause.) Get ready. Touch I. *III.*
c. Again. Repeat *b* until firm.
d. Get ready to say all the sounds when I touch them.
e. Alternate touching **ch, c, e, o, l, u, ō,** and **I** three or four times. Point to the sound. (Pause one second.) Say: Get ready. Touch the sound. *The children respond.*

TASK 4 Individual test

Call on different children to identify one or more sounds in task 3.

Lesson 144

SOUNDS

TASK 1 Sounds firm-up

a. Get ready to say the sounds when I touch them.

b. Alternate touching **oo** and **r.** Point to the sound. (Pause one second.) Say: Get ready. Touch the sound. *The children respond.*

c. When **oo** and **r** are firm, alternate touching **oo, r, x,** and **w** until all four sounds are firm.

TASK 2 Individual test

Call on different children to identify **oo, r, x,** or **w.**

TASK 3 Teacher introduces cross-out game

a. Use acetate and crayon.

b. I'll cross out the sounds on this part of the page when you can tell me every sound.

c. Remember—when I touch it, you say it.

d. Go over the sounds until the children can identify all the sounds in order.

TASK 4 Individual test

Call on different children to identify two or more sounds in task 4.

TASK 5 Teacher crosses out sounds

a. You told me every sound. Get ready to do it again. This time I'll cross out each sound when you tell me what it is.

b. Point to each sound. (Pause.) Say: Get ready. Touch the sound. *The children respond.* As you cross out the sound, say:

Goodbye, _____ .

READING VOCABULARY

TASK 5   Children read the fast way

a. Get ready to read these words the fast way.
b. Touch the ball for **slēēp.** (Pause three seconds.) Get ready.
(Signal.) *Sleep.*

c. Repeat *b* for the remaining words on the page.

TASK 6   Children read the fast way again

a. Get ready to do these words again. Watch where I point.
b. Point to a word. (Pause one second.) Say: Get ready.   (Signal.)
The children respond. Point to the words in this order:
big, bit, but, slēēp.

c. Repeat *b* until firm.

TASK 7   Individual test

Call on different children to read one word the fast way.

sl**ēē**p

bit

but

big

TASK 21   Picture comprehension

a. Everybody, look at the picture.
b. Ask these questions:
   1. What is that bug doing?   *The children respond.*
                                          Sitting on the shore.
   2. I wonder why he doesn't swim across that lake.
                    The children respond. He doesn't want to get wet.
   3. I wonder why he doesn't take his car to the other side.
                    The children respond. He doesn't have one.
   4. What would you do if you were that bug?   *The children respond.*

Take-Home 143

SUMMARY OF INDEPENDENT ACTIVITY

TASK 22   Introduction to independent activity

a. Pass out Take-Home 143 to each child.
b. Everybody, you're going to do this take-home on your own.
                    Tell the children when they will work the items.
                    Let's go over the things you're going to do.

TASK 23   Story items

a. Hold up side 1 of your take-home and point to the story-items
                                          exercise.
b. Everybody, read item 1 about the story the fast way. First word.
        Check children's responses. Get ready.   Clap for each word as
                    the children read *the bug sat on the shore of . . . .*
c. Everybody, what's the answer?   (Signal.) *A lake.*
d. Think about what happened in the story and circle the right
                                          answer for each item.

TASK 24   Sound writing

a. Point to the sound-writing exercise. Here are the sounds you're
                    going to write today. I'll touch the sounds. You say them.
b. Touch each sound. *The children respond.*
c. Repeat the series until firm.

TASK 25   Reading comprehension

a. Point to the boxed sentences in the reading-comprehension
                                          exercise.
b. Everybody, get ready to read the sentences the fast way.
c. First word.   Check children's responses. Get ready.   Clap for
                    each word as the children read *a boy had a box.*
d. Have the children reread the sentence until firm.
e. Get ready to read the next sentence.   Repeat *c* and *d* for **a fox
                                          went in the box.**
f. Point to items 1 and 2. These items tell about the story in the
                    box. You're going to read each item and circle the right
                                          answer.

TASK 26   Sentence copying

a. Hold up side 2 of your take-home and point to the dotted sentence
                    in the sentence-copying exercise.
b. You're going to trace the words in this sentence. Then you're
                    going to write the sentence on the other lines.
c. Reading the fast way. First word.   Check children's responses.
                    Get ready.   Clap for each word.
d. After you finish your take-home, you get to draw a picture about
                    the sentence, **a bug sat at the lāke.** You'll draw your picture
                    on a piece of plain paper.

TASK 27   Pair relations

a. Point to the pair-relations exercise. You're going to read each
                    sentence. Then draw a line from the sentence to the right
                                          picture.
b. When the children finish their take-homes, give them sheets of
                    plain paper. Remind them to draw a picture that shows **a bug
                                          sat at the lāke.**

END OF LESSON 143

TASK 8 Children sound out the word and tell what word

a. Touch the ball for **bīte**. Sound it out.
b. Get ready. Touch **b, ī, t**, as the children say *bīīt*.

If sounding out is not firm, repeat *b*.

c. What word? (Signal.) *Bite.* Yes, **bite**.

TASK 9 Children sound out the word and tell what word

a. Touch the ball for **tub**. Sound it out.
b. Get ready. Touch **t, u, b** as the children say *tuuub*.

If sounding out is not firm, repeat *b*.

c. What word? (Signal.) *Tub.* Yes, **tub**.

TASK 10 Children sound out an irregular word (walk)

a. Touch the ball for **walk**. Sound it out.
b. Get ready. Quickly touch each sound as the children say *wwwaaalllk*.

To correct	If the children do not say the sounds you touch
	1. Say: You've got to say the sounds I touch.
	2. Repeat *a* and *b* until firm.

c. Again. Repeat *b* until firm.
d. That's how we <u>sound out</u> the word. Here's how we <u>say</u> the word.
Walk. How do we <u>say</u> the word? (Signal.) *Walk.*
e. Now you're going to <u>sound out</u> the word. Get ready.

Touch each sound as the children say *wwwaaalllk*.
f. Now you're going to say the word. Get ready. (Signal.) *Walk.*
g. Repeat *e* and *f* until firm.
h. Yes, this word is **walk**. Let's go for a walk.

TASK 11 Individual test

Call on different children to do *e* and *f* in task 10.

TASK 12 Children read the words the fast way

Have the children read the words on this page the fast way.

TASK 13 Individual test

Call on different children to read one word the fast way.

Do not touch any small letters.

bīte

tub

walk

Story 143

TASK 18 First reading—children read the title and first three sentences

a. Pass out Storybook 3.

b. Open your book to page 12. You're going to read the first part of this story today.

c. Everybody, touch the title of the story and get ready to read the words in the title the fast way.

d. First word. Check children's responses. (Pause two seconds.) Get ready. Clap. *The*.

e. Clap for each remaining word in the title.

f. After the children have read the title, ask: What's this story about? (Signal.) *The other side of the lake.* Yes, **the other side of the lake**.

g. Everybody, get ready to read this story the fast way.

h. First word. Check children's responses. (Pause two seconds.) Get ready. Clap. *A*.

i. Clap for the remaining words in the first sentence. Pause at least two seconds between claps.

j. Repeat *h* and *i* for the next two sentences. Have the children reread the first three sentences until firm.

TASK 19 Individual children or the group read sentences to complete the first reading

a. I'm going to call on different children to read a sentence. Everybody, follow along and point to the words. If you hear a mistake, raise your hand.

b. Call on a child. Read the next sentence. Do not clap for the words. Let the child read at his own pace, but be sure he reads the sentence correctly.

To correct	Have the child sound out the word. Then return to the beginning of the sentence.

c. Repeat *b* for most of the remaining sentences in the story. Occasionally have the group read a sentence. When the group is to read, say: Everybody, read the next sentence. (Pause two seconds.) Get ready. Clap for each word in the sentence. Pause at least two seconds between claps.

TASK 20 Second reading—individual children or the group read each sentence; the group answer questions

a. You're going to read the story again. This time I'm going to ask questions.

b. Starting with the first word of the title. Check children's responses. Get ready. Clap as the children read the title. Pause at least two seconds between claps.

c. Call on a child. Read the first sentence. *The child responds.*

d. Repeat *b* and *c* in task 19. Present the following comprehension questions to the entire group.

After the children read:	You say:
The other side of the lake.	What's this story about? (Signal.) *The other side of the lake.*
The bug said, "I need to get to the other side of this big lake."	What did he say? (Signal.) *I need to get to the other side of this big lake.* Where was he? (Signal.) *On the shore.*
"But I do not like to get wet."	What did the bug say? *The children respond.* He said, "I like to sleep and I like to ride in a car. But I do not like to get wet."
So he sat and sat on the shore of the lake.	What did he do? (Signal.) *He sat and sat on the shore of the lake.* I wonder how he'll get to the other side of the lake. We'll find out when we read the next part of the story.

TASK 14   Children sound out an irregular word (talk)

a. Touch the ball for **talk.**   Sound it out.

b. Get ready. Quickly touch each sound as the children say *taaalllk.*

c. Again. Repeat *b until firm.*

d. That's how we <u>sound out</u> the word. Here's how we <u>say</u> the word.
Talk. How do we <u>say</u> the word. (Signal.) *Talk.*

e. Now you're going to <u>sound out</u> the word. Get ready.
Touch each sound as the children say *taaalllk.*

f. Now you're going to say the word. Get ready. (Signal.) *Talk.*

g. Repeat *e* and *f* until firm.

h. Yes, this word is **talk.** I am **talking** to you now.

i. Call on different children to do *e* and *f* in task 14.

TASK 15   Children read a word beginning with two consonants (stop)

a. Cover **s.** Point to **top.**   You're going to read this part of the word
the fast way. (Pause three seconds.)   Get ready. (Signal.) *Top.*
Yes, **top.**

b. Uncover **s.** Point to **s.**   You're going to say this first.
Move your finger quickly under **top.**   Then you're going to say
(pause)   **top.**

c. Point to **s.**   What are you going to say first? (Signal.) *sss.*
What are you going to say next? (Signal.) *Top.*

d. Repeat *c* until firm.

e. Touch the ball for **stop.**   Remember—first you say **sss**; then you
say **top.**   Get ready. Move to **s,** then quickly along the arrow.
Ssstop.

f. Say it fast. (Signal.) *Stop.*   Yes, what word? (Signal.) *Stop.*
Yes, **stop.** Good reading.

g. Again. Repeat *e* and *f* until firm.

h. Now you're going to sound out (pause)   **stop.** Get ready. Touch
s, t, o, p as the children say *ssstooop.*   What word? (Signal.) *Stop.*
Yes, stop.

TASK 16   Children read the words the fast way

Have the children read the words on this page the fast way.

TASK 17   Individual test

Call on different children to read one word the fast way.

TASK 12   Children identify, then sound out an irregular word (other)

a. Touch the ball for **other.**   Everybody, you're going to read this word the fast way. (Pause three seconds.)   Get ready. Move your finger quickly along the arrow. *Other.*   Yes, **other.**

b. Now you're going to sound out the word. Get ready. Quickly touch **o, th, er** as the children say *ooothththerrr.*

c. Again. Repeat *b.*

d. How do we say the word? (Signal.) *Other.*   Yes, **other.**

e. Repeat *b* and *d* until firm.

TASK 13   Individual test

Call on different children to do *b* and *d* in task 12.

Do not touch any small letters.

TASK 14   Children identify, then sound out an irregular word (you)

a. Touch the ball for **you.**   Everybody, you're going to read this word the fast way. (Pause three seconds.)   Get ready. Move your finger quickly along the arrow. *You.*   Yes, **you.**

b. Now you're going to sound out the word. Get ready. Quickly touch **y, o, u** as the children say *yyyooouuu.*

c. Again. Repeat *b.*

d. How do we say the word? (Signal.) *You.*   Yes, **you.**

e. Repeat *b* and *d* until firm.

TASK 15   Individual test

Call on different children to do *b* and *d* in task 14.

TASK 16   Children identify, then sound out an irregular word (are)

a. Touch the ball for **are.**   Everybody, you're going to read this word the fast way. (Pause three seconds.)   Get ready. Move your finger quickly along the arrow. *Are.*   Yes, **are.**

b. Now you're going to sound out the word. Get ready. Quickly touch **a, r** as the children say *aaarrr.*

c. Again. Repeat *b.*

d. How do we say the word? (Signal.) *Are.*   Yes, **are.**

e. Repeat *b* and *d* until firm.

TASK 17   Individual test

Call on different children to do *b* and *d* in task 16.

Story 129

TASK 18   First reading—children read the story the fast way

Have the children reread any sentences containing words that give them trouble. Keep a list of these words.

a. Pass out Storybook 2.
b. Open your book to page 34.
c. Everybody, touch the title of the story and get ready to read the words in the title the fast way.
d. First word. Check children's responses. (Pause two seconds.) Get ready. Clap. *The.*
e. Clap for each remaining word in the title.
f. After the children have read the title, ask: What's this story about? (Signal.) *The man and his bed.* Yes, the man and his bed.
g. Everybody, get ready to read this story the fast way.
h. First word. Check children's responses. (Pause two seconds.) Get ready. Clap. *A.*
i. Clap for the remaining words in the first sentence. Pause at least two seconds between claps.
j. Repeat *h* and *i* for the next two sentences. Have the children reread the first three sentences until firm.
k. The children are to read the remainder of the story the fast way, stopping at the end of each sentence.
l. After the first reading of the story, print on the board the words that the children missed more than one time. Have the children sound out each word one time and tell what word.
m. After the group's responses are firm, call on individual children to read the words.

TASK 19   Individual test

a. Look at page 34. I'm going to call on different children to read a whole sentence.
b. Call on different children to read a sentence. Do not clap for each word.

TASK 20   Second reading—children read the story the fast way and answer questions

a. You're going to read the story again the fast way and I'll ask questions.
b. Starting with the first word of the title. Check children's responses. Get ready. Clap. *The.*
c. Clap for each remaining word. Pause at least two seconds between claps. Pause longer before words that gave the children trouble during the first reading.
d. Ask the comprehension questions below as the children read.

After the children read:	You say:
The man and his bed.	What's this story about? (Signal.) *The man and his bed.*
He said, "I like to sit in the tub and rub, rub, rub."	What did the man say? (Signal.) *I like to sit in the tub and rub, rub, rub.*
Then the man said, "Now I will sleep in this bed."	What did the man say? (Signal.) *Now I will sleep in this bed.*
But a dog was in his bed.	What was in his bed? (Signal.) *A dog.*
"So he can sleep with me."	Will the man let the dog sleep in the bed? (Signal.) *Yes.*
And the dog did not bite the man.	Does the dog like to bite? (Signal.) *No.* Did he bite the man? (Signal.) *No.*

TASK 21   Picture comprehension

a. What do you think you'll see in the picture? *The children respond.*
b. Turn the page and look at the picture.
c. Ask these questions:
   1. What is in the man's bed? *A dog.*
   2. What would you do if a dog wanted to sleep in your bed? *The children respond.*

TASK 9   Children read slide and slider

Do not touch any small letters.

a. Cover **s.** Run your finger under l͞īde. You're going to sound out this part. Get ready. Touch **l, ī, d** as the children say *Illīīīd.*

b. Say it fast. (Signal.) *Līde.* Yes, this part is l͞īde.

c. Uncover **s.** Point to **s.** You're going to say this first. Move your finger quickly under l͞īde. Then you're going to say (pause) l͞īde.

d. Point to **s.** What are you going to say first? (Signal.) *sss.* What are you going to say next? (Signal.) *Līde.*

e. Repeat *d* until firm.

f. Touch the ball for **slide.** Get ready. Move to **s,** then quickly along the arrow. *Ssslīde.*

g. Say it fast. (Signal.) *Slide.* Yes, what word? (Signal.) *Slide.* Yes, **slide.** Good reading.

h. Again. Repeat *f* and *g* until firm.

i. Now you're going to sound out (pause) **slide.** Get ready. Touch **s, l, ī, d** as the children say *sssllīīīd.* What word? (Signal.) *Slide.* Yes, **slide.**

j. Point to slīde. This word is slide.

k. Tap under **er** in slīder. So this must be . . . . Touch the ball for **slīder** and move your finger quickly along the arrow. *Slider.* Yes, **slider.**

l. Repeat *j* and *k* until firm.

m. Now you're going to sound out (pause) **slider.** Get ready. Touch **s, l, ī, d, er** as the children say *sssllīīīderrr.* What word? (Signal.) *Slider.* Yes, **slider.**

TASK 10   Children identify, then sound out an irregular word (car)

a. Touch the ball for **car.** Everybody, you're going to read this word the fast way. (Pause three seconds.) Get ready. Move your finger quickly along the arrow. *Car.* Yes, **car.**

b. Now you're going to sound out the word. Get ready. Quickly touch **c, a, r** as the children say *caaarrr.*

c. Again. Repeat *b.*

d. How do we say the word? (Signal.) *Car.* Yes, **car.**

e. Repeat *b* and *d* until firm.

TASK 11   Individual test

Call on different children to do *b* and *d* in task 10.

slīde

slīder

car

Take-Home 129

SUMMARY OF INDEPENDENT ACTIVITY

TASK 22 Introduction to independent activity

a. Pass out Take-Home 129 to each child.

b. Everybody, you're going to do this take-home on your own. Tell the children when they will work the items. Let's go over the things you're going to do.

TASK 23 Sentence copying

a. Hold up side 1 of your take-home and point to the dotted sentence in the sentence-copying exercise.

b. You're going to trace the words in this sentence. Then you're going to write the sentence on the other lines.

c. Reading the fast way. First word. Check children's responses. Get ready. Clap. *A.*

d. Next word. Check children's responses. Get ready. Clap. *Man.*

e. Repeat *d* for the remaining words.

f. After you finish your take-home, you get to draw a picture about the sentence **a man had a tub**. You'll draw your picture on a piece of plain paper.

TASK 24 Cross-out game

a. Point to the boxed words in the Cross-out Game. Everybody, what word are you going to circle? (Signal.) *Hat.* Yes, **hat**.

b. What word are you going to cross out? (Signal.) *Hate.* Yes, **hate**.

TASK 25 Reading comprehension

a. Point to the boxed sentences in the reading-comprehension exercise.

b. Everybody, get ready to read the sentences the fast way.

c. First word. Check children's responses. Get ready. Clap for each word as the children read *the man had a tub.*

d. Have the children reread the sentence until firm.

e. Get ready to read the next sentence. Repeat *c* and *d* for **hē said, "I līke to rub, rub."**

f. Point to items 1 and 2. These items tell about the story in the box. You're going to read each item and circle the right answer.

TASK 26 Sound writing

a. Point to the sound-writing exercise on side 2. Here are the sounds you're going to write today. I'll touch the sounds. You say them.

b. Touch each sound. *The children respond.*

c. Repeat the series until firm.

TASK 27 Pair relations

a. Point to the pair-relations exercise. You're going to read each word. Then draw a line from the word to the picture.

b. When the children finish their take-homes, give them sheets of plain paper. Remind them to draw a picture that shows **a man had a tub**.

END OF LESSON 129

READING VOCABULARY

Do not touch any small letters.

TASK 6   Children sound out the word and tell what word

a. Touch the ball for **shōre.** Sound it out.
b. Get ready.   Touch **sh, ō, r** as the children say *shshshōōōrrr.*
   If sounding out is not firm, repeat *b.*
c. What word? (Signal.) *Shore.* Yes, **shore.**

TASK 7   Children read the fast way

a. Get ready to read these words the fast way.
b. Touch the ball for **tāke.** (Pause three seconds.) Get ready.
                                                    (Signal.) *Take.*
c. Repeat *b* for the remaining words on the page.

TASK 8   Children read the fast way again

a. Get ready to do these words again. Watch where I point.
b. Point to a word. (Pause one second.) Say: Get ready.   (Signal.)
   The children respond. Point to the words in this order:
   shōre, tāke, lāke, eāgle, wet.
c. Repeat *b* until firm.

Individual test

Call on different children to read one word the fast way.

shōre

tāke

ēagle

wet

lāke

Lesson 130

SOUNDS

TASK 1   Teacher and children play the sounds game

a. Use acetate and crayon. Write the sounds in the symbol box. Keep score in the score box.
b. **I'm smart. I bet I can beat you in a game.**
c. **Here's the rule. When I touch a sound, you say it.**
d. Play the game.
Make one symbol at a time in the symbol box. Use the symbols **b, ing, ē,** and **e.**
Make each symbol quickly. (Pause.) Touch the symbol.
Play the game for about two minutes.
Then ask: **Who won?** Draw a mouth on the face in the score box.

TASK 2   Child plays teacher

a. Use acetate and crayon.
b. **[Child's name] is going to be the teacher.**
c. **He is going to touch the sounds. When he touches a sound, you say it.**
d. The child points to and touches the sounds. You circle any sound that is not firm.
e. After the child has completed the page, present all the circled sounds to the children.

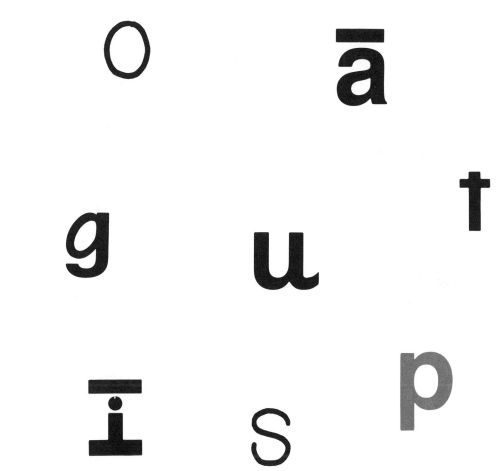

TASK 3   Individual test

Call on different children. **If you can say the sound when I call your name, you may cross it out.**

Lesson 143

Groups that are firm on Mastery Tests 26 and 27 should skip this lesson and do lesson 144 today.

SOUNDS

TASK 1 Teaching **oo** as in **moon** (not **look**)

a. Point to **oo**. My turn. (Pause.) Touch **oo** and say: *oooo*.
b. Point to **oo**. Your turn. When I touch it, you say it. (Pause.)
Get ready. Touch **oo**. *oooo*. Lift your finger.
c. Again. Touch **oo**. *oooooooo*. Lift your finger.
d. Repeat *c* until firm.

TASK 2 Sounds firm-up

a. Get ready to say the sounds when I touch them.
b. Alternate touching **oo** and **w**. Point to the sound. (Pause one second.)
Say: Get ready. Touch the sound. *The children respond.*
c. When **oo** and **w** are firm, alternate touching **oo**, **w**, **o**, and **ō** until all four sounds are firm.

TASK 3 Individual test

Call on different children to identify **oo**, **w**, **o**, or **ō**.

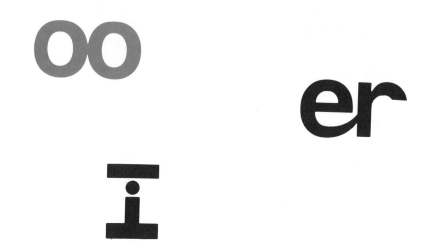

TASK 4 Sounds firm-up

a. Point to **oo**. When I touch the sound, you say it.
b. (Pause.) Get ready. Touch **oo**. *oooo*.
c. Again. Repeat *b* until firm.
d. Get ready to say all the sounds when I touch them.
e. Alternate touching **oo**, **er**, **ī**, **x**, **b**, **e**, **ā**, and **y** three or four times. Point to the sound.
(Pause one second.) Say:
Get ready. Touch the sound. *The children respond.*

TASK 5 Individual test

Call on different children to identify one or more sounds in task 4.

215

130

READING VOCABULARY

TASK 4 Children read the fast way

a. Get ready to read these words the fast way.
b. Touch the ball for **them.** (Pause three seconds.) Get ready.

(Signal.) *Them.*

c. Repeat *b* for the remaining words on the page.

TASK 5 Children read the fast way again

a. Get ready to do these words again. Watch where I point.
b. Point to a word. (Pause one second.) Say: Get ready. (Signal.)
The children respond. Point to the words in this order:
cats, bed, fishing, gōing, them.
c. Repeat *b* until firm.

TASK 6 Individual test

Call on different children to read one word the fast way.

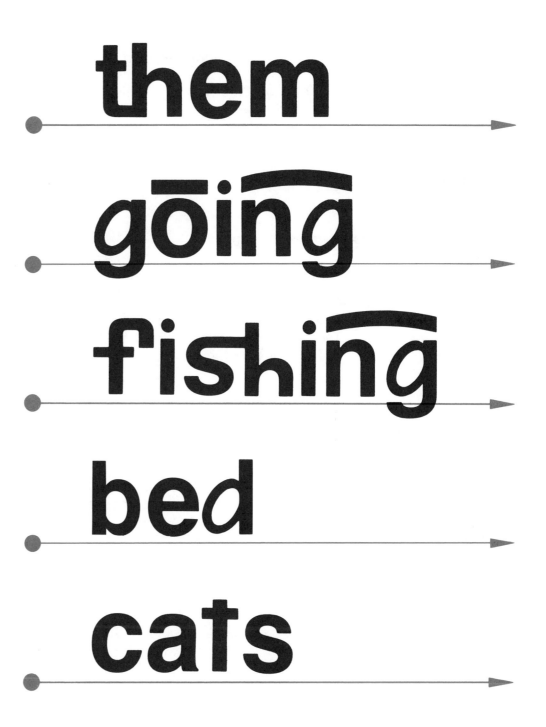

them

gōing

fishing

bed

cats

TASK 21   Picture comprehension

a. Everybody, look at the picture.
b. Ask these questions:
   1. What do you see in the box? *The children respond.*
                                       The fat fox and his brother.
   2. I wonder which is the fat fox and which is his brother?
       The children respond. I can see why it got hot in that box
                           with two foxes hitting it.

Take-Home 142

SUMMARY OF INDEPENDENT ACTIVITY

TASK 22   Introduction to independent activity

a. Pass out Take-Home 142 to each child.
b. Everybody, you're going to do this take-home on your own.
          Tell the children when they will work the items.
          Let's go over the things you're going to do.

TASK 23   Story items

a. Hold up side 1 of your take-home and point to the story-items
                       exercise.
b. Everybody, read item 1 about the story the fast way. First word.
   Check children's responses. Get ready. Clap for each word as the
             children read *a fat fox went in . . . .*
c. Everybody, what's the answer? (Signal.) *A box.*
d. Think about what happened in the story and circle the right
               answer for each item.

TASK 24   Sound writing

a. Point to the sound-writing exercise. Here are the sounds you're
         going to write today. I'll touch the sounds. You say them.
b. Touch each sound. *The children respond.*
c. Repeat the series until firm.

TASK 25   Reading comprehension

a. Point to the boxed sentences in the reading-comprehension exercise.
b. Everybody, get ready to read the sentences the fast way.
c. First word. Check children's responses. Get ready. Clap for
           each word as the children read *a boy had a toy.*
d. Have the children reread the sentence until firm.
e. Get ready to read the next sentence. Repeat *c* and *d* for
                    the toy was red.
f. Point to items 1 and 2. These items tell about the story in the box.
       You're going to read each item and circle the right answer.

TASK 26   Sentence copying

a. Hold up side 2 of your take-home and point to the dotted sentence
              in the sentence-copying exercise.
b. You're going to trace the words in this sentence. Then you're
           going to write the sentence on the other lines.
c. Reading the fast way. First word. Check children's responses.
             Get ready. Clap for each word.
d. After you finish your take-home, you get to draw a picture about
       the sentence, **I love to hit a box.** You'll draw your picture on
              a piece of plain paper.

TASK 27   Pair relations

a. Point to the pair-relations exercise. You're going to read each
       sentence. Then draw a line from the sentence to the right picture.
b. When the children finish their take-homes, give them sheets of
       plain paper. Remind them to draw a picture that shows **I love to hit
                    a box.**

END OF LESSON 142

TASK 7   Children identify, then sound out an irregular word (walk)

a. Touch the ball for **walk**. Everybody, you're going to read this word the fast way. (Pause three seconds.) Get ready. Move your finger quickly along the arrow. *Walk*. Yes, **walk**.

b. Now you're going to sound out the word. Get ready. Quickly touch **w, a, l, k** as the children say *wwwaaalllk*.

c. Again. Repeat *b*.

d. How do we say the word? (Signal.) *Walk*. Yes, **walk**.

e. Repeat *b* and *d* until firm.

TASK 8   Individual test

Call on different children to do *b* and *d* in task 7.

TASK 9   Children identify, then sound out an irregular word (talking)

a. Touch the ball for **talking**. Everybody, you're going to read this word the fast way. (Pause three seconds.) Get ready. Move your finger quickly along the arrow. *Talking*. Yes, **talking**.

b. Now you're going to sound out the word. Get ready. Quickly touch **t, a, l, k, ing** as the children say *taaalllkiiing*.

c. Again. Repeat *b*.

d. How do we say the word? (Signal.) *Talking*. Yes, **talking**.

e. Repeat *b* and *d* until firm.

TASK 10   Individual test

Call on different children to do *b* and *d* in task 9.

TASK 11   Children read the words the fast way

a. Now you get to read the words on this page the fast way.

b. Touch the ball for **talking.** (Pause three seconds.) Get ready. Move your finger quickly along the arrow. *Talking*.

c. Repeat *b* for **walk.**

TASK 12   Individual test

Call on different children to read one word the fast way.

Story 142

TASK 18 First reading—children read the title and first three sentences

a. Pass out Storybook 3.
b. Open your book to page 9.
c. Everybody, touch the title of the story and get ready to read the words in the title the fast way.
d. First word. Check children's responses. (Pause two seconds.) Get ready. Clap. *The.*
e. Clap for each remaining word in the title.
f. After the children have read the title, ask: What's this story about? (Signal.) *The fat fox and his brother.* Yes, the fat fox and his brother.
g. Everybody, get ready to read this story the fast way.
h. First word. Check children's responses. (Pause two seconds.) Get ready. Clap. *A.*
i. Clap for the remaining words in the first sentence. Pause at least two seconds between claps.
j. Repeat *h* and *i* for the next two sentences. Have the children reread the first three sentences until firm.

TASK 19 Individual children or the group read sentences to complete the first reading

a. I'm going to call on different children to read a sentence. Everybody, follow along and point to the words. If you hear a mistake, raise your hand.
b. Call on a child. Read the next sentence. Do not clap for the words. Let the child read at his own pace, but be sure he reads the sentence correctly.

To correct	Have the child sound out the word. Then return to the beginning of the sentence.

c. Repeat *b* for most of the remaining sentences in the story. Occasionally have the group read a sentence. When the group is to read, say: Everybody, read the next sentence. (Pause two seconds.) Get ready. Clap for each word in the sentence. Pause at least two seconds between claps.

TASK 20 Second reading—individual children or the group read each sentence; the group answer questions

a. You're going to read the story again. This time I'm going to ask questions.
b. Starting with the first word of the title. Check children's responses. Get ready. Clap as the children read the title. Pause at least two seconds between claps.
c. Call on a child. Read the first sentence. *The child responds.*
d. Repeat *b* and *c* in task 19. Present the following comprehension questions to the entire group.

After the children read:	You say:
The fat fox and his brother.	What's this story about? (Signal.) *The fat fox and his brother.*
His brother said, "Sitting in a box is not a lot of fun."	What did his brother say? (Signal.) *Sitting in a box is not a lot of fun.* Where were the fat fox and his brother? (Signal.) *In a big box.* Did the fat fox like to sit in a box? (Signal.) *No.*
So he hit and hit.	What happened? *The children respond.* He hit the box with his hand, nose, and tail.
"Let's stop hitting."	What did the fat fox say? (Signal.) *Let's stop hitting.*
"Sleeping in a box is fun."	What did his brother say? (Signal.) *Sleeping in a box is fun.* Why are the foxes tired? *The children respond.* From hitting the box.

TASK 13 Children sound out the word and tell what word

a. Touch the ball for **dīve.** Sound it out.

b. Get ready. Touch **d, ī, v,** as the children say *dīīvvv.*
                    If sounding out is not firm, repeat *b.*

c. What word? (Signal.) *Dive.* Yes, **dive.**

TASK 14 Children sound out the word and tell what word

a. Touch the ball for **līke.** Sound it out.

b. Get ready. Touch **l, ī, k** as the children say *lllīīīk.*
    If sounding out is not firm, repeat *b.*

c. What word? (Signal.) *Like.* Yes, **like.**

**TASK 15 Children read a word beginning with two consonants
      (slīding)**

a. Cover **s.** Run your finger under **līding.** You're going to sound out
    this part. Get ready. Touch **l, ī, d, ing** as the children say *llīīīdiiing.*

b. Say it fast. (Signal.) *Līding.* Yes, this part is **liding.**

c. Uncover **s.** Point to **s.** You're going to say this first.
    Move your finger quickly under **liding.** Then you're going to say
                    (pause) **līding.**

d. Point to **s.** What are you going to say first? (Signal.) *sss.*
                    What are you going to say next? (Signal.) *Līding.*

e. Repeat *d* until firm.

f. Touch the ball for **slīding.** Remember—first you say **sss**; then you
                    say **līding.** Get ready. Move to **s,** then quickly along the
                    arrow. *Ssslīding.*

g. Say it fast. (Signal.) *Sliding.* Yes, what word? (Signal.) *Sliding.*
                    Yes, **sliding.** Good reading.

h. Again. Repeat *f* and *g* until firm.

i. Now you're going to sound out (pause) **sliding.** Get ready.
                    Touch **s, l, ī, d, ing** as the children say *ssslllīīīdiiing.*
                    What word? (Signal.) *Sliding.* Yes, **sliding.**

TASK 16 Children read the words the fast way

a. Now you get to read the words on this page the fast way.

b. Touch the ball for **slīding.** (Pause three seconds.) Get ready.
                    Move your finger quickly along the arrow. *Sliding.*

c. Repeat *b* for **dīve.**

Do not touch any small letters.

TASK 17 Individual test

Call on different children to read one word the fast way.

142

TASK 12   Children read the fast way

Touch the ball for **stop.** Get ready to read this word the fast way.
(Pause three seconds.) Get ready. (Signal.) *Stop.*

TASK 13   Children sound out the word and tell what word

a. Touch the ball for **they.** Sound it out.
b. Get ready. Touch **th, e, y** as the children say *thththeeeyyy.*
If sounding out is not firm, repeat *b.*
c. What word? (Signal.) *They.* Yes, **they.**

TASK 14   Children sound out the word and tell what word

Repeat the procedures in task 13 for **ever.**

TASK 15   Children rhyme with box

a. Touch the ball for **box.** You're going to read this word the fast way.
(Pause three seconds.) Get ready.
Move your finger quickly along the arrow. *Box.*
b. Touch the ball for **fox.** This word rhymes with (pause) **box.**
Move to **f,** then quickly along the arrow. *Fffox.*
Yes, what word? (Signal.) *Fox.*

TASK 16   Children read the words the fast way

Have the children read the words on this page the fast way.

TASK 17   Individual test

Call on different children to read one word the fast way.

stop

they

ever

box

fox

212

Story 130

TASK 18   First reading—children read the story the fast way

Have the children reread any sentences containing words that give them trouble. Keep a list of these words.

a. Pass out Storybook 2.
b. Open your book to page 37.
c. Everybody, touch the title of the story and get ready to read the words in the title the fast way.
d. First word. Check children's responses. (Pause two seconds.) Get ready. Clap. *The.*
e. Clap for each remaining word in the title.
f. After the children have read the title, ask: What's this story about? (Signal.) *The talking cat.* Yes, **the talking cat.**
g. Everybody, get ready to read this story the fast way.
h. First word. Check children's responses. (Pause two seconds.) Get ready. Clap. *The.*
i. Clap for the remaining words in the first sentence. Pause at least two seconds between claps.
j. Repeat *h* and *i* for the next two sentences. Have the children reread the first three sentences until firm.
k. The children are to read the remainder of the story the fast way, stopping at the end of each sentence.
l. After the first reading of the story, print on the board the words that the children missed more than one time. Have the children sound out each word one time and tell what word.
m. After the group's responses are firm, call on individual children to read the words.

TASK 19   Individual test

a. Turn back to page 37. I'm going to call on different children to read a whole sentence.
b. Call on different children to read a sentence. Do not clap for each word.

TASK 20   Second reading—children read the story the fast way and answer questions

a. You're going to read the story again the fast way and I'll ask questions.
b. Starting with the first word of the title. Check children's responses. Get ready. Clap. *The.*
c. Clap for each remaining word. Pause at least two seconds between claps. Pause longer before words that gave the children trouble during the first reading.
d. Ask the comprehension questions below as the children read.

After the children read:	You say:
The talking cat.	What's this story about? (Signal.) *The talking cat.*
She met a fat cat.	What did she meet? (Signal.) *A fat cat.* Where was the girl going when she met the cat? (Signal.) *For a walk.*
"But I do not talk to girls."	What did the cat say? (Signal.) *But I do not talk to girls.* Who is the cat talking to? (Signal.) *The girl.* That cat is silly.
The cat said, "I will not talk to girls."	What did the cat say? (Signal.) *I will not talk to girls.* Who is that cat talking to? (Signal.) *The girl.* That cat is silly.
"And I do not give fish to cats I do not like."	What did the girl say? (Signal.) *And I do not give fish to cats I do not like.* What do you think the cat will do now? *The children respond.* Let's read and find out.
The cat said, "I like fish so I will talk to this girl."	What did the cat say? (Signal.) *I like fish, so I will talk to this girl.* Why is the cat talking to her? (Signal.) *Because the cat likes fish.*
So the girl and the cat ate fish.	What did the girl and the cat do? (Signal). *They ate fish.*

READING VOCABULARY

Do not touch any small letters.

TASK 7   Children sound out the word and tell what word

a. Touch the ball for **ōver.** Sound it out.
b. Get ready. Touch **ō, v, er** as the children say *ōōōvvverrr.*
    If sounding out is not firm, repeat *b.*
c. What word? (Signal.) *Over.* Yes, **over.**

TASK 8   Children sound out the word and tell what word

Repeat the procedures in task 7 for **ēagle.**

TASK 9   Children read the fast way

a. Get ready to read these words the fast way.
b. Touch the ball for **sitting.** (Pause three seconds.) Get ready.
                              (Signal.) *Sitting.*

c. Repeat *b* for the remaining words on the page.

TASK 10   Children read the words the fast way

Have the children read the words on this page the fast way.

TASK 11   Individual test

Call on different children to read one word the fast way.

ōver

ēagle

sitting

hitting

sleeping

130

TASK 21 Picture comprehension

a. Everybody, look at the picture.

b. Ask these questions:

1. What are the girl and the cat doing? *The children respond.* Eating.

2. Does that cat look happy now? (Signal.) *Yes.*

3. Do you think he'll talk to the girl after he eats? *The children respond.*

4. He's such a silly cat. What would you do if you had a talking cat? *The children respond.*

Take-Home 130

SUMMARY OF INDEPENDENT ACTIVITY

TASK 22 Introduction to independent activity

a. Pass out sides 1 and 2 of Take-Home 130 to each child.

b. Everybody, do a good job on your take-home today and I'll give you a bonus take-home.

c. Hold up side 1 of your take-home. You're going to do this take-home on your own. Tell the children when they will work the items. Let's go over some of the things you're going to do.

TASK 23 Sentence copying

a. Point to the dotted sentence in the sentence-copying exercise.

b. You're going to trace the words in this sentence. Then you're going to write the sentence on the other lines.

c. Reading the fast way. First word. Check children's responses. Get ready. Clap. *She.*

d. Next word. Check children's responses. Get ready. Clap. *Met.*

e. Repeat *d* for the remaining words.

f. After you finish your take-home, you get to draw a picture about the sentence, **shē met a fat cat.** You'll draw your picture on a piece of plain paper.

TASK 24 Reading comprehension

a. Point to the boxed sentences in the reading-comprehension exercise.

b. Everybody, get ready to read the sentences the fast way.

c. First word. Check children's responses. Get ready. Clap for each word as the children read *"can cats talk?" the girl said.*

d. Have the children reread the sentence until firm.

e. Get ready to read the next sentence.

Repeat *c* and *d* for **the cat said, "I can talk."**

f. Point to items 1 and 2. These items tell about the story in the box. You're going to read each item and circle the right answer.

TASK 25 Other independent activity: sides 1, 2, 3, 4

Remember to do all the parts of the take-home and to read all the parts carefully. After you draw your picture, I'll give you a bonus take-home.

INDIVIDUAL CHECKOUT: STORYBOOK

TASK 26 3-minute individual checkout

a. As you are doing your take-home, I'll call on children one at a time to read the **whole story.** Remember, you get two stars if you read the story in less than three minutes and make no more than three errors.

b. Call on a child. Tell the child: Start with the title and read the story carefully the fast way. Go. Time the child. Tell the child any words the child misses. Stop the child as soon as the child makes the fourth error or exceeds the time limit.

c. If the child meets the rate-accuracy criterion, record two stars on your chart for lesson 130. Congratulate the child. Give children who do not earn two stars a chance to read the story again before the next lesson is presented.

107 words/3 min = 36 wpm [3 errors]

END OF LESSON 130

Before presenting lesson 131, give Mastery Test 25 to each child.
Do not present lesson 131 to any groups that are not firm on this test.

Lesson 142

oo

r

o

w

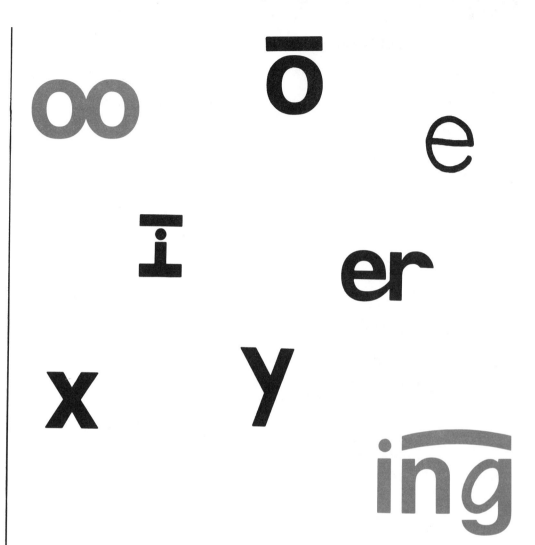

SOUNDS

TASK 1   Teaching oo as in moon (not look)

a. Point to **oo.** Here's a new sound.
b. My turn. (Pause.) Touch **oo** and say: **oooo.**
c. Again. Touch **oo** for a longer time. **ooooooo.** Lift your finger.
d. Point to **oo.** Your turn. When I touch it, you say it. (Pause.) Get ready. Touch **oo.** *oooo.* Lift your finger.
e. Again. Touch **oo.** *oooooooo.* Lift your finger.
f. Repeat e until firm.

TASK 2   Individual test

Call on different children to identify **oo.**

TASK 3   Sounds firm-up

a. Get ready to say the sounds when I touch them.
b. Alternate touching **oo** and **r.** Point to the sound. (Pause one second.) Say: Get ready. Touch the sound. *The children respond.*
c. When **oo** and **r** are firm, alternate touching **oo, r, o,** and **w** until all four sounds are firm.

TASK 4   Individual test

Call on different children to identify **oo, r, o,** or **w.**

TASK 5   Sounds firm-up

a. Point to **oo.** When I touch the sound, you say it.
b. (Pause.) Get ready. Touch **oo.** *oooo.*
c. Again. Repeat b until firm.
d. Get ready to say all the sounds when I touch them.
e. Alternate touching **oo, ō, e, ī, er, x, y,** and **ing** three or four times. Point to the sound. (Pause one second.) Say: Get ready. Touch the sound. *The children respond.*

TASK 6   Individual test

Call on different children to identify one or more sounds in task 5.

210

Mastery Test 25 after lesson 130, before lesson 131

a. Get ready to read these words the fast way.
b. (test item) Touch the ball for **sent.** (Pause three seconds.)
Get ready. (Signal.) *Sent.*
c. (test item) Touch the ball for **gōing.** (Pause three seconds.)
Get ready. (Signal.) *Going.*
d. (test item) Touch the ball for **bugs.** (Pause three seconds.)
Get ready. (Signal.) *Bugs.*
e. (test item) Touch the ball for **walk.** (Pause three seconds.)
Get ready. (Signal.) *Walk.*

Total number of test items: **4**

A group is weak if more than one-third of the children missed any of the items on the test.

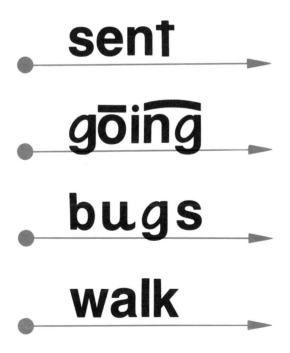

WHAT TO DO

If the group is firm on Mastery Test 25 and was firm on Mastery Test 24:

Present lessons 131 and 132, and then skip lesson 133. If more than one child missed any of the items on the test, present the firming procedures specified below to those children.

If the group is firm on Mastery Test 25 but was weak on Mastery Test 24:

Present lesson 131 to the group during the next reading period. If more than one child missed any of the items on the test, present the firming procedures specified below to those children.

If the group is weak on Mastery Test 25:

A. Present these firming procedures to the group during the next reading period.
   1. Lesson 127, Reading Vocabulary, pages 119–120, tasks 7 through 14.
   2. Lesson 128, Reading Vocabulary, page 126, tasks 12 through 16.
   3. Lesson 129, Reading Vocabulary, page 131–132, tasks 5 through 13.
   4. Lesson 130, Reading Vocabulary, pages 137–138, tasks 4 through 12.
B. After presenting the above tasks, again give Mastery Test 25 individually to members of the group who failed the test.
C. If the group is firm (less than one-third of the total group missed any items on the retest), present lesson 131 to the group during the next reading period.
D. If the group is still weak (more than one-third of the total group missed any items on the retest), repeat *A* and *B* during the next reading period.

Take-Home 141

END OF LESSON 141

SUMMARY OF INDEPENDENT ACTIVITY

TASK 26   Introduction to independent activity

a. Pass out Take-Home 141 to each child.
b. Everybody, you're going to do this take-home on your own.
Tell the children when they will work the items.
Let's go over the things you're going to do.

TASK 27   Story items

a. Hold up side 1 of your take-home and point to the story-items
exercise.
b. Everybody, read item 1 about the story the fast way. First word.
Check children's responses. Get ready. Clap for each word as the
children read *his mother liked . . . .*
c. Everybody, what's the answer? (Signal.) *Little toys.*
d. Think about what happened in the story and circle the right answer
for each item.

TASK 28   Sound writing

a. Point to the sound-writing exercise. Here are the sounds you're
going to write today. I'll touch the sounds. You say them.
b. Touch each sound. *The children respond.*
c. Repeat the series until firm.

TASK 29   Reading comprehension

a. Point to the boxed sentences in the reading-comprehension exercise.
b. Everybody, get ready to read the sentences the fast way.
c. First word. Check children's responses. Get ready. Clap for
each word as the children read *a duck did not like to walk.*
d. Have the children reread the sentence until firm.
e. Get ready to read the next sentence. Repeat c and d for **sō the
duck went in the lāke.**
f. Point to items 1 and 2. These items tell about the story in the box.
You're going to read each item and circle the right answer.

TASK 30   Sentence copying

a. Hold up side 2 of your take-home and point to the dotted sentence
in the sentence-copying exercise.
b. You're going to trace the words in this sentence. Then you're going
to write the sentence on the other lines.
c. Reading the fast way. First word. Check children's responses.
Get ready. Clap for each word.
d. After you finish your take-home, you get to draw a picture about
the sentence, **hē māde a duck big.** You'll draw your picture
on a piece of plain paper.

TASK 31   Pair relations

a. Point to the pair-relations exercise. You're going to read each
sentence. Then draw a line from the sentence to the right picture.
b. When the children finish their take-homes, give them sheets of
plain paper. Remind them to draw a picture that shows
hē māde a duck big.

END OF LESSON 141

Lesson 131

y

v

SOUNDS

TASK 1 Teaching y as in yes

a. Point to **y.** Here's a new sound.

b. My turn. (Pause.) Touch **y** and say: yyy.

c. Again. Touch **y** for a longer time. yyyyy. Lift your finger.

d. Point to **y.** Your turn. When I touch it, you say it. (Pause.) Get ready. Touch **y.** *yyy.* Lift your finger.

e. Again. Touch **y.** *yyyyyy.* Lift your finger.

f. Repeat *e* until firm.

TASK 2 Individual test

Call on different children to identify **y.**

TASK 3 Sounds firm-up

a. Get ready to say the sounds when I touch them.

b. Alternate touching **y** and **v.** Point to the sound. (Pause one second.) Say: Get ready. Touch the sound. *The children respond.*

c. When **y** and **v** are firm, alternate touching **y, v, w,** and **i** until all four sounds are firm.

TASK 4 Individual test

Call on different children to identify **y, v, w,** or **i.**

y

n

o

e

ō

ī

TASK 5 Sounds firm-up

a. Point to **y.** When I touch the sound, you say it.

b. (Pause.) Get ready. Touch **y.** *yyy.*

c. Again. Repeat *b* until firm.

d. Get ready to say all the sounds when I touch them.

e. Alternate touching **y, n, o, ō, e, ī, ing,** and **b** three or four times. Point to the sound. (Pause one second.) Say: Get ready. Touch the sound. *The children respond.*

TASK 6 Individual test

Call on different children to identify one or more sounds in task 5.

Story 141

TASK 22 First reading—children read the title and first three sentences

a. Pass out Storybook 3.

b. Open your book to page 7. Now you're going to finish the story about the boy who liked big toys.

c. Everybody, touch the title of the story and get ready to read the words in the title the fast way.

d. First word. Check children's responses. (Pause two seconds.) Get ready. Clap. *Going.*

e. Clap for each remaining word in the title.

f. After the children have read the title, ask: What's this story about? (Signal.) *Going to the toy shop.* Yes, **going to the toy shop.**

g. Everybody, get ready to read this story the fast way.

h. First word. Check children's responses. (Pause two seconds.) Get ready. Clap. *A.*

i. Clap for the remaining words in the first sentence. Pause at least two seconds between claps.

j. Repeat *h* and *i* for the next two sentences. Have the children reread the first three sentences until firm.

TASK 23 Individual children or the group read sentences to complete the first reading

a. I'm going to call on different children to read a sentence. Everybody, follow along and point to the words. If you hear a mistake, raise your hand.

b. Call on a child. Read the next sentence. Do not clap for the words. Let the child read at his own pace, but be sure he reads the sentence correctly.

To correct	Have the child sound out the word. Then return to the beginning of the sentence.

c. Repeat *b* for most of the remaining sentences in the story. Occasionally have the group read a sentence. When the group is to read, say: Everybody, read the next sentence. (Pause two seconds.) Get ready. Clap for each word in the sentence. Pause at least two seconds between claps.

TASK 24 Second reading—individual children or the group read each sentence; the group answer questions

a. You're going to read the story again. This time I'm going to ask questions.

b. Starting with the first word of the title. Check children's responses. Get ready. Clap as the children read the title. Pause at least two seconds between claps.

c. Call on a child. Read the first sentence. *The child responds.*

d. Repeat *b* and *c* in task 23. Present the following comprehension questions to the entire group.

After the children read:	You say:
"They are big and little."	What did the man say? *The children respond.* He said, "I have toys that you will like. They are big and little." I wonder how toys can be big <u>and</u> little. Let's read and find out.
He got a little toy duck and he made it big.	I wonder how he did that. *The children respond.*

TASK 25 Picture comprehension

a. Everybody, look at the picture.

b. Ask these questions:

1. Now I see how he made the little duck big. How did he do that? *The children respond.* He blew it up.
2. Is that duck big <u>and little</u>? Yes.
3. When is it big? *The children respond.* After it's blown up.
4. When is it little? *The children respond.* Before it's blown up.
5. Did you ever have a toy that you could blow up and make big? *The children respond.*

131

READING VOCABULARY

TASK 7 Children sound out the word and tell what word

a. Touch the ball for **rabbit**. Sound it out.
b. Get ready. Touch **r, a,** between the **b**'s, **i, t** as the children say *rrraaabiiit*. If sounding out is not firm, repeat *b*.
c. What word? (Signal.) *Rabbit*. Yes, **rabbit**.

TASK 8 Children read the fast way

a. Get ready to read these words the fast way.
b. Touch the ball for **fishing**. (Pause three seconds.) Get ready.
(Signal.) *Fishing*.
c. Repeat *b* for the remaining words on the page.

TASK 9 Children read the fast way again

a. Get ready to do these words again. Watch where I point.
b. Point to a word. (Pause one second.) Say: Get ready. (Signal.)
The children respond. Point to the words in this order:
slēēping, mōre, sitting, fishing.
c. Repeat *b* until firm.

TASK 10 Individual test

Call on different children to read one word the fast way.

Do not touch any small letters.

rabbit

fishing

sitting

slēēping

mōre

TASK 17   Children sound out an irregular word (come)

a. Touch the ball for **come**.   Sound it out.
b. Get ready.   Quickly touch each sound as the children say

cooommmeee.

To correct	If the children do not say the sounds you touch
	1. Say: **You've got to say the sounds I touch.**
	2. Repeat *a* and *b* until firm.

c. Again.   Repeat *b* until firm.
d. That's how we <u>sound out</u> the word. Here's how we <u>say</u> the word.
Come. How do we <u>say</u> the word?   (Signal.) *Come.*
e. Now you're going to <u>sound out</u> the word. Get ready.
Touch each sound as the children say *cooommmeee.*
f. Now you're going to say the word. Get ready.   (Signal.) *Come.*
g. Repeat *e* and *f* until firm.
h. Yes, this word is **come**. **Come** with me to the store.

TASK 18   Individual test

Call on different children to do *e* and *f* in task 17.

TASK 19   Children read the fast way

a. Get ready to read these words the fast way.
b. Touch the ball for **līke**. (Pause three seconds.)   Get ready.
(Signal.) *Like.*
c. Repeat *b* for the remaining words on the page.

TASK 20   Children read the fast way again

a. Get ready to do these words again. Watch where I point.
b. Point to a word. (Pause one second.) Say: Get ready.   (Signal.)
The children respond. Point to the words in this order:
līke, getting, fox.
c. Repeat *b* until firm.

TASK 21   Individual test

Call on different children to read one word on the page the fast way.

Do not touch any small letters.

131

TASK 11 Children read the fast way

a. Get ready to read these words the fast way.

b. Touch the ball for **slēēps.** (Pause three seconds.) Get ready.
(Signal.) *Sleeps.*

c. Repeat *b* for the remaining words on the page.

TASK 12 Children read the fast way again

a. Get ready to do these words again. Watch where I point.

b. Point to a word. (Pause one second.) Say: Get ready. (Signal.)
The children respond. Point to the words in this order:
ōr, dīve, slēēps, them, with.

c. Repeat *b* until firm.

TASK 13 Individual test

Call on different children to read one word the fast way.

Do not touch any small letters.

slēēps

ōr

with

dīve

them

145

TASK 13   Children sound out the word and tell what word

a. Touch the ball for **topper.**   Sound it out.
b. Get ready. Touch **t, o,** between the **p**'s, **er** as the children say
tooooperrr. If sounding out is not firm, repeat *b.*
c. What word? (Signal.) *Topper.*   Yes, **topper.**

topper

**TASK 14   Children read a word beginning with two consonants
(stopper)**

a. Cover **s.** Run your finger under **topper.**   You're going to sound
out this part. Get ready. Touch **t, o,** between the **p**'s, **er** as the
children say *tooooperrr.*
b. Say it fast. (Signal.) *Topper.*   Yes, this part is **topper.**
c. Uncover **s.** Point to **s.**   You're going to say this first.
Move your finger quickly under **topper.**   Then you're going to say
(pause)   **topper.**
d. Point to **s.**   What are you going to say first? (Signal.) *sss.*
What are you going to say next? (Signal.) *Topper.*
e. Repeat *d* until firm.
f. Touch the ball for **stopper.**   Remember, first you say **sss;** then
you say **topper.** Get ready. Move to **s,** then quickly along the
arrow. *Ssstopper.*
g. Say it fast. (Signal.) *Stopper.*   Yes, what word? (Signal.) *Stopper.*
Yes, **stopper.** Good reading.
h. Again. Repeat *f* and *g* until firm.
i. Now you're going to sound out (pause)   **stopper.** Get ready.
Touch **s, t, o,** between the **p**'s, **er** as the children say *ssstoooperrr.*
What word? (Signal.) *Stopper.*   Yes, **stopper.**

stopper

TASK 15   Children read the words the fast way

a. Now you get to read the words on this page the fast way.
b. Touch the ball for **topper.** (Pause three seconds.)   Get ready.
Move your finger quickly along the arrow. *Topper.*
c. Repeat *b* for **stopper.**

TASK 16   Individual test

Call on different children to read one word the fast way.

Story 131

146

TASK 14   First reading—children read the story the fast way

Have the children reread any sentences containing words that give them trouble. Keep a list of these words.

a. Pass out Storybook 2.
b. Open your book to page 40.
c. Everybody, touch the title of the story and get ready to read the words in the title the fast way.
d. First word. Check children's responses. (Pause two seconds.) Get ready. Clap. *The.*
e. Clap for each remaining word in the title.
f. After the children have read the title, ask: What's this story about? (Signal.) *The dog that ate fish.* Yes, **the dog that ate fish.**
g. Everybody, get ready to read this story the fast way.
h. First word. Check children's responses. (Pause two seconds.) Get ready. Clap. *A.*
i. Clap for the remaining words in the first sentence. Pause at least two seconds between claps.
j. Repeat *h* and *i* for the next two sentences. Have the children reread the first three sentences until firm.
k. The children are to read the remainder of the story the fast way, stopping at the end of each sentence.
l. After the first reading of the story, print on the board the words that the children missed more than one time. Have the children sound out each word one time and tell what word.
m. After the group's responses are firm, call on individual children to read the words.

TASK 15   Individual test

a. Look at page 40. I'm going to call on different children to read a whole sentence.
b. Call on different children to read a sentence. Do not clap for each word.

TASK 16   Second reading—children read the story the fast way and answer questions

a. You're going to read the story again the fast way and I'll ask questions.
b. Starting with the first word of the title. Check children's responses. Get ready. Clap. *The.*
c. Clap for each remaining word. Pause at least two seconds between claps. Pause longer before words that gave the children trouble during the first reading.
d. Ask the comprehension questions below as the children read.

After the children read:	You say:
The dog that ate fish.	What's this story about? (Signal.) *The dog that ate fish.*
The girl did not like the dog to eat fish.	Who went fishing? (Signal.) *The girl and the dog.* Did the dog eat fish? (Signal.) *Yes.* How did the girl feel about the dog eating fish? *The children respond.* She did not like the dog to eat fish.
"Give me the five fish," the dog said.	What did the dog say? (Signal.) *Give me the five fish.* How many fish did the girl catch? (Signal.) *Five.* Do you think the girl will give the fish to the dog? *The children respond.*
"No," the girl said.	What did the girl say? (Signal.) *No.* Did she want to give the fish to the dog? (Signal.) *No.*
"Dive in and get them."	What did the girl say? *The children respond.* She said, "More fish are in the lake. Dive in and get them." Do you think the dog will do that? *The children respond.*
And the girl went to sleep.	Did the dog go in the lake? (Signal.) *Yes.* What did the girl do? (Signal.) *Sleep.*

READING VOCABULARY

Do not touch any small letters.

TASK 7 Children sound out the word and tell what word

a. Touch the ball for **box.** Sound it out.

b. Get ready. Touch **b, o, x** as the children say *booox.*

If sounding out is not firm, repeat *b.*

c. What word? (Signal.) *Box.* Yes, **box.**

TASK 8 Children sound out the word and tell what word

a. Touch the ball for **hand.** Sound it out.

b. Get ready. Touch **h, a, n, d** as the children say *haaannnd.*

If sounding out is not firm, repeat *b.*

c. What word? (Signal.) *Hand.* Yes, **hand.**

TASK 9 Children sound out the word and tell what word

a. Touch the ball for **bīke.** Sound it out.

b. Get ready. Touch **b, ī, k** as the children say *bīīīk.*

If sounding out is not firm, repeat *b.*

c. What word? (Signal.) *Bike.* Yes, **bike.**

TASK 10 Children sound out the word and tell what word

a. Touch the ball for **thēse.** Sound it out.

b. Get ready. Touch **th, ē, s** as the children say *thththēēēsss.*

If sounding out is not firm, repeat *b.*

c. What word? (Signal.) *These.* Yes, **these.**

TASK 11 Children read the words the fast way

a. Now you get to read the words on this page the fast way.

b. Touch the ball for **box.** (Pause three seconds.) Get ready.

Move your finger quickly along the arrow. *Box.*

c. Repeat *b* for each word on the page.

TASK 12 Individual test

Call on different children to read one word the fast way.

box

hand

bīke

thēse

TASK 17 Picture comprehension

a. What do you think you'll see in the picture? *The children respond.*

b. Turn the page and look at the picture.

c. Ask these questions:

1. How many fish does the girl have? *Five.*

2. What do you think she's saying to that dog?

The children respond.

3. I wonder what's in that can near the girl.

The children respond. Yes, worms.

4. Did you ever go fishing and catch five fish?

The children respond.

Take-Home 131

STORY ITEMS
The children will need pencils.

TASK 18 Children complete sentences and answer story questions

a. Pass out Take-Home 131 to each child.

b. Point to the story-items exercise on side 1. These items are about the story you just read.

c. Everybody, read item 1 the fast way. First word. Check children's responses. Get ready. Clap for each word as the children read *the girl got . . . .*

d. The story told that the girl went fishing, and the girl got . . . . Everybody, what did the girl get? (Signal.) *Five fish.* Yes, **five fish**.

e. Touch the right words in item 1. Check children's responses. Circle the words. Check children's responses.

To correct	Have the children read the appropriate sentence in the story. Then repeat *d* and *e*.

f. Everybody, read item 2 the fast way. First word. Check children's responses. Get ready. Clap for each word as the children read *did she give fish to the dog?*

g. Everybody, did she give fish to the dog? (Signal.) *No.*

h. Touch the right word in item 2. Check children's responses. Circle the word. Check children's responses.

i. Everybody, read item 3 the fast way. First word. Check children's responses. Get ready. Clap for each word as the children read *the dog went . . . .*

j. Everybody, where did the dog go? (Signal.) *In the lake.* Yes, **in the lake**.

k. Touch the right words in item 3. Check children's responses. Circle the words. Check children's responses.

Lesson 141

Groups that are firm on Mastery Tests 26 and 27 should skip this lesson and do lesson 142 today.

SOUNDS

TASK 1   Teaching **x** as in **ox**

a. Point to **x.** My turn. When I touch it, I'll say it. (Pause.)
Touch **x** for an instant, saying: **ks.** Do not say **ecks.**
b. Point to **x.** Your turn. When I touch it, you say it. (Pause.)
Get ready. Touch **x.** *ks.*

c. Again. Touch **x.** *ks.*
d. Repeat *c* until firm.

TASK 2   Sounds firm-up

a. Get ready to say the sounds when I touch them.
b. Alternate touching **x** and **k.** Point to the sound. (Pause one second.) Say: Get ready. Touch the sound. *The children respond.*
c. When **x** and **k** are firm, alternate touching **x, k, s,** and **ch** until all four sounds are firm.

TASK 3   Individual test

Call on different children to identify **x, k, s,** or **ch.**

TASK 4   Teacher introduces cross-out game

a. Use acetate and crayon.
b. I'll cross out the sounds on this part of the page when you can tell me every sound.

c. Remember—when I touch it, you say it.
d. Go over the sounds until the children can identify all the sounds in order.

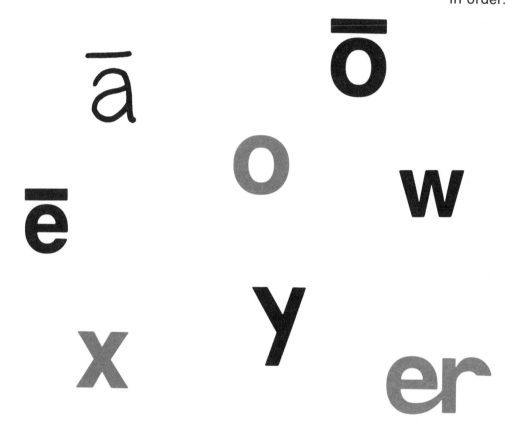

TASK 5   Individual test

Call on different children to identify two or more sounds in task 4.

TASK 6   Teacher crosses out sounds

a. You told me every sound. Get ready to do it again. This time I'll cross out each sound when you tell me what it is.
b. Point to each sound. (Pause.) Say: Get ready. Touch the sound. *The children respond.* As you cross out the sound, say:
Goodbye, _____ .

SUMMARY OF INDEPENDENT ACTIVITY

TASK 19   Introduction to independent activity

a. Hold up Take-Home 131.

b. Everybody, you're going to finish this take-home on your own.
Tell the children when they will work the remaining items.
Let's go over the things you're going to do.

TASK 20   Sound writing

a. Point to the sound-writing exercise on side 1. Here are the sounds
you're going to write today. I'll touch the sounds. You say them.

b. Touch each sound. *The children respond.*

c. Repeat the series until firm.

TASK 21   Reading comprehension

a. Point to the boxed sentences in the reading-comprehension exercise.

b. Everybody, get ready to read the sentences the fast way.

c. First word.   Check children's responses. Get ready.
Clap for each word as the children read *a man had a car.*

d. Have the children reread the sentence until firm.

e. Get ready to read the next sentence.   Repeat *c* and *d* for **the car
was red.**

f. Point to items 1 and 2. These items tell about the story in the
box. You're going to read each item and circle the right answer.

TASK 22   Sentence copying

a. Hold up side 2 of your take-home and point to the dotted sentence
in the sentence-copying exercise.

b. You're going to trace the words in this sentence. Then you're going
to write the sentence on the other lines.

c. Reading the fast way. First word.   Check children's responses.
Get ready.   Clap for each word.

d. After you finish your take-home, you get to draw a picture about
the sentence, **shē got fīve fish.** You'll draw your picture on a
piece of plain paper.

TASK 23   Pair relations

a. Point to the pair-relations exercise. You're going to read each
sentence. Then draw a line from the sentence to the right
picture.

b. When the children finish their take-homes, give them sheets of
plain paper. Remind them to draw a picture that shows **shē got
fīve fish.**

END OF LESSON 131

Look Ahead

Mastery Tests

Skill Tested	Implications
Test 28 (Lesson 135) Reading the story the fast way; children set pace	During these last 20 lessons, be sure that children are firm on sounds and vocabulary, and that they are able to meet criterion on the Checkouts.
Test 29 (Lesson 150) Reading words the fast way **Test 30** (Lesson 155) Reading the story the fast way; children set pace	

Reading Checkouts

Lessons 145, 150, 155, 160

Read the Items

- Read the Items activities allow for practice in comprehension and following directions in a game-like format. Children respond well to the challenge of "This one's tough! I bet you can't do it!" followed by praise when they do succeed.

Reading Activities

Help children develop comprehension skills by using the following activities.

Story Maps (Lessons 141–160)

Reinforce the story grammars by having children make maps or illustrations of the headings: where, who, problem, ending. Children work with partners or in small groups. To illustrate *where,* children would make a map of the places visited in the story. To illustrate *who,* children would make a picture of the main characters. With different groups making pictures of different headings of the story, the class makes an illustrated story grammar.

Ready to Write (Lessons 157–158)

Help students establish the story grammar for Lessons 157 and 158 by completing a story grammar chart. On the chart, list the following elements: Title, Where, Who, Problem, Events, Ending. First help children complete the chart using the fat eagle and tiger stories. Then show children how to create a new story by changing the characters, the problem, the events, the setting, and the title of the story. Write a group story or have children write their own. Extend the activity to include editing, revising, and publishing.

Poetry Corner (Lesson 145)

After children have finished reading story 145, have them write a cinquain to help capture the main idea of a story. A cinquain is an unrhymed, five-line poem in which the thought is stressed. The cinquain specifications and an example are shown below.

Specifications:

Line 1   One word describing the title

Line 2   Two words describing the character

Line 3   Three words expressing an action

Line 4   Four words expressing a feeling or an opinion

Line 5   One word, a synonym for the title

The Pig That Bit His Leg

Pig
Very silly
Bit his leg
The bug tricked him
Oink

Lesson 132

SOUNDS

TASK 1 Teaching **y** as in **yes**

a. Point to **y**. My turn. (Pause.) Touch **y** and say: yyy.
b. Point to **y**. Your turn. When I touch it, you say it. (Pause.)
Get ready. Touch **y**. *yyy*. Lift your finger.
c. Again. Touch **y**. *yyyy*. Lift your finger.
d. Repeat *c* until firm.

TASK 2 Sounds firm-up

a. Get ready to say the sounds when I touch them.
b. Alternate touching **y** and **i**. Point to the sound. (Pause one second.)
Say: Get ready. Touch the sound. *The children respond.*
c. When **y** and **i** are firm, alternate touching **y, i, k,** and **e** until all
four sounds are firm.

TASK 3 Individual test

Call on different children to identify **y, i, k,** or **e.**

TASK 4 Sounds firm-up

a. Point to **y**. When I touch the
sound, you say it.
b. (Pause.) Get ready. Touch **y**.
yyy.
c. Again. Repeat *b* until firm.
d. Get ready to say all the sounds
when I touch them.
e. Alternate touching **y, ing, u, sh,
l, ch, ī,** and **b** three or four times.
Point to the sound.
(Pause one second.) Say:
Get ready. Touch the sound.
The children respond.

TASK 5 Individual test

Call on different children to identify
one or more sounds in task 4.

y

i

k

e

ing

u

sh

I

ch

b

i

149

Making Progress

	Since Lesson 1	Since Lesson 121
Word Reading	33 sounds 283 regular words 34 irregular words Reading words the fast way Reading stories the fast way Individuals taking turns reading	6 sounds 73 regular words 15 irregular words Individuals taking turns reading
Comprehension	**Picture Comprehension** Predicting what the picture will show Answering comprehension questions about the picture **Story Comprehension** Answering *who, what, when, where* and *why* questions about the story Finding periods, question marks, and quotation marks Answering written comprehension questions about the day's story and short passages	**Story Comprehension** Answering written comprehension questions about the day's story and short passages

What to Use

Teacher	Students
Presentation Book C (pages 204–344) **Teacher's Guide** (page 49) **Teacher's Take-Home Book and Answer Key** **Spelling Book**	**Storybook 3** (pages 7–64) **Take-Home Book C** plain paper (Sentence picture) lined paper (Spelling)

What's Ahead in Lessons 141–160

New Skills
- Story length will increase from 106 to 136 words.
- Children will begin reading two-part stories.
- Children will do "Read the Item" activities involving both comprehension and following directions.
- Children will do picture completion items which involve both comprehension and spelling.

New Sounds
- Lesson 142 – **oo** as in *moon*
- Lesson 145 – **J** as in *jump* (quick sound)
- Lesson 149 – **ȳ** as in *my*
- Lesson 152 – **wh** as in *why*
- Lesson 154 – **qu** as in *quick*
- Lesson 156 – **z** as in *zap*
- Lesson 158 – **ū** as in *use*

New Vocabulary
- *Regular words:*

  (141) bike, box, fox, stopper, these, topper
  (142) eagle, hitting, over
  (143) shore, slider
  (144) broom, chore, dime, room
  (145) better, chip, moon, pile, than
  (146) brush, brushed, day, must, soon
  (147) either, jump, pool, store, tore
  (148) broke, jumped, jumps, swimming
  (149) bring, bringing, fill, teacher
  (150) horse, riding,
  (151) bill, fine, liked, nine
  (152) filled, fly, gold, my
  (153) six
  (154) rushing, slipped, times, tooth, when, where, white
  (155) shine, smile, smiled, why
  (156) after, fatter, from, tiger, tree, under, yelled
  (157) even, fast, slow, stands, steps, things
  (158) head, life, picks, show, thing, wife

- *Irregular words:*

  (145) talked, walked
  (147) loved
  (149) start, tart
  (150) your
  (152) book
  (153) look, touch
  (154) took
  (156) looked

Lessons 141–160

READING VOCABULARY

Do not touch any small letters.

TASK 6 Children read the fast way

a. Get ready to read these words the fast way.

b. Touch the ball for **having.** (Pause three seconds.) Get ready.
(Signal.) *Having.*

c. Repeat *b* for the remaining words on the page.

TASK 7 Children read the fast way again

a. Get ready to do these words again. Watch where I point.

b. Point to a word. (Pause one second.) Say: Get ready. (Signal.)
The children respond. Point to the words in this order:
top, gōing, having, sāme.

c. Repeat *b* until firm.

TASK 8 Individual test

Call on different children to read one word the fast way.

top

sāme

WHAT TO DO

a. Get ready to read these words the fast way.

b. **(test item)** Touch the ball for **went.** (Pause three seconds.) Get ready. (Signal.) *Went.*

c. **(test item)** Touch the ball for **other.** (Pause three seconds.) Get ready. (Signal.) *Other.*

d. **(test item)** Touch the ball for **you.** (Pause three seconds.) Get ready. (Signal.) *You.*

e. **(test item)** Touch the ball for **card.** (Pause three seconds.) Get ready. (Signal.) *Card.*

Total number of test items: **4**

A group is weak if more than one-third of the children missed any of the items on the test.

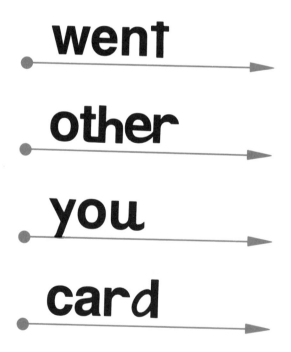

If the group is firm on Mastery Test 27 and was firm on Mastery Test 26:

Skip lesson 141, present lesson 142, then skip lesson 143. If more than one child missed any of the items on the test, present the firming procedures specified below to those children.

If the group is firm on Mastery Test 27 but was weak on Mastery Test 26:

Present lesson 141 to the group during the next reading period. If more than one child missed any of the items on the test, present the firming procedures specified below to those children.

If the group is weak on Mastery Test 27:

A. Present these firming procedures to the group during the next reading period.
 1. Lesson 137, Reading Vocabulary, pages 180–181, tasks 4 through 13.
 2. Lesson 138, Reading Vocabulary, pages 187–188, tasks 9 through 17.
 3. Lesson 140, Reading Vocabulary, pages 198–199, tasks 6 through 16.

B. After presenting the above tasks, again give Mastery Test 27 individually to members of the group who failed the test.

C. If the group is firm (less than one-third of the total group missed any items on the retest), present lesson 141 to the group during the next reading period.

D. If the group is still weak (more than one-third of the total group missed any items on the retest), repeat A and B during the next reading period.

TASK 9   Children read a word beginning with two consonants (slīde)

a. Cover **s.** Run your finger under **līde.** You're going to sound out this part. Get ready. Touch **l, ī, d** as the children say *Illīīīd.*

b. Say it fast. (Signal.) *Līde.* Yes, this part is **līde.**

c. Uncover **s.** Point to **s.** You're going to say this first. Move your finger quickly under **līde.** Then you're going to say (pause) **līde.**

d. Point to **s.** What are you going to say first? (Signal.) *sss.* What are you going to say next? (Signal.) *Līde.*

e. Repeat *d* until firm.

f. Touch the ball for **slīde.** Remember—first you say **sss**; then you say **līde.** Get ready. Move to **s,** then quickly along the arrow. *Ssslīde.*

g. Say it fast. (Signal.) *Slide.* Yes, what word? (Signal.) *Slide.* Yes, **slide.** Good reading.

h. Again. Repeat *f* and *g* until firm.

i. Now you're going to sound out (pause) **slide.** Get ready. Touch **s, l, ī, d** as the children say *ssslllīīīd.* What word? (Signal.) *Slide.* Yes, **slide.**

Do not touch any small letters.

TASK 10   Children read a word beginning with two consonants (slid)

a. Cover **s.** Run your finger under **lid.** You're going to sound out this part. Get ready. Touch **l, i, d** as the children say *Illiiid.*

b. Say it fast. (Signal.) *Lid.* Yes, this part is **lid.**

c. Uncover **s.** Point to **s.** You're going to say this first. Move your finger quickly under **lid.** Then you're going to say (pause) **lid.**

d. Point to **s.** What are you going to say first? (Signal.) *sss.* What are you going to say next? (Signal.) *Lid.*

e. Repeat *d* until firm.

f. Touch ball for **slid.** Remember—first you say **sss**; then you say **lid.** Get ready. Move to **s,** then quickly along the arrow. *Ssslid.*

g. Say it fast. (Signal.) *Slid.* Yes, what word? (Signal.) *Slid.* Yes, **slid.** Good reading.

h. Again. Repeat *f* and *g* until firm.

i. Now you're going to sound out (pause) **slid.** Get ready. Touch **s, l, i, d** as the children say *ssslllliiid.* What word? (Signal.) *Slid.* Yes, **slid.**

TASK 11   Individual test—Have children read one word the fast way.

TASK 23 Picture comprehension

a. What do you think you'll see in the picture? *The children respond.*
b. Ask these questions:
  1. Where are the boy and his mother in this picture?
    The children respond. In a toy shop.
  2. What kind of toys do you see? *The children respond.*
  3. Which toy would you like the best? *The children respond.*
  4. Are big toys more fun than little toys? *The children respond.*

Take-Home 140

SUMMARY OF INDEPENDENT ACTIVITY

TASK 24 Introduction to independent activity

a. Pass out sides 1 and 2 of Take-Home 140 to each child.
b. Everybody, do a good job on your take-home today and I'll give you a bonus take-home.
c. Hold up side 1 of your take-home. You're going to do this take-home on your own. Tell the children when they will work the items. Let's go over some of the things you're going to do.

TASK 25 Story items

a. Point to the story-items exercise.
b. Everybody, read item 1 about the story the fast way. First word. Check children's responses. Get ready. Clap for each word as the children read, *A boy went to a . . . .*
c. Everybody, what's the answer? (Signal.) *Toy shop.*
d. Think about what happened in the story and circle the right answer for each item.

TASK 26 Reading comprehension

a. Point to the boxed sentences in the reading-comprehension exercise.
b. Everybody, get ready to read the sentences the fast way.
c. First word. Check children's responses. Get ready. Clap for each word as the children read *his mother got a card.*
d. Have the children reread the sentence until firm.

e. Get ready to read the next sentence. Repeat c and d for **it said, "I love you."**
f. Point to items 1 and 2. These items tell about the story in the box. You're going to read each item and circle the right answer.

TASK 27 Sentence copying

a. Hold up side 2 of your take-home and point to the dotted sentence in the sentence-copying exercise.
b. You're going to trace the words in this sentence. Then you're going to write the sentence on the other lines.
c. Reading the fast way. First word. Check children's responses. Get ready. Clap for each word.
d. After you finish your take-home, you get to draw a picture about the sentence, **hē is in a toy shop.** You'll draw your picture on a piece of plain paper.

TASK 28 Other independent activity: sides 1, 2, 3, 4

Remember to do all the parts of the take-home and to read all the parts carefully. After you draw your picture, I'll give you a bonus take-home.

INDIVIDUAL CHECKOUT: STORYBOOK

TASK 29 2½-minute individual checkout

a. As you are doing your take-home, I'll call on children one at a time to read the **whole story.** Remember, you get two stars if you read the story in less than two and a half minutes and make no more than three errors.
b. Call on a child. Tell the child: Start with the title and read the story carefully the fast way. Go. Time the child. Tell the child any words the child misses. Stop the child as soon as the child makes the fourth error or exceeds the time limit.
c. If the child meets the rate-accuracy criterion, record two stars on your chart for lesson 140. Congratulate the child. Give children who do not earn two stars a chance to read the story again before the next lesson is presented.

92 words/2.5 min = 37 wpm **[3 errors]**　　　**END OF LESSON 140**

Before presenting lesson 141, give Mastery Test 27 to each child.
Do not present lesson 141 to any groups that are not firm on this test.

TASK 12   Children sound out the word and tell what word

a. Touch the ball for **rabbit.** Sound it out.

b. Get ready. Touch **r, a,** between the **b**'s, **i, t** as the children say
rrraaabiiit. If sounding out is not firm, repeat b.

c. What word? (Signal.) Rabbit. Yes, **rabbit.**

TASK 13   Children sound out the word and tell what word

Repeat the procedures in task 12 for **time.**

TASK 14   Children sound out the word and tell what word

Repeat the procedures in task 12 for **tell.**

TASK 15   Children read do and doing

a. Touch the ball for **do.** You're going to read this word the fast way.
(Pause three seconds.) Get ready.   Move your finger quickly
along the arrow. Do.

b. Return to the ball for **do.** Yes, this word is **do.**

c. Touch the ball for **doing.** So this must be **do** . . . . Touch **ing.**
Ing. What word? (Signal.) Doing. Yes, **doing.**

d. Again. Repeat b and c until firm.

e. Touch the ball for **do.** This word is **do.**

f. Touch the ball for **doing.** So this must be . . . .
Quickly run your finger under **do** and tap **ing.**
Doing. Yes, **doing.**

g. Again. Repeat e and f until firm.

h. Now you're going to sound out (pause) **doing.** Get ready.
Touch **d, o, ing** as the children say doooiiing.

i. How do we say the word? (Signal.) Doing. Yes, **doing.**

TASK 16   Children read the words the fast way

Have the children read the words on this page the fast way.

TASK 17   Individual test

Call on different children to read one word the fast way.

Do not touch any small letters.

rabbit

time

tell

do

doing

Story 140

TASK 20 First reading—children read the title and first three sentences

a. Pass out Storybook 3.

b. **Open your book to page 4. You're going to read the first part of this story today.**

c. **Everybody, touch the title of the story and get ready to read the words in the title the fast way.**

d. **First word.** Check children's responses. (Pause two seconds.) **Get ready.** Clap. *Going.*

e. Clap for each remaining word in the title.

f. After the children have read the title, ask: **What's this story about?** (Signal.) *Going to the toy shop.* **Yes, going to the toy shop.**

g. **Everybody, get ready to read this story the fast way.**

h. **First word.** Check children's responses. (Pause two seconds.) **Get ready.** Clap. *A.*

i. Clap for the remaining words in the first sentence. Pause at least two seconds between claps.

j. Repeat *h* and *i* for the next two sentences. Have the children reread the first three sentences until firm.

TASK 21 Individual children or the group read sentences to complete the first reading

a. **I'm going to call on different children to read a sentence. Everybody, follow along and point to the words. If you hear a mistake, raise your hand.**

b. Call on a child. **Read the next sentence.** Do not clap for the words. Let the child read at his own pace, but be sure he reads the sentence correctly.

To correct	Have the child sound out the word. Then return to the beginning of the sentence.

c. Repeat *b* for most of the remaining sentences in the story. Occasionally have the group read a sentence. When the group is to read, say: **Everybody, read the next sentence.** (Pause two seconds.) **Get ready.** Clap for each word in the sentence. Pause at least two seconds between claps.

TASK 22 Second reading—individual children or the group read each sentence; the group answers questions

a. **You're going to read the story again. This time I'm going to ask questions.**

b. **Starting with the first word of the title.** Check children's responses. **Get ready.** Clap as the children read the title. Pause at least two seconds between claps.

c. Call on a child. **Read the first sentence.** *The child responds.*

d. Repeat *b* and *c* in task 21. Present the following comprehension questions to the entire group.

After the children read:	You say:
Going to the toy shop.	**What's this story about?** (Signal.) *Going to the toy shop.*
"I like big toys."	**What did the boy say?** (Signal.) *I like big toys.* **Where was the boy?** (Signal.) *In a toy shop.* **Who went with him to get toys?** (Signal.) *His mother.*
"So we will get little toys."	**Did his mother like big toys?** (Signal.) *No.* **What kind of toys did she like?** (Signal.) *Little toys.*
"And I like big toys."	**What did the boy say?** *The children respond.* **He said, "I am not a dog. I am a boy. And I like big toys." I wonder how he's going to get a big toy if his mother doesn't like big toys.** *The children respond.* **We'll find out in the next part of the story.**

Story 132

TASK 18 First reading—children read the story the fast way

Have the children reread any sentences containing words that give them trouble. Keep a list of these words.

a. Pass out Storybook 2.
b. Open your book to page 43.
c. Everybody, touch the title of the story and get ready to read

d. First word. Check children's responses. (Pause two seconds.)
Get ready. Clap. The.

e. Clap for each remaining word in the title.
f. After the children have read the title, ask: What's this story about?
(Signal.) The rat got a sore nose.
Yes, the rat got a sore nose.

g. Everybody, get ready to read this story the fast way.
h. First word. Check children's responses. (Pause two seconds.)
Get ready. Clap. A.

i. Clap for the remaining words in the first sentence. Pause at
least two seconds between claps.

j. Repeat <i>h</i> and <i>i</i> for the next two sentences. Have the children reread
the first three sentences until firm.

k. The children are to read the remainder of the story the fast way,
stopping at the end of each sentence.

l. After the first reading of the story, print on the board the words
that the children missed more than one time. Have the children
sound out each word one time and tell what word.

m. After the group's responses are firm, call on individual children
to read the words.

TASK 19 Individual test

a. Turn back to page 43. I'm going to call on different children to
read a whole sentence.

b. Call on different children to read a sentence: Do not clap for each
word.

TASK 20 Second reading—children read the story the fast way and answer questions

a. You're going to read the story again the fast way and I'll ask
questions.

b. Starting with the first word of the title. Check children's
responses. Get ready. Clap. The.

c. Clap for each remaining word. Pause at least two seconds between
claps. Pause longer before words that gave the children trouble
during the first reading.

d. Ask the comprehension questions below as the children read.

After the children read:	You say:
The rat got a sore nose.	What's this story about? (Signal.) *A rat got a sore nose.*
The rabbit went down on his tail.	Who went down the slide? (Signal.) *A rat and a rabbit.* How did the rabbit go down the slide? (Signal.) *On his tail.*
The rat went up to the top of the slide and slid down on his nose.	How did the rat go down the slide? (Signal.) *On his nose.*
But he came down on his nose.	How did the rat come down the slide this time? (Signal.) *On his nose.*
The rabbit said, "That rat can not tell if he is on his nose or his tail."	What did the rabbit say? (Signal.) *That rat can not tell if he is on his nose or his tail.*

TASK 21 Picture comprehension

a. Everybody, look at the picture.
b. Ask these questions:
  1. Who's going down the slide? *The rat.*
  2. What do you think the rabbit is saying? *The children respond.*
  3. How did the rabbit go down the slide? *The children respond.*
  On his tail.

TASK 17 Children read **shop** and **shopping**

a. Touch the ball for **shop.** You're going to read this word the fast way. (Pause three seconds.) Get ready. Move your finger quickly along the arrow. *Shop.*

b. Return to the ball for **shop.** Yes, this word is **shop.**

c. Touch the ball for **shopping.** So this must be **shop** . . . . Touch **ing.** *Ing.* What word? (Signal.) *Shopping.* Yes, **shopping.**

d. Again. Repeat *b* and *c* until firm.

e. Touch the ball for **shop.** This word is **shop.**

f. Touch the ball for **shopping.** So this must be . . . . Quickly run your finger under **shop** and tap **ing.** *Shopping.* Yes, **shopping.**

g. Again. Repeat *e* and *f* until firm.

h. Now you're going to sound out (pause) **shopping.** Get ready. Touch **sh, o,** between the **p**'s, **ing** as the children say *shshshooopiiing.* Yes, what word? (Signal.) *Shopping.* Yes, **shopping.**

TASK 18 Children read the word the fast way

a. Get ready to read this word the fast way.

b. Touch the ball for **bōy.** (Pause three seconds.) Get ready. (Signal.) *Boy.* Yes, **boy.**

c. Repeat *b* for **ever** and **never.**

TASK 19 Children read the fast way again

a. Get ready to do these words again. Watch where I point.

b. Point to a word. (Pause one second.) Say: Get ready. (Signal.) *The children respond.* Point to the words in this order: **bōy, shopping, ever, never, shop.**

shop

shopping

bōy

ever

never

Take-Home 132

STORY ITEMS
The children will need pencils.

TASK 22 Children complete sentences and answer questions

a. Pass out Take-Home 132 to each child.
b. Point to the story-items exercise on side 1. These items are about the story you just read.
c. Everybody, read item 1 the fast way. First word. Check children's responses. Get ready. Clap for each word as the children read *the rabbit went down on his . . . .*
d. The story told that a rat and a rabbit went down a slide. The rabbit went down on his . . . . Everybody, what did the rabbit go down the slide on? (Signal.) *His tail.* Yes, his **tail.**
e. Touch the right word in item 1. Check children's responses. Circle the word. Check children's responses.

To correct	Have the children read the appropriate sentence in the story. Then repeat *d* and *e*.

f. Everybody, read item 2 the fast way. First word. Check children's responses. Get ready. Clap for each word as the children read *the rat slid down on his . . . .*
g. Everybody, what did the rat go down the slide on? (Signal.) *His nose.* Yes, his **nose.**
h. Touch the right word in item 2. Check children's responses. Circle the word. Check children's responses.
i. Repeat *f* through *h* for item 3.

SUMMARY OF INDEPENDENT ACTIVITY

TASK 23 Introduction to independent activity

a. Hold up Take-Home 132.
b. Everybody, you're going to finish this take-home on your own. Tell the children when they will work the remaining items. Let's go over the things you're going to do.

TASK 24 Sound writing

a. Point to the sound-writing exercise on side 1. Here are the sounds you're going to write today. I'll touch the sounds. You say them.
b. Touch each sound. *The children respond.*
c. Repeat the series until firm.

TASK 25 Reading comprehension

a. Point to the boxed sentences in the reading-comprehension exercise.
b. Everybody, get ready to read the sentences the fast way.
c. First word. Check children's responses. Get ready. Clap for each word as the children read *the girl went for a walk.*
d. Have the children reread the sentence until firm.
e. Get ready to read the next sentence. Repeat *c* and *d* for **shē met a fat pig.**
f. Point to items 1 and 2. These items tell about the story in the box. You're going to read each item and circle the right answer.

TASK 26 Sentence copying

a. Hold up side 2 of your take-home and point to the dotted sentence in the sentence-copying exercise.
b. You're going to trace the words in this sentence. Then you're going to write the sentence on the other lines.
c. Reading the fast way. First word. Check children's responses. Get ready. Clap for each word.
d. After you finish your take-home, you get to draw a picture about the sentence, **hē slid on his nōse.** You'll draw your picture on a piece of plain paper.

TASK 27 Pair relations

a. Point to the pair-relations exercise. You're going to read each sentence. Then draw a line from the sentence to the right picture.
b. When the children finish their take-homes, give them sheets of plain paper. Remind them to draw a picture that shows **hē slid on his nōse.**

END OF LESSON 132

TASK 12 Children read the word the fast way

a. Get ready to read this word the fast way.
b. Touch the ball for **tōy.** (Pause three seconds.) Get ready.
(Signal.) *Toy.* Yes, **toy.** That is a very nice (pause) **toy.**
c. Repeat *b* until firm.

TASK 13 Individual test

Call on different children to do *b* in task 12.

TASK 14 Children read the fast way

a. Get ready to read these words the fast way.
b. Touch the ball for **līke.** (Pause three seconds.) Get ready.
(Signal.) *Like.*
c. Repeat *b* for the remaining words on the page.

TASK 15 Children read the fast way again

a. Get ready to do these words again. Watch where I point.
b. Point to a word. (Pause one second.) Say: Get ready. (Signal.)
The children respond. Point to the words in this order:
went, stop, līke.
c. Repeat *b* until firm.

TASK 16 Individual test

Call on different children to read one word on the page the fast way.

Do not touch any small letters.

Lesson 133

Groups that are firm on Mastery Tests 23 and 24 should skip this lesson and do lesson 134 today.

y

i

ē

ī

SOUNDS

TASK 1 Teaching y as in yes

a. Point to **y**. My turn. (Pause.) Touch **y** and say: yyy.
b. Point to **y**. Your turn. When I touch it, you say it. (Pause.) Get ready. Touch **y**. *yyy.* Lift your finger.
c. Again. Touch **y**. *yyyy.* Lift your finger.
d. Repeat *c* until firm.

TASK 2 Sounds firm-up

a. Get ready to say the sounds when I touch them.
b. Alternate touching **y** and **i**. Point to the sound. (Pause one second.) Say: Get ready. Touch the sound. *The children respond.*
c. When **y** and **i** are firm, alternate touching **y, i, ē,** and **ī** until all four sounds are firm.

TASK 3 Individual test

Call on different children to identify **y, i, ē,** or **ī.**

TASK 4 Teacher introduces cross-out game

a. Use acetate and crayon.
b. I'll cross out the sounds on this part of the page when you can tell me every sound.
c. Remember—when I touch it, you say it.
d. Go over the sounds until the children can identify all the sounds in order.

TASK 5 Individual test

Call on different children to identify two or more sounds in task 4.

TASK 6 Teacher crosses out sounds

a. You told me every sound. Get ready to do it again. This time I'll cross out each sound when you tell me what it is.
b. Point to each sound. (Pause.) Say: Get ready. Touch the sound. *The children respond.* As you cross out the sound, say: Goodbye, _____.

READING VOCABULARY

TASK 6 Children sound out an irregular word (come)

a. Touch the ball for **come.** Sound it out.
b. Get ready. Quickly touch each sound as the children say
cooommmeee.
c. Again. Repeat *b* until firm.
d. That's how we <u>sound out</u> the word. Here's how we <u>say</u> the word.
Come. How do we <u>say</u> the word? (Signal) *Come.*
e. Now you're going to <u>sound out</u> the word. Get ready.
Touch each sound as the children say *cooommmeee.*
f. Now you're going to say the word. Get ready. (Signal.) *Come.*
g. Repeat *e* and *f* until firm.

TASK 7 Children rhyme with an irregular word (come)

a. Touch the ball for **come.** Everybody, you're going to read
this word the fast way. Get ready. (Signal.) *Come.*
b. Touch the ball for **some.** This word rhymes with (pause) **come.**
Get ready. Move to **s**, then quickly along the arrow. *Sssome.*
c. Repeat *a* and *b* until firm.

TASK 8 Children sound out some

Have the children sound out **some.** *Sssooommmeee.* How do we say
the word? (Signal.) *Some.* Yes, **some. Some** dogs are mean.

TASK 9 Children sound out the word and tell what word

a. Touch the ball for **hop.** Sound it out.
b. Get ready. Touch **h, o, p** as the children say *hooop.*
If sounding out is not firm, repeat *b.*
c. What word? (Signal.) *Hop.* Yes, **hop.**

TASK 10 Children read the words the fast way

Have the children read the words on this page the fast way.

TASK 11 Individual test

Call on different children to read one word the fast way.

READING VOCABULARY

Do not touch any small letters.

TASK 7 Children sound out an irregular word (into)

a. Touch the ball for **into.** Sound it out.
b. Get ready. Quickly touch each sound as the children say *iiinnntooo.*

To correct	If the children do not say the sounds you touch
	1. Say: **You've got to say the sounds I touch.**
	2. Repeat *a* and *b* until firm.

c. Again. Repeat *b* until firm.
d. That's how we <u>sound out</u> the word. Here's how we <u>say</u> the word.
　　　　　　　　　Into. How do we <u>say</u> the word? (Signal.) *Into.*
e. Now you're going to <u>sound out</u> the word. Get ready.
　　　　　　　　Touch each sound as the children say *iiinnntooo.*
f. Now you're going to say the word. Get ready. (Signal.) *Into.*
g. Repeat *e* and *f* until firm.
h. Yes, this word is **into.** He went **into** the store.

TASK 8 Individual test

Call on different children to do *e* and *f* in task 7.

TASK 9 Children read the fast way

a. Get ready to read these words the fast way.
b. Touch the ball for **stops.** (Pause three seconds.) Get ready.
　　　　　　　　　　　　　　　　(Signal.) *Stops.*

c. Repeat *b* for the remaining words on the page.

TASK 10 Children read the fast way again

a. Get ready to do these words again. Watch where I point.
b. Point to a word. (Pause one second.) Say: Get ready. (Signal.)
　　　　　　The children respond. Point to the words in this order:
　　　　　　　　　　stopping, stops, līke, rich.
c. Repeat *b* until firm.

TASK 11 Individual test

Call on different children to read one word on the page the fast way.

into

stops

rich

līke

stopping

Lesson 140

SOUNDS

TASK 1 Teaching **x** as in **ox**

a. Point to **x.** My turn. When I touch it, I'll say it. (Pause.)
Touch **x** for an instant, saying: *ks.* Do not say **ecks.**

b. Point to **x.** Your turn. When I touch it, you say it. (Pause.)
Get ready. Touch **x.** *ks.*

c. Again. Touch **x.** *ks.*
d. Repeat *c* until firm.

s

k er

TASK 2 Sounds firm-up

a. Get ready to say the sounds when I touch them.
b. Alternate touching **x** and **s.** Point to the sound. (Pause one second.)
Say: Get ready. Touch the sound. *The children respond.*
c. When **x** and **s** are firm, alternate touching **x, s, k,** and **er** until all
four sounds are firm.

TASK 3 Individual test

Call on different children to identify **x, s, k,** or **er.**

TASK 4 Sounds firm-up.

a. Point to **x.** When I touch the
sound, you say it.
b. (Pause.) Get ready. Touch **x.**
ks.
c. Again. Repeat *b* until firm.
d. Get ready to say all the sounds
when I touch them.
e. Alternate touching **x, l, sh, y, b,
v, I,** and **e** three or four times.
Point to the sound.
(Pause one second.) Say:
Get ready. Touch the sound.
The children respond.

TASK 5 Individual test

Call on different children to identify
one or more sounds in task 4.

x

l sh

y

b v

I e

TASK 12 Children rhyme with an irregular word (park)

a. Touch the ball for **park.** Everybody, you're going to read this word the fast way. (Pause three seconds.) Get ready. Move your finger quickly along the arrow. *Park.* Yes, **park.**

b. Quickly touch the ball for **dark.** This word rhymes with (pause) **park.** Move to **d,** then quickly along the arrow. *Dark.* Yes, **dark.**

c. Repeat *a* and *b* until firm.

park

TASK 13 Children sound out dark

a. Touch the ball for **dark.** You're going to sound out this word. Get ready. Quickly touch **d, a, r, k** as the children say *daaarrrk.*

b. How do we say the word? (Signal.) *Dark.* Yes, **dark.**

At night it is **dark** outside.

c. If *a* and *b* are not firm, say: Again. Repeat *a* and *b*.

dark

TASK 14 Individual test—Have children do *a* and *b* in task 13.

TASK 15 Children sound out the word and tell what word

a. Touch the ball for **digging.** Sound it out.

b. Get ready. Touch **d, i,** between the **g**'s, **ing** as the children say *diiigiiing.* If sounding out is not firm, repeat *b*.

c. What word? (Signal.) *Digging.* Yes, **digging.**

digging

TASK 16 Children rhyme with red

a. Touch the ball for **red.** You're going to read this word the fast way. (Pause three seconds.) Get ready. Move your finger quickly along the arrow. *Red.*

b. Touch the ball for **led.** This word rhymes with (pause) **red.** Move to **l,** then quickly along the arrow. *Led.* Yes, what word? (Signal.) *Led.*

red

TASK 17 Children read the words the fast way

Have the children read the words on this page the fast way.

led

TASK 18 Individual test—Have children read one word the fast way.

TASK 26   Picture comprehension

a. Everybody, look at the picture.
b. Ask these questions:
  1. What's happening in the picture? *The children respond.*
  2. What do you think that mother duck is saying to the pig?
     The children respond. I think that pig picked on the wrong
     mother duck.
  3. Did you ever see a real duck? *The children respond.*
     Was that duck mean? *The children respond.*

Take-Home 139

SUMMARY OF INDEPENDENT ACTIVITY

TASK 27   Introduction to independent activity

a. Pass out Take-Home 139 to each child.
b. Everybody, you're going to do this take-home on your own.
      Tell the children when they will work the items.
      Let's go over the things you're going to do.

TASK 28   Story items

a. Hold up side 1 of your take-home and point to the story-items
      exercise.
b. Everybody, read item 1 about the story the fast way. First word.
      Check children's responses. Get ready. Clap for each word as
      the children read *the ducks went for a . . . .*
c. Everybody, what's the answer? (Signal.) *Walk.*
d. Think about what happened in the story and circle the right answer
      for each item.

TASK 29   Sound writing

a. Point to the sound-writing exercise. Here are the sounds you're
      going to write today. I'll touch the sounds. You say them.
b. Touch each sound. *The children respond.*
c. Repeat the series until firm.

TASK 30   Reading comprehension

a. Point to the boxed sentences in the reading-comprehension
      exercise.
b. Everybody, get ready to read the sentences the fast way.
c. First word. Check children's responses. Get ready. Clap for
       each word as the children read *a deer came up to them.*
d. Have the children reread the sentence until firm.
e. Get ready to read the next sentence. Repeat *c* and *d* for **ann said,
       "are you a pet?"**
f. Point to items 1 and 2. These items tell about the story in the box.
       You're going to read each item and circle the right answer.

TASK 31   Sentence copying

a. Hold up side 2 of your take-home and point to the dotted sentence
      in the sentence-copying exercise.
b. You're going to trace the words in this sentence. Then you're going
      to write the sentence on the other lines.
c. Reading the fast way. First word. Check children's responses.
      Get ready. Clap for each word.
d. After you finish your take-home, you get to draw a picture about
      the sentence, **the ducks met a pig.** You'll draw your picture
      on a piece of plain paper.

TASK 32   Pair relations

a. Point to the pair-relations exercise. You're going to read each
      sentence. Then draw a line from the sentence to the right
      picture.
b. When the children finish their take-homes, give them sheets of
      plain paper. Remind them to draw a picture that shows
      the ducks met a pig.

END OF LESSON 139

TASK 19 Children sound out an irregular word (you)

a. Touch the ball for **you.** Sound it out.
b. Get ready. Quickly touch each sound as the children say *yyyooouuu.*
c. Again. Repeat *b* until firm.
d. That's how we <u>sound out</u> the word. Here's how we <u>say</u> the word.
          You. How do we <u>say</u> the word? (Signal.) *You.*
e. Now you're going to <u>sound out</u> the word. Get ready.
        Touch each sound as the children say *yyyooouuu.*
f. Now you're going to say the word. Get ready. (Signal.) *You.*
g. Repeat *e* and *f* until firm.
h. Yes, this word is **you. You** are working hard today.

TASK 20 Individual test

Call on different children to do *e* and *f* in task 19.

TASK 21 Children sound out the word and tell what word

a. Touch the ball for **bōy.** Sound it out.
b. Get ready. Touch **b, ō, y** as the children say *bōōōyyy.*
    If sounding out is not firm, repeat *b.*
c. What word? (Signal.) *Boy.* Yes, **boy.**

TASK 22 Individual test

Call on different children to do *b* and *c* in task 21.

TASK 23 Children read the words the fast way

Have the children read the words on this page the fast way.

TASK 24 Individual test

Call on different children to read one word the fast way.

Story 139

TASK 23 First reading—children read the story the fast way

Have the children reread any sentences containing words that give them trouble. Keep a list of these words.

a. Pass out Storybook 3.

b. Open your book to page 1.

c. Everybody, touch the title of the story and get ready to read the words in the title the fast way.

d. First word. Check children's responses. (Pause two seconds.) Get ready. Clap. *The.*

e. Clap for each remaining word in the title.

f. After the children have read the title, ask: What's this story about? (Signal.) *The duck and the mean pig.* Yes, the duck and the mean pig.

g. Everybody, get ready to read this story the fast way.

h. First word. Check children's responses. (Pause two seconds.) Get ready. Clap. *A.*

i. Clap for the remaining words in the first sentence. Pause at least two seconds between claps.

j. Repeat *h* and *i* for the next two sentences. Have the children reread the first three sentences until firm.

k. The children are to read the remainder of the story the fast way, stopping at the end of each sentence.

l. After the first reading of the story, print on the board the words that the children missed more than one time. Have the children sound out each word one time and tell what word.

m. After the group's responses are firm, call on individual children to read the words.

TASK 24 Individual test

a. Turn back to page 1. I'm going to call on different children to read a whole sentence.

b. Call on different children to read a sentence. Do not clap for each word.

TASK 25 Second reading—children read the story the fast way and answer questions

a. You're going to read the story again the fast way and I'll ask questions.

b. Starting with the first word of the title. Check children's responses. Get ready. Clap. *The.*

c. Clap for each remaining word. Pause at least two seconds between claps. Pause longer before words that gave the children trouble during the first reading.

d. Ask the comprehension questions below as the children read.

After the children read:	You say:
The duck and the mean pig.	What's this story about? (Signal.) *The duck and the mean pig.*
A big mean pig met them on the road.	Who met them? (Signal.) *A big mean pig.* How many little ducks were walking with the mother duck? (Signal.) *Nine.* I wonder what that pig will do. *The children respond.* Let's read and find out.
"I eat beds and I eat bugs."	Oh, oh. I wonder what that mother duck will do.
"And I bite pigs that are mean."	Was the mother duck afraid of the pig? (Signal.) *No.* What do you think the pig will do? *The children respond.*
So the pig ran.	What did the pig do? (Signal.) *The pig ran.*

Story 133

TASK 25 First reading—children read the story the fast way

Have the children reread any sentences containing words that give them trouble. Keep a list of these words.

a. Pass out Storybook 2.

b. Open your book to page 46.

c. Everybody, touch the title of the story and get ready to read the words in the title the fast way.

d. First word. Check children's responses. (Pause two seconds.)
Get ready. Clap. *The.*

e. Clap for each remaining word in the title.

f. After the children have read the title, ask: What's this story about? (Signal.) *The rich pig.* Yes, **the rich pig.**

g. Everybody, get ready to read this story the fast way.

h. First word. Check children's responses. (Pause two seconds.)
Get ready. Clap. *A.*

i. Clap for the remaining words in the first sentence. Pause at least two seconds between claps.

j. Repeat *h* and *i* for the next two sentences. Have the children reread the first three sentences until firm.

k. The children are to read the remainder of the story the fast way, stopping at the end of each sentence.

l. After the first reading of the story, print on the board the words that the children missed more than one time. Have the children sound out each word one time and tell what word.

m. After the group's responses are firm, call on individual children to read the words.

TASK 26 Individual test

a. Look at page 46. I'm going to call on different children to read a whole sentence.

b. Call on different children to read a sentence. Do not clap for each word.

TASK 27 Second reading—children read the story the fast way and answer questions

a. You're going to read the story again the fast way and I'll ask questions.

b. Starting with the first word of the title. Check children's responses. Get ready. Clap. *The.*

c. Clap for each remaining word. Pause at least two seconds between claps. Pause longer before words that gave the children trouble during the first reading.

d. Ask the comprehension questions below as the children read.

After the children read:	You say:
The rich pig.	What's this story about? (Signal.) *The rich pig.*
It was dark in the park.	Where was the dog? (Signal.) *In the park.* What was it like in the park? (Signal.) *Dark.*
"Pigs live on farms."	What did the dog say? (Signal.) *Pigs live on farms.* Who did the dog run into? (Signal.) *A pig.*
"I am a rich pig."	What did the pig say? (Signal.) *I am a rich pig.*
But the waves made the ship rock.	What happened to the ship? (Signal.) *The ship rocked.* How does a ship rock? *The children respond.*
And the dog got sick.	What happened to the dog? (Signal.) *She got sick.* Why? (Signal.) *The ship rocked.*

TASK 28 Picture comprehension

a. What do you think you'll see in the picture? *The children respond.*

b. Turn the page and look at the picture.

c. Ask these questions:

1. Who's on that ship? *The children respond.* A pig and a dog.
2. What is the ship doing? *The children respond.* Rocking.
3. What's making the ship rock? *The children respond.* The waves. Show me the waves. *The children respond.*
4. Were you ever on a boat or a ship? *The children respond.*

TASK 17   Children sound out the word and tell what word

a. Touch the ball for **tōys.** Sound it out.
b. Get ready.   Touch **t, ō, y, s** as the children say *tōōōyyysss.*
  If sounding out is not firm, repeat *b.*
c. What word?   (Signal.) *Toys.*   Yes, **toys. Toys** are fun to play with.

TASK 18   Individual test

Call on different children to do *b* and *c* in task 17.

TASK 19   Children identify, then sound out an irregular word (other)

a. Touch the ball for **other.** Everybody, you're going to read this word
                       the fast way.   (Pause three seconds.) Get ready.
    Move your finger quickly along the arrow. *Other.* Yes, **other.**
b. Now you're going to sound out the word. Get ready.
            Quickly touch **o, th, er** as the children say *ooothththerrr.*
c. Again.   Repeat *b.*
d. How do we say the word?   (Signal.) *Other.* Yes, **other.**
e. Repeat *b* and *d* until firm.

TASK 20   Individual test—Have children do *b* and *d* in task 19.

TASK 21   Children read the words the fast way

a. Now you get to read the words on this page the fast way.
b. Touch the ball for **other.** (Pause three seconds.) Get ready.
                  Move your finger quickly along the arrow. *Other.*
c. Repeat *b* for **tōys.**

TASK 22   Individual test

Call on different children to read one word the fast way.

Take-Home 133

STORY ITEMS
The children will need pencils.

TASK 29 Children complete sentences and answer questions

a. Pass out Take-Home 133 to each child.

b. Point to the story-items exercise on side 1. **These items are about the story you just read.**

c. **Everybody, read item 1 the fast way. First word.** Check children's responses. **Get ready.** Clap for each word as the children read *the dog said, "pigs live . . . ."*

d. **The story told that the dog said, "pigs live . . . ."**
Everybody, where did the dog say pigs live? (Signal.)
On farms. **Yes, on farms.**

e. **Touch the right words in item 1.** Check children's responses.
Circle the words. Check children's responses.

To correct	Have the children read the appropriate sentence in the story. Then repeat *d* and *e*.

f. **Everybody, read item 2 the fast way. First word.** Check children's responses. **Get ready.** Clap for each word as the children read *the pig said, "I am a . . . ."*

g. **Everybody, the pig said, "I am a . . . ."** (Signal.) *Rich pig.*

h. **Touch the right words in item 2.** Check children's responses.
Circle the words. Check children's responses.

i. **Everybody, read item 3 the fast way. First word.** Check children's responses. **Get ready.** Clap for each word as the children read *the ship rocked and the dog . . . .*

j. **Everybody, the ship rocked and the dog . . . .** (Signal.) *Got sick.*
Yes, got sick.

k. **Touch the right words in item 3.** Check children's responses.
Circle the words. Check children's responses.

SUMMARY OF INDEPENDENT ACTIVITY

TASK 30 Introduction to independent activity

a. Hold up Take-Home 133.

b. **Everybody, you're going to finish this take-home on your own.**
Tell the children when they will work the remaining items.
Let's go over the things you're going to do.

TASK 31 Sound writing

a. Point to the sound-writing exercise on side 1. **Here are the sounds you're going to write today. I'll touch the sounds. You say them.**

b. Touch each sound. *The children respond.*

c. Repeat the series until firm.

TASK 32 Reading comprehension

a. Point to the boxed sentences in the reading-comprehension exercise.

b. **Everybody, get ready to read the sentences the fast way.**

c. **First word.** Check children's responses. **Get ready.** Clap for each word as the children read *a girl went fishing.*

d. Have the children reread the sentence until firm.

e. **Get ready to read the next sentence.** Repeat *c* and *d* for **shē did not get fish.**

f. Point to items 1 and 2. **These items tell about the story in the box. You're going to read each item and circle the right answer.**

TASK 33 Sentence copying

a. Hold up side 2 of your take-home and point to the dotted sentence in the sentence-copying exercise.

b. **You're going to trace the words in this sentence. Then you're going to write the sentence on the other lines.**

c. **Reading the fast way. First word.** Check children's responses. **Get ready.** Clap for each word.

d. **After you finish your take-home, you get to draw a picture about the sentence, I live on a ship. You'll draw your picture on a piece of plain paper.**

TASK 34 Pair relations

a. Point to the pair-relations exercise. **You're going to read each sentence. Then draw a line from the sentence to the right picture.**

b. When the children finish their take-homes, give them sheets of plain paper. Remind them to draw a picture that shows **I live on a ship.**

END OF LESSON 133

TASK 11   Children read the word the fast way

a. Get ready to read this word the fast way.
b. Touch the ball for **bōys.** (Pause three seconds.) Get ready.
(Signal.) *Boys.* Yes, **boys.**
c. Repeat *b* until firm.

bōys

TASK 12   Individual test

Call on different children to do *c* in task 11.

TASK 13   Children identify, then sound out an irregular word (mother)

a. Touch the ball for **mother.** Everybody, you're going to read this
word the fast way.   (Pause three seconds.) Get ready.
Move your finger quickly along the arrow. *Mother.* Yes, **mother.**
b. Now you're going to sound out the word. Get ready.
Quickly touch **m, o, th, er** as the children say *mmmooothththerrr.*
c. Again.   Repeat *b.*
d. How do we say the word?   (Signal.) *Mother.* Yes, **mother.**
e. Repeat *b* and *d* until firm.

mother

TASK 14   Individual test

Call on different children to do *b* and *d* in task 13.

TASK 15   Children read the words the fast way

a. Now you get to read the words on this page the fast way.
b. Touch the ball for **bōys.** (Pause three seconds.) Get ready. Move
your finger quickly along the arrow. *Boys.*
c. Repeat *b* for **mother.**

TASK 16   Individual test

Call on different children to read one word the fast way.

Lesson 134

SOUNDS

TASK 1 Teacher and children play the sounds game

a. Use acetate and crayon. Write the sounds in the symbol box. Keep score in the score box.

b. I'm smart. I bet I can beat you in a game.

c. Here's the rule. When I touch a sound, you say it.

d. Play the game.
Make one symbol at a time in the symbol box. Use the symbols **r, w, e,** and **b.**
Make each symbol quickly. (Pause.) Touch the symbol.
Play the game for about two minutes.
Then ask: Who won? Draw a mouth on the face in the score box.

TASK 2 Child plays teacher

a. Use acetate and crayon.

b. [Child's name] is going to be the teacher.

c. [He or She] is going to touch the sounds. When [he or she] touches a sound, you say it.

d. The child points to and touches the sounds. You circle any sound that is not firm.

e. After the child has completed the page, present all the circled sounds to the children.

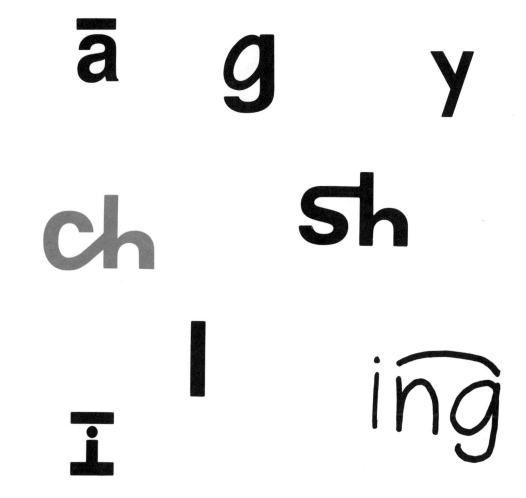

TASK 3 Individual test

Call on different children. If you can say the sound when I call your name, you may cross it out.

READING VOCABULARY

Do not touch any small letters.

TASK 7 **Children sound out the word and tell what word**

a. Touch the ball for **bēans**. Sound it out.

b. Get ready. Touch **b, ē, n, s** as the children say *bēēēnnnsss*.
If sounding out is not firm, repeat *b*.

c. What word? (Signal.) *Beans.* Yes, **beans**.

TASK 8 **Children read the fast way**

a. Get ready to read these words the fast way.

b. Touch the ball for **ever.** (Pause three seconds.) Get ready.
(Signal.) *Ever.*

c. Repeat *b* for the remaining words on the page.

TASK 9 **Children read the fast way again**

a. Get ready to do these words again. Watch where I point.

b. Point to a word. (Pause one second.) Say: Get ready. (Signal.)
The children respond. Point to the words in this order:
never, ever, shopping.

c. Repeat *b* until firm.

TASK 10 **Individual test**

Call on different children to read one word on the page the fast way.

READING VOCABULARY

Do not touch any small letters.

TASK 4   Children sound out the word and tell what word

a. Touch the ball for **tōld.** Sound it out.

b. Get ready. Touch **t, ō, l, d** as the children say *tōōōllld.*

If sounding out is not firm, repeat *b.*

c. What word? (Signal.) *Told.* Yes, **told.**

TASK 5   Children sound out the word and tell what word

Repeat the procedures in task 4 for **hōle.**

TASK 6   Children sound out the word and tell what word

Repeat the procedures in task 4 for **yes.**

TASK 7   Children sound out an irregular word (you)

a. Touch the ball for **you.** Sound it out.

b. Get ready. Quickly touch each sound as the children say *yyyooouuu.*

c. Again. Repeat *b* until firm.

d. That's how we <u>sound out</u> the word. Here's how we <u>say</u> the word.

You. How do we <u>say</u> the word? (Signal.) *You.*

e. Now you're going to <u>sound out</u> the word. Get ready.

Touch each sound as the children say *yyyooouuu.*

f. Now you're going to say the word. Get ready. (Signal.) *You.*

g. Repeat *e* and *f* until firm.

h. Yes, this word is **you.** I like **you.**

TASK 8   Individual test

Call on different children to do *e* and *f* in task 7.

TASK 9   Children read the words the fast way

Have the children read the words on this page the fast way.

TASK 10   Individual test

Call on different children to read one word the fast way.

tōld

hōle

yes

you

Lesson 139

x

k

s

ch

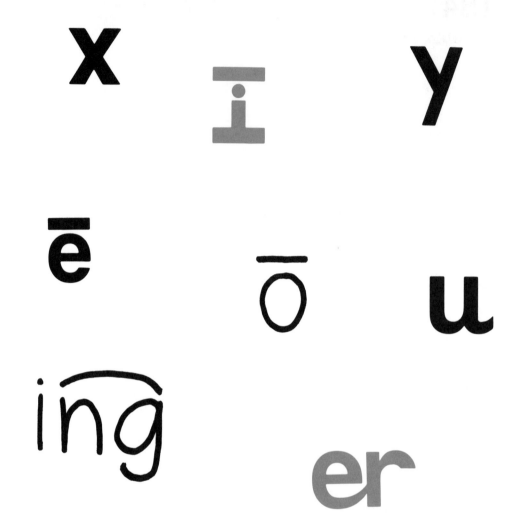

SOUNDS

TASK 1   Teaching x as in ox

a. Point to **x.** Here's a new sound. It's a quick sound.

b. My turn. (Pause.) Touch **x** for an instant, saying: ks.
Do not say **ecks.**

c. Again. Touch **x** and say: ks.

d. Point to **x.** Your turn. When I touch it, you say it. (Pause.) Get ready. Touch **x.** *ks.*

e. Again. Touch **x.** *ks.*

f. Repeat *e* until firm.

TASK 2   Individual test

Call on different children to identify **x.**

TASK 3   Sounds firm-up

a. Get ready to say the sounds when I touch them.

b. Alternate touching **x** and **k.** Point to the sound. (Pause one second.) Say: Get ready. Touch the sound. *The children respond.*

c. When **x** and **k** are firm, alternate touching **x, k, s,** and **ch** until all four sounds are firm.

TASK 4   Individual test

Call on different children to identify **x, k, s,** or **ch.**

TASK 5   Sounds firm-up

a. Point to **x.** When I touch the sound, you say it.

b. (Pause.) Get ready. Touch **x.** *ks.*

c. Again. Repeat *b* until firm.

d. Get ready to say all the sounds when I touch them.

e. Alternate touching **x, ī, y, ē, ō, u, ing,** and **er** three or four times. Point to the sound. (Pause one second.) Say: Get ready. Touch the sound. *The children respond.*

TASK 6   Individual test

Call on different children to identify one or more sounds in task 5.

TASK 11   Children sound out an irregular word (yard)

a. Touch the ball for **yard.**   Sound it out.

b. Get ready. Quickly touch each sound as the children say *yyyaaarrrd.*

To correct	If the children do not say the sounds you touch
	1. Say: You've got to say the sounds I touch.
	2. Repeat *a* and *b* until firm.

c. Again. Repeat *b* until firm.

d. That's how we <u>sound out</u> the word. Here's how we <u>say</u> the word. **Yard.** How do we <u>say</u> the word?   (Signal.) *Yard.*

e. Now you're going to <u>sound out</u> the word. Get ready.
 Touch each sound as the children say *yyyaaarrrd.*

f. Now you're going to say the word. Get ready.   (Signal.) *Yard.*

g. Repeat *e* and *f* until firm.

h. Yes, this word is **yard.**

TASK 12   Individual test

Call on different children to do *e* and *f* in task 11.

TASK 13   Children read the fast way

a. Get ready to read these words the fast way.

b. Touch the ball for **dug.** (Pause three seconds.)   Get ready. (Signal.) *Dug.*

c. Repeat *b* for the remaining words on the page.

TASK 14   Children read the fast way again

a. Get ready to do these words again. Watch where I point.

b. Point to a word. (Pause one second.) Say: Get ready. (Signal.) *The children respond.* Point to the words in this order: **lived, dug, līne.**

c. Repeat *b* until firm.

TASK 15   Individual test

Call on different children to read one word on the page the fast way.

Do not touch any small letters.

yard

dug

līne

lived

TASK 21   Picture comprehension

a. Everybody, look at the picture.
b. Ask these questions:
  1. Who is that in the picture? *The children respond.*
                                                  The boy and his mother.
  2. What do you think the card says? *The children respond.*
                                                  Mother, I love you.
  3. Did you ever send a pretty card to your mother?
                                                  The children respond.

Take-Home 138

SUMMARY OF INDEPENDENT ACTIVITY

TASK 22   Introduction to independent activity

a. Pass out Take-Home 138 to each child.
b. Everybody, you're going to do this take-home on your own.
                    Tell the children when they will work the items.
                    Let's go over the things you're going to do.

TASK 23   Story items

a. Hold up side 1 of your take-home and point to the story-items
                                                              exercise.
b. Everybody, read item 1 about the story the fast way. First word.
            Check children's responses. **Get ready.** Clap for each word
                        as the children read *a boy sent a card to his . . . .*
c. Everybody, what's the answer? (Signal.) *Mother.*
d. Think about what happened in the story and circle the right
                                                  answer for each item.

TASK 24   Sound writing

a. Point to the sound-writing exercise. Here are the sounds you're
                    going to write today. I'll touch the sounds. You say them.
b. Touch each sound. *The children respond.*
c. Repeat the series until firm.

TASK 25   Reading comprehension

a. Point to the boxed sentences in the reading-comprehension
                                                              exercise.
b. Everybody, get ready to read the sentences the fast way.
c. First word. Check children's responses. **Get ready.** Clap for
                        each word as the children read *a girl met a boy.*
d. Have the children reread the sentence until firm.
e. Get ready to read the next sentence. Repeat *c* and *d* for
                        shē said, "let's dig a hōle."
f. Point to items 1 and 2. These items tell about the story in the
                box. You're going to read each item and circle the right answer.

TASK 26   Sentence copying

a. Hold up side 2 of your take-home and point to the dotted sentence
                        in the sentence-copying exercise.
b. You're going to trace the words in this sentence. Then you're
                        going to write the sentence on the other lines.
c. Reading the fast way. First word. Check children's responses.
                        Get ready. Clap for each word.
d. After you finish your take-home, you get to draw a picture about
                        the sentence, **hē gāve mom a card.** You'll draw your
                        picture on a piece of plain paper.

TASK 27   Pair relations

a. Point to the pair-relations exercise. You're going to read each
                        sentence. Then draw a line from the sentence to the right
                                                              picture.
b. When the children finish their take-homes, give them sheets of
                        plain paper. Remind them to draw a picture that shows
                        hē gāve mom a card.

END OF LESSON 138

TASK 16 Children read dig and digging

a. Touch the ball for **dig.** You're going to read this word the fast way.
(Pause three seconds.) Get ready.
Move your finger quickly along the arrow. *Dig.*
b. Return to the ball for **dig.** Yes, this word is **dig.**
c. Touch the ball for **digging.** So this must be **dig** . . . . Touch **ing.**
Ing. What word? (Signal.) *Digging.* Yes, **digging.**
d. Again. Repeat *b* and *c* until firm.
e. Touch the ball for **dig.** This word is **dig.**
f. Touch the ball for **digging.** So this must be . . . . Quickly run
your finger under **dig** and tap **ing.** *Digging.* Yes, **digging.**
g. Again. Repeat *e* and *f* until firm.
h. Now you're going to sound out (pause) **digging.** Get ready.
Touch **d, i,** between the **g**'s, **ing** as the children say *diiigiiing.*
Yes, what word? (Signal.) *Digging.* Yes, **digging.**

TASK 17 Individual test

Call on different children to read one word the fast way.

Story 138

TASK 18 First reading—children read the story the fast way

Have the children reread any sentences containing words that give them trouble. Keep a list of these words.

a. Pass out Storybook 2.
b. Open your book to page 62.
c. Everybody, touch the title of the story and get ready to read the words in the title the fast way.
d. First word. Check children's responses. (Pause two seconds.)
Get ready. Clap. *A.*
e. Clap for each remaining word in the title.
f. After the children have read the title, ask: What's this story about? (Signal.) *A card for mother.* Yes, **a card for mother.**
g. Everybody, get ready to read this story the fast way.
h. First word. Check children's responses. (Pause two seconds.)
Get ready. Clap. *A.*
i. Clap for the remaining words in the first sentence. Pause at least two seconds between claps.
j. Repeat *h* and *i* for the next two sentences. Have the children reread the first three sentences until firm.
k. The children are to read the remainder of the story the fast way, stopping at the end of each sentence.
l. After the first reading of the story, print on the board the words that the children missed more than one time. Have the children sound out each word one time and tell what word
m. After the group's responses are firm, call on individual children to read the words.

TASK 19 Individual test

a. Turn back to page 62. I'm going to call on different children to read a whole sentence.
b. Call on different children to read a sentence. Do not clap for each word.

TASK 20 Second reading—children read the story the fast way and answer questions

a. You're going to read the story again the fast way and I'll ask questions.
b. Starting with the first word of the title. Check children's responses. Get ready. Clap. *A.*
c. Clap for each remaining word. Pause at least two seconds between claps. Pause longer before words that gave the children trouble during the first reading.
d. Ask the comprehension questions below as the children read.

After the children read:	You say:
A card for mother.	What's this story about? (Signal.) *A card for mother.*
But his mother did not get the card.	Who sent the card? (Signal.) *A boy.* Who did he send the card to? (Signal.) *His mother.* What did the card say? (Signal.) *Mother, I love you.* Did his mother get the card? (Signal.) *No.*
A cop got the card.	Who got the card? (Signal.) *A cop.*
They met the boy.	Who did they meet? (Signal.) *The boy.* Who were they looking for? (Signal.) *Mother.*
"Give me that card."	What did the boy say? (Signal.) *Give me that card.* Do you think the cop and her brother will give the boy the card? *The children respond.* Let's read and find out.
So they gave him the card.	Did they give the boy the card? (Signal.) *Yes.*
And he gave the card to his mother.	What did the boy do? (Signal.) *He gave the card to his mother.*

Story 134

TASK 18   First reading—children read the story the fast way

Have the children reread any sentences containing words that give them trouble. Keep a list of these words.

a. Pass out Storybook 2.
b. Open your book to page 49.
c. Everybody, touch the title of the story and get ready to read the words in the title the fast way.
d. First word. Check children's responses. (Pause two seconds.) Get ready. Clap. *Digging.*
e. Clap for each remaining word in the title.
f. After the children have read the title, ask: What's this story about? (Signal.) *Digging in the yard.* Yes, **digging in the yard.**
g. Everybody, get ready to read this story the fast way.
h. First word. Check children's responses. (Pause two seconds.) Get ready. Clap. *A.*
i. Clap for the remaining words in the first sentence. Pause at least two seconds between claps.
j. Repeat *h* and *i* for the next two sentences. Have the children reread the first three sentences until firm.
k. The children are to read the remainder of the story the fast way, stopping at the end of each sentence.
l. After the first reading of the story, print on the board the words that the children missed more than one time. Have the children sound out each word one time and tell what word.
m. After the group's responses are firm, call on individual children to read the words.

TASK 19   Individual test

a. Look at page 49. I'm going to call on different children to read a whole sentence.
b. Call on different children to read a sentence. Do not clap for each word.

TASK 20   Second reading—children read the story the fast way and answer questions

a. You're going to read the story again the fast way and I'll ask questions.
b. Starting with the first word of the title. Check children's responses. Get ready. Clap. *Digging.*
c. Clap for each remaining word. Pause at least two seconds between claps. Pause longer before words that gave the children trouble during the first reading.
d. Ask the comprehension questions below as the children read.

After the children read:	You say:
Digging in the yard.	What's this story about? (Signal.) *Digging in the yard.*
The dog dug a hole in the yard.	Where did the dog live? (Signal.) *In the yard.* What did the dog do? (Signal.) *Dug a hole.* Do you think the man will like that? *The children respond.* Let's read and find out.
The little man got mad.	Did the man like the dog to dig? (Signal.) *No.*
The man got a cop.	Who did the man get? (Signal.) *A cop.*
The cop said, "Dogs can not dig in this yard."	What did the cop say? (Signal.) *Dogs can not dig in this yard.*
"Can I be a cop dog?"	What did the dog ask? (Signal.) *Can I be a cop dog?*
"I need a cop dog."	What did the cop say? (Signal.) *Yes. I need a cop dog.*

138

TASK 14   Children sound out an irregular word (mother)

a. Touch the ball for **mother.** Sound it out.
b. Get ready. Quickly touch each sound as the children say
mmmooothththerrr.
c. Again. Repeat *b* until firm.
d. That's how we <u>sound out</u> the word. Here's how we <u>say</u> the word.
Mother. How do we <u>say</u> the word? (Signal.) *Mother.*
e. Now you're going to <u>sound out</u> the word. Get ready.
Touch each sound as the children say *mmmooothththerrr.*
f. Now you're going to say the word. Get ready. (Signal.) *Mother.*
g. Repeat *e* and *f* until firm.
h. Yes, this word is **mother.** His **mother** took him to school.
i. Call on different children to do *e* and *f.*

TASK 15   Children read the word the fast way

a. Get ready to read this word the fast way.
b. Touch the ball for **bōy.** (Pause three seconds.)   Get ready.
(Signal.) *Boy.*   Yes, **boy.**
c. Repeat *b* until firm.

TASK 16   Children sound out an irregular word (other)

a. Touch the ball for **other.**   Sound it out.
b. Get ready. Quickly touch each sound as the children say
ooothththerrr.
c. Again. Repeat *b* until firm.
d. That's how we <u>sound out</u> the word. Here's how we <u>say</u> the word.
Other. How do we <u>say</u> the word? (Signal.) *Other.*
e. Now you're going to <u>sound out</u> the word. Get ready.
Touch each sound as the children say *ooothththerrr.*
f. Now you're going to say the word. Get ready. (Signal.) *Other.*
g. Repeat *e* and *f* until firm.
h. Yes, this word is **other.** The **other** day we went to a show.
i. Call on different children to do *e* and *f.*

TASK 17   Children read the words the fast way

Have the children read the words on this page the fast way.

mother

bōy

other

TASK 21   Picture comprehension

a. Everybody, look at the picture.
b. Ask these questions:
   1. What is the dog doing? *The children respond.* Digging a hole.
   2. What is he using to dig? *A shovel.*
   3. Do dogs really use shovels? *The children respond.*
   4. Did you ever dig a hole with a shovel? *The children respond.*

Take-Home 134

SUMMARY OF INDEPENDENT ACTIVITY

TASK 22   Introduction to independent activity

a. Pass out Take-Home 134 to each child.
b. Everybody, you're going to do this take-home on your own.
Tell the children when they will work the items.
Let's go over the things you're going to do.

TASK 23   Story items

a. Hold up side 1 of your take-home and point to the story-items exercise.
b. Everybody, read item 1 about the story the fast way. First word.
Check children's responses. Get ready. Clap for each word as the children read *the dog dug a hole in the . . . .*
c. Everybody, what's the answer? (Signal.) *Yard.*
d. Think about what happened in the story and circle the right answer for each item.

TASK 24   Sound writing

a. Point to the sound-writing exercise. Here are the sounds you're going to write today. I'll touch the sounds. You say them.
b. Touch each sound. *The children respond.*
c. Repeat the series until firm.

TASK 25   Reading comprehension

a. Point to the boxed sentences in the reading-comprehension exercise.
b. Everybody, get ready to read the sentences the fast way.
c. First word. Check children's responses. Get ready. Clap for each word as the children read *a rat likes to eat.*
d. Have the children reread the sentence until firm.
e. Get ready to read the next sentence. Repeat c and d for **hē ēats a red lēaf.**
f. Point to items 1 and 2. These items tell about the story in the box. You're going to read each item and circle the right answer.

TASK 26   Sentence-copying

a. Hold up side 2 of your take-home and point to the dotted sentence in the sentence-copying exercise.
b. You're going to trace the words in this sentence. Then you're going to write the sentence on the other lines.
c. Reading the fast way. First word. Check children's responses. Get ready. Clap for each word.
d. After you finish your take-home, you get to draw a picture about the sentence, **the dog dug a hōle.** You'll draw your picture on a piece of plain paper.

TASK 27   Pair relations

a. Point to the pair-relations exercise. You're going to read each sentence. Then draw a line from the sentence to the right picture.
b. When the children finish their take-homes, give them sheets of plain paper. Remind them to draw a picture that shows **the dog dug a hōle.**

END OF LESSON 134

TASK 9 Children sound out the word and tell what word

a. Touch the ball for **her.** Sound it out.

b. Get ready. Touch **h, er** as the children say *herrr.*

If sounding out is not firm, repeat *b.*

c. What word? (Signal.) *Her.* Yes, **her.**

her

TASK 10 Children sound out an irregular word (card)

a. Touch the ball for **card.** Sound it out.

b. Get ready. Quickly touch each sound as the children say *caaarrrd.*

c. Again. Repeat *b* until firm.

d. That's how we <u>sound out</u> the word. Here's how we <u>say</u> the word.
Card. How do we <u>say</u> the word? (Signal.) *Card.*

e. Now you're going to <u>sound out</u> the word. Get ready. Touch each
sound as the children say *caaarrrd.*

f. Now you're going to say the word. Get ready. (Signal.) *Card.*

g. Repeat *e* and *f* until firm.

h. Yes, this word is **card.** She got a birthday **card.**

i. Call on different children to do *e* and *f.*

card

TASK 11 Children sound out an irregular word (love)

a. Touch the ball for **love.** Sound it out.

b. Get ready. Quickly touch each sound as the children say
lllooovvveee.

c. Again. Repeat *b* until firm.

d. That's how we <u>sound out</u> the word. Here's how we <u>say</u> the word.
Love. How do we <u>say</u> the word? (Signal.) *Love.*

e. Now you're going to <u>sound out</u> the word. Get ready. Touch each
sound as the children say *lllooovvveee.*

f. Now you're going to say the word. Get ready. (Signal.) *Love.*

g. Repeat *e* and *f* until firm.

h. Yes, this word is **love.** I **love** to eat cookies.

i. Call on different children to do *e* and *f.*

love

TASK 12 Children read the words the fast way

Have the children read the words on this page the fast way.

TASK 13 Individual test

Call on different children to read one word the fast way.

Lesson 135

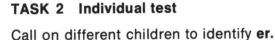

SOUNDS

TASK 1 Teaching **er** as in **brother**

a. Point to **er**. Here's a new sound.

b. My turn. (Pause.) Touch **er** and say: **errr (urrr).**

c. Again. Touch **er** for a longer time. **errrrrr.** Lift your finger.

d. Point to **er**. Your turn. When I touch it, you say it. (Pause.) Get ready. Touch **er**. *errr.* Lift your finger.

e. Again. Touch **er**. *errrrrr.* Lift your finger.

f. Repeat *e* until firm.

TASK 2 Individual test

Call on different children to identify **er**.

TASK 3 Sounds firm-up

a. Get ready to say the sounds when I touch them.

b. Alternate touching **er** and **r**. Point to the sound. (Pause one second.) Say: Get ready. Touch the sound. *The children respond.*

c. When **er** and **r** are firm, alternate touching **er, r, y,** and **e** until all four sounds are firm.

TASK 4 Individual test

Call on different children to identify **er, r, y,** or **e.**

TASK 5 Sounds firm-up

a. Point to **er**. When I touch the sound, you say it.

b. (Pause.) Get ready. Touch **er**. *errr.*

c. Again. Repeat *b* until firm.

d. Get ready to say all the sounds when I touch them.

e. Alternate touching **ing, ī, er, i, v, p, b,** and **w** three or four times. Point to the sound. (Pause one second.) Say: Get ready. Touch the sound. *The children respond.*

TASK 6 Individual test

Call on different children to identify one or more sounds in task 5.

167

READING VOCABULARY

Do not touch any small letters.

TASK 4   Children sound out an irregular word (brother)

a. Touch the ball for **brother.** Sound it out.

b. Get ready. Quickly touch each sound as the children say
                                            brrrooothththerrr.

c. Again. Repeat **b** until firm.

d. That's how we <u>sound out</u> the word. Here's how we <u>say</u> the word.
          Brother. How do we <u>say</u> the word? (Signal.) *Brother.*

e. Now you're going to <u>sound out</u> the word. Get ready.
          Touch each sound as the children say *brrrooothththerrr.*

f. Now you're going to say the word. Get ready. (Signal.) *Brother.*

g. Repeat *e* and *f* until firm.

h. Yes, this word is **brother.** Do you have a **brother**?

brother

TASK 5   Individual test

Call on different children to do *e* and *f* in task 4.

gīve

TASK 6   Children read the fast way

a. Get ready to read these words the fast way.

b. Touch the ball for **give.** (Pause three seconds.) Get ready.
                                            (Signal.) *Give.*

c. Repeat *b* for the remaining words on the page.

gāve

TASK 7   Children read the fast way again

a. Get ready to do these words again. Watch where I point.

b. Point to a word. (Pause one second.) Say: Get ready. (Signal.)
          The children respond. Point to the words in this order:
                                            gāve, sent, give.

c. Repeat *b* until firm.

sent

TASK 8   Individual test

Call on different children to read one word on the page the fast way.

READING VOCABULARY

TASK 7   Children sound out the word and tell what word

a. Touch the ball for **dad.** Sound it out.
b. Get ready.   Touch **d, a, d** as the children say *daaad.*
                             If sounding out is not firm, repeat *b.*
c. What word?   (Signal.) *Dad.* Yes, **dad.**

dad

TASK 8   Children sound out the word and tell what word

a. Touch the ball for **they.** Sound it out.
b. Get ready.   Touch **th, e, y** as the children say *thththeeeyyy.* If sounding out is not firm, repeat *b.*
c. What word?   (Signal.) *They.* Yes, **they.**

they

TASK 9   Children read the fast way

a. Get ready to read these words the fast way.
b. Touch the ball for **mom.** (Pause three seconds.) Get ready.
                                   (Signal.) *Mom.*
c. Repeat *b* for the remaining words on the page.

mom

TASK 10 Children read the fast way again

a. Get ready to do these words again. Watch where I point.
b. Point to a word. (Pause one second.) Say: Get ready.   (Signal.)
   The children respond. Point to the words in this order:
   then, bed, mom.
c. Repeat *b* until firm.

then

Individual test

Call on different children to read one word on the page the fast way.

bed

Lesson 138

Groups that are firm on Mastery Tests 25 and 26 should skip this lesson and do lesson 139 today.

SOUNDS

TASK 1 Teacher and children play the sounds game

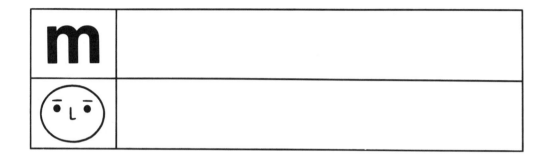

a. Use acetate and crayon. Write the sounds in the symbol box. Keep score in the score box.

b. **I'm smart. I bet I can beat you in a game.**

c. **Here's the rule. When I touch a sound, you say it.**

d. Play the game.
Make one symbol at a time in the symbol box. Use the symbols **y, ī, b,** and **t.**
Make each symbol quickly.
(Pause.) Touch the symbol.
Play the game for about two minutes.
Then ask: **Who won?** Draw a mouth on the face in the score box.

TASK 2 Child plays teacher

a. Use acetate and crayon.

b. **[Child's name] is going to be the teacher.**

c. **[He or She] is going to touch the sounds. When [he or she] touches a sound, you say it.**

d. The child points to and touches the sounds. You circle any sound that is not firm.

e. After the child has completed the page, present all the circled sounds to the children.

TASK 3 Individual test

Call on different children. **If you can say the sound when I call your name, you may cross it out.**

135

TASK 11 Children sound out the word and tell what word

a. Touch the ball for **bōy.** Sound it out.
b. Get ready. Touch **b, ō, y** as the children say *bōōōyyy.*
   If sounding out is not firm, repeat *b.*
c. What word? (Signal.) *Boy.* Yes, **boy.**

TASK 12 Individual test

Call on different children to do *b* and *c* in task 11.

TASK 13 Children read the fast way

a. Get ready to read these words the fast way.
b. Touch the ball for **yes.** (Pause three seconds.) Get ready.
                                                     (Signal.) *Yes.*
c. Repeat *b* for the remaining words on the page.

TASK 14 Children read the fast way again

a. Get ready to do these words again. Watch where I point.
b. Point to a word. (Pause one second.) Say: Get ready. (Signal.)
           The children respond. Point to the words in this order:
                                        yes, fīnd, red.
c. Repeat *b* until firm.

TASK 15 Individual test

Call on different children to read one word on the page the fast way.

bōy

yes

red

fīnd

TASK 23 Picture comprehension

a. Everybody, look at the picture.

b. Ask these questions:
1. **What is Ann doing?** *The children respond.* Petting a deer.
2. **Where do you think they are?** *The children respond.*
3. **Have you ever seen a deer?** *The children respond.*

Take-Home 137

SUMMARY OF INDEPENDENT ACTIVITY

TASK 24 Introduction to independent activity

a. Pass out Take-Home 137 to each child.

b. Everybody, you're going to do this take-home on your own.
Tell the children when they will work the items.
Let's go over the things you're going to do.

TASK 25 Story items

a. Hold up side 1 of your take-home and point to the story-items
exercise.

b. Everybody, read item 1 about the story the fast way. First word.
Check children's responses. Get ready. Clap for each word as
the children read *ann and her dad went hunting for . . . .*

c. Everybody, what's the answer? (Signal.) *Deer.*

d. Think about what happened in the story and circle the right answer
for each item.

TASK 26 Sound writing

a. Point to the sound-writing exercise. Here are the sounds you're
going to write today. I'll touch the sounds. You say them.

b. Touch each sound. The children respond.

c. Repeat the series until firm.

TASK 27 Reading comprehension

a. Point to the boxed sentences in the reading-comprehension exercise.

b. Everybody, get ready to read the sentences the fast way.

c. First word. Check children's responses. Get ready. Clap for
each word as the children read *a boy had red paint.*

d. Have the children reread the sentence until firm.

e. Get ready to read the next sentence. Repeat *c* and *d* for **sō hē
mād̄e a car red.**

f. Point to items 1 and 2. These items tell about the story in the
box. You're going to read each item and circle the right answer.

TASK 28 Sentence copying

a. Hold up side 2 of your take-home and point to the dotted sentence
in the sentence-copying exercise.

b. You're going to trace the words in this sentence. Then you're going
to write the sentence on the other lines.

c. Reading the fast way. First word. Check children's responses.
Get ready. Clap for each word.

d. After you finish your take-home, you get to draw a picture about
the sentence, **the girl has pets.** You'll draw your picture
on a piece of plain paper.

TASK 29 Pair relations

a. Point to the pair-relations exercise. You're going to read each
sentence. Then draw a line from the sentence to the right picture.

b. When the children finish their take-homes, give them sheets of
plain paper. Remind them to draw a picture that shows
the girl has pets.

END OF LESSON 137

Story 135

TASK 16 First reading—children read the story the fast way

Have the children reread any sentences containing words that give them trouble. Keep a list of these words.

a. Pass out Storybook 2.
b. Open your book to page 52.
c. Everybody, touch the title of the story and get ready to read the words in the title the fast way.
d. First word. Check children's responses. (Pause two seconds.) Get ready. Clap. *Ron.*
e. Clap for each remaining word in the title.
f. After the children have read the title, ask: What's this story about? (Signal.) *Ron said, "Yes."* Yes, **Ron said,** "**Yes.**"
g. Everybody, get ready to read this story the fast way.
h. First word. Check children's responses. (Pause two seconds.) Get ready. Clap. *Ron's.*
i. Clap for the remaining words in the first sentence. Pause at least two seconds between claps.
j. Repeat *h* and *i* for the next two sentences. Have the children reread the first three sentences until firm.
k. The children are to read the remainder of the story the fast way, stopping at the end of each sentence.
l. After the first reading of the story, print on the board the words that the children missed more than one time. Have the children sound out each word one time and tell what word.
m. After the group's responses are firm, call on individual children to read the words.

TASK 17 Individual test

a. Turn back to page 52. I'm going to call on different children to read a whole sentence.
b. Call on different children to read a sentence. Do not clap for each word.

TASK 18 Second reading—children read the story the fast way and answer questions

a. You're going to read the story again the fast way and I'll ask questions.
b. Starting with the first word of the title. Check children's responses. Get ready. Clap. *Ron.*
c. Clap for each remaining word. Pause at least two seconds between claps. Pause longer before words that gave the children trouble during the first reading.
d. Ask the comprehension questions below as the children read.

After the children read:	You say:
Ron said, "Yes."	What did Ron say? (Signal.) *Yes.*
"Yes," Ron said.	What did Ron's dad tell him to do? (Signal.) *Sleep in bed.* What did Ron say? (Signal.) *Yes.*
He got the paint and made the bed red.	What did his mom tell him to do? (Signal.) *Paint the bed red.* What did Ron say? (Signal.) *Yes.* Did he paint the bed? (Signal.) *Yes.*
And he made the car red.	What did the big boy ask? (Signal.) *Can Ron paint a car red?* What did Ron say? (Signal.) *Yes.* Did he make the car red? (Signal.) *Yes.*
Now Ron is not red.	Is Ron red now? (Signal.) *No.* Why not? *The children respond.* He went to the tub and went rub, rub, rub.

170

Story 137

TASK 20 First reading—children read the story the fast way

Have the children reread any sentences containing words that give them trouble. Keep a list of these words.

a. Pass out Storybook 2.
b. Open your book to page 59.
c. Everybody, touch the title of the story and get ready to read the words in the title the fast way.
d. First word. Check children's responses. (Pause two seconds.)
Get ready. Clap. *Hunting.*
e. Clap for each remaining word in the title.
f. After the children have read the title, ask: What's this story about?
(Signal.) *Hunting for a deer.* Yes, **hunting for a deer.**
g. Everybody, get ready to read this story the fast way.
h. First word. Check children's responses. (Pause two seconds.)
Get ready. Clap. *Ann.*
i. Clap for the remaining words in the first sentence. Pause at least two seconds between claps.
j. Repeat *h* and *i* for the next two sentences. Have the children reread the first three sentences until firm.
k. The children are to read the remainder of the story the fast way, stopping at the end of each sentence.
l. After the first reading of the story, print on the board the words that the children missed more than one time. Have the children sound out each word one time and tell what word.
m. After the group's responses are firm, call on individual children to read the words.

TASK 21 Individual test

a. Turn back to page 59. I'm going to call on different children to read a whole sentence.
b. Call on different children to read a sentence. Do not clap for each word.

TASK 22 Second reading—children read the story the fast way and answer questions

a. You're going to read the story again the fast way and I'll ask questions.
b. Starting with the first word of the title. Check children's responses.
Get ready. Clap. *Hunting.*
c. Clap for each remaining word. Pause at least two seconds between claps. Pause longer before words that gave the children trouble during the first reading.
d. Ask the comprehension questions below as the children read.

After the children read:	You say:
Hunting for a deer.	What's this story about? (Signal.) *Hunting for a deer.*
Ann said, "Let's go find a deer for a pet."	Why does Ann want a deer? (Signal.) *For a pet.* Who is Ann talking to? (Signal.) *Her dad.*
"And cats are pets."	Are dogs pets? (Signal.) *Yes.* And are cats pets? (Signal.) *Yes.* Are deer pets? (Signal.) *No.*
"But I will let a girl and her dad pet me."	Who is talking? (Signal.) *The deer.* I think it might be fun to pet a deer.
It was.	A deer is big. Show me how you would pet a deer. *The children respond.*
They go with her to hunt for the deer that she can pet.	Does she have pets now? (Signal.) Yes. What are they? *The children respond.* Yes, a pet dog and a pet cat.

TASK 19 Picture comprehension

a. Everybody, look at the picture.
b. Ask these questions:
  1. What's that stuff all over Ron? *The children respond.* Red paint.
  2. What's Ron doing? *The children respond.* Painting a car.
  3. Ron sure is silly. How's he going to get that red paint off himself? *The children respond.* By taking a bath.

Take-Home 135

SUMMARY OF INDEPENDENT ACTIVITY

TASK 20 Introduction to independent activity

a. Pass out sides 1 and 2 of Take-Home 135 to each child.
b. Everybody, do a good job on your take-home today and I'll give you a bonus take-home.
c. Hold up side 1 of your take-home. You're going to do this take-home on your own. Tell the children when they will work the items. Let's go over some of the things you're going to do.

TASK 21 Story items

a. Point to the story-items exercise.
b. Everybody, read item 1 about the story the fast way. First word. Check children's responses. Get ready. Clap for each word as the children read, *Ron said, ...*
c. Everybody, what's the answer? (Signal.) *Yes.*
d. Think about what happened in the story and circle the right answer for each item.

TASK 22 Reading comprehension

a. Point to the boxed sentences in the reading-comprehension exercise.
b. Everybody, get ready to read the sentences the fast way.
c. First word. Check children's responses. Get ready. Clap for each word as the children read *a man went on a ship.*
d. Have the children reread the sentence until firm.
e. Get ready to read the next sentence. Repeat c and d for **the ship was big.**

f. Point to items 1 and 2. These items tell about the story in the box. You're going to read each item and circle the right answer.

TASK 23 Sentence copying

a. Hold up side 2 of your take-home and point to the dotted sentence in the sentence-copying exercise.
b. You're going to trace the words in this sentence. Then you're going to write the sentence on the other lines.
c. Reading the fast way. First word. Check children's responses. Get ready. Clap for each word.
d. After you finish your take-home, you get to draw a picture about the sentence, **ron got the pāint.** You'll draw your picture on a piece of plain paper.

TASK 24 Other independent activity: sides 1, 2, 3, 4

Remember to do all the parts of the take-home and to read all the parts carefully. After you draw your picture, I'll give you a bonus take-home.

INDIVIDUAL CHECKOUT: STORYBOOK
TASK 25 3-minute individual checkout

a. As you are doing your take-home, I'll call on children one at a time to read the **whole story.** Remember, you get two stars if you read the story in less than three minutes and make no more than three errors.
b. Call on a child. Tell the child: Start with the title and read the story carefully the fast way. Go. Time the child. Tell the child any words the child misses. Stop the child as soon as the child makes the fourth error or exceeds the time limit.
c. If the child meets the rate-accuracy criterion, record two stars on your chart for lesson 135. Congratulate the child. Give children who do not earn two stars a chance to read the story again before the next lesson is presented.

112 words/3 min = 37 wpm [3 errors]

END OF LESSON 135

Before presenting lesson 136, give Mastery Test 26 to each child. Do not present lesson 136 to any groups that are not firm on this test.

TASK 15 **Children sound out an irregular word (love)**

a. Touch the ball for **love**. Sound it out.

b. Get ready. Quickly touch each sound as the children say

Illlooovvveee.

To correct	If the children do not say the sounds you touch
	1. Say: **You've got to say the sounds I touch.**
	2. Repeat *a* and *b* until firm.

c. Again. Repeat *b* until firm.

d. That's how we <u>sound out</u> the word. Here's how we <u>say</u> the word.
Love. How do we <u>say</u> the word? (Signal.) *Love.*

e. Now you're going to <u>sound out</u> the word. Get ready.
Touch each sound as the children say *Illlooovvveee.*

f. Now you're going to say the word. Get ready. (Signal.) *Love.*

g. Repeat *e* and *f* until firm.

h. Yes, this word is **love**. I **love** you.

TASK 16 **Individual test**

Call on different children to do *e* and *f* in task 15.

TASK 17 **Children sound out the word and tell what word**

a. Touch the ball for **dēēr**. Sound it out.

b. Get ready. Touch **d,** between the **e**'s, **r** as the children say *dēēērrr.*
If sounding out is not firm, repeat *b*.

c. What word? (Signal.) *Deer.* Yes, **deer**.

TASK 18 **Children read the words the fast way**

a. Now you get to read the words on this page the fast way.

b. Touch the ball for **love**. (Pause three seconds.) Get ready.
Move your finger quickly along the arrow. *Love.*

c. Repeat *b* for **deer**.

TASK 19 **Individual test**

Call on different children to read one word the fast way.

Mastery Test 26 after lesson 135, before lesson 136

a. **Get ready to read this story the fast way.**
b. **(test item)** First word. (Pause two seconds.) **Get ready.** Clap. *A.*
c. **(15 test items)** Clap one time for each remaining word in the story. Pause two seconds between claps.

Total number of test items: **16**

A group is weak if more than one-third of the children missed two or more words on the test.

WHAT TO DO

If the group is firm on Mastery Test 26 and was firm on Mastery Test 25:

Skip lesson 136, and present lesson 137, and skip lesson 138. If more than one child missed two or more words on the test, present the firming procedures specified in the next column to those children.

If the group is firm on Mastery Test 26 but was weak on Mastery Test 25:

Present lesson 136 to the group during the next reading period. If more than one child missed two or more words on the test, present the firming procedures specified below to those children.

If the group is weak on Mastery Test 26:

A. Present these firming procedures to the group during the next reading period. Present each story until the children make no more than three mistakes. Then proceed to the next story.
   1. Lesson 133, Story, page 159, tasks 25, 26.
   2. Lesson 134, Story, page 165, tasks 18, 19.
   3. Lesson 135, Story, page 170, tasks 16, 17.
B. After presenting the above tasks, again give Mastery Test 26 individually to members of the group who failed the test.
C. If the group is firm (less than one-third of the total group missed two or more words in the story on the retest), present lesson 136 to the group during the next reading period.
D. If the group is still weak (more than one-third of the total group missed two or more words in the story on the retest), repeat A and B during the next reading period.

a rat and a rabbit

went down a slɪde.

the rabbit went down

on his tāil.

TASK 9   Children identify, then sound out an irregular word (you)

a. Touch the ball for **you.** Everybody, you're going to read this word
the fast way. (Pause three seconds.) Get ready.
Move your finger quickly along the arrow. *You.* Yes, **you.**

b. Now you're going to sound out the word. Get ready.
Quickly touch **y, o, u** as the children say *yyyooouuu.*

c. Again. Repeat *b.*

d. How do we say the word? (Signal.) *You.* Yes, **you.**

e. Repeat *b* and *d* until firm.

TASK 10   Individual test—Have children do *b* and *d* in task 9.

you

TASK 11   Children sound out an irregular word (other)

a. Touch the ball for **other.** Sound it out.

b. Get ready. Quickly touch each sound as the children say
ooooothththerrr.

c. Again. Repeat *b* until firm.

d. That's how we <u>sound out</u> the word. Here's how we <u>say</u> the word.
Other. How do we <u>say</u> the word? (Signal.) *Other.*

e. Now you're going to <u>sound out</u> the word. Get ready.
Touch each sound as the children say *ooooothththerrr.*

f. Now you're going to <u>say</u> the word. Get ready. (Signal.) *Other.*

g. Repeat *e* and *f* until firm.

other

TASK 12   Children rhyme with an irregular word (other)

a. Touch the ball for **other.** Everybody, you're going to read this
word the fast way. Get ready. (Signal.) *Other.*

b. Touch the ball for **mother.** This word rhymes with (pause) **other.**
Get ready. Move to **m,** then quickly along the arrow. *Mother.*

c. Repeat *a* and *b* until firm.

mother

TASK 13   Children sound out mother

Have the children sound out **mother.** *Mmmooothththerrr.*
How do we say the word? (Signal.) *Mother.* Yes, **mother.**
Mother is feeding the baby.

TASK 14   Individual test—Have children read one word the fast way.

Lesson 136

Groups that are firm on Mastery Tests 25 and 26 should skip this lesson and do lesson 137 today.

SOUNDS

TASK 1 Teaching **er** as in **brother**

a. Point to **er**. My turn. (Pause.) Touch **er** and say: **errr (urrr).**

b. Point to **er**. Your turn. When I touch it, you say it. (Pause.)
Get ready. Touch **er**. *errr.* Lift your finger.

c. Again. Touch **er**. *errrr.* Lift your finger.

d. Repeat *c* until firm.

TASK 2 Sounds firm-up

a. Get ready to say the sounds when I touch them.

b. Alternate touching **er** and **ē**. Point to the sound. (Pause one second.)
Say: Get ready. Touch the sound. *The children respond.*

c. When **er** and **ē** are firm, alternate touching **er, ē, r,** and **e** until all four sounds are firm.

TASK 3 Individual test

Call on different children to identify **er, e, r,** or **ē.**

TASK 4 Teacher introduces cross-out game

a. Use acetate and crayon.

b. I'll cross out the sounds on this part of the page when you can tell me every sound.

c. Remember—when I touch it, you say it.

d. Go over the sounds until the children can identify all the sounds in order.

TASK 5 Individual test

Call on different children to identify two or more sounds in task 4.

TASK 6 Teacher crosses out sounds

a. You told me every sound. Get ready to do it again. This time I'll cross out each sound when you tell me what it is.

b. Point to each sound. (Pause.) Say: Get ready. Touch the sound. The children respond. As you cross out the sound, say: Goodbye, ———.

READING VOCABULARY

TASK 4   Children sound out an irregular word (brother)

a. Touch the ball for **brother.** Sound it out.

b. Get ready. Quickly touch each sound as the children say
brrrooothththerrr.

To correct	If the children do not say the sounds you touch
	1. Say: **You've got to say the sounds I touch.**
	2. Repeat *a* and *b* until firm.

c. Again. Repeat *b* until firm.

d. That's how we <u>sound out</u> the word. Here's how we <u>say</u> the word.
Brother. How do we <u>say</u> the word? (Signal.) *Brother.*

e. Now you're going to <u>sound out</u> the word. Get ready.
Touch each sound as the children say *brrroooththherrr.*

f. Now you're going to say the word. Get ready.   Signal.) *Brother.*

g. Repeat *e* and *f* until firm.

h. Yes, this word is **brother.** I have a big **brother.**

TASK 5   Individual test

Call on different children to do *e* and *f* in task 4.

TASK 6   Children read the fast way

a. Get ready to read these words the fast way.

b. Touch the ball for **hunting.** (Pause three seconds.) Get ready.
(Signal.) *Hunting.*

c. Repeat *b* for the remaining words on the page.

TASK 7   Children read the fast way again

a. Get ready to do these words again. Watch where I point.

b. Point to a word. (Pause one second.) Say: Get ready. (Signal.)
The children respond. Point to the words in this order:
hunt, hunting, but, sēēn.

c. Repeat *b* until firm.

TASK 8   Individual test

Call on different children to read one word on the page the fast way.

brother

hunting

sēēn

but

hunt

READING VOCABULARY

Do not touch any small letters.

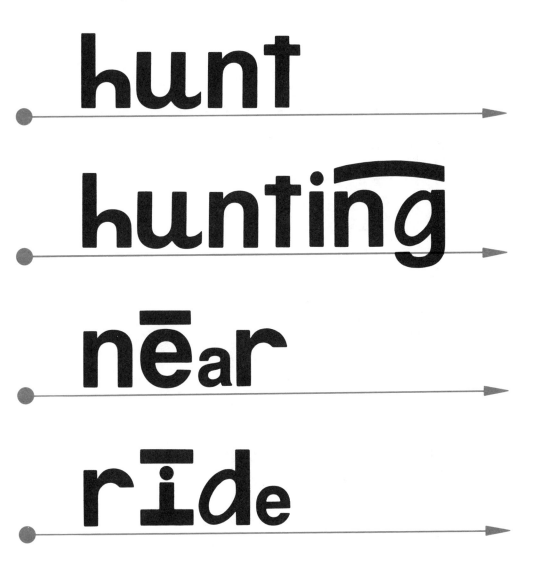

TASK 7 Children read hunt and hunting

a. Touch the ball for **hunt.** Sound it out.

b. Get ready. Touch **h, u, n, t,** as the children say *huuunnnt.*

If sounding out is not firm, repeat *b.*

c. What word? (Signal.) *Hunt.* Yes, **hunt.**

d. Return to the ball for **hunt.** This word is **hunt.**

e. Touch the ball for **hunting.** So this must be **hunt** . . . . Touch **ing.**

Ing. What word? (Signal.) *Hunting.* Yes, **hunting.**

f. Again. Repeat *d* and *e* until firm.

g. Touch the ball for **hunt.** This word is **hunt.**

h. Touch the ball for **hunting.** So this must be . . . . Run your finger

under **hunt** and tap **ing.** *Hunting.* Yes, **hunting.**

i. Again. Repeat *g* and *h* until firm.

j. Now you're going to sound out (pause) **hunting.** Get ready.

Touch **h, u, n, t, ing** as the children say *huuunnnntiiing.*

Yes, what word? (Signal.) *Hunting.* Yes, **hunting.**

TASK 8 Children read the fast way

a. Get ready to read these words the fast way.

b. Touch the ball for **nēar.** (Pause three seconds.) Get ready.

(Signal.) *Near.*

c. Repeat *b* for the remaining words on the page.

TASK 9 Children read the fast way again

a. Get ready to do these words again. Watch where I point.

b. Point to a word. (Pause one second.) Say: Get ready. (Signal.)

The children respond. Point to the words in this order:

gun, nēar, rīde.

c. Repeat *b* until firm.

TASK 10 Individual test

Call on different children to read one word on the page the fast way.

Lesson 137

SOUNDS

TASK 1 Teacher and children play the sounds game

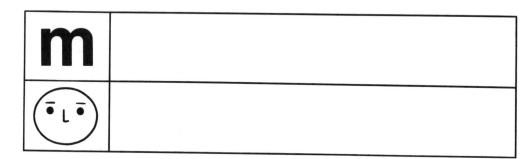

a. Use acetate and crayon. Write the sounds in the symbol box. Keep score in the score box.
b. **I'm smart. I bet I can beat you in a game.**
c. **Here's the rule. When I touch a sound, you say it.**
d. Play the game.
Make one symbol at a time in the symbol box. Use the symbols **y, b, er,** and **c.**
Make each symbol quickly. (Pause.) Touch the symbol.
Play the game for about two minutes.
Then ask: **Who won?** Draw a mouth on the face in the score box.

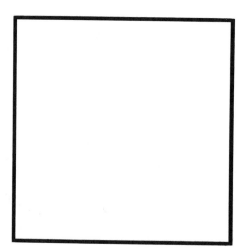

TASK 2 Child plays teacher

a. Use acetate and crayon.
b. **[Child's name] is going to be the teacher.**
c. **[He or She] is going to touch the sounds. When [he or she] touches a sound, you say it.**
d. The child points to and touches the sounds. You circle any sound that is not firm.
e. After the child has completed the page, present all the circled sounds to the children.

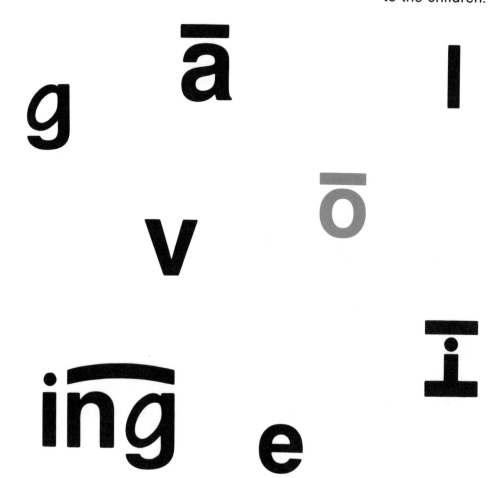

TASK 3 Individual test

Call on different children. **If you can say the sound when I call your name, you may cross it out.**

TASK 11   Children sound out the word and tell what word

a. Touch the ball for **hēre.** Sound it out.

b. Get ready. Touch **h, ē, r** as the children say *hēēērrr.*

If sounding out is not firm, repeat *b.*

c. What word? (Signal.) *Here.* Yes, **here.**

TASK 12   Children identify, then sound out an irregular word (walk)

a. Touch the ball for **walk.** Everybody, you're going to read this word the fast way. (Pause three seconds.) Get ready. Move your finger quickly along the arrow. *Walk.* Yes, **walk.**

b. Now you're going to sound out the word. Get ready. Quickly touch **w, a, l, k** as the children say *wwwaaalllk.*

c. Again. Repeat *b.*

d. How do we say the word? (Signal.) *Walk.* Yes, **walk.**

e. Repeat *b* and *d* until firm.

TASK 13   Individual test

Call on different children to do *b* and *d* in task 12.

TASK 14   Children read the words the fast way

Have the children read the words on this page the fast way.

TASK 15   Individual test

Call on different children to read one word the fast way.

Do not touch any small letters.

TASK 25   Picture comprehension

a. What do you think you'll see in the picture?
b. Turn the page and look at the picture.
c. Ask these questions:
   1. What are the boy and the girls doing? *The children respond.*
                                     Running to the park.
   2. Do you think they're near the park in the picture? (Signal.) *Yes.*
      How do you know? *The children respond.*
   3. I'll bet they're tired. Did you ever run a long, long way?
                                     The children respond.

Take-Home 136

SUMMARY OF INDEPENDENT ACTIVITY

TASK 26   Introduction to independent activity

a. Pass out Take-Home 136 to each child.
b. Everybody, you're going to do this take-home on your own.
               Tell the children when they will work the items.
               Let's go over the things you're going to do.

TASK 27   Story items

a. Hold up side 1 of your take-home and point to the story-items
                                                    exercise.
b. Everybody, read item 1 about the story the fast way. First word.
      Check children's responses. Get ready. Clap for each word as
               the children read *the boy said, "let's go to . . . ."*
c. Everybody, what's the answer? (Signal.) *The park.*
d. Think about what happened in the story and circle the right answer
                                                    for each item.

TASK 28   Sound writing

a. Point to the sound-writing exercise. Here are the sounds you're
               going to write today. I'll touch the sounds. You say them.
b. Touch each sound. *The children respond.*
c. Repeat the series until firm.

TASK 29   Reading comprehension

a. Point to the boxed sentences in the reading-comprehension exercise.
b. Everybody, get ready to read the sentences the fast way.
c. First word. Check children's responses. Get ready. Clap for each
                              word as the children read *a dog dug a hole.*
d. Have the children reread the sentence until firm.
e. Get ready to read the next sentence. Repeat *c* and *d* for **a man fell
                              in the hōle.**
f. Point to items 1 and 2. These items tell about the story in the box.
               You're going to read each item and circle the right answer.

TASK 30   Sentence copying

a. Hold up side 2 of your take-home and point to the dotted sentence
                              in the sentence-copying exercise.
b. You're going to trace the words in this sentence. Then you're going
                              to write the sentence on the other lines.
c. Reading the fast way. First word. Check children's responses.
                              Get ready. Clap for each word.
d. After you finish your take-home, you get to draw a picture about
               the sentence, **they ran to the park.** You'll draw your picture on
                              a piece of plain paper.

TASK 31   Pair relations

a. Point to the pair-relations exercise. You're going to read each
               sentence. Then draw a line from the sentence to the right picture.
b. When the children finish their take-homes, give them sheets of
               plain paper. Remind them to draw a picture that shows
                              they ran to the park.

END OF LESSON 136

TASK 16 Children sound out the word and tell what word

a. Touch the ball for **bōy.** Sound it out.
b. Get ready. Touch **b, ō, y** as the children say *bōōōyyy.*
   If sounding out is not firm, repeat *b.*
c. What word? (Signal.) *Boy.* Yes, **boy.**

TASK 17 Individual test

Call on different children to do *b* and *c* in task 16.

TASK 18 Children sound out an irregular word (**you**)

a. Touch the ball for **you.** Sound it out.
b. Get ready. Quickly touch each sound as the children say *yyyooouuu.*
c. Again. Repeat *b* until firm.
d. That's how we <u>sound out</u> the word. Here's how we <u>say</u> the word.
   You. How do we <u>say</u> the word? (Signal.) *You.*
e. Now you're going to <u>sound out</u> the word. Get ready.
   Touch each sound as the children say *yyyooouuu.*
f. Now you're going to say the word. Get ready. (Signal.) *You.*
g. Yes, this word is **you. You** are smart today.

TASK 19 Individual test

Call on different children to do *e* and *f* in task 18.

TASK 20 Children read the words the fast way

a. Now you get to read the words on this page the fast way.
b. Touch the ball for **bōy.** (Pause three seconds.) Get ready.
   Move your finger quickly along the arrow. *Boy.*
c. Repeat *b* for **you.**

TASK 21 Individual test

Call on different children to read one word the fast way.

Story 136

TASK 22 First reading—children read the story the fast way

Have the children reread any sentences containing words that give them trouble. Keep a list of these words.

a. Pass out Storybook 2.

b. Open your book to page 56.

c. Everybody, touch the title of the story and get ready to read the words in the title the fast way.

d. First word. Check children's responses. (Pause two seconds.) Get ready. Clap. *Going.*

e. Clap for each remaining word in the title.

f. After the children have read the title, ask: What's this story about? (Signal.) *Going to the park.* Yes, going to the park.

g. Everybody, get ready to read this story the fast way.

h. First word. Check children's responses. (Pause two seconds.) Get ready. Clap. *A.*

i. Clap for the remaining words in the first sentence. Pause at least two seconds between claps.

j. Repeat *h* and *i* for the next two sentences. Have the children reread the first three sentences until firm.

k. The children are to read the remainder of the story the fast way, stopping at the end of each sentence.

l. After the first reading of the story, print on the board the words that the children missed more than one time. Have the children sound out each word one time and tell what word.

m. After the group's responses are firm, call on individual children to read the words.

TASK 23 Individual test

a. Look at page 56. I'm going to call on different children to read a whole sentence.

b. Call on different children to read a sentence. Do not clap for each word.

TASK 24 Second reading—children read the story the fast way and answer questions

a. You're going to read the story again the fast way and I'll ask questions.

b. Starting with the first word of the title. Check children's responses. Get ready. Clap. *Going.*

c. Clap for each remaining word. Pause at least two seconds between claps. Pause longer before words that gave the children trouble during the first reading.

d. Ask the comprehension questions below as the children read.

After the children read:	You say:
Going to the park.	What's this story about? (Signal.) *Going to the park.*
He said, "Let's go to the park."	What did the boy say? (Signal.) *Let's go to the park.* Who is he talking to? (Signal.) *Five girls.*
"Is the park near here?"	What did a girl say to the boy? *The children respond.* She said, "We can not see the park. Is the park near here?"
"We need a car to get to the park."	What did the boy say? (Signal.) *We need a car to get to the park.*
"How will we get to the park?"	Can they ride to the park? (Signal.) *No.* Can they walk to the park? (Signal.) *No.* How do you think they'll get to the park? *The children respond.* Let's read and find out.
So the boy and the girls ran to the park.	What happened? (Signal.) *The boy and the girls ran to the park.*